SpringerWienNewYork

Hans Kelsen

Secular Religion

A Polemic against the Misinterpretation of Modern Social Philosophy, Science, and Politics as "New Religions"

Edited from the estate of Hans Kelsen
by Robert Walter†, Clemens Jabloner and Klaus Zeleny

SpringerWienNewYork

em. Univ.-Prof. DDr. Dr. h. c. Robert Walter †
Univ.-Prof. Dr. Dr. h. c. Clemens Jabloner
Dr. Klaus Zeleny
Hans Kelsen-Institut, Vienna, Austria

Financial support was given by *Bundesministerium für Wissenschaft und Forschung in Wien.*

Printed in Germany

SpringerWienNewYork is part of
Springer Science + Business Media
springer.at

Typesetting: Jung Crossmedia Publishing GmbH, 35633 Lahnau, Germany
Printing: Strauss GmbH, 69509 Mörlenbach, Germany

Printed on acid-free and chlorine-free bleached paper
SPIN 80021438

CIP data applied for

ISBN 978-3-7091-0765-2 SpringerWienNewYork

Table of Contents

Introductionary Remarks

By Richard Potz

With his last opus Hans Kelsen follows up on a long and intense theoretical debate with Eric Voegelin, and in so doing also addresses a subject which, surprisingly, assumed new importance at the end of the 20th and the beginning of the 21st century.

In the subtitle Kelsen describes his work as "A Polemic against the Misinterpretation of Modern Social Philosophy, Science, and Politics as 'New Religions'."

The central purpose of the text is to show that concepts of the Enligthenment leading from Lessing and Comte to Marx and Nietzsche have been fundamentally misunderstood as a gnostic theology of modern times.

Kelsen first describes the strong trends in 20th century cultural theory, which point at the similarities of the most important philosophical and sociological theories and political ideologies of modern times with the theological speculation and religious movements of the late antiquity and the Middle Ages, most notably messianic chiliasm, gnosis, Augustinian theology and the trinitarian theology of history of Joachim of Fiore, branded as father of all European revolutions.

For Voegelin, the most important representative of this theory, a well-ordered political community is impossible without a sense of transcendence. If the transcendent principle of order is lost, than the result is what he calls a Gnostic immanentism, which leads to the divinization of man as the basic malady of modern times and finally culminates in the quasi-religious totalitarisms of the 20th century. Consequently, the replacement of a cyclical thinking by a linear philosophy of history is seen as a result of the Judeo-Christian history of salvation, leading directly up to the belief in progress of modernity. Kelsen refers to Fritz Gerlich, who, in "Der Kommunismus als Lehre vom tausendjährigen Reich" (1920), described Communism as a secularized Judeo-Christian religion of redemption. The fact that National Socialism also explicitly adopted the millenaristic image of the "Thousand-Year Reich" seems to fit with this intellectual commonplace of the 20th century.

For Kelsen the crucial point in the position of Voegelin is that not only totalitarian concepts with their quasi-religious claims, but practically all scientific and intellectual movements of modern times finally fall under the suspicion of Gnosticism. The theory of modern gnosis is based on the assumption that in social sciences and philosophy lucid and satisfactory explanations are only possible on the condition of a "theological understanding". In that perspective, even politics is always inherently religious (by its nature) and cannot be separated from religion. Under modern conditions – that is, given the loss of a transcendent principle of order – this would necessarily result in the fatal escape into Gnostic concepts of secular religions and their sham offers of absolute values. On the one hand, science and philosophy would have to view themselves once again as theology, and on the other hand, the return of politics to religion as an inherent necessity would be almost inescapable (cf. preface).

Kelsen sees this interpretation with its religious appropriation of modernity as being extremely dangerous, as it obscures and even covers up the fact that modern science would not have been possible without its emancipation from religion and theology. At the end of the book Kelsen points out his credo: "For science is not, as the Marxists pretend, a mere intellectual superstructure over political reality – a view which the anti-Marxists, without being aware of it, confirm by attributing to science the function of justifying a definite political system. Science can only describe and explain, it cannot justify reality. It has the immanent tendency to be independent of politics and, as a rational and objective cognition of reality, can not presuppose in the description and explanation of its object the existence of a transcendent authority beyond any possible human experience."

The existence of an objective and independent science replacing the scientific truth claim of religious revelations texts, therefore, was and is t h e very criterion of modern times. For Kelsen – as for Hans Blumenberg – the legitimacy of Modernity is grounded in the overcoming of the Gnostic temptation of imagining that one can possess an absolute truth.

The central concern of Kelsen is the necessity to defend the claim of modern science against this abuse. He clearly recognizes the danger of connecting a totalitarian monopolization of (quasi-)scientific results with a quasi-religious truth claim. Both the "scientific materialism" of Marxist provenance, as well as the "scientific" racial theory of National Socialism made use of quasi-religious components and symbols. The 20th century was no doubt characterized by the phenomenon that "scientifically" grounded Weltanschauungen were offered not only as a substitute for religion but also as an alternative legitimacy for a modern political order, thereby replacing democracy, rule of law and private autonomy by an (quasi-)ontological order of being.

In responding to Voegelin, Kelsen untiringly rejects the thesis that there is a Gnostic concept underlying not only the totalitarian quasi-religious Weltanschauungen but also Western democracy, meaning, in other words, that democratic Western society is also afflicted with the Gnostic disease.

The manuscript was written in the early 1960s, when the end of real socialism as an unsuccessful implementation of a totalitarian "Gnostic" concept not at all was in sight, although Kelsen had anticipated this end.

The question, however, is whether the formation of new political religions is possible after the decline of the "Gnostic" totalitarianism which can be interpreted as a defeat of the "secular religions" which have failed to redeem their salvation claim and have been unable to replace religion by quasi-science-based gnosticism. Or else, the result would 'only' be the return of fundamentalist religion. The beginning of a "Revanche de Dieu" (Gilles Kepel, 1990) following the demise of the communist empire maybe has to been seen as such a consequence and certainly took many by surprise.

This phenomenon also reflects the remarkable resurgence of the discussion of the secularization thesis at the end of the 20th century. Throughout the last century, the prevailing view was that secularity is a central and for the most part irreversible feature of modern Europe, reaching far beyond the legal and political structures. Even though a broader understanding of secularisation as covering all areas has increasingly been criticized in the second half of the 20th century (Löwith, Blumenberg, Gogarten, Lübbe), its importance for the political and legal foundations of modernity was generally not questioned by these authors.

Recent decades have seen a change. American social and political scholars in particular speak of an emerging post-secular society. They note a "cultural" and even "religious turn" in the global political order, which comes as a surprise especially for Europeans who assume that modernization without secularization would be unthinkable. In my view, this is the result of confusion. One has to distinguish between a secularized society with privatization of religion on the one hand and a secular political order on the other hand, which combines an institutional separation of State and Church with the involvement of religions in the "overlapping consensus" of a pluralistic society by giving public space for the activities of religious communities.

The question of whether and in what form religion will return to politics and theology to science (Kelsen's Conclusion) has become relevant to an extent that was, perhaps, not even expected by Kelsen himself. This is all the more reason to remember the risks that Kelsen detected.

We must not forget that pseudoscientific findings and explanations can easily entail a process of ideologization, succumbing to what we can call the gnostic temptation. Even after the end of the Cold War chaos and uncertainty continue to exist and so the danger of the emergence of new secular religions is not entirely banished. In a globalized world they – more than ever – could be used for promoting particular political interests and as an instrument in conflicts based on the continued existence of global inequalities and discriminations.

In this context, we also have to discuss the global spread of religious fundamentalism. Searching for new gnostic dreamers, theorists of modern gnosis have thus discovered Islamism as a new form of gnosticism after the end of real socialism. Samuel Huntington's question on the possibility of a "Clash of Civilizations" therefore must also be addressed in the discussion inspired by this book of Hans Kelsen.

A crucial point remains. Are we facing a crisis caused by an inherent defect of modernity, namely the loss of the inner relationship between politics and the religious sphere or a crisis caused by the continuing difficulties in coping with the challenges of modernity – a modernity which is certainly based on the separation of religion and politics but is not afraid of granting religions an appropriate place in public life.

Regardless of its time-related aspects, this final work of Hans Kelsen and its sensitivity for the risks mentioned above offers valuable impulses that merit consideration in the ongoing discussion of the relationship of politics, religion and science at the beginning of the 21st century.

Editorial Remarks

By Clemens Jabloner, Klaus Zeleny and Gerhard Donhauser

Among other papers the unpublished works of the famous jurist Hans Kelsen contain an extensive bundle of texts concerning the relationship between modern science on the one hand and religion as well as metaphysics on the other hand. Kelsen's considerations on that subject are elaborated in great detail in the manuscript "Secular Religion". The text is written in English. In 1964 Kelsen withdrew the manuscript from printing although galley proofs existed. Kelsen's treatise is – as it turns out from the author's preface – directed against the attempt to interpret important works of modern philosophy in spite of their explicit antireligious tendency as "disguised or degenerated" religion as well as certain political ideologies of modernity as "secular religions". According to Kelsen this attempt was going so far to identify the nature of modern age – and especially of modern science as its characteristic element – with "Gnosticism". By most of them who interpreted modern age in the mentioned way this term was used as a synonym for "false religion" or heresy. This kind of view seemed to be dangerous to Kelsen because it wanted to submit science to the yoke of religion, a yoke that science had shaken off at the age of Enlightenment. As Kelsen says:

> *"If any criterion distinguishes modern times from the Middle Ages it is – in Western civilization – the existence of objective and independent science. A retrogression of science to metaphysics and theology means the return to the spirit of the Middle Ages. The literature against which this book is written seriously endangers the existence of an objective and independent science and therefore the spirit of modern times."*

The starting point of Kelsen's considerations was the book "The New Science of Politics", published in 1952 by Kelsen's former student Eric Voegelin.[I] Kelsen obviously started to deal with Voegelin's work just after its publication and

I See Eckhart Arnold, Eric Voegelin, in: Robert Walter/Clemens Jabloner/Klaus Zeleny (eds.), Der Kreis um Hans Kelsen. Die Anfangsjahre der Reinen Rechtslehre, Wien: Verlag Manz (2008) pp. 513–552.

completed a manuscript entitled "A New Science of Politics". This manuscript covered 125 pages, was written in English (as the "reviewed" book) and constituted a very thorough and profound analysis of Voegelin's book.[II] In July 1954 Kelsen sent the manuscript to Voegelin. Since January 1954 they were in correspondence on Voegelin's book and Kelsen's review. Unfortunately no statement of Voegelin's on Kelsen's criticism has survived. We only know that Voegelin "warned" Kelsen of publishing his critical view, because Voegelin thought such a publication might damage Kelsen's reputation.

Indeed, Kelsen did not publish his review on Voegelin's book, probably for two reasons: on the one hand his treatise had taken such proportions that it could hardly be called a review; on the other hand Kelsen made plans to carry out a more extensive examination of neometaphysical doctrines, containing also his criticism of Voegelin.[III]

However, another possible reason for Kelsen's decision not to publish the manuscript – as well as for Vogelin's warning – might be found in the fact that Kelsen's text contains a positive valuation of Marx's criticism of religion. Kelsen was already suspected to sympathize with Marxism.[IV] During the fifties and sixties such a suspicion could have had far-reaching personal consequences for the suspect. For lack of remarks of Kelsen about that it is an open question whether such conjectures are true or not.

So Kelsen postponed publication and carried on working on his manuscript. He extended it and entitled it "Defense of Modern Times". In 1955 he sent it to the publishing house Routledge and Kegan Ltd. in London. This attempt of publication failed, details are unknown because the correspondence of Kelsen preserved in his estate is obviously incomplete. In 1958 the University of California Press accepted the manuscript "Defense of Modern Times" for publication.

Again, despite acceptance for publication, Kelsen continued to rework his text which now – in the early sixties – came under the title "Religion without God?".[V] In 1962 a special "intermezzo" took place: In the middle of that year Kelsen sent a brief manuscript entitled "Is modern civilization 'Gnosticism'?" to the journal "Social Research" in New York. This text contains a note with the remark "Editor's note – This paper, in slightly different form, is a chapter in the author's forthcoming book entitled ***Theology without God?*** A Polemic

II It is part of Kelsen's estate.
See Eckhart Arnold, Nachwort: Voegelins "Neue Wissenschaft" im Lichte von Kelsens Kritik, in: Hans Kelsen, A New Science of Politics, Frankfurt and Lancaster: ontos Verlag (2004) p. 111.

III See Arnold, Nachwort, p. 116.

IV See Oliver Rathkolb, Hans Kelsen und das FBI während des McCarthysmus in den USA, in: Robert Walter/Werner Ogris/Thomas Olechowski (eds.), Hans Kelsen: Leben – Werk – Wirksamkeit, Wien: Verlag Manz (2009) pp. 339–348.

V It is part of Kelsen's estate.

Against a Misinterpretation of Modern Philosophy and Science. It is reprinted here with the permission of The University of California Press, Berkeley."[VI] If Kelsen has initiated this operation as some kind of promotion campaign for his planned book cannot be said certainly; in any case the journal was willing to accept the article, though only for 1963 because it was too late for the edition of 1962.

During the year 1962 Kelsen sent the whole manuscript to the mentioned journal. It is possible that the University of California Press has beforehand refused to add the extensive proposed changes of Kelsen into the manuscript or to pursue working on Kelsen's book that maybe seemed to be too extensive on the whole. The journal "Social Research" was willing to publish the whole work, but then the University of California Press obviously changed its mind and Kelsen demanded the manuscript back from the mentioned journal at the beginning of 1963. To this end he wrote a brief telegram ("return manuscript"). "Social Research" fulfilled Kelsen's demand with an expressing of regret.

Still in 1963 the University of California Press drew up galley proofs (again), still entitled "Religion without God?"[VII] Once more Kelsen revised the text. In 1964 Kelsen received further galley proofs, this time entitled "Secular Religion".[VIII] The galleys were changed slightly by Kelsen, but then the work was broken off: Kelsen withdrew the document from publication. He paid a large sum to the University of California Press to reimburse their costs. Rudolf A. Métall reported in his Kelsen-biography that Kelsen has done so because the manuscript included Kelsen's view that no concept of religion could go without the idea of a personal god. But then Kelsen would have attached great value to the views of Huxley and Russell. According to them religious feelings were possible without any metaphysical belief in a god.[IX]

Kelsen died in 1973. His unpublished works were handed to his student, friend and biographer Rudolf A. Métall.[X] After Métall's death (1975) the Hans Kelsen-Institut got hold of Kelsen's unpublished works.

In 1979 the Hans Kelsen-Institut finished a first examination of the question if the withdrawn manuscript should be published. With reference to Métall the institute took the opinion that Kelsen's will should be respected and a publication should not be done.

VI It is part of Kelsen's estate.

VII It is part of Kelsen's estate.

VIII It is part of Kelsen's estate.

IX See Rudolf A. Métall, Hans Kelsen, Wien: Deuticke Verlag (1969) p. 91; Arnold, Nachwort, p. 116.

X See Nicoletta Bersier Ladavac, Rudolf Aladár Métall, in: Robert Walter/Clemens Jabloner/Klaus Zeleny (eds.), Der Kreis um Hans Kelsen. Die Anfangsjahre der Reinen Rechtslehre, Wien: Verlag Manz (2008) pp. 315–324.

In 1983 Kelsen's daughter Maria Feder (1915–1994) brought to the institute that Lewis Feuer,[XI] who would have advocated the publication, had told her that Kelsen had said to him (Feuer) in 1964 (after Kelsen had pulled back the manuscript), Feuer could do his own thing after Kelsen's death. Feuer also mentioned in a letter from the year 1980 that Kelsen had authorized him (Feuer) to publish the manuscript. Feuer had received a copy of "Religion without God?" from Kelsen in 1963 and wrote in 1980 that "much to the chagrin of the University of California Press, Professor Kelsen at the last moment refused to allow the book to be published". Kelsen's daughter agreed with the publication and informed the institute that apart from Feuer also Max Knight,[XII] who had also a copy of the manuscript, wanted it to be published.

After further considerations the board of trustees (Kuratorium) of the Hans Kelsen-Institut decided to take first steps for a publication. A first consultation was in favour of a publication, especially because the manuscript contained criticism of Voegelin. Then it was possible to interest the publishing house Philosophia in Munich for the project, because the University of California Press had refused to publish the manuscript. But another consultation voiced against the publication because Kelsen's polemics would come to nothing. Besides that Kelsen would not give a lucid explanation for the question what else (if not "secular religions") modern totalitarian systems should be. Finally the board of trustees of the Hans Kelsen-Institut refused a publication in 1989.

In 2003 Eckhart Arnold came up to the Hans Kelsen-Institut with the idea to publish the critical review of Kelsen against Voegelin from 1954. This text was even very closely dedicated to Voegelin's book. The board of trustees of the Hans Kelsen-Institut gave Arnold permission to do so, namely with reference to an examination, which declared itself in favor of a publication, especially because Kelsen's text was a very well-developed contribution, interesting as a contemporary document. It would also deal with problems of sociology of religion, a topic receiving increased international attention since the turn of the millennium. The volume was published in the same year.[XIII] Since then it has been translated into Spanish and Italian.

XI Lewis Samuel Feuer (1912–2002) was a reader of Kelsen's manuscript for the University of California Press in 1963; he taught sociology at the University of California, Berkeley, later as a professor of sociology at the University of Toronto, at last at the University of Virginia.

XII Max Knight (born Max Eugen Kühnel, 1909–1993) studied law at the University of Vienna and political science at the University of California, Berkeley, both under Kelsen; he translated the 2nd edition of Kelsen's Pure Theory of Law (German 1960, English 1967, published by the University of California Press); he was Principal Editor of the University of California Press (1951–1976); he was essayist and translator of many works.

XIII Hans Kelsen, A New Science of Politics, Frankfurt and Lancaster: ontos Verlag (2004).

Subsequent to the mentioned publication the Hans Kelsen-Institut tried again for publishing the text of 1964. In 2006 Richard Potz – the author of the Introductionary Remarks to this publication – granted on his request access to the files. In his expert's view he categorized the manuscript as significant because its subject had reached topicality again just recently. Any trend towards a "new" de-secularization was to see exactly with Kelsen's criticism. Furthermore, any trend towards a "new" theologization, no matter whether under the mask of scientific character or not, would hold the danger of totalitarianism. In this context Kelsen's text would offer an excellent contribution to a current discussion. In 2008 the board of trustees of the Hans Kelsen-Institut came to the conclusion that Kelsen's manuscript of 1964 should be published. The renowned Springer Verlag could be won to publish the manuscript. At this point we also want to express our thanks to Springer for the admission of "Secular Religion" into its publisher's list. Finally, we would like to thank Mag. Susanne Gmoser and MMMag. Ramon Pils for their proof-reading skills.

"Secular Religion" is published on the basis of the galley proofs from 1964. In order to guarantee the greatest possible degree of authenticity, a very restrictive editing regime has been applied: apart from adding Kelsen's remarks, correcting typing errors and some standardization concerning the quotations and the bibliography the text has been left completely unrevised. This method was chosen in order to make sure Kelsen's very personal style – being an Austrian scholar working primarily in German – is preserved. To further facilitate access to the text, subject and name indices, an introductionary and an editorial report have been added.

To my faithful friend
Dr. Rudolf A. Métall

Preface

This Book is directed against the attempt of various recent writers to interpret the most important works of social philosophy, especially philosophy of history, of modern times, in spite of their outspoken antitheological tendency, as disguised or degenerated theology, and certain political ideologies of our time as "secular religions." This attempt goes so far as to identify the nature of modernity and in particular scientism, its most characteristic element, with Gnosticism, stigmatized as a false religion, as a heresy.

The author wants to show the fundamental misinterpretation in seeing theology in the thought of men who, like the philosophers of the Enlightenment, Lessing, Comte, Marx, Nietzsche, tried to emancipate human thinking from the bondage of theology. This misinterpretation is, in the author's opinion, dangerous: for it implies the view, consciously or unconsciously, that a social science or philosophy (and especially a science or philosophy of history) independent of theology can have no satisfactory results because it does not lead to the absolute values that can be based only on true religion and without which society and history are meaningless; that politics is by its very nature religion or cannot be separated from it; and that, consequently, the open return of science and philosophy to theology, the return of politics to religion, is indispensable.

That such a misinterpretation is advanced by professional theologians who explain reality in general, social and historical reality in particular, from the point of view of their belief in the existence of an all-powerful and all-just God, the creator and ruler of this world, is understandable because it may be considered to be the consequence of their creed; although one would expect that theologians particularly would decline to confound the idea of religion with atheistic philosophy and politics. However this may be, this book is not written against theologians. It would be futile to direct an attack against them from the point of view of someone who in his scientific view of the world does not presuppose their creed.

If, however, the mentioned misinterpretation is presented not in the name of theology but in the name of *science*, it must be refuted; even if it is not intended to be reactionary but to free social science and philosophy from theological implications. For then it has the undesirable effect of being taken by the theologians as an involuntary confirmation of their view.

The development of modern science is the result of its emancipation from religion and theology. This emancipation is particularly important to social science and especially to historical science, for in these areas of thought theology serves definite political interests, and submission to it is incompatible with an objective science of society and history.

If any criterion distinguishes modern times from the Middle Ages it is – in Western civilization – the existence of objective and independent science. A retrogression of science to metaphysics and theology means the return to the spirit of the Middle Ages. The literature against which this book is written seriously endangers the existence of an objective and independent science and therefore the spirit of modern times.

I wish to thank Miss Lucie E. N. Dobbie, Executive Editor of the University of California Press, Professor John Herz of the City College of New York, Dr. Hans Georg Schenk of the University College, Oxford, and Professor Sheldon Wolin of the University of California, Berkeley, for calling my attention to some writers who exhibit in their interpretation of modern social philosophy the tendency against which this polemic is directed, and Professor Lewis S. Feuer of the University of California, Berkeley, for valuable advice.

Berkeley, California, 1964 Hans Kelsen

Introduction

Recent theories of culture show a tendency to read into the most characteristic philosophical and sociological doctrines, and political ideologies and movements of our time similarities with theological speculations and religious movements of late antiquity and the Middle Ages, especially Messianic chiliasm, the gnosis, St. Augustine's theology, and Joachim of Flora's trinitarian construction of history envisaged as Gnosticism by some writers. Probably the first of such attempts is that of Fritz Gerlich, a distinguished German journalist, who, in his study of communism (*Der Kommunismus als Lehre vom tausendjährigen Reich, 1920*),[1] tries to show theological implications in an outspoken antireligious, atheistic doctrine. He characterizes communism as a secularized "religion of redemption," and regards it as chiliasm. He rejects the view that there is merely a minor parallelism between the Judaeo-Christian belief in the Kingdom of God as a realm of a thousand years and Karl Marx's prediction of the future Communist society; Marx's prediction, Gerlich emphasizes, must be understood as derived from the former belief.

In 1932 Ernst Cassirer, generally recognized as an authority in the history of philosophy, published his *Philosophie der Aufklärung*.[2] He refuses to accept the traditional view that "the Enlightenment was an age basically irreligious and inimical to religion, for such a view runs the risk of overlooking precisely the highest positive achievements of the period. Skepticism as such is incapable of such achievements. The strongest intellectual forces of the Enlightenment do not lie in its rejection of belief but rather in the new form of faith which it proclaims, and in the new form of religion which it embodies."

In the same year the historian Carl L. Becker developed similar ideas in *The Heavenly City of the Eighteenth-Century Philosophers.*[3] He tries to show that

1 Fritz Gerlich, Der Kommunismus als Lehre vom tausendjährigen Reich (München, 1920), pp. 19, 22.

2 Ernst Cassirer, Die Philosophie der Aufklärung (Tübingen, 1932). English translation by Fritz C. A. Koelln and James P. Pettegrove, The Philosophy of the Enlightenment (Boston, 1955), pp. 135 seq.

3 Carl L. Becker, The Heavenly City of the Eighteenth-Century Philosophers (New Haven, 1932).

it is a mistake to consider the eighteenth century, the century of the Enlightenment, as the age of reason, and to contrast it with the Middle Ages as the age of faith. He says: "We are accustomed to think of the eighteenth century as essentially modern in its temper. Certainly, the *Philosophes* themselves made a great point of having renounced the superstition and hocus-pocus of medieval Christian thought, and we have usually been willing to take them at their word. Surely, we say, the eighteenth century was preeminently the age of reason, surely the *Philosophes* were a skeptical lot, atheists in effect if not by profession, addicted to science and the scientific method, always out to crush the infamous, valiant defenders of liberty, equality, fraternity, freedom of speech, and what you will. All very true. And yet I think the *Philosophes* were nearer the Middle Ages, less emancipated from the preconceptions of medieval Christian thought, than they quite realized or we have commonly supposed ... I shall attempt to show that the *philosophes* demolished the Heavenly City of St. Augustine only to rebuild it with more up-to-date materials."[4]

Similar attempts were later made by Charles Frankel, professor of philosophy at Columbia University, whose study *The Faith of Reason* endeavors "to relate the *philosophes'* ideas on progress to the larger metaphysical prepossessions which they inherited" from the theological speculations passionately combated by them.[5]

On a much broader basis, Karl Löwith, professor of philosophy at Heidelberg University, in *Meaning in History*[6] tries to point out the theological implications of modern philosophies of history. He asserts "that philosophy of history originates with the Hebrew and Christian faith in a fulfilment, and that it ends with the secularization of its eschatological pattern,"[7] and that modern historians "elaborate a philosophy of history by secularizing theological principles and applying them to an ever increasing number of empirical facts." The historical consciousness of the Christian Occident, he says, is "determined by an eschatological motivation, from Isaiah to Marx, from Augustine to Hegel, from Joachim to Schelling."[8] He sees an essential influence of Joachim of Flora – or Floris, a twelfth-century abbot, native of Calabria – on Gotthold Ephraim Lessing's outspoken antitheological *Education of the Human Race*[9] and seriously asserts that the radically antitheistic social doctrine of Proudhon was "deeply marked by Christianity."[10]

4 Ibid., pp. 8, 29, 31.
5 Charles Frankel, The Faith of Reason. The Idea of Progress in the French Enlightenment (New York, 1948), p. 2.
6 Karl Löwith, Meaning in History: The Theological Implications of the Philosophy of History (Chicago, 1949).
7 Ibid., p. 2.
8 Ibid., pp. 18, 19.
9 Ibid., p. 208.
10 Ibid., p. 65.

Comte's and Marx's positivistic and materialistic schemes are, according to Löwith's interpretation, a reappearance of Joachim's eschatological expectations.[11] These created, as early as the thirteenth century, the intellectual climate and perspective in which the modern philosophies of history became possible that are the bases of the American, French, and Russian revolutions. For, none of these revolutions could have happened in the absence of the idea of progress and "no idea of secular progress toward fulfilment without the original faith in a Kingdom of God" is conceivable according to Löwith.[12] The idea of progress that is the basis of modern philosophy of history is "Christian by derivation"[13] and in opposition to "the classical notion of time as an eternal cycle."[14]

Löwith's reinterpretation of modern philosophy of history is astonishingly similar to the views of the French Dominican, Father A. G. Sertillanges, in his *Le Christianisme et les Philosophies.*[15] The tendency of this work is to show that "the evangelical ferment was such that it enabled the Christian Church to establish its own philosophy, to recover all philosophies of the past by rectifying and perfecting them and to influence all philosophies of the future"; that "without Christianity no acceptable philosophy would exist. All those which have appeared after the Gospel owe their best points to the latter, and those which have preceded the Gospel, useful as they may have been by being incorporated, would be of no use by themselves for our civilization." "Modern philosophy, like modern history, at least in the Western world, has its origin in the cross: the Good Tiding is its absolute beginning. When Jesus invites Nathaniel to revive, he invites also philosophy."[16]

In accordance with this view, predetermined by his religious faith, Sertillanges insists on the Christian origin of the idea of progress, and maintains that this Christian idea is "the basis of the discipline called philosophy of history. Antiquity developed but unshaped embryos of such a concept of progress. The idea of cycle was too dominant and paralyzing. When modern thinkers resumed it in the name of reason, they only laicized the Christian thought. This is true of August Comte, Condorcet, and Voltaire."[17] Consequently Sertillanges declares: "The philosophical humanitarianism as understood by August Comte and Herder is evidently derived from the Christian concept of the Kingdom of God on earth. Without this conception their philosophies would not have been born. However, this conception, by becoming simply philo-

11 Ibid., p. 159.

12 Ibid., p. 212.

13 Ibid., p. 61.

14 Ibid., pp. 7, 160.

15 [Antonin-Gilbert] Sertillanges [O.P.], Le Christianisme et les Philosophies, Vol. I: Le Ferment Evangelique, L'Elaboration Séculaire, La Synthèse Thomiste, 2nd ed. (Paris, n. d.); Vol. II: Les Temps Modernes (Paris, 1941).

16 Ibid., I, pp. 5, 7.

17 Ibid., I, p. 71.

sophical, is depraved and falsified, like all those which pass from the Christian domain to the laicized domain of the mind."[18]

Sertillanges says that Marxism "has spun a great dream, and this dream has a religious and [in particular] an essentially Christian character";[19] that Marx's ideal, the Communist society of the future, is specifically Christian because it is "the vision of a totalitarian civilization, concentrating all material forces in a unified and organized humanity ... The science of his time, impregnated by Darwinism and the principle of Carnot, has not inspired this vision. It is rather prophetism or Christian millenarianism."[20] Consequently Marxism is a "laicized mysticism." "In his description of the communist society of the future, Marx was not aware – or perhaps he was? – that he simply described the evangelical Kingdom of God ... Briefly, what he visualizes as the status after the realization of his ideal communism, is a *parousie laïque*; it is the corpus *mysticum* of Christ in its perfection."[21]

Sertillange's analysis of Nietzsche's philosophy results in the statement that "what he wants to get from the poor life as it presents itself to our experience, is to be found in the Kingdom of God; hence it is this Kingdom which he is looking for ... In the last analysis this destroyer is a great mystic. This antichrist is a Christian!"[22]

In the same vein lies the work of the Jesuit Henri de Lubac *Proudhon* et le Christianisme[23] in which the blasphemous atheist Proudhon is presented as a Christian theologian.

Protestant theology, too, seems to be interested in interpreting modern atheistic philosophies as secularized religions. Reinhold Niebuhr, in *Faith and History, A Comparison of Christian and Modern Views of History*,[24] asserts that "the Marxist movement of the nineteenth century presented a secularized version of sectarian perfectionism. In this version the working class, more particularly the class of industrial workers, were constituted into a messianic class whose triumph over their foes would prove, according to their faith, to be not merely a triumph over particular foes but the final triumph over evil in history... The Christian myth of the Fall was reinterpreted so that an original state of innocence was posited as existing before the rise of private property. In this state man had not lost the communal essence of his existence. The rise

18 Ibid., I, p. 103.

19 Ibid., II, p. 221.

20 Ibid., II, pp. 221 seq.

21 Ibid., II, p. 223.

22 Ibid., II, pp. 447 seq.

23 Henry de Lubac, S.J., Proudhon et le Christianisme (Paris, 1945). English translation by R. E. Scantlebury, The Un-Marxian Socialist. A Study of Proudhon (New York, 1948).

24 Reinhold Niebuhr, Faith and History, a Comparison of Christian and Modern Views of History (New York, 1949).

of private property constituted the Fall, and the socialization of all property was therefore expected to usher in the kingdom of perfect love on earth, in which, when fully developed, everyone 'would give according to his ability and take according to his need.' ... There is no question about the religious character of this whole program, despite its ostensible scorn for religion and its pretension to a 'scientific' interpretation of the 'laws of motion' in history. A 'dialectical' process becomes surrogate for the absent God."[25]

Another Protestant theologian, Rudolf Bultmann, in his Gifford lectures, *History and Eschatology*, calls the *Communist Manifesto* of 1848 "a Messianic message," "a secularized eschatology."[26] A collection of essays entitled *Christian Faith and Communist Faith, A Series of Studies by Members of the Anglican Communion*, edited by D. M. MacKinnon,[27] has, as its title shows, similar tendencies.

It is therefore not astonishing that a theologizing historian like Arnold J. Toynbee[28] sees in communism a "Christian heresy," and this is equally true of the theologizing philosopher Karl Jaspers[29] who finds in Nietzsche's anti-Christian philosophy "Christian impulses."

In the wake of the theologian Sertillanges follows the Roman Catholic writer Etienne Gilson, in *Les Metamorphosis de la Cité de Dieu*.[30] He propounds the thesis that the ideas of a universal society, comprising the whole of mankind, at which the works of Bacon, Dante, Nicolas of Cues, Campanella,

25 Ibid., pp. 209 seq.

26 Rudolf Bultmann, History and Eschatology (Edinburgh, 1957), pp. 56 seqq., 69.

27 Christian Faith and Communist Faith. A Series of Studies by Members of the Anglican Communion. Edited by D. M. MacKinnon (London, 1953).

28 Arnold J. Toynbee, A Study of History (London, New York, Toronto, 1954), VIII, IX. Toynbee says: Men "swallowed the word which Communism gave them without pausing to ask whether this was God's word or Antichrist's" (VIII, 469); he considers communism "a Christian heresy" in which "the stone of Communism had been substituted for the bread of the Gospel" in the sense of Matt., 7:9 and Luke, 11:11 (IX, 644); he speaks of the "Marxian Gospel" and of Marxists as of men who "had gone a whoring after other Gods," quoting Judges, 2:17 (IX, 449); he interprets the conflict between communism and liberalism as a religious conflict, since "this economic issue masked a religious one," a conflict between two idolatries: "a conflict between two incompatible versions of the cult of a human idol. Communism was preaching that Man's divinity lay in Man's collective material power, while Liberalism was preaching that it lay in men's individual and personal freedom" (IX, 620–621). Toynbee's own philosophy of history is expressed in the statement: "The meaning behind the facts of History ... is a revelation of God and a hope of communion with Him; but in this quest for a Beatific Vision that is visible to a communion of Saints we are ever in danger of being diverted from our search for God to a glorification of Man ..." (X, 126).

29 Karl Jaspers, Nietzsche und das Christentum (Hameln, n. d.), pp. 9 seqq. See below, pp. 199 seqq.

30 Etienne Gilson, Les Metamorphoses de la Cité de Dieu (Louvain and Paris, 1952).

Abbé de Saint-Pierre, Leibniz, and of atheists like Saint-Simon and Comte were aimed, are but "avatars" or parodies of St. Augustine's City of God. "History and our own time abound with parodies of the City of God," as the result of the attempt to temporalize it.[31] Gilson considers St. Augustine "the father of all philosophies of history, even if he has not wanted them, and even if they do not recognize themselves as that which they really are: remains of a vaster edifice in which alone they could find the authentic meaning, of which they are not aware, and thus the full justification of their proper truth."[32] "The sequence of the metamorphoses of the City of God... is the history of a stubborn effort to make a temporal city out of this eternal city by substituting for the faith some natural, comprehensible bond as a uniting force of this society."[33]

A few years after the work of Sertillanges had appeared, Raymond Aron, a writer belonging to the left wing of the French anti-Vichy movement, published an article "L'Avenir des religions séculières" (1944).[34] Under this title he discusses socialism, especially Marxism, as well as national socialism and fascism; finally he declares that almost all political theories of our time are "secular religions." With reference to the future communist society, predicted by Marx, Aron speaks of a "socialist eschatology" and with reference to the revolutionary destruction of capitalism of an "apocalyptic catastrophe." Without referring to the work of Sertillanges and probably without sharing the Dominican's intention to restore the authority of Christian theology, Aron's interpretation of Marxism is exactly the same as that of the theologian, and thus Aron, unintentionally, supports Sertillange's reactionary tendency. With respect to the interpretation of Marxian socialism, there is perfect agreement between the Catholic theologian and the Jewish philosopher Martin Buber who, referring to Marx, speaks of "the socialist secularization of eschatology" and of Marx's apocalyptic position.[35] Like Gerlich in 1920, J. L. Talmon, a professor at the Hebrew University in Jerusalem, characterizes the political system of bolshevism, which he considers a "totalitarian democracy," as "political Messianism" and "secular religion."[36] Whereas, however, according to this and most of the other theological interpretations of communism, the secular religion implied in this political system is a corrupted form of the Judaeo-Chris-

31 Ibid., pp. VIII, IX.

32 Ibid., pp. 70–71.

33 Ibid., p. 288.

34 Raymond Aron, "L'Avenir des religions séculières," La France Libre, VIII (London, 1944), pp. 210–217, 269–277.

35 Martin Buber, Paths in Utopia, transl. by R. F. C. Hull (London, 1949), p. 10.

36 J. L. Talmon, The Rise of Totalitarian Democracy (Boston, 1952), pp. 1, 8, 12.

tian faith, the French sociologist Jules Monnerot discovered in it the Mohammedan religion: he proclaims it as "the twentieth-century Islam."[37]

In his *History of Western Morals*,[38] Crane Brinton of Harvard University, referring to Carl Becker and Raymond Aron, characterizes the philosophy of the Enlightenment as "the new religion of the modern West," and a "secular religion."[39] He speaks of "Christianity and the Enlightenment" as "of these two rival, but by no means wholly antithetical faiths."[40] He considers the philosophy of the Enlightenment as the mother of what may be called the world view of modern times, and characterizes this view and the intellectual systems based on it, such as positivism, materialism, humanism, Marxism, as well as the political ideologies of nationalism, democratism, even scientism as "faiths," "theologies," "heresies," "eschatologies," and the like. He admits, however, that all these "religions," "faiths," "theologies," "heresies," "eschatologies" do not imply a belief in God; he speaks of "religious atheists"[41] and "theology without a *theos*,"[42] "secular faith,"[43] "metaphysical rationalism."[44] He says: "I am going to use from time to time, as the generic term for this religion ["the Enlightenment-born religion which in many of its forms specifically declares itself to be anti-Christian"] the term 'free thought,'"[45] which means that the religion of the Enlightenment is – in Brinton's opinion – a free-thought religion. He says: "There are in our modern West millions of free thinkers of all shades, none of them theologically, eschatologically, ethically, emotionally quite Christians."[46] But although they are not Christians, Brinton implies that they have nevertheless a "secular," a "free-thought" religion – a theology without God, an eschatology without an eschaton. "I must insist," he says, "that the range of free thinking is very great, that, like Christianity, this new religion is not monolithic."[47] Free thinking is, then, like Christianity, a "religion." Brinton admits that the eighteenth-century Enlightenment produced a "revolutionary new idea," an idea that this philosophy "fashioned into a new world view of a universe without God, a universe where everything was natural,

37 Jules Monnerot, Sociologie du Communisme (Paris, 1949); English translation by Jane Degras and Richard Rees, Sociology and Psychology of Communism (Boston, 1953), pp. 9 seqq.

38 Crane Brinton, A History of Western Morals (New York, 1959).

39 Ibid., pp. 306, 29, 118, and passim.

40 Ibid., p. 455.

41 Ibid., p. 472.

42 Ibid., p. 471.

43 Ibid., p. 175.

44 Ibid., p. 269.

45 Ibid., p. 306.

46 Ibid., p. 307.

47 Ibid., p. 308.

nothing supernatural."[48] If, as he asserts, this world view is a "religion," it is a religion without the supernatural.

In his evaluation of Joachim's importance for modern philosophy of history as the basis of revolutionary movements Löwith follows Eugen Rosenstock-Huessy, professor of philosophy at Dartmouth College. The latter asserts that Joachim, with his prediction of an age of perfect religious life, "has recognized the new law, whose last executor was to be Lenin," and thereby "has identified the first revolution [i. e., the "revolution" launched by the pope against the emperor at the beginning of our millennium] with the entire millennium of revolutionary dialectic." Thus Joachim "has baptized our millennium by its political revolutions."[49] Before Rosenstock, Alois Dempf, professor of philosophy at Munich University, glorified Joachim as "the prophet of a new time" and asserted that the new time predicted by Joachim was "the modern times."[50] Löwith goes so far as to recognize Joachim's third age, which has an exclusively religious character, in political events such as the Third International and above all the Third Reich of National Socialism. "The third dispensation of the Joachites reappeared as a third International and a third Reich, inaugurated by a *dux* or a *Führer* who was acclaimed as a savior and greeted by millions with *Heil!*"[51]

Hans Jonas, professor at the New School of Social Research, the author of a study on the gnosis,[52] discovers Gnostic elements in modern existentialism.[53] Jakob Taubes,[54] professor of religion at Columbia University, characterizes the atheistic-materialistic philosophies of our time (Feuerbach, Marx, Nietzsche) as "apocalyptic."[55] He asserts a decisive affinity between the apocalyptic speculation and the gnosis on the one hand, and these philosophies, especially Marxism, on the other; he considers Hegel's dialectic, taken over by Marx, as a specifically apocalyptic-Gnostic method of thinking.[56] Taubes sees in the peri-

48 Ibid., p. 341.

49 Eugen Rosenstock-Huessey, Die europäischen Revolutionen (Jena, 1931), pp. 10 seq. He says: "The oldest revolutionary in Europe is the pope" because the first European revolution is the pope's attempt to recover Italy from the emperor. "From the revolution of the pope in Italy to the Bolshevik recovery of the Russian earth for the peasants a unitary intellectual current is rolling on" (p. 13). In his study The Christian Future; or The Modern Mind Outrun (London, 1947), Rosenstock writes: "Men like Karl Marx and Friedrich Nietzsche kept the flames of eschatology alive" (p. 70).

50 Alois Dempf, Sacrum Imperium (München/Berlin, 1929), pp. 12, 269, 281.

51 Löwith, Meaning in History, p. 159.

52 Hans Jonas, Gnosis und spätantiker Geist. Vol. I: Die mythologische Gnosis (Göttingen, 1934).

53 Hans Jonas, "Gnosticism and Modern Nihilism," Social Research, XIX (1952), pp. 430 seqq.

54 Jakob Taubes, Abendländische Eschatologie (Bern, 1947).

55 Ibid., p. 6.

56 Ibid., pp. 35 seqq.

odization of history into Antiquity, Middle Ages, and Modern Times a secularized version of Joachim's distinction of three ages (conforming to the concept of the holx trinity) – the ages of God Father, God Son, and God Holy Spirit.[57] He even traces to Joachim of Flora the beginning of the Copernican – in opposition to the Ptolemaic – picture of the world, one of the most characteristic elements of modern civilization.[58] This is possible only by a theological interpretation of the two astronomical hypotheses that Taubes takes over from the German theologian Erwin Reisner. The latter asserts that the view of the world in any epoch is determined by the concept of the relationship between earth and heaven.[59] The Ptolemaic view of the world, he suggests, is characterized by the idea of a heaven above the earth, housing God; and just as man is an image of God, earth is an image of heaven. The Copernican view of the world knows no such heaven; the earth is moving in empty space, surrounded by unlimited, meaningless nothing; living below a godless heaven, man becomes homeless on earth, and hence tries to create for himself a new home in the future, according to Reisner. The areligious Copernican ethics is oriented toward the future, says Reisner, and leads to activism – a specifically "plebeian" ideal, the ideal of the laboring man working for the future. "The victory of the ethos of labor is the victory of the proletariat, of the swarming multitude, a population of ants, who indefatigably crawl the earth and know nothing of the heaven above it."[60] Although Reisner does not say so expressly, he undoubtedly implies in his theological interpretation of the Copernican view of the world that Marxism is an activistic philosophy directed at the future. It is evidently this orientation toward the future which induces Taubes to place the origin of the Copernican view of the world in Joachim's eschatological interpretation of history. Following Rosenstock, Taubes characterizes the "history of the European eschatology ... as the history of the European revolutions"[61] and does not hesitate to conceive of "the law of modern times" as apocalyptic eschatology.[62]

One of the most conspicuous representatives of this school of thought is the outstanding political scientist Eric Voegelin, professor at the University of Munich. Under the influence of Löwith, Jonas, and Taubes, this author, in attempting to lay the foundations of "a new science of politics," which "must at the same time be a theory of history,"[63] declares the nature of modernity to be Gnosticism.[64] He characterizes as Gnosticism the humanistic and encyclope-

57 Ibid., p. 81.
58 Ibid., p. 88.
59 Erwin Reisner, Die christliche Botschaft im Wandel der Epochen (München, 1935), pp. 99 seqq.
60 Ibid., p. 125.
61 Taubes, Abendländische Eschatologie, p. 87.
62 Ibid., pp. 85 seqq.
63 Eric Voegelin, The New Science of Politics: An Introduction (Chicago, 1952), pp. 1 seqq.
64 Ibid., pp. 107 seqq.

dist periodization of history, Hegel's spiritualistic and Marx's materialistic philosophy of history, Feuerbach's critique of religion, Nietzsche's philosophy of the superman; but also Comte's positivism, the ideologies of the Russian Caesaropapism, the political theories of bolshevism and National Socialism, and even modern scientism. Gnostic politicians are, according to this new science of politics, Ivan the Terrible, but also Lenin, Hitler, but also the democratic opponents of communism and National Socialism, especially those who, like President Woodrow Wilson, advocate the abolition of war through an international organization.[65]

The Gnosis has been condemned by the Church as heretical; and Voegelin, following the judgment of the Church, considers Gnosticism, or what he imagines to be Gnosticism, a false religion, a heresy, and hence a dangerous error. In a pamphlet published in 1959, *Wissenschaft, Politik und Gnosis*,[66] he expresses the opinion that modern positivistic moral and social sciences constitute a "low state of science" [*"Tiefstand der Wissenschaft"*], responsible for the fact that the knowledge of the Gnostic character of "a main trend in European and especially German thinking" [*"eine Hauptlinie der europäischen und im besonderen der deutschen Denkbewegung"*] has been blocked. In this respect his new science of politics, which is directed against the antimetaphysical social science of the nineteenth and twentieth century, points in the same direction as Rosenstock's theologically oriented social philosophy. The latter, assuming that "the Gnostics taught that life had truth without need of historic Revelation," thinks "we can overcome the new hordes who make vitality their God only with a sword whose steel contains no alloy of Gnosticism or Humanism." By the "new hordes" he means modern "mechanizing science which makes man a mere derivation of antecedent causes" and hence is tempting us "to worship crude vitality, sensationalism, life at any price."[67]

This comparative philosophy of culture is more or less modeled after Oswald Spengler's intuitive, rather than scientific, and, to a great extent, fantastic morphology of history. According to Spengler, cultures of different ages, for instance the Hellenistic-Roman and our modern civilizations, are considered "contemporary" spiritual, cultural, or political epochs if they show certain real or imagined analogies.[68] In this sense Spengler assumes that the theology of history of Joachim of Flora, who wrote toward the end of the twelfth century, "corresponds" ["entspricht"] to the eschatological speculation of the gnosis, which flourished in the first Christian centuries.[69] Löwith applies

65 Ibid., pp. 111 seqq., 116, 124 seqq., 172 seqq.
66 Eric Voegelin, Wissenschaft, Politik und Gnosis (München, 1959), pp. 9, 10, 11.
67 Rosenstock-Huessy, The Christian Future, pp. 121–122.
68 Oswald Spengler, The Decline of the West (New York, 1932), Vol. I, Tables I-III.
69 Ibid., II, p. 250.

Spengler's concept of "pseudo-morphosis" – he characterizes the Communist creed "as a pseudo-morphosis of Jewish-Christian Messianism";[70] Jonas and Taubes refer to Spengler, for whose philosophy of history they profess great admiration.[71]

70 Löwith, op. cit., p. 46.

71 Jonas, Gnosis und spätantiker Geist, pp. 73 seqq.; Taubes, Abendländische Eschatologie, p. 22. Jonas, in "Gnosticism and Modern Nihilism," pp. 433 seq. writes: "The existence of an affinity or analogy across the ages, such as is here alleged, is not so surprising if we remember that in more than one respect the cultural situation in the Greco-Roman world of the first Christian centuries shows broad parallels with the modern situation. Spengler went so far as to declare the two ages 'contemporaneous' in the sense of being identical phases in the life cycle of their respective cultures. In this analogical sense we would now be living in the period of the early Ceasars. However that may be, there is certainly more than mere coincidence in the fact that we recognize ourselves in so many facets of later postclassical antiquity. Gnosticism is one of those facets ..."

Chapter I The Search for Parallelisms and Its Dangers

The search for parallelisms in the problems raised in different fields of knowledge, such as social theory and theology, politics, and religion, is a legitimate, useful, and undoubtedly scientific task. But this comparative method has two dangers. First, the tendency to find affinities may induce the author to overestimate similarities and to underestimate, even to ignore, essential differences between two phenomena, and second, to see identity where there is only the appearance of an analogy owing to the use of the same terms (such as "revolution," "liberty," "progress"), covering different meanings.[72]

A characteristic example of misinterpreting analogy as identity is Carl Schmitt, *Politische Theologie: Vier Kapitel zur Lehre von der Souveränität.*[73] He says: "All important concepts of modern political theory are secularized

72 I, too, have called attention to a certain parallelism between problems of jurisprudence and theology. For a scientific description, the state as an acting person is but the personification of a national legal order; but if this personification is hypostatized and thus the fiction of the state as a really existing thing different from and independent of the law is produced, the sham problem of a relationship between state and law arises; which resembles in many respects the theological problem of the relationship between God and world. See my Der soziologische und der juristische Staatsbegriff (Tübingen, 1922), pp. 219 seqq. However, the demonstration of this parallelism is meant only as an epistemological criticism of the dualistic theory of state and law. It does not imply the assumption that this dualism is a disguise of the theological dualism of God and world. I am far from turning the analogy into an identity. True, I characterize the dualism of state and law as state theology; but I say: "The postulate that the theory of state should cease to be a theology of state [meaning: should abandon its dualistic construction and be aware that the state is a legal order] is directed exclusively against its systematic dualism, which is characteristic of theology. It is from this dualism that the parallelism of sham problems and antinomies results. To recognize their inadmissibility is our foremost task. So far as theology presents itself as theory of a system of religious norms – and that means only as ethics – its methodological relationship to a theory of legal norms cannot be denied" (p. 253).

73 Carl Schmitt, Politische Theologie: Vier Kapitel zur Lehre von der Souveränität (München und Leipzig, 1922).

theological concepts."[74] But he demonstrates this thesis only on the concept of sovereignty: "Sovereign is he who decides about the state of emergency."[75] To establish a state of emergency (*Ausnahmezustand*) means to suspend the constitution or some of its provisions. But from the fact that the so-called sovereign is competent to establish a state of emergency does not follow that "sovereignty" is nothing else but this competence. A state whose constitution does not authorize the establishment of a state of emergency remains sovereign, if sovereignty is considered to be an essential quality of the state. The state of emergency is an exception in any case; and it is a paradox to see the decisive criterion of the normal quality in an exception. In order to justify it Schmitt goes so far as to declare: "The normal proves nothing, the exception proves everything."[76] Thus he tries – in vain – to make a virtue out of this necessity.

There is, indeed, a certain analogy between the sovereignty of the state, interpreted as "omnipotence" of the legislator, and the omnipotence of God. But Schmitt says: "The 'omnipotence' of the modern legislator to which all textbooks of political science refer, is not only linguistically taken over from theology."[77] That means it is a theological concept. But every scientific and not politically determined definition of the so-called omnipotence of the legislator stresses the difference between this concept and the omnipotence of God. The omnipotence of God is unlimited: the so-called omnipotence of the legislator means only his competence to make and unmake positive law. His omnipotence is restricted to the process of legislation. Only the ideologists of the absolute monarchy who present the power of the head of state as derived from God and the head of state as the representative and image of God try to make the people believe the power of the head of state is an image of the power of God. Thus, for example, Jean Bodin[78] says: "Puis qu'il n'y a rien plus grand en terre apres Dieu que les Princes souverains, et qu'ils sont etablis de lui comme ses lieutenants, pour commander aux autres hommes, il est besoin de prendre garde a leur qualité, afin de respecter et reverer leur maiesté en toute obeissance, sentir et parler d'eux en tout honneur: ca qui mesprise son Prince souverain, il mesprise Dieu, duquel il est l'image en terre."[79] But even Bodin defines sovereignty as the power to make and unmake the law. He says: "Et par ainsi nous conclurons que la premiere marque du prince souverain, c'est la puissance de donner loy à tous en general, et à chacun en particulier."[80] And: "Sous ceste mesme puissance de donner et casser la loy, sont compris tous les

74 Ibid., p. 37.
75 Ibid., p. 9.
76 Ibid., p. 15.
77 Ibid., p. 38.
78 Jean Bodin, Les Six Livres de la Republique (1599).
79 Ibid., p. 211–212.
80 Ibid., p. 221.

autres droits et marques de souveraineté: de sorte qu'à parler proprement on peut dire qu'il n'y a que ceste seule marque de souverineté attendu que tous les autres droits sont compris en cestui-là: comme decerner la guerre, ou faire la paix ... qui sont les vrayes marques de souveraineté, comprises sous la puissance de donner la loy à tous en general, et à chacun en particulier, et ne la recevoir que de Dieu."[81] It is, therefore, not correct, if Schmitt, in order to justify his definition of sovereignty, refers to the theory of Bodin who, as Schmitt,[82] considers the right to *annul* the positive law as the proper mark of sovereignty and therefore tries to derive all the other marks from it: "Darum ist die Befugnis, das geltende Gesetz aufzuheben – sei es generell, sei es im einzelnen Fall –, so sehr das eigentliche Kennzeichen der Souveränität, dass Bodin alle anderen Merkmale (Kriegserklärung und Friedensschluss ...) daraus ableiten will." It is – as the quoted sentences show – not the right to *annul* the positive law, but the right "to make and to unmake the law," that is, the power of legislation, from which Bodin derives the other marks of sovereignty.

Misused in this way, the method of a comparative theory of culture may deteriorate into empty verbalism. A typical example is the use – or misuse – of the word "revolution." In the language of our time the word has the specifically political meaning of the overthrow by force, in a mass movement, of a government which, actually or allegedly, suppresses natural rights. The attraction that the idea of revolution exerts on intellectuals and the masses derives from its connotation of liberation from suppression, material and spiritual. This ideological element is decisive in our idea of the two great revolutions – the French revolution of the eighteenth and the Russian revolution of the twentieth century. Both are directed against a religious ideology used by a government to maintain its authority. But how can this ideology be defended against the reproach of suppression? By showing that it is "revolutionary" itself – that the representative of this ideology, the pope, as Rosenstock tries to prove, inaugurated the first European revolution, a "world revolution spreading over Europe."[83] This can be done only by describing as "revolution" the pope's attempt to recover Italy from the emperor. According to Rosenstock, the "revolutionary" element of this *recuperatio* consists "in the intervention of the pope in the territorial questions of the Apennine Peninsula." The recuperation is at the same time a "renovation." "This is the catchword which stands at the top of all revolutions," says Rosenstock. "But it sounds also in the mouth of the spiritual revolutionary, who successfully rebelled against the – only apparently renovating – empire, the pope." "The revolutionaries and the pope have far too long considered themselves as absolute adversaries, because of their ideologies.

81 Ibid., p. 223.
82 Schmitt, Politische Theologie: Vier Kapitel zur Lehre von der Souveränität, p. 11.
83 For this passage, and those immediately following, see Rosenstock, Die europäische Revolutionen, pp. 11, 12.

Both, however, are born from the same spirit, the fates of both are revolutionary. The Russian revolution, too, still contains a remnant of that syllable 're' which we meet in all true revolutions. They are all rebellions of the recovery of a primary right [*Urrecht*], a natural condition of the world. Thus misapplying the word "revolution" to the pope's policy of recovering from the emperor the dominion over Italy, the policy of the head of Christianity is interpreted as the model for the Bolshevik revolution against the Christian religion as the ideology of capitalism! You are mistaken, the author says to the revolutionaries, to fight the Church as your enemy, for it is as "revolutionary" as yourselves. The difference between the pope's fight and the Russian revolution is ignored. But this difference is so essential that the minor similarity between the pope's opposition to the emperor, and the Bolshevik's fight against the capitalist government is irrelevant.

Another example of such pseudoparallelism is Dempf's glorification of Joachim as the prophet of modern times for predicting that in 1260 an epoch of monarchism, and thus of a perfect religious life, will begin. Dempf must admit that the time predicted by Joachim was the time of the *spiritualis intelligentia*, an intellectual ideal of the Christian Middle Ages, whereas the modern times are the time of science,[84] which is the opposite intellectual ideal. The difference is fundamental. The fact that a monk at the end of the twelfth century wrongly predicted the realization of a Christian religious ideal is certainly insufficient reason to attribute to him the inauguration of a period supposed to be the realization of a rationalistic, areligious principle.

History may be interpreted in two fundamentally different ways. One is to regard the evolution of mankind as the realization of the will of man, the other as the realization of the will of God. One is philosophy of history; the other is theology of history. Löwith, in his study on the meaning in history, tries to obliterate this difference by using the term "philosophy of history" to denote "a systematic interpretation of universal history in accordance with a principle by which historical events and successions are unified and directed toward an ultimate meaning."[85] On the basis of this definition, he unveils the modern philosophies of history (which imply the idea of progress and predict the future state of a perfect society) as "secularized" theology in general and as a "modern transfiguration" of Joachim of Flora's theology of history in particular. Löwith thus uses the same conceptual device which Sertillanges employs in the phrase "laicize the Christian thought,"[86] or in the formula "secularized parousia."[87] Voegelin, too, speaks of a "parousia of reality [*Parusie des Seins*]",

84 Dempf, Sacrum Imperium, pp. 280 seq.

85 Löwith, Meaning in History, p. 1.

86 Sertillanges, Le Christianisme, I, p. 71.

87 Ibid., II, p. 223; or the statement: "le mystère éclair à sa façon [the mystery makes clear]", I, p. 15.

which is substituted for the "parousia of Christ." This "parousia of reality" means "the expectation of a salvation in which the power of reality is substituted for the power of God."[88] However, "secularized" theology, just like "laicized Christian thought," "secularization" of an "eschatological pattern,"[89] or a "secular religion,"[90] are contradictions in terms, for to secularize an institution or a doctrine means to exclude all religious elements from it. A "secular religion" is a dereligionized religion, which means no religion at all. Secularization or laicization implies an intellectual attitude opposed to that of theology or religion. The idea of *parousia*, that is, the presence of the divine in earthly things (especially of Christ on earth, his second coming) cannot be "laic" because the meaning of "laic" is incompatible with that attitude; and to say, that the parousia of Christ is replaced by the "parousia of reality" is an inadmissible misuse of the word parousia, for a parousia of reality in which the divine is absent, is no paraousia in the only proper sense of this term. Similarly, an eschatological pattern cannot be secularized because a secular view of the word denies an *eschaton*. "Eschaton" means the "ultimate," that is, the absolutely final state of man or mankind – "absolutely" final because predestined by the absolute will of God, the absolute *par excellence*. The eschaton is a metaphysical-transcendental idea of the future. But the future predicted by a secular philosophy of history is directly opposed to the Christian eschaton, which is a spiritual, religiously perfect state of the individual soul, the state of salvation, that is, the deliverance from sin through the atoning and redemptive work of Jesus Christ; whereas a secular philosophy of history foresees an entirely temporal state of social welfare, a relative optimum of social organization achieved through the work of man without any religious implication.

Rosenstock, too, speaks of a secularized eschaton, saying that Marx preaches the eschatology of the Old Testament. Rosenstock defines, correctly, the essence of eschatology as "the infinity; it asks complete surrender to something outside the existing order of things."[91] But it is precisely the "existing order of things," the order of *this* world, to which the specifically modern philosophies of history refer. A "secularized" eschatology is the negation of eschatology.

The self-contradictory concept of a "secularized eschatology" is consciously or unconsciously used because it implies that in the philosophy or sociology of the authors concerned the eschatology of the Christian faith still lingers despite their attempt to abandon it. Their attempt is in vain: Their intellectual aim cannot be reached without the Christian belief in the last things.[92]

---

88 Voegelin, Wissenschaft, Politik und Gnosis, p. 60.

89 Löwith, Meaning in History, p. 2.

90 Aron, L'Avenir, pp. 210 seqq.

91 Rosenstock-Huessy, The Christian Future, pp. 70 f.

92 Bultmann, History and Eschatology, p. 59, says that "for the Christian historians we cannot speak of a meaning which is immanent in the process of history. The meaning is im-

Raymond Aron tries to justify the view that certain antireligious doctrines are "secular religions" (see below, pp. 25 seqq.). He says: "I propose to call 'se-

posed on history by the divine providence." This is a teleological view of history. "The teleological view of history could be secularized, as could also Augustine's conception of the struggle between the 'Civitas terrena' and the 'Civitas Dei.' The concept of teleology made it possible to understand the struggle in secular terms as the struggle between the dark powers of nature and unreasonableness on the one hand, and the enlightened reason on the other. Even the idea of the fall of Adam as the origin of history could be taken over, if the fall was no longer understood as a unique historical event, but interpreted as a symbol of the fall of men from the good. The idea of the eschatological consummation could be interpreted as the victory of reason regarded as the necessary end of the historical development" (p. 61). But if the struggle between the "Civitas terrena" and the "Civitas Dei" is understood as the struggle between dark and light powers, that is to say, between evil and good, and if Adam's fall is interpreted not as a unique event but as the fall of men from the good, neither Augustin's two cities nor Adam's fall play any part in the philosophy of history and, then, eschatology is not secularized but abandoned. If there is no metaphysical implication, no connection with the transcendental will of God, there is no eschatology in the antagonism between good and evil; whereas in eschatology the antagonism between good and evil is essentially inherent. In other words eschatology is by its nature a good-evil speculation, but a good-evil speculation is not necessarily eschatological. It may have a purely secular character. "The historiography of the Renaissance," says Bultmann, "furthers the process of secularization only indirectly, in so far as it adopts a profane understanding of history after the example of the Ancients. According to this it is man, not God, who sets the historical process going. The apocalyptic tradition with its scheme of the four world-empires of Daniel is abandoned and the idea of the eschatological end of history is dropped" (p. 63). This means that, according to Bultmann's own words, secularizing eschatology is equivalent to abandoning it, to accepting a view opposite to eschatology.

It is understandable that a theologian like Bultmann makes use of the self-contradictory concept of secularized eschatology. For, from the point of view of theology the meaning of historicity is revealed only in the eschatology of the Christian faith, and every attempt to find a meaning in history is consciously or unconsciously eschatology. "There can be no doubt," he says, "that the radical understanding of the historicity of man has appeared in Christianity, the way being prepared in the Old Testament. This is proved by the fact that real autobiography arose for the forst time within Christianity. From this origin the understanding of the human beiing as historical became effective in the West, and it remained vivid even when it was divorced from Christian faith and secularized as in the modern philosophy of existence which finds its extreme form in Sartre" – who is an atheist (p. 149). "Jesus Christ is the eschatological event, not as an established fact of past time but as repeatedly present, as addressing you and me here and now in preaching" (pp. 151–152). "Every instant has the possibility of being an eschatological instant and in Christian faith this possibility is realised" (p. 154). "The meaning in history lies always in the present, and when the present is conceived as the eschatological present by Christan faith the meaning in history is realised" (p. 155).

R. G. Collingwood, in The Idea of History (Oxford, 1951, p. 54) says: "Eschatology is always an intrusive element in history. The historian's business is to know the past, not to know the future; and whenever historians claim to be able to determine the future in cular religions' the doctrines that take in the minds of our contemporaries the place of the vanished faith and transfer the salvation of mankind to this world in the form of a social order to be established in a remote future."[93] The first statement that some doctrines, such as socialism, take the place of faith in the minds of men presupposes that these doctrines have the same character as the vanished faith, that is, the character of a religion. This, however, is still the question which Aron is obviously begging. The second statement implies the idea that the "salvation of mankind" at which doctrines such as socialism are aiming is the same as the salvation of mankind at which a religion such as Christianity is directed. Only if the two salvations are thus equated may these doctrines be called "religions." But the social order which, according to Marxian socialism, is to be established in the future on this earth, guaranteeing as much happiness as possible to everyone without regard to his merits, is evidently something totally different from the "salvation," which the Christian religion promises only to those who believe in the divine Saviour and conduct their lives in conformity with his teaching, as a reward for their piety. Aron seems to be aware of this fact because he speaks of an "earthly salvation [*salut terrestre*]".[94] But this is not salvation in the sense that this term has in Christian religion. To use this term for two different things obscures their essential difference and hence the difference between socialism and religions – "true religions"[95] or, as Aron himself occasionally says: the "religions of salvation."[96] By obscuring these differences Aron arrives at his contradictory term: "secular religion." Aron knows that this terminology will encounter objections based on the fact that what he calls "religion" has no transcendent object. But he thinks he can reject these objections. "The psychologist or sociologist [this is, of course, Aron himself] will tell us: 'A man is religious not only when he worships a divinity, but also when he puts all resources of his mind, all devotions of his will, all the ardor of fanaticism in the service of a cause or of something

advance of its happening, we may know with certainty that something has gone wrong with their fundamental conception of history." He states that from the Christian point of view God's, not man's, purpose is decisive and that the only force that determines the course of history is divine nature. "Hence the divine nature being revealed, those to whom it is revealed by faith can see by faith what the future must be" (p. 55). An attempt to predict the future does not necessarily presuppose Christian eschatology. The possibility of predicting future events is according to a widespread opinion the consequence of knowing the laws of causality determining nature als well as society. On this basis Comte, Nietzsche, Marx try to predict the future of society. True, they were not historians, but sociologists or social philosophers. But this difference is irrelevant with respect to the noneschatological character of their predictions.

93 Aron, op. cit., p. 210.

94 Ibid., p. 217.

95 Ibid., p. 217.

96 Ibid., p. 277.

which has become the purpose and the end of his sentiments and actions.' Now it is a fact that secular religions are capable of converting minds to the same devotion, the same intransigence, the same unconditional fervour as religious faiths at the time of their most imperious and most universal rise."[97] It is a logical fallacy to conclude from *the intensity of the feelings* with which men cling to some ideas, anything about *the nature* of these ideas, so that a doctrine is a "religion," if the intensity with which a man is convinced of its truth is the same as the intensity with which a man believes in the existence of an all-just and all-powerful God. Even a scientific doctrine, rejecting any presupposition of a transcendent, supernatural power, could then be presented as a religion.[98]

---

97 Ibid., p. 210.

98 Bernard Bosanquet, in Baldwin's Dictionary of Philosophy and Psychology (New York and London, 1911), in the article on Philosophy of Religion defines religion as follows: "A man's real religion, it may be said, is that set of objects, habits, and convictions, whatever it might prove to be, which he would die for rather than abandon, or at least would feel himself excommunicated from humanity if he did abandon." With reference to the first part of the definition Walter Kaufmann, in Critique of Religion and Philosophy (New York, 1958, p. 72), says correctly: "Few people would die for their religion rather than abandon it and many more would die for other things." James Martineau's definition in A Study of Religion (New York, 1888, I, p. 1) that religion is "belief in an Everliving God, that is, a Divine Mind and Will ruling the Universe and holding Moral relations with mankind," is too narrow, because it does not apply to primitive religions. James H. Leuba, in A Psychological Study of Religion (New York, 1912), p. 52, defines: "Religion is that part of human experience in which man feels himself in relation with powers of psychic nature, usually personal powers, and makes use of them." This definition is acceptable only if by "powers" superhuman or supernatural powers are to be understood. The typical argument against a definition of religion as a belief in a supernatural power on which the fate of man depends (i. e., a belief in God or God-like beings) is that Buddhism knows no such belief and yet is called a religion. See C. J. Ducasse, A Philosophical Scrutiny of Religion (New York, 1953, pp. 17 seq., 22 seq.). However, a definition of religion which – following the uncritical usage of language – tries to comprehend in one conception all the essentially different objects that actually are called "religion," such as Judaism, Christianity, Mohammedanism and in addition also Buddhism, is worthless. Besides, such a definition is misleading, because it obliterates the fundamental difference between the belief in God and a philosophy which includes no such belief or which even denies the existence of supernatural powers. Ducasse, pp. 22–23, admits that "the gods were no objects of worship in the religion he [Buddha] founded. They played no part in it ... Buddhism, which is one of the noblest religions of mankind ... is also the outstanding instance of a religion 'atheistic' in the sense just indicated." But Buddhism is not an atheistic or, as Ducasse later (p. 35) formulates it, a "nontheistic" religion, but an atheistic philosophy of being, and specifically an atheistic doctrine about a morally perfect life – an atheistic ethics. See Fritz Mauthner, Der Atheismus und seine Geschichte im Abendland (Stuttgart and Berlin, 1920–1923, IV, p. 415 seq.).
An outstanding authority in the field of history of religion, Max Müller, in his work, Lectures on the Science of Religion (New York, 1874), considers the belief in God to be an essential element of religion. He says: "The intention of religion, wherever we meet it,

Aron himself makes this objection. He says of the quoted attempt to justify his term "secular religion": "This argument, if isolated, would be of no great importance. For it would amount to calling religion every doctrine which produces ardent passions and, simultaneously, nurtures the intolerance and violence of faith. But it seems to me that certain doctrines of our time deserve the name of secular religions in a more precise sense." His new argument is: The function of religion is to determine the supreme values directing human existence; and since the political doctrines of our time, especially Marxian socialism, determine such supreme values, they are essentially religious. This conclusion is the result of an erroneous identification of religion with morals, that is, a system of moral norms based on values inevitably presupposed to be supreme (which does not mean, as Aron seems to assume, that they are absolute values). Such a system is not necessarily religious. Some moral systems have no relation to any religion. The moral values of a religion are characterized by the belief that they are established by the will of God or a godlike transcendent being and hence are absolute. As long as a moral-political doctrine – such as Marxian socialism – does not base its values on the will of a superhuman, supernatural being, there is no reason to call it a religion, or – as Aron does – "Manicheism."[99] Any system of moral-political values, by its nature, implies the distinc-

is always holy. However imperfect, however childish a religion may be, it always places the human soul in the presence of God; and however imperfect and however childish the conception of God may be, it always represents the highest ideal of perfection which the human soul, for the time being, can reach and grasp. Religion therefore places the human soul in the presence of its highest ideal, it lifts it above the level of ordinary goodness, and produces at least a yearning after a higher and better life – a life in the light of God" (p. 116). But quite inconsistently he speaks of Buddhism as of a religion although he can not deny that in the teachings of Buddha there is no place for a god. He says: "In no religion are we so constantly reminded of our own as in Buddhism, and yet in no religion has man drawn away so far from the truth as in the religion of Buddha. Buddhism and Christianity are indeed the two opposite poles with regard to the most essential points of religion; Buddhism ignoring all feeling of dependence on a higher power, and therefore denying the very existence of a supreme Deity; Christianity resting entirely on a belief in God as the Father, in the Son of Man as the Son of God, and making us all children of God by faith in his Son" (p. 113). It is true that Müller takes into consideration the possibility of distinguishing between Buddhism and the teaching of Buddha (p. 138). But he denies that such a separation is practicable for us. As far as the decisive point is concerned, the atheism, he does not think that any one passage from the books of the Buddhist canon can be quoted which "presupposes the belief in a personal God or a Creator" (p. 139). And in open contradiction to his quoted definition of religion Müller speaks of "atheistic religions" and says that "the religion of Buddha was from the beginning purely atheistic" (p. 52). Cf. T. W. Rhys Davids, Buddhism, its History and Literature (New York and London, 1896), p. 5, where the author refers to that contradiction in Müller's work.

99 Aron, L'Avenir, p. 215.

tion between good and evil – a distinction which is possible without recourse to God or godlike beings, and without referring to absolute values; hence, a moral-political interpretation of history may – without assuming religious character – see in the flux of events a permanent struggle between good and evil tendencies of the men making history. Although Marxism denies that its doctrine contains moral ideals, it implies such a view. But though, as a political theory, Marxism actually presupposes moral values, it does not consider them as established by God. Manicheism, however, is a true religion. For, the fight between good and evil forces – the forces of light and the forces of darkness, which according to this religion, exist in the reality of nature – is the struggle between supernatural beings, hence totally different from the struggle between good and evil tendencies of men, even if these tendencies are, erroneously, hypostatized as good and evil "forces."

Only on the basis of the inadmissible identification of religion and morals can Aron assert that the political doctrines of our time – including Marxism – show traits which are characteristics of religious dogmas.[100] A dogma is a truth revealed by God and proclaimed by the Church. This proclamation implies the obligation to believe in this truth, an obligation sanctioned by divine punishment. The Marxian doctrine contains nothing that could be considered as a dogma in the proper sense of this term. There is no truth revealed by God, and no truth which Marxists are "obliged" to believe in. That a man who does not believe in the truth of the Marxian doctrine is not considered a Marxist, is different from the obligation to believe, implied in the concept of a religious dogma.

Another argument for the religious character of political doctrine is Aron's statement that they furnish "*une interpretation globale du monde*," which probably means a view of the entire cosmos, a cosmology. This is certainly not true for Marxian socialism, which is only an interpretation of human history, as Aron, correcting his statement, admits by adding in parenthesis: "at least of the historical world." He says further that the political doctrines of our time, especially Marxism, "explain the meaning of catastrophes through which unhappy mankind is passing, and permit the perceiving of the far-away outcome of these tragic trials." The attempt to foresee and explain disastrous situations of human society has in itself no religious character, but the way in which these catastrophes are explained can be "religious." Marx's doctrine does not explain the facts which it considers catastrophes, as Christian religion explains analogous facts: as a punishment which God inflicts upon men for their sins. Marxian doctrine explains catastrophes as the natural effect of social causes; and it predicts the outcome of the trial not, as Christian religion does, as a divine intervention into human history, but as the effect of human action. The end of the trial, according to Marxism, is the future communist society. Aron calls it "the future community of saved mankind [*la communauté future*

100 Ibid., p. 211.

de l'humanité sauvée]". The word "*sauvée*" is ambiguous. It means simply "rescued," delivered from an evil. In this sense humanity, in the future state of communism, may be called "*sauvée*". But the term has also a specific religious meaning: "blessed," "blissful," a state of the mind delivered from sin, the effect of the redemption, the work of the divine Saviour. In this sense certainly there will be no "*humanité sauvée*" in the future communist society according to Marxian doctrine. To call Marxian socialism a "religion" because it predicts a "*communauté future de l'humanité sauvée*" is the misuse of the ambiguity of a term.

Crane Brinton tries to justify his interpretation of the philosophy of the Enlightenment and its offsprings as secular religion in a way similar to that of Aron. For Brinton as a historian of morals and ethics, the relation between morals and religion, theology and ethics is a fundamental problem. "We must," he says, "examine the very thorny problem of what we mean by religion and what religion has to do with morals. The problem is thorny for us largely because a great number of educated Westerners today consider that they have no religion but do have morals, and that the separation of religion and morals is a natural, normal part of Western life." Brinton asserts: "Historically speaking, this is simply not so; religion and morals have been intimately related, though it makes little sense to say that either is the 'cause' of the other." He does not tell, in this context, what he means by religion; he says only: "Any sort of religious belief, including most emphatically our own secular religions like nationalism, Marxism, the various positivist or rationalist beliefs stemming mostly from the eighteenth-century Enlightenment, gives our judgments on all forms of religion an inescapable emotional bias."[101] The relation between religion and morals, he says, is "so close as to be, in real life for real people, a felt unity." "The old debate as to whether religion and morals *can* be divorced ought at least to be somewhat affected by what seems to me the fact that in Western experience they *never have been* divorced."[102] He goes so far as to assert – without restricting himself to a historical approach: "I consider the concept of a society without a religion as much nonsense as the concept of a human society without human beings;"[103] and since, in his opinion, "morality is at once a part of man's being and the whole of it,"[104] we assume as his view that there is no morality without religion – a view whose truth can hardly be demonstrated if it refers not only to the past but also to the future of mankind, but which precisely in this general significance is one of the most favored arguments advanced by theology for the necessity of religion.

101 Brinton, A History of Western Morals, pp. 38–39.

102 Ibid,. p. 28.

103 Ibid., p. 468.

104 Ibid., p. 6.

The relationship which Brinton supposes to exist between religion and morals determines his concept of religion. He says, the statement that religion and morals have never been divorced in Western experience "does, indeed, imply a definition of religion that by no means all Westerners will accept."[105] What is this definition? Brinton gives no clear answer to this question. He distinguishes two kinds of religions: religions with and religions without a supernatural godhead. "I am being quite fashionable today when I note modern Marxism as one of these religions without supernatural godhead. What the Marxist believes about the nature of the universe – his religion – seems to me to have some relation to what he believes about the nature of man and his place in that universe – his morals. The same is true of the positivist, the rationalist, the member of an ethical-culture society, and all the other varieties of what M. Raymond Aron calls a 'secular religion'."[106] The "nature of the universe" is the problem of a natural science, called "cosmology," and not of a social science; and Marxism claims to be a social, not a natural science. Consequently there is no specific Marxian belief about the nature of the universe, no Marxian cosmology, as there is a Marxian "belief," that is, a theory about the nature of man and his place – not in the universe, but in society and history.

Since Marxism is an atheistic social theory, it implies the rejection of the belief that man as a social being is created by God and that human history is governed by divine will. It is true that Marxism has ethical implications which may have some relation to its atheism, but they stand in no relation to its nonexistent cosmology. A Marxist's beliefs about the nature of man and his place in society and history are not identical with his morals. Morals are a system of norms prescribing human behavior. A theory of the nature of man and his place in society may have no normative character at all, and has very little of it in the Marxian sociological theory of history.

From Brinton's statement quoted above it seems to follow that he considers a theory about the nature of the universe (even if it does not presuppose the existence of a supernatural godhead) as a religion, namely a secular religion, in contradistinction to a belief in the existence of such a godhead, that is a nonsecular religion, a religious religion the one being a contradiction in terms, the other a pleonasm. But he does not explain why he designates as religion an atheistic belief about the nature of the universe.

There is not only an accepted term to designate a theory about the nature of the universe, namely cosmology; but also a generally accepted distinction between a metaphysical-religious or theological cosmology, such as presented in the first chapter of *Genesis*, and a secular, that is, areligious cosmology, presented by modern empirical science. To call both "religions" amounts to obscuring the essential difference between these two kinds of cosmologies and –

105 Ibid., p. 28.
106 Ibid., p. 29.

in the last analysis – between religion and science. As we shall see later, Brinton's work shows clear tendencies in this direction (see below, pp. 31 seqq.). Now the question arises: What is the purpose – or effect – of obscuring this difference whose recognition is fundamental to the spirit of modern times? The answer is to be found in works of theologians who welcome this reinterpretation of modern philosophy and science; who want us to go back to religion, to let theology again rule over science.

It seems that Brinton himself had some scruples about Aron's "secular religion." He says: "Since words like 'religion' and 'theology' applied, say, to modern Western nationalism, or to Marxism, or to any form of Enlightenment clearly do offend many Christians, I shall reluctantly fall back at times on that horrid Germanism 'world view' ['*Weltanschauung*'] (p. 29). To call antireligious, atheist doctrines "religions" does not offend Christians as much as it offends atheistic, antitheological thinkers whose views are called "religions." As a matter of fact, Christian theologians like Sertillanges, Niebuhr, Bultmann, and religiously minded writers like Gerlich,[107] Löwith, Gilson, Voegelin, and others applied this terminology long before Brinton. It is objectionable not because it wounds religious feelings, but because it is logically inadmissible, implying a contradiction in terms. Besides, the meaning of *Weltanschauung* is not identical with "belief about the nature of the universe." This German term means a speculation about the essence and meaning of the world and of human life, ethics being an essential part of it. Its meaning is different from that of the word "religion." For there are two kinds of world views strictly opposed to each other: a religious and an areligious (even antireligious) or secular world view. Hence the term "world view" cannot be substituted for the term "religion." By substituting, at times, the "horrid Germanism 'world view'" for the term "religion," Brinton does not escape the obligation to justify his concept of a "secular religion."

That seems to be his own feeling. For, toward the end of his work, in which he consistently speaks of the Enlightenment and its offspring as of religions, immediately after a passage in which he refers to the Enlightenment as to "the new faith," he again mentions that "to many [it] does not even seem to be a religion"; "the word 'religion' is for most people reserved for Christianity and other theisms, and for what the anthropologist calls religion. In the Communist world and among the anti-Christians in the free world rebellion against Christian theism is so strong that the word 'religion' is for them an indecent word. It would be nice if we had another word that would do the work of 'religion,' and tie together instances of human behavior that the classifying intellect finds; it useful to put together, not at the species level, but at the genus level. But I know of no such useful word, and refuse to coin one."[108] Which are

107 Gerlich became a convert to Roman Catholicism in 1931.

108 Brinton, A History of Western Morals, p. 375.

these "instances of human behavior" for which Brinton can find no other words but "secular religion"? Until now he used this term not to characterize "instances of human behavior" but philosophical and political doctrines, such as rationalism, materialism, evolutionarism, positivism, democratism, and above all Marxism. What he means by "instances of human behavior" he tries perhaps to explain when he says later: "In the eighteenth century an important number of human beings in the West came to take toward man's fate here on earth an attitude only a few human beings had taken previously, an attitude nowhere better summed up than in the words of one of the leaders of those who took this new view: all men on earth have rights to 'life, liberty and the pursuit of happiness.' These rights were more important because Jefferson and many of his fellows were fairly sure that no one had any other life anywhere save his own present one on this earth." Jefferson's famous proclamation of these human rights is a typical expression of moral ideas of the Enlightenment – its ideas about man's duties and rights, which are the core of its secular ethics. "Now," says Brinton, "I shall call this set of attitudes toward man's fate the 'faith' of the Enlightenment, thus dodging temporarily at least the word 'religion,' though clinging to the word faith to what seems to me inescapable in man's fate." It is not possible to dodge the word "religion" by using the word "faith" because both words have the same meaning and are actually employed by Brinton as synonymous. He tries to justify his calling some attitudes toward man's fate "faith" by adding: "for us all, both 'seeing is believing' and 'believing is seeing' are true and necessary statements, but the latter usually prevails in a conflict." It certainly is not correct that the two statements are "for us all" true and necessary; and Brinton himself immediately admits: "The rationalism of the eighteenth century of course denied the second proposition."[109] However that may be, Brinton understands by "faith of the Enlightenment" its moral ideas, its ethics. His previous attempt at explaining "secular religion" as an areligious cosmology, is abandoned. By secular religion he means secular morals. Since he considers morals "inseparable" from religion, since he assumes that the two form "in real life for real people" a "felt unity," he is so near to identify morals with religion that he finally thinks primarily of morals when he speaks of religion. Immediately before the quoted passage concerning the attitudes toward man's fate Brinton says: "The new faith [meaning the "new faith of the Enlightenment"] has an ethical code that makes material satisfactions in themselves a good ... The new faith has a melioristic, even an idealistic, ethics;" "in its orthodox form of nationalist democracy" it has made a "kind of compromise with its ideals." He speaks of "the heresies of the new faith,"[110] and since these "heresies" include the ethics of the new faith, this ethics, as a heresy, must be a religion. As a matter of fact it is only the "ethical code" of the new faith

109 Ibid., p. 376.
110 Ibid., p. 374.

which is the "secular religion" that Brinton sees in the Enlightenment and its offspring. Since the morals of the Enlightenment and its offspring, especially Marxism, are decidedly secular and their ethics nontheological and antireligious, he calls them "secular religions." In this respect, too, he follows Aron.

Brinton refers in numerous passages to morals as to religion. Although he characterizes the Enlightenment throughout his work as a "new religion,"[111] he says at the beginning of the chapter "The Age of Reason;"[112] "In the course of the eighteenth century a 'New Moral World,' to borrow the phrase of Robert Owen, one of the most hopeful prophets of this world, came into full competition with the complex of older moral worlds we Westerners had been living in." If a moral world has a "prophet," morals is conceived as a religion. Brinton continues: "By this sweeping statement I do not at all wish to deny that the origins of the 'new morality' go back well into the medieval centuries." In this connection he speaks of "the fundamental positions of this new morality, this new world view" of the Enlightenment. The "horrid Germanism" – "world view" – is the term he "at times" substitutes for the normally used word "religion." As the characteristic element of this "new world view" or "new morality" he refers to the fact that it sought to substitute "for the *transcendental* God-determined Christian otherworldly heaven a this-world *transformed* by human reason guiding human action into ... well, the phrase is inadequate, but 'a heaven on earth' will have to do."

Brinton admits that it is "inadequate" to characterize the social ideas of the Enlightenment as a "heaven on earth." Yet only on the basis of this inadequate figure of speech can he call, in the following passage, the enlightened doctrine of progress toward a morally satisfactory state of society the "basic article of faith of the eighteenth-century Enlightenment," an "eighteenth-century eschatology," a "messianic belief."[113] To answer the question as to how this "inadequate" figure of speech could be taken literally, the statement in which this astonishing jump of thought takes place must be quoted: "Now Americans today are so used to this basic article of faith of the eighteenth-century Enlightenment – though not by any means in its fresh, revolutionary, immediacy of 1789, when it took on intensities worth comparing with early Christian expectance of a Second Coming, when, indeed, this eighteenth-century eschatology was a messianic belief – that it is hard for us to realize that, as at least belief that for *all* human beings the 'pursuit of happiness' and the attainment of comfort here on earth are normal and expected aims, this world view is new indeed." Since the conviction of the justice of the principle that all men on earth have the rights to life, liberty, and the pursuit of happiness, *took on inten-*

111 In the Index, under "Enlightenment," we read: "as new religion: 297 seqq., 306 seqq., 370 n., 374 seqq., 450 seqq."

112 Brinton, A History of Western Morals, p. 293.

113 Ibid., p. 294.

sity worth comparing with Christian expectance of a Second Coming, this conviction is the belief in an article of faith, an eschatology, a Messianic belief, and consequently the philosophy of the Enlightenment which proclaimed this ethical-political principle is, to Brinton, a religion.

In another connection Brinton, after having referred to the Christian crusades, calls the wars into which the French and the Russian revolutions resulted "the secular crusades that followed hard on the establishment of the two most active forms of the faith of the Enlightenment: that of French Jacobins and that of the Russian Bolsheviks."[114]

Then he adds: "Even plain nationalism, not raised to very religious intensity, has inspired men to fight and resist with more than ordinary persistence, fury, and intolerance. There is no escaping the commonplace; men do fight best when they fight for a cause, fight best of all to help God, or Reason, or Dialectical Materialism bring about the inevitable." The decisive point in this statement is the concept of "religious intensity": If the intensity with which men cling to a certain idea has a certain degree, it is "religious," which means the idea has a religious character. Since the Jacobins and the Bolsheviks were so intensely convinced of the justice of their ideas that they even resorted to war for them, their ideas were forms of a (secular) faith and the wars (secular) crusades.

In another connection Brinton says about Russian Communists: "The mere passage of time must gradually lessen the intensity of their religious faith, their revolutionary desire to conquer and convert. Russians moved by nationalism alone, by mere pooled self-esteem, may be less formidable than Russians moved by a spiritual *élan* we do not really understand, but which we have seen in the revolutionary France of 1794, in Christian crusades, and in Moslem jihads."[115] The "intensity" with which the Russians fight for communism, then, makes their atheistic doctrine a "religious faith." If we have seen their "spiritual *elan*" in the wars which the Christians and Moslems waged for their religions, then the *elan* with which the Soviets try to establish communism over the earth is a religious *elan*, a "religiously derived *elan*." This is the same logical fallacy on which Brinton's authority, Raymond Aron, first tried to base his concept of a "secular religion," but which Aron finally dropped (see above, pp. 24 seq.).

Unfortunately even Bertrand Russel and Julian Huxley, whose antitheological attitudes are beyond doubt, define religion in a way that justifies the self-contradictory concept of a secular religion. Bertrand Russel, in *Religion and* Science[116], presents two different characteristics of religion. First he says:

114 Ibid., p. 429.

115 Ibid., p. 412.

116 Bertrand Russell, Religion und Science. First published 1935, and reprinted (= The Home University Library of Modern Knowledge, 178; London, New York, Toronto, 1956).

"Religion, considered socially, is a more complex phenomenon than science. Each of the great historical religions has three aspects: (1) a church, (2) a creed, and (3) a code of personal morals."[117] "A religious creed differs from a scientific theory in claiming to embody eternal and absolutely certain truth, whereas science is always tentative, expecting that modifications in its present theories will sooner or later be found necessary, and aware that its method is one which is logically incapable of arriving at a complete and final demonstration."[118] "Science thus encourages abandonment of the search for absolute truth."[119]

However, that a religious creed claims to embody eternal and absolute truth, is not its primary characteristic; it is only the consequence of the belief in the existence of a transcendent being, that is, a being whose existence is beyond any human experience and endowed with absolute authority – a being which because of these characteristics is called "God." A religious creed proclaims its truth to be absolute because it supposes this truth to originate in a transcendent being, the personification of the absolute. A religious creed differs from a scientific theory because science, as a pursuit of knowledge by observation and reasoning, refuses to assert the existence of such a transcendent being and therefore, if consistent, cannot claim to arrive at absolute truth. Thus it is primarily the absence of the belief in God or a godlike entity by which science differs from religion. Russel's first characterization of religion refers to a secondary, not to the primary, essential element.

His second characterization of religion is presented in the following statements: "Religion has been associated not only with creeds and churches, but with the personal life of those who felt its importance ... The man, who feels deeply the problem of human destiny, the desire to diminish the sufferings of mankind, and the hope that the future will realize the best possibilities of our species, is nowadays often said to have a religious outlook, however little he may accept of traditional Christianity." Insofar as "religion consists in a way of feeling rather than in a set of beliefs,"[120] "many freethinkers have shown in their lives that this way of feeling has no essential connection with a creed."[121] Hence freethinkers may have a religion, a secular religion, as Aron and Brinton say.

On the basis of this definition of religion as a kind of feeling Russell speaks of communism and fascism (including national socialism) as of "new religions."[122] He says of these political movements: "new religions have arisen, with all the persecuting zeal of vigorous youth, and with as great a readiness

117 Ibid., p. 8.
118 Ibid., p. 14.
119 Ibid., p. 15.
120 Ibid., p. 17.
121 Ibid., p. 18.
122 Ibid., p. 7.

to oppose science as characterized the Inquisition in the time of Galileo. If you maintain in Germany [1935] that Christ was a Jew, or in Russia that the atom has lost its substantiality and become a mere series of events, you are liable to very severe punishment – perhaps nominally economic rather than legal, but none the milder on that account."[123] In National Socialist Germany and in Communist Russia "there is a body of dogma promulgated by the Government" and consequently there is "orthodoxy" and "heresy" from the point of view of both political systems.[124]

It is evident that Russel uses the word "religion" to designate two phenomena, which – in spite of a certain similarity – are so essentially different that such a terminology is inadmissible. He could not use this terminology, which enables him to speak of fascism, national socialism, and communism as of new "religions," and of religious atheism, if his first characterization of religion had not missed the essential point: the belief in God or gods. How detrimental this double-faced terminology – double-faced in the literary sense of this term – is to his own work is shown by the fact that it remarkably weakens his statement: "Between religion and science there has been a prolonged conflict, in which, until the last few years, science has invariably proved victorious." For he is forced to admit: "In so far as religion consists in a way of feeling, rather than in a set of beliefs, science cannot touch it."[125]

Nor are the consequences acceptable. From the definition of religion as a kind of feeling does not follow that something other than the belief in God – such as fascism, national socialism, and communism, is a religion. For fascism, national socialism, and communism are not feelings. They are political systems, that is, doctrines, ideas. The definition from which the interpretation of these political systems as religions follows is: Religion is any doctrine or idea

123 Ibid., p. 247.

124 Ibid., pp. 248–249. In his work A History of Western Philosophy (New York, 1945), pp. 363 seq., Bertrand Russell says: "The Jewish pattern of history, past and future, is such as to make a powerful appeal to the oppressed and unfortunate at all times. Saint Augustine adapted this pattern to Christianity, Marx to Socialism. To understand Marx psychologically one should use the following dictionary:
Yaweh = Dialectical Materialism
The Messiah = Marx
The Elect = The Proletariat
The Church = The Communist Party
The Second Coming = The Revolution
Heil = Punishment of the Capitalists
The Millennium = The Communist Commonwealth
The terms on the left give the emotional content of the terms on the right, and it is this emotional content, familiar to those who have had a Christian or Jewish upbringing, that makes Marx's eschatology credible."

125 Russell, Religion and Science, pp. 7, 17.

to which a certain kind of feeling refers or which a certain kind of feeling arouses. The main reason for Russell's interpretation is the "persecuting zeal" – the "persecution of intellectuals," which in Germany under the National Socialist regime took place and in Russia under the Communist regime still takes place.[126] If the specific feeling manifests itself in a hostile reaction against adversaries or those who are considered to be adversaries because their attitude is, rightly or wrongly, judged as detrimental to the established order, any political system that defends itself in this way is a religion; and every political system will react in this way. Even in a liberal democracy, which recognizes the principle of tolerance, people who show their antidemocratic conviction will be subjected to some discriminating treatment, for instance by not being admitted to government positions, apart from the fact that those who try to overthrow the democratic government by force and to establish a dictatorship will be punished. The elimination of the belief in God from the concept of religion almost completely obliterates the difference between religion and politics. Russell reproaches not only fascism, national socialism, and communism with the "brunt of persecution." He says: "In England – now, as always, an exceptionally tolerant country – a man whose views on economics are obnoxious to the government, will escape all penalties if he keeps his opinions to himself, or expresses them only in books of a certain length. But even in England, the expression of *communist* opinions in speeches or cheap pamphlets exposes a man to loss of livelihood and occasional periods in prison."[127] Such an anti-Communist reaction, such a "brunt of persecution", is even stronger in the United States. Would it not be absurd to consider – for this reason – the political system prevailing in the United States and England, which guarantees the freedom of religion, that is, the freedom of everybody to adhere to any religion whatever or to no *religion* at all, to be itself a religion?

Julian Huxley, in his recently published *Religion Without Revelation*,[128] sustains the view that "belief in supernatural beings is not an essential or integral part of the religious way of life,"[129] that "the essence of religion springs from man's capacity for awe and reverence, that the objects of religion ... are in origin and essence those things, events, and ideas which arouse the feeling of sacredness."[130] The feeling a man has when he considers an object "sacred" is a kind of reverence, but not every feeling of reverence is a feeling of sacredness. A man may feel reverence for his parents or his teacher, without considering these persons "sacred." The only possibility of differentiating the feeling of sacredness from other feelings of reverence is the fact that the object of re-

126 Ibid., p. 247.
127 Ibid., p. 248.
128 Julian Huxley, Religion Without Revelation (New York, 1957).
129 Ibid., p. 10.
130 Ibid., p. 120.

verence is considered to be in some relation to supernatural powers. It is just the supernatural that arouses awe. "Sacred" in the original and proper sense of the term, according to the Old Testament, is the specific quality of God, or the quality of a person or thing devoted to God. The German word for "sacred" is *heilig*; and Windelband, a German authority in the history of philosophy, characterized *das Heilige* as the realm of values, "in so far as they are related to a suprasensuous reality."[131] To illustrate his view, Huxley gives a characteristic example: "Human love and marriage can possess this sanctity [which pertains to certain ideas and to certain basic human relations], can be a sacrament, just as well to two complete atheists as to two devot Christians, just as fully if regarded as a human development from animal mating relationships as if supposed to be divinely ordained."[132] The statement that marriage is a "sacrament" has its specific meaning only if it expresses the idea that marriage is a divine institution and as such opposed to the view that marriage is a human institution. The term "sacrament" is defined in Baldwin's *Dictionary of Philosophy and Psychology*,[133] as follows: "A solemn rite of religion administered according to prescribed forms, which is supposed to carry with it the divine sanction and to communicate needed grace to the believing recipient." An atheist may be of the opinion that marriage is an important social institution, that monogamy is the relatively best form of marriage, that the law should not permit divorce, but never can he believe that marriage is a "sacrament," provided this term is used in its proper, generally accepted sense. In the statement: "An atheist may consider marriage to be a 'sacrament,'" this term is used to designate an idea that is in direct opposition to the idea which this term designates. To designate by the same term two contradictory ideas is an inadmissible terminology, for it obliterates an essential difference – in this instance the difference between an atheist and a theist.

Huxley refers to Rudolf Otto's *The Idea of the Holy.*[134] According to Otto, the feeling of sacredness is essentially connected with the belief in the existence of something which he calls *"das Numinose"* the "Numinous." It is the reflex of the fact that a certain object is considered to be, or experienced as, something "numinous." The Latin word *numen*, on the basis of which Otto coined the German adjective *numinos* ("numinous"), is translated by him expressly as *"übernatürliches Wesen"* ("supernatural being").[135] Otto says: *"numinose*

131 Wilhelm Windelband, An Introduction to Philosophy, transl. by Joseph McCabe (London, 1921), pp. 324 seqq.

132 Huxley, Religion without Revelation, p. 26.

133 Baldwin's Dictionary of Philosophy and Psychology (1911), II, pp. 483–484.

134 Rudolf Otto, Das Heilige. Über das Irrationale in der Idee des Göttlichen und sein Verhältnis zum Rationalen, 14th ed. (Gotha, 1926) transl. by John W. Harvey, The Idea of the Holy (London, 1925).

135 Otto, Das Heilige, p. 253.

Gemütsgestimmtheit," that is, the fact which Huxley calls "the feeling of sacredness," takes place "*wo ein Objekt als numinoses verneint worden ist*" (p. 7), ("where an object is considered to be numinous"). If the word "numinous" is taken from the Latin word "numen" and "numen" means "supernatural being," then to consider an object to be numinous means to consider it to be supernatural. It is true that Otto rejects the "supernaturalistic" theory (p. 185 f.). This is not quite consistent with his theory of the "numinous" and his characterization of religion as belief in something "suprasensous" ("*ein Übersinnliches*") (pp. 1, 184). Besides, his rejection of the supernaturalistic theory is directed against the opinion that, since there are facts that cannot be explained by the laws of nature, having no natural cause, they must have a supernatural cause. Otto supposes that "Divination," that is recognizing the Holy in its appearances, has nothing to do with the law of nature and the relation or lack of relation to it. It is not concerned with the way in which *das Übersinnliche* comes into existence. But by "supernatural" not necessarily a specific kind of causation but just the same may be meant as by the word das *Übersinnliche*.

Otto characterizes[136] the feeling which an object considered to be "numinous" evokes as "dämonischer Schein [demonic awe]". He says: "The feeling of the numinous at its higher stages is very different from the mere demoniac awe." But even at this stage its origin and affinity [with the demoniac awe] is evident. Even if the belief in demons has been long ago raised to a belief in Gods, the "Gods" as numina are still felt as something "ghostly [etwas Gespenstisches]" (p. 19). Hence we may assume that the "demoniac awe" which a numinous object evokes at the lower stage of evolution is the awe of demons; the term "demon" – as Otto insists (p. 98) – not in the ordinary sense of something opposed to the *Theion* (the divine) i. e. in the sense of an "anti-God [*Gegengott*]", but in the sense of a "pre-God [*Vorgott*]". It is "a low stage of the *numina* out of which gradually the 'God' as a higher form comes forth." Demons in this sense are certainly, though not yet Gods, god-like, suprasensuous beings; and an object considered to be "numinous" evokes demoniac awe because this object is considered to be in some relation to a demon. But Otto says (p. 16) that "demons" and "gods" spring from this demoniac awe, that they are "objectifications (*Verdinglichungen*)" of this feeling. There is, however, no reason why an object perceptible by a man's senses should evoke in him this specific awe if he would not believe that this effect is in some relation to a God or God-like suprasensuous being to a demon. Otto's rejection of animism (p. 16/17) is unfounded. To consider an object as sacred *presupposes* the belief in the existence of something supernatural in the sense of *suprasensuous*. Huxley says "that religion arose as a feeling of the sacred";[137] but it is just the other way around: the feeling of the sacred arose from religion as the belief in super-

136 Otto, Das Heilige, pp. 16, 19, 97.
137 Huxley, Religion Without Revelation, p. 10.

natural or suprasensous beings. The conscious or unconscious purpose of the various attempts to define religion without referring to the supernatural or suprasensous is: to save religion, to defend it against the attack by science. The main concern of Huxley's book is to show, "how, in principle at least, science and religion can be reconciled."[138] He emphasizes that "there should no longer be any talk of conflict between science and religion."[139] Thus he does a great favor to theology, which he, as a scientist, rejects.[140]

138 Ibid., p. 239.

139 Ibid., p. 212.

140 Ibid., pp. 114–116. In defending science against theology but not against religion, Huxley shows a tendency similar to that of Andrew Dickson White who in his A History of the Warfare of Science with Theology in Christendom (New York, 1896, reprinted New York, 1960) – in opposition to John W. Draper, History of the Conflict Between Science and Religion (3rd ed. New York, 1875), who regarded the conflict as one between science and religion – declared (Introduction, p. XII): "My conviction is that Science, though it has evidently conquered Dogmatic Theology based on biblical texts and ancient modes of thought, will go hand in hand with Religion." It is, however, impossible to seperate theology from religion and thus avoid to recognize the conflict between science and religion. For religion, and that means in the only proper sense of the word: the belief in the existence of God or god-like beings, is the necessary presupposition of theology, the science of God, the vain attempt to convey knowledge of something that, by its very nature, is beyond human knowledge.

Chapter II Doctrine of Progress: and Eschatology

It is primarily the idea of progress, which Brinton and others interpret as eschatology. It is true that both eschatological speculations and some modern philosophies of history presuppose the principle of progress, that is, the idea of an improvement of the past and present in the future. But in view of the fundamental antagonism in the meaning of this improvement, "progress" in the Christian eschatological sense and "progress" in the philosophical secular sense are concepts which have nothing in common but this word.

Progress is not a specifically Christian idea, "the gift of the Christian era,"[141] as Rosenstock says: the Jewish-Christian theology is not the only religious ideology that refers to an improvement in the evolution of mankind. Such improvement is the specific meaning of the Greek Prometheus myth. A fragment by Xenophanes runs as follows: "The gods have not revealed all things to men from the beginning, but by seeking they find in time what is better."[142] Sophocles in *Antigone* praises the technical progress of mankind,[143] and the ideal of progress is unequivocally expressed in the myth which Plato puts in the mouth of Protagoras in the dialogue named after this great thinker.[144] The principle of progressive evolution appears in the philosophy of Democritus and the Epicureans, especially in that of Diogenes of Oionoanda and Lucretius.[145] In the philosophy of the Stoa we may find the idea that the world in its temporal course is a progressive realization of reason.[146] J. Thyssen, in a monograph, says that "the great problem of the beginning of civilization and evolution, which naturally is the center of philosophy of history (the problem of progress!), can be found already circumstantially expounded in antiquity."[147] Moreover, the principle of progress on which some modern philo-

141 Rosenstock-Huessy, The Christian Future, p. 75.

142 John Burnet, Early Greek Philosophy, 4th ed. (London, 1930), p. 119.

143 Sophocles, Antigone, pp. 332 seqq.

144 Plato, Protagoras, 320c seqq. See W. K. C. Guthrie, In the Beginning (London, 1957), pp. 80 seqq.

145 See Hans Leisegang, Denkformen, 2nd ed. (Berlin, 1951), pp. 360 seq.

146 See Hans Eibl, Metaphysik und Geschichte (Leipzig and Wien, 1913), p. 195.

147 Johannes Thyssen, Geschichte der Geschichtsphilosophie (Berlin, 1936), p. 7.

sophies of history are based differs from the Christian expectation of the coming Kingdom of God not only in the meaning of improvement implied in the two ideologies: The former assumes a steady development of mankind from its lowest stage to higher stages of civilization; according to the latter, just as in the myth of the Golden Age,[148] the highest stage – paradise – is at the beginning of an evolution that continues not with progress but with regress, the fall of man and the loss of paradise. Hence, the later stages are not exactly those of a true progress but – so far as the last stage is conceived in the original Jewish version as a heaven on earth – of a return to the first stage, the Kingdom of God being a second paradise, the reestablishment of an original situation.[149]

148 J. B. Bury, in The Idea of Progress (New York, 1932), p. 8, says: "The old legend of a 'golden age' of simplicity, from which man had fallen away, was generally accepted as truth, and leading thinkers combined it with the doctrine of a gradual sequence of social and material improvements during the subsequent period of decline" [Plato's Laws, Dicaearchus]. He refers also to Seneca's prediction of a steady increase of knowledge in his statement: "The day will come when time and human diligence will clear up problems which are now obscure ... One day our posterity will marvel at our ignorance of causes so clear to them" (p. 13). Even if Seneca did not believe that this increase of knowledge will bring about a progress of humanity – as Bury emphasizes – he advocated a doctrine of progress, not of an absolute and universal but of a relative and partial progress. These facts are sufficient to consider the opinion that the idea of progress is a monopoly of Christian religion as highly doubtful.

149 St. Augustine, one of the outstanding authorities of Christian theology, believed that no true progress is to be found in the course of human history (see Th. E. Mommsen, "St. Augustine and the Christian Idea of Progress," Journal of the History of Ideas, XII [1951], p. 374); and Sertillanges, Le Christianisme, I, p. 70, correctly says with respect to the Christian idea of progress "that in the Christian system progress in the sense of an increase of value – instead of a movement toward a goal – must not be sought in the future, in conformity with the ideas of Condorcet and the Encyclopedists. It is not at the end of, but above, history that it is to be achieved. It is not horizontal, it is vertical. In its horizontal sense the course of humanity depends on the masses, that is to say on the inferior or average instincts rather than on sovereign values. The latter are realized by heroes, geniuses and saints; they are individual and they can be imparted to the masses only to a limited extent and at the risk of being abolished by passionate infidelity or indifference. For this reason progress in itself is independent of time. The greatest progress of humanity has already been accomplished; it is the rise of one of us to the 'grace of union,' which makes all the spiritual brothers of the divine Chosen one participants of the very Divinity." It is evident that the Christian idea of the "grace of union" has nothing to do with the principle of progress which is at the basis of certain modern philosophies of history. On the other hand, Plato's metaphysical speculation implies a conception not very different from that which Sertillanges considers to be the Christian idea of progress – the sun as the visible reality, the offspring of the invisible God, the idea of the absolute good, of which a few chosen individuals may reach a mystic vision. Cf. Plato, Republic 508a-e; Seventh Letter, 341c. See my "Platonic Justice," Ethics, XLVIII (1937–38), pp. 367–400.

If the concept of philosophy of history is restricted to speculations about an "ultimate meaning" of history, the "philosophy" is indeed identical with theology of history, and then it is not necessary to have recourse to the logical fallacy of "secularized theology." For the "ultimate" meaning of history, to use Löwith's own words, is the answer to "ultimate questions concerning first and last things," which "cannot be answered on the basis of empirical knowledge."[150] The "ultimate" meaning of history can only be the meaning which history has according to the absolute will of God. The ultimate meaning of history is, indeed, the Christian eschaton; and only a theology of history, not a scientific philosophy of history, can ask such a question. Modern times know several such theologies of history, and Hegel's so-called philosophy of history is certainly one of them. But only with the aid of the logically fallacious formula of a secularized theology can outspokenly antitheological or antimetaphysical philosophies (such as the philosophies of Lessing, Comte, and Marx) be classified as theologies, as implying theological elements, or as entirely depending on theology. Neither Lessing with his *Education of the Human Race* nor Comte with his positive philosophy nor Marx with his economic materialism intended to answer "ultimate" questions. These writers predict as possible and probable a future state of mankind that is to be considered as an improvement over that of the past and present; but in this future state they do not see the realization of the "ultimate" meaning of history. They intend to make a scientific, not a religious prediction. It is of the same type – though not of the same degree of probability – as the prediction of a physicist that a heated metallic body will expand. Their statements about the future are based on the experience of the past and not on divine inspiration. The statements constitute the application of objective laws of causality, as conceived by the human mind, not the result of a mystic insight in the will of a personal God revealed in Scripture. These philosophers believed in the progress of mankind in conformity with the law of evolution; but, as rationalistic, empirical thinkers who did not pretend to be provided with supernatural forces of cognition, they were fully aware of the fact that their knowledge of the laws of nature and of history, as a merely human knowledge, was limited and open to error. When they spoke of a "necessary" evolution toward a future state of improvement, they only meant – though they did not always expressly declare it – what to human knowledge appears to be necessary, that is, a certain degree of probability. Consequently, they did not assume, as is sometimes imputed to them, that the future state, which they thought themselves able to foresee, constituted a definite end of the evolution; that it meant the absolute end of history, as the advent of the Kingdom of God. And end of evolution is incompatible with the idea of a law of evolution because this law, which is the basis of progress,

150 Löwith, Meaning in History, p. 3.

must be conceived as prevailing also in the future stage of mankind, although its results are not foreseen.

Löwith contrasts philosophy – as distinguished from theology – with science (pp. 1, 3). But the two most important philosophies of history whose theological implications he tries to show, those of Comte and Marx, present themselves as scientific; and since their authors try to establish verifiable general laws of history, based on observed facts and not on religious belief or metaphysical speculation, they fulfill the requirements of science. Whether their results prove to be true is not decisive for the question of their scientific character. It is the fate of any scientific doctrine to be rejected as erroneous and to be replaced by another which may have the same fate. It is not the result that counts, but the method. It is especially the negative element of this method, the exclusion of any religious or metaphysical presupposition, which allows us to consider a philosophy of history as "scientific" in contradistinction to "theological"; and this in spite of the fact that some of these philosophies imply the logically fallacious idea of a social value immanent in social reality and, consequently, the illusion that social evolution is necessarily combined with social improvement, that is, with progress. This illusion is ultimately based on the lack of insight in the fundamental difference between reality and value, between the "is" and the "ought." The tendency to ignore this difference and to infer by an act of human reason, from that which *is* that which *ought* to be, is inherent not only in theological speculation, where it is based on the assumption of a reality created by God, it is also inherent in rationalistic thinking, which conceives of value not as implanted into reality from the outside by the will of God, but as immanent in it from the beginning.

It is true that the immanence of value in reality and the idea of an absolute value can be consistently maintained only on the theological presupposition that reality is the creation of the absolutely good will of God;[151] and it is true that a rationalistic, nonmetaphysical doctrine, which cannot avoid distinguishing value and reality, has no answer to the question how value can become immanent in reality, and consequently has no basis for the assumption of absolute values; there is some foundation in the argument that such a doctrine is not consistent if it maintains the immanence of value in reality and claims absolute value for its ideals but at the same time rejects the theological assumption of God as the creator of reality. But these rationalistic doctrines have to be taken as inconsistent as they are, and not as they would be if they were consistent. It is not permissible to attribute to them a theological element which they – though inconsistently – reject. The difference between a theological and a rationalistic ontology – the difference between the immanence of value in reality in the two systems – is so decisive that their similarity in this point is of minor

151 Cf. Hans Kelsen, "Die Grundlage der Naturrechtslehre" in F. Schmölz, ed., Das Naturrecht in der politischen Theorie (Wien, 1963), pp. 1–37.

importance. The view that value is immanent in reality and that consequently human reason can infer from that which is that which ought to be, is in rationalistic thinking certainly not a derivation of theological speculation. It is rather the result of overestimating the faculties of human reason, a tendency which originates not in a dependency on, but in the antagonism to, theology and metaphysics. Restricting the concept of philosophy of history to an interpretation in which historic events have an "ultimate," that is, eschatological, meaning, and considering at the same time the doctrines of Lessing, Comte, and Marx as "philosophies" of history, consciously or unconsciously obliterates the difference between theology and scientific philosophy.

If, then, the first danger facing the comparative theory of culture is the interpretation of progress as eschatology, the second, and more serious, danger is the attempt to find analogies between Christian theology and modern social theory, and especially between religion and politics, with the intention or the effect of belittling or obscuring the fundamental difference between them. Behind this attempt may well be a reactionary tendency to reorient social theory toward theology. If modern social theory is secularized theology and if political ideologies are disguised or degenerated religion, are we then to think that this secularization, disguise, or degeneration are the fundamental errors of modern civilization, that our social theory and politics are moving in a wrong direction and should return to their original, but forgotten or wrongly denied, model? As a consequence of this doctrine a desecularization of science and political ideologies is necessary. Only then will they be able to reach the truth, which, of course, can only be the truth of God. Thus the emancipation of science and political ideology from theology and religious authority, to which modern civilization owes its existence, shall be undone.

This may be the goal of the theological interpretation of modern philosophy. Its most consistent representative, Father Sertillanges, as a Catholic theologian, has no reason to hide this goal. He says: "Philosophy has been more and more separated from theology, but not to its advantage. We do not speak of its autonomy, to a great extent recognized for two centuries. However, autonomy and separation are two different things ... Thinking is free, but when it ceases to center in God it derails, and if it derails it is dispersed. Faith is the lodestar of the free thinker. Without applying coercion it saves him from great errors."[152] "Autonomy of science" under the authority of theology! Freedom of thought within the boundaries of the Christian religion!

152 Sertillanges, Le Christianisme, II, p. 12. He speaks of a "symbiose" of science with theology and declares: "Philosopy, 'the secretary of state' of theology, to use an excellent formula by Jacques Maritain, could only benefit by keeping company with its sovereign ["ne puvait manquer de s'enrichir au commerce de son souverain"]", (ibid., I, p. 22). To see in philosophy the secretary of state of theology, and in theology its sovereign amounts exactly to the same thing as the old formula: philosophia ancilla theologiae.

Niebuhr,[153] as pointed out, characterizes Marxism as a secularized version of Messianism; but he disqualifies this version as a "perversion of a profound truth." This value judgment implies an appeal to withdraw from Marxism and return to the true Christian faith. Niebuhr admits that "the struggle between rich and poor, between the owners and the workers in modern industrial society, is a fact which Marxism illumined, and which both orthodox Christianity and liberalism were inclined to obscure." But he says: "Marxism falsely made it into a final fact of history which was supposed to bear within itself the possibility of an ultimate redemption of history. The illusions of Marxism are thus the end-products of a Christian civilization which either failed to realize the highest possibilities of life in history or which claimed the realization of a perfection which can never be achieved in history." To the illusions of Marxism Niebuhr opposes the reality of the Christian view of history, which he formulates as follows: "The divine judgment ... remains over all historical achievements and realizations of meaning. The goodness of Christ must be embodied in the stuff of history. But it can never be so embodied that it does not also stand in contradiction to history in judgment and become the completion of history only by divine mercy rather than by human achievement." Philosophy of history has to be Christian theology of history.

This is also Toynbee's view; he characterizes communism as a, "substitute for Christianity," in order to stress that "in the long run ... this 'ideology' – offering, as it did, a stone for bread – might prove to be an unsatisfying substitute for Religion."[154] He tries thus to convince his readers that it is necessary to give up a materialistic interpretation of history and to adopt a theological one.

Gilson affirms that none of the schemes aiming at a universal society, after the model of Augustine's City of God, has succeeded "in providing the universal society with the necessary bond which since the time of Augustine the Christian wisdom of faith has offered them." The "lesson we may draw from this experience of almost twenty centuries" is this: "In their attempt to establish a universal society by only the means of which man disposes without God, our contemporaries desire a Christian end without desiring the Christian means ... It is necessary either to renounce the ideal of a universal society or to redemand the bond of union with the Christian faith. There may be a city of men [the other universal society according to St. Augustine] – and it will not be established without politicians, jurists, scholars, philosophers – but it will still less be established without the Church and theologians."[155] But what do the Church and the theologians teach? "The spiritual power is not subjected to the temporal power ... but the temporal power is subjected to the spiritual power; the pope who has authority over the spiritual has therefore

153 Niebuhr, Faith and History, pp. 210, 212–213.

154 Toynbee, A Study of History, IX, p. 583.

155 Gilson, Les Metamorphoses, p. 268.

also authority over the temporal as far as the temporal depends on the spiritual ... The pope is not the political sovereign of any of the nations of this earth, but he has sovereign authority over the way all nations execute their policy. Representative of Christ the King, he judges all in His name and in virtue of His authority."[156] "The city of man can be built, in the shadow of the cross, only as a suburb of the City of God."[157] There can be no doubt about the tendency of this interpretation of atheist philosophies as metamorphoses of St. Augustine's City of God. It is important to consider carefully this tendency in order to see the possible consequences of interpretations similar to those of a professional theologian or to those of an author openly oriented by theology, if these interpretations are advocated by writers who present themselves as men of science and hence are not in a position to be as sincere as Sertillanges or Gilson, and may not even be conscious of these consequences.

When Löwith emphasizes that modern philosophy of history is determined by an eschatological motivation, he says: "The significance of this vision of an ultimate end, as both *finis* and *telos*, is that it provides a scheme of progressive order and meaning, a scheme which has been capable of overcoming the ancient fear of fate and fortune. Not only does the *eschaton* delimit the process of history by an end, it also articulates and fulfils it by a definite goal. The bearing of the eschatological thought on the historical consciousness of the Occident is that it conquers the flux of historical time, which wastes away and devours its own creations unless it is defined by an ultimate goal. Comparable to the compass which gives us orientation in space, and thus enables us to conquer it, the eschatological compass gives orientation in time by pointing to the Kingdom of God as the ultimate end and purpose."[158] This is more than an objective, value-free inquiry into the theological implication of modern philosophies of history. In comparing the eschaton with a compass, Löwith ignores the difference between the geographical compass, which actually gives orientation in space, and the eschatological compass, which only pretends to give orientation in time. The difference between the two is that of a real and an illusionary effect; thus, the reader is left in doubt whether Löwith considers theological speculation about the eschaton as reliable as the scientific device of the compass.

Rosenstock is less ambiguous in his opinion about the value of theology as compared with that of science.[159] He says: "Whenever modern planning has seceded from Christianity, war and slavery have seemed quite normal to the secular mind. So today, economic order without respect for the human soul will mean, and already means, class war, racism, and even return of bloody sac-

156 Ibid., pp. 275–276.

157 Ibid., p. 291.

158 Löwith, Meaning in History, p. 18.

159 Rosenstock-Huessy, The Christian Future, p. 160.

rifices." As if war and slavery did not exist under the undisputed domination of Christianity and had not been justified by Christian theology![160] In a footnote he adds: "Contemporary neo-savagery comes directly in the wake of the final triumph of natural science over its rival, theology. Man has been conquered by an idol his own mind made: Nature with a capital N. He is an artificially produced African." Rosenstock says that modern social sciences have a "prehistoric," "precrucial" standard. For "they do not admit that in the center of time our own nature became conscious of itself and thereby was definitely transformed [by the teachings of Buddha, Laotse, Abraham and, above all, of Christ]. They do not admit that the very existence of any science proves the existence of creation instead of causation." He openly postulates a "Christian" science, based on value judgments, "without which no talk about social process is possible;" and these "value judgments ... must be based on the frank admission that we already know, from the Cross of created human nature, what the full freedom, the full creativity, the wholehearted fellowship, and the perfect service of mankind ought to be."[161]

This can only mean that social science has to be theology.

Reisner, whose theological interpretation of the Ptolemaic geocentric and the Copernican heliocentric astronomy is influenced by Rosenstock[162] and in turn influenced Taubes, shows frankly his preference for the Ptolemaic picture of the world, which conceives of the earth as placed below a divine heaven. He must admit that the Ptolemaic view "cannot be defended and maintained with human means," but he emphasizes that "it is, at least, worth being defended and maintained, whereas the Copernican view [of an earth without heaven] as the typical view of a man who has alienated himself from God whom he has deserted, can never be justified from the point of view of revelation."[163] "Thinking scientifically means thinking in terms of *causality*, and causality prevails where the creator is missing. For only so far as things are no longer regarded as created, as originating in the free will of God, do they *seem* to condition each other, which means they follow the law of causality. The law in all possible forms – as moral law, logical law, law of nature – is the necessary result of man's running away from his creator, of man's being deaf to the creative word 'Let there be,' and the personal command 'You shall.' ... The [Ptolemaic]

160 The Catholic writer August M. Knoll, Katholische Kirche und scholastisches Naturrecht (Wien, Frankfurt am Main, Zürich, 1962), p. 31, calls attention to the fact that the scholastic natural-law doctrine defended slavery as an institution ordered by God and Nature; and that Thomas Aquinas (Summa theologica I, 21, a. 1, ad 3) justifies slavery by the principle suum cuique: "Dicitur esse suum alicuius quod ad ipsum ordinatur. Sicut servus est domini, et non e converso: nam liberum est, quod sui causa est." (Knoll, op. cit., pp. 24, 97).

161 Rosenstock-Huessy, The Christian Future, pp. 194 seqq.

162 Rosenstock-Huessy, Die europäischen Revolutionen, p. 3.

163 Reisner, Die christliche Botschaft, p. 119.

earth below [divine] heaven knows nothing of causality and the like; only the terrestrian globe senselessly driven around in space *seems* to be determined by causality; and causality is the very expression of its senselessness."[164] (Italics mine.)

The symbol of modern science, as opposed to theology, is the Protagorean formula: Man is the measure of all things. Of this principle, Taubes says:[165] "Man, forgetting the divine measure, becomes more and more presumptuous and takes himself for the measure of all things. By taking himself for the measure of all things, man obscures the true connection of things." Taubes asks: "Why does this error delude man particularly, this error which drives man farthest from God?" It is a fateful error for man to consider himself the measure of all things. "Man in himself is nothing, unless he participates in God. Then only is the veil removed which covers the world, then only the fog disappears; the presumptuous human measures fall and God as the true measure of things becomes manifest." There can be no doubt about the consequences to be drawn from these statements concerning the relationship between science and theology.

Examining the effects of the "old," that is, Judaeo-Christian religion and the "new religion" of Enlightenment and its offspring Marxism-Leninism on "the mental and moral health of the individual, on his disposition toward one or another kind of conduct," Brinton finds a difference between the old and new religion; he declares: "The differences between them in this respect may be slight, but nonetheless important."[166] The difference is "that emotionally and intellectually the new religion in its extreme form does fulfill *less successfully than traditional Christianity the useful and indeed necessary role the Marxists call scornfully that of 'opium of the people'*; or at any rate, that the new religion is not *a satisfactory sedative* for the intellectuals, who seem nowadays to need a sedative badly." (Italics mine.) Brinton believes that "men in the West throughout their history, and especially their leaders both in thought and in action, have tended to be over-active rather than underactive, have stood in need rather of being quieted than of being pricked." Since, on the whole, the new religion has a stimulating effect whereas the old religion has a quieting effect on the minds of men, Brinton suggests – "as a mere hypothesis," to be sure – "that the two centuries of experience we have had with the religion of the Enlightenment show that this faith is weak in consoling power and, as a *faith*, intellectually disturbing." Finally, he says: "I think it reasonably clear a priori that the new religion can but produce as consoling elements in the cure of souls substitutes that do their work less effectively than did the consoling elements of the old religion." In connection with his attempt to present de-

164 Ibid., pp. 122 seq.
165 Taubes, Abendländische Eschatologie, pp. 193 seq.
166 Brinton, A History of Western Morals, pp. 457, 458.

mocratic nationalism as a religion Brinton says: "Christianity would seem to be ... the most consoling faith ... Marianne of the French Republic is a lively and charming lady whom we all know from the cartoonists' sketches; but she is no substitute for Our Lady of Sorrows. Nationalism has its surrogates for the saints; but not even Abraham Lincoln seems to fit into prayer."[167] (Two pages earlier Brinton had said: "There are clearly national saints – Washington, Lincoln, Lenin ..."[168])

Now we see why it is necessary to interpret the philosophy of the Enlightenment and its offspring, especially Marxism, as religions! For only if they are religions can they be compared with Christianity, and can the question be asked which of the two religions is preferable. The answer is obvious, if, as Brinton affirms, without attempting to prove it, that "men are generally more in need of sedation than stimulation."[169] They need consolation rather than stimulation to action. Then it is only consistent to demand that modern civilization should turn from the new insufficient religion to the old, satisfactory one. Brinton himself does not draw expressly this consequence of his interpretation of the Enlightenment and Marxism. But his *History of Western Morals* opens the way to it. It is enough that he emphatically rejects Marx's word of the "opium of the people," that he ascertains that the "new religion" is "less successful" than the old one; and that he insists on the latter's "useful, and indeed necessary role."[170] He openly declares that his own position "is ultimately a metaphysical one."[171] If he had published his book a dozen years earlier, Father Sertillanges would have found in it a welcome confirmation of his attempt to bring philosophy and science again under the authority of theology.

Voegelin is quite sincere in this respect. His attempt to lay the foundation of a new science of politics that at the same time has to be a philosophy of history is directed against the areligious and anti-metaphysical positivism of the nineteenth century, which he accuses of having destroyed the political science founded, as he asserts, by Plato.[172] The destructiveness of positivism consists, according to Voegelin, above all in the fact that it "contracted" political science "to a description of existing institutions."[173] This contraction stems from the tendency (1) to distinguish between objectively verifiable judgments about reality and value judgments based on subjective emotions of wish and fear; and (2) to eliminate the latter from a scientific description and explanation of reality in general, and social-political reality in particular. Although the oppo-

167 Ibid., p. 334.
168 Ibid., p. 332.
169 Ibid., p. 457.
170 Ibid., pp. 433, 457.
171 Ibid., p. 448.
172 Voegelin, The New Science of Politics, pp. 1, 4.
173 Ibid., p. 2.

site position (namely, that value can*not* be separated from reality because the first is immanent in the second) is the most characteristic consequence of a theological-metaphysical view of the world, it is accepted also by representatives of positivism such as Comte and Marx. However, Voegelin's attempt to restore political science by expanding it "to its full grandeur as the science of human existence in society and history, as well as of the principles of order [that is, principles of value]" aims at a return in social science to theology and metaphysical speculation. Three times in Western history, he says, have such attempts been made, in "epochs of a revolutionary and crucial nature." "The foundation of political science through Plato and Aristotle marked the Hellenic crises; St. Augustine's *Civitas Dei* marked the crisis of Rome and Christianity; and Hegel's philosophy of law and history marked the first major earthquake of the Western crisis." Hence, "restoration of political science" means "a return to the consciousness of principles, not perhaps a return to the specific content of an earlier attempt. One cannot restore political science today through Platonism, Augustinianism, or Hegelianism." But: "Much can be learned, to be sure, from the earlier philosophers concerning the range of problems, as well as concerning their theoretical treatment."

What Voegelin really means by his "restoration of political science to its principles" becomes clear in the following statements: "If, for instance, in our prescientific participation in the order of a society, in our prescientific experiences of right and wrong, of justice and injustice, we should feel the desire to penetrate to a theoretical understanding of the source of order and its validity, we may arrive in the course of our endeavors at the theory that the justice of human order depends on its participation in the Platonic Agathon, or the Aristotelian Nous, or the Stoic Logos, or the Thomistic *ratio aeterna*. For one reason or another, none of these theories may satisfy us completely; [that they are satisfying at least to a certain extent, is presupposed] but we know that we are in search for an answer of this type. If, however, the way should lead us to the notion that social order is motivated by will to power and fear, we know that we have lost the essence of the problem somewhere in the course of our inquiry – however valuable the results may be in clarifying other essential aspects of social order." Because a still more essential aspect is that of justice: "In looking back from the answer to the question, we know, therefore, that the methods of a psychology of motivations are not adequate for the exploration of the problem [which means evidently the problem of justice, a value problem] and that in this concrete case it would be better to rely on the methods of metaphysical speculation and theological symbolization."[174] In his recent study *Wissenschaft, Politik und Gnosis*, Voegelin becomes even more explicit. Here he designates as the aim of science in general and of social science

174 Ibid., p. 6.

in particular "the cognition of the order of being [*"Erkenntnis der Seinsordnung"*], the understanding that above the hierarchy of the universe a transcendent source of being and its order exists. This understanding has its root in the real movement of the human soul toward the transcendently experienced divine being ["... die Einsicht, dass die innerhalb der Welt unterscheidbaren Seinsstufen überhöht werden von einer jenseitigen Quelle des Seins und seiner Ordnung. Und die Einsicht wieder hat ihre Wurzel in den realen Bewegungen der menschlichen Geistseele auf das als jenseitig erlebte, göttliche Sein hin"]". This "transcendent source of being and its order" is evidently God who, according to the Scripture, has created the world and governs its course. This is the specifically theological view of Voegelin's science of politics. Only if this understanding is reached, "is it possible to examine, whether the actually existing opinions about the right social order agree with the transcendent order of being [that is, with the divine order originating in the transcendent source of being] ["... ist es möglich die Meinungen über die rechte Ordnung, die in der Gesellschaft im Umlauf sind, darauf hin zu prüfen, ob sie mit der Seinsordnung zusammenstimmen"]".[175] This examination is the essential function of Voegelin's new science of politics. The divine order, which is the criterion of this examination, is the one revealed in the Scripture. Voegelin gives an example of the examination to be undertaken by the new science of politics: "If the strong and successful is highly estimated [the new science of politics] can oppose to him the man who possesses the virtue of *phronesis*, of wisdom, the man who lives *sub specie mortis* and acts in view of the last judgment... When ardent youths are repelled by the vulgarity of democracy, Plato may call their attention to the fact that energy, pride, and will to power can, it is true, found a regime of force of an intellectually dirty elite [*"das Gewaltregime einer geistig ungewaschenen Elite"*]", but not a just government; when democrats are enthusiastic about equality and liberty and forget that government requires spiritual education and intellectual discipline, he [Plato] may warn them that they are driving toward tyranny."[176] This antidemocratic tendency is characteristic of the new science of politics. That it is oriented, in the main, toward Christian theology becomes particularly evident from the sentence which closes the preface. "The escape of the Gnostics [of antiquity] from the really wicked, embarrassing, and depressing state of the world is understandable. However, the order of the world of antiquity has been renewed by a movement, which endeavored to set going again the 'serious play' (to use Plato's formula) through works of love, by Christianity ["Die Flucht der Gnostiker aus einem wahrhaft heillosen, verwirrenden und erdrückenden Zustand der Welt ist verständlich. Aber die Ordnung der alten Welt wurde erneuert durch die Bewegung, die

175 Voegelin, Wissenschaft, Politik und Gnosis, pp. 26–27.
176 Ibid., pp. 27, 28.

sich bemühte, das 'ernste Spiel' (um Platons Formel zu gebrauchen) durch liebendes Tun wieder in Gang zu bringen – durch das Christentum"]".[177]

Of course, Voegelin must be prepared for the objection that speculations about a "transcendent source of the being and its order," that is, the other world of theology, has nothing to do with science because it refers to an imaginary subject of which we have no knowledge; and that knowledge of something which, by its nature, transcends our knowledge is a meaningless contradiction in terms. Hence, turning the tables, he declares this speculation to be true science; he interprets the view that the other world is beyond scientific cognition (that in the name of science no assertion about such a subject is possible), as *"Frageverbot"*[178] that is, as prohibition of the question about the transcendent source of the empirical world. He says the opposition against truth – that is, against the belief in a transcendent source of being, the belief in the existence of God – becomes "radical and dangerous when the philosophical questioning [the questioning about the transcendent source of the being] itself is called in question, when the *doxa* [Plato's term for mere opinion in opposition to *episteme*, true knowlege] assumes philosophical form, when it arrogates to itself the title of science and prohibits the [true] science [of the other-world] as nonscience ["... wenn das philosophische Fragestellen selbst in Frage gestellt wird, wenn die *Doxa* philosophische Form annimmt, wenn sie den Titel der Wissenschaft arrogiert und die Wissenschaft als Nicht-Wissenschaft verbietet"]".[179] Those who prohibit the question about the other world "know that they cannot, and know why they cannot, stand a critical analysis of their view and hence make the prohibition of examining their premises the content of their dogma ["... es handelt sich um Meinungen, deren Vertreter wissen, dass und warum sie einer kritischen Analyse nicht standhalten, und die darum das Verbot der Prüfung ihrer Prämissen zum Inhalt ihres Dogmas machen"]".[180] Those who prohibit the questions are Gnostics, and since they do it because they know that the questions would lead to the breakdown of their doctrine, they commit an "intellectual swindle."[181] "The gnostic thinker indeed commits an intellectual swindle – and he knows that he does it ["Der gnostische Denker begeht in der Tat einen intellektuellen Schwindel und er weiss, dass er es tut"]".[182]

In modern, positivistic antimetaphysical science and philosophy against which Voegelin is fighting, there is no such a thing as a *"Frageverbot"*; and especially no prohibition of the question about a transcendent source of being.

177 Ibid., p. 19.
178 Ibid., p. 29 seqq.
179 Ibid., p. 29.
180 Ibid., p. 31.
181 Ibid., pp. 38 seqq.
182 Ibid., p. 44.

Science as a function of cognition does not and cannot prohibit any questions; for prohibiting is a function of will, not of cognition. One of the most characteristic representatives of the positivistic science of scientific philosophy is Hans Reichenbach.[183] What does he say about the transcendent source of being and its order, that is, the creation and government of the world by God? Does he prohibit the question who created the world and who governs it? By no means! He simply declares that to answer this question by referring to a transcendent source of being, namely, "to God" is a naïve "pseudo-explanation."[184] How spurious this alleged *"Frageverbot"* is can be seen in the fact that Voegelin tries to demonstrate its existence only in Marx's' early writings, especially in a manuscript dealing with economic and philosophical problems of 1844, and in Comte's *Philosophie positive.*[185] We shall see later that the alleged *"Frageverbot"* does not exist in either work (see below, pp. 148 seq.). Marx as an atheist simply refuses to accept the answer that Christian theology gives to the question of the origin of the world and abstains from – but does not forbid – the asking of the question. Hence Voegelin calls him "an intellectual swindler."[186] Comte, in the first lecture of the *Cours de Philosophie*, to which Voegelin refers without quoting a definite sentence and without indicating the page on which the *"Frageverbot"* is formulated, says only that in the scientific age the human mind will abstain from asking about the origin and destination of the universe (see below, p. 149). Voegelin does not seem to be aware that the question about the origin of the world necessarily leads into a *regressus in infinitum* and that consequently the question must stop somewhere. From the point of view of positivistic science it stops at the borderline of empirical rational cognition. What could Voegelin answer if someone should ask him about the origin of the "transcendent source of being and its order"? He would certainly not restrict himself to saying that to such a ques-

183 Hans Reichenbach, The Rise of Scientific Philosophy (Berkeley and Los Angeles, 1951).

184 Ibid., pp. 8 seq. The passage concerned runs as follows: "The desire to understand the physical world has at all times led to the question of how the world began. The mythologies of all peoples include primitive versions of the origin of the universe. The best known story of creation, a product of Hebrew imaginative spirit, is given in the Bible and dates about the ninth century B.C. It explains the world as the creation of God. Its explanation is of the naïve type that satisfies a primitive mind, or a childlike mind, proceeding by anthropomorphic analogies: as humans make homes and tools and gardens, God made the world. One of the most general and fundamental questions, that of the genesis of the physical world, is answered by an analogy with experiences of the daily environment. That pictures of this kind do not constitute an explanation, that, if they were true, they would make the problem of an explanation only more difficult to solve, has often been rightly argued. The story of the creation is a pseudo-explanation."

185 Voegelin, Wissenschaft, Politik und Gnosis, pp. 33 seqq.

186 Voegelin, Wissenschaft, Politik und Gnosis, pp. 38 seq.

tion there is no answer; he would probably say that it is forbidden to ask such a question because it constitutes a violation of the awe we owe to this "transcendent source of being and its order." If a *"Frageverbot"* exists at all, it could be issued only from the point of view of a theological dogma.

Voegelin's new science of politics might have the effect of restoring the hegemony of theology over science; science, then, would become nothing but a handmaiden of theology. It was not so very long ago that political science was still in this position. The progress of natural science in modern times has resulted from the emancipation from the bonds in which theology had held it during the Middle Ages. The emancipation of political science from theology does not go back as far in time as the emancipation of natural science. Until the end of the eighteenth century, theology kept political science under its strict control. The doctrine that the state is a divine institution and the ruler an authority ordained by God was generally accepted. It is, therefore, not exactly a "new" science of politics at which Voegelin, according to the title of his book, is aiming. It is a very old one, which has been abandoned because it was exposed as a pseudoscience, the instrument of definite political powers.[187] It is a retrogressive movement, of which Voegelin's book and the entire literature to which it belongs bear witness.[188] It tends to make the spirit of the Middle Ages

187 One of the objections which Voegelin puts forward against a positivistic political science is its attempt to be free of value judgments about the object of its cognition (The New Science of Politics, pp. 14 seqq). It is the most characteristic consequence of a really value-free science of politics that if emphatically refuses to justify – morally or politically – any actually established social order, that it restricts itself to an objective description of political phenomena. But Voegelin says: "The contraction of political science to a description of existing institutions and the apology of their principles, that is, the degradation of political science to a handmaid of the powers that be, has been typical for stable situations" (ibid., p. 2). If political science is "contracted" to a description of existing institutions, this science cannot, at the same time, convey an apology of their principles and thus become a handmaid of the powers that be. The apology or, what amounts to the same, the condemnation of existing institutions by a so-called political science is possible only – and as a matter of fact, is its ultimate end – if this "science" pretends to be able to determine the political values to be realized. Plato condemns democracy, Aristotle glorifies monarchy. It is precisely to a political-metaphysical speculation of the Platonic or Aristotelian type that Voegelin wishes to turn back modern political science.

188 There is a striking parallelism between this literature and the reactionary romanticism that flourished in France and Germany at the beginning of the nineteenth century as an intellectuel movement directed against the Enlightenment of the eighteenth century and the democratic principles of the French Revolution. The Catholic writers Joseph de Maistre and the Vicomte de Bonald called for a return to political absolutism and a control of the state by the Church. Karl Ludwig von Haller, Friedrich Schlegel, and Adam Müller advocated similar ideas. These three writers were converted to Catholicism. It is significant that the title of Voegelin's book, The New Science of Politics, is almost a copy of *Restauration der Staatswissenschaft*, the title of Haller's work (published

carry over into modern times. "Go back to God!", these writers call to modern science. But God seems to be more progressive than they are. For, when there was darkness upon the face of the deep, he said: Let there be light! Whereas they want darkness to prevail again. This attempt must not go unchallenged.

1816), and that its tendency is clearly expressed in the title of a pamphlet Adam Müller published in 1820: *Von der Notwendigkeit einer theologischen Grundlage der gesamten Staatswissenschaft*. In this pamphlet Adam Müller rejects the rationalistic, anti-theological idea of the state as a sovereign, that is to say, as a supreme authority. He says: "I see in the general enthusiasm for the chimerae of the absolute state, the absolute law, and the absolute reason nothing but the drive of an unfortunate generation at a personal God whom it has deserted ... an obvious idolatry." He states that in his time, just as in the first days of the French Revolution, "the fatal delusion prevails that man creates his God, and not God man." Adam Müller, Schriften zur Staatsphilosophie, ed. by Rudolf Kohler, with a preface by P. Erich Przywara, S. J. (München, n. d.), p. 180. "Posterity will recognize in the convulsive movements of this time nothing but the awakening of religion" (ibid., p. 245). See David Owen Evans, Social Romanticism in France (Oxford, 1951), p. 96, and Wilhelm Metzger, Gesellschaft, Recht und Staat in der Ethik des deutschen Idealismus (Heidelberg, 1917, pp. 251 seqq.). Evans mentions (p. 98, note 1) that de Maistre took up the prophecy of Joachim of Flora that a Reign of the Holy Ghost would dawn in the year 1260.

Chapter III Joachim of Flora's and St. Augustine's Theologies of History

Joachim of Flora

Jakob Taubes characterizes the "law of modern times" as "apocalyptic" in the sense of Joachim of Flora's prediction of a third age as the age of the *ecclesia spiritualis*;[189] Eric Voegelin advocates the doctrine that the nature of modern civilization is Gnosticism as manifested in Joachim of Flora's eschatological theology of history. This theology, Voegelin asserts, decisively affected the way in which "Western political societies interpret the meaning of their existence."[190] The essence of Joachim's Gnosticism, and consequently of modern civilization, is, according to Voegelin, a "re-divinization" of society in opposition to its "de-devinization," which, – and this is one of the paradoxes of Voegelin's new science of politics – is the result of the victory of Christianity over the polytheism of Roman civilization.[191] Voegelin, especially, makes Augustine's theology responsible for this de-divinization, for it articulated the one Christian society into a spiritual and a temporal order with the pope and the emperor as the supreme representatives.[192] This de-divinization brought about

189 Taubes, Abendländische Eschatologie, p. 85. Taubes does not say expressly that Joachim of Flora is a Gnostic. He calls his theology of history "apocalyptic." But using freequently the term "apocalyptic-Gnostic" (pp. 22, 25, 27, 35) he identifies, more or less, "apocalyptic" with "Gnostic." He says (p. 9) of the "apocalyptic": "The world is the antidivine, and God is the anti-worldly [Die Welt ist das Gegengöttliche, und Gott ist das Gegenweltliche]". "God is strange in the world and unknown [Gott ist in der Welt fremd und unbekannt]". These are essential elements of the gnosis. Taubes considers Hegel's philosophy of history to be "apocalyptic-Gnostic" (pp. 35, 159) and at the same time stresses the similarity between Joachim's theology and Hegel's philosophy of history (pp. 91, 159).

190 Voegelin, The New Science of Politics, p. 118.

191 Ibid., pp. 106–107.

192 Ibid., pp. 109–110. "The spiritual destiny of man in the Christian sense cannot be represented on earth by the power organization of a political society; it can be represented only by the church. The sphere of power is radically de-divinized; it has become temporal. The double representation of man in society through church and empire lasted

a "desire for a re-divinization of society," and this desire was satisfied by Joachim who "broke with the Augustinian conception of Christian society when he applied the symbol of the Trinity to the course of history."[193] The essential point in Joachim's trinitarian theology of history is the prediction of a third age. After the age of God Father, which was an age of the layman, and the age of God Son, which was that of the priest, the third age will be that of God the Holy Spirit. It will be an age of the monk and as such an age of religious perfection – men will live *secundum spiritum*. A monastic order will rise over the whole world, an *ecclesia spiritualis*, and the members of this spiritual church will know God not only allegorically – as at the present time – but directly as he really is.[194]

Since, according to Voegelin's interpretation, Joachim's trinitarian theology of history is decisive for the Gnosticism of modern civilization, the questions arise why Joachim has to be considered as a Gnostic, and why his allegedly Gnostic interpretation of history implied – as Voegelin asserts – a re-divinization of society de-divinized by Augustinian theology.

The view that Joachim's trinitarian theology of history is Gnosticism, is highly problematical because the gnosis has been condemned by the Church as heretic, but Joachim's orthodoxy has been decidedly recognized by Pope Honorius III.[195] Voegelin's answers to the just formulated questions are not convincing. He considers Joachim as a Gnostic:

First, because among the "aggregate of symbols" created by Joachim, is a "prophet of the new age." Voegelin seems to assume that the idea of a prophet is a specific Gnostic element. For he says "the Gnostic prophet or, in the later stages of secularization, the Gnostic intellectual becomes an appurtenance of modern civilization. Joachim himself is the first instance of the species."[196]

Second, another element of the gnosis is "the attempt at immanentizing the meaning of existence ... an attempt at bringing our knowledge of transcendence into a firmer grip than the *cognitio fidei*, the cognition of faith [of ortho-

through the Middle-Ages. The specifically modern problems of representation are connected with the re-divinization of society" (ibid., p. 106).

193 Ibid., pp. 110 seq.

194 Ernst Benz, Ecclesia spiritualis (Stuttgart, 1934), pp. 15, 38.

195 Cf. Johannes Chrysostomus Huck, Joachim von Floris und die joachitische Literatur (Freiburg im Breisgau, 1938), pp. 266 seqq. Huck emphasizes Joachim's orthodoxy. Cf. also Henry Bett, Joachim of Flora (London, 1931), p. 28: "Joachim is a loyal Catholic"; and p. 65. Bett rejects (p. 51) the suggestion that Joachim's theology of history came "from some of the heretics who derived from the East like the Cathari ... the supposition is discounted by Joachim's particular abhorence of heretics."

196 Voegelin, The New Science of Politics, pp. 111–112. Voegelin (op. cit., p. 139) goes as far as to say that "in the Joachitic movement the works of Joachim of Flora played this role" – that is the role of a "Gnostic Koran" – "under the title of Evangelium aeternum."

dox Christianity], will afford; and Gnostic experiences offer this firmer grip in so far as they are an expansion of the soul to the point where God is drawn into the existence of man." "These Gnostic experiences, in the amplitude of their variety, are the core of the re-divinization of society, for the men who fall into these experiences divinize themselves by substituting more massive modes of participation in divinity for faith in the Christian sense."[197]

This is the typical experience of the mystics, and Joachim is, according to Voegelin, a mystic Gnostic. Joachim's attempt to find a meaning – or, as Voegelin prefers to formulate it: an "eidos" – of history, not provided in the Augustinian, that is, the orthodox Christian theology, was an attempt at an "immanentization of meaning." The new age predicted by Joachim "would bring an increase of fulfilment within history, but the increase would not be due to an immanent eruption: it would come through a new transcendental irruption of the spirit." By this mysterious statement, Voegelin probably means that redemption – or, as he formulates it: "the soteriological truth of Christianity," the "perfection through grace," the "Christian transcendental fulfilment" or the "Christian eschaton" – takes place according to Joachim's theology of history in *this* world but according to Augustine's theology in the *other* world, so that history in the Augustinian conception can have no meaning. "The problem of an eidos in history ... arises only when Christian transcendental fulfilment becomes immanentized." Since Voegelin believes that history has no meaning, he declares the "immanentist hypostasis of the eschaton" to be a "theoretical fallacy." "The course of history as a whole is no object of experience; history has no eidos because the course of history extends into the unknown future. The meaning of history, thus, is an illusion; and this illusionary eidos is created by treating a symbol of faith as if it were a proposition concerning an object of immanent experience"[198].

Voegelin does not say that the symbol of faith, that is, faith in the Kingdom of God to come, is an illusion. History has no meaning if interpreted from the point of view of empirical cognition based on "immanent," that is, human, experience. But interpreted from the point of view of faith it may have a meaning that is not illusionary. The term "immanentization," which plays a decisive part in the new science of politics, is ambiguous. It covers two different facts. First, the attempt to endow human history with a meaning, especially with the meaning of an evolution toward a perfect condition of society; used in this sense, immanentization is a specifically social category – it implies a positive and optimistic attitude toward this world and humanity living in it. Second, the mystic-Gnostic experience of "the expansion of the soul to the point where God is drawn into the existence of man," the *unio mystica*, brought about in a state of ecstasy; in this sense, immanentization is the expression of a highly in-

197 Ibid., p. 124.

198 Ibid., pp. 119–120.

dividualistic attitude without any social implication. The mystic is asocial because his union with God isolates him from the others. The mystic experience of a union with God is no basis of social cooperation with others as equals.[199]

199 A very characteristic example of the asocial, even antisocial, attitude of true mysticism is the teaching on justice of one of the most famous German mystics of the fourteenth century, Meister Eckhart. There are two sermons dealing with this problem. In one of them (Meister Eckhart: A Modern Translation, by Raymond Bernard Blackney [New York, 1957], pp. 178 seqq.) Eckhart starts from the Wisdom of Solomon 5:15: "The just shall live forever" and asks "Who are the just?") His answer is: "A Scripture says: 'He is just who gives to each what belongs to him.'" This is a translation of the Institutes of Justinian: "Justitia est constans et perpetua voluntas ius suum cuique tribuendi." Eckahart interprets this formula to mean: "Thus, they are just who give to God what is his, to the angels what is theirs, and to their fellow men what is theirs." Justinian's definition of justice, however, refers only to men, not to God and the angels. As far as justice with respect to men is concerned, Eckhart says: "We should give help to those in hell-fire and betterment to the living." This has evidently nothing to do with the justice to which Justinian's Institutes refer. But Eckhart does not stick to this first definition of justice. He replaces it by the statement: Persons are just "who take everything from God evenly [die alle Dinge von Gott als gleich hinnehmen], just as it comes, great and small, desirable and undesirable, one thing like another all the same, and none more or less. If one thing means more than another to you, you are unjust. You must always put your will aside ... The just have no will at all: whatever God wants, it is *all one to them,* however great the discomfort of it may be." This is what he calls in another work "detachment [Abgeschiedenheit]". "To the just person nothing is so hard to bear or so painful as anything opposed to justice, that is to say, as not feeling impartially the same about everything that happens ... If one thing makes them happy and another depressed, they are not just" (op. cit., p. 179). Thus justice is detachment (and not, as Eckhart's doctrine is sometimes interpreted, detachment the condition of justice). This is an open rejection of justice as the "will" to attribute to everyone his due; and insofar as it implies the renunciation of the distinction between good and evil – for everything comes from God, and everything which comes from God must be accepted as equal, that is to say, without regard to its being good or evil from the human point of view – the abandonment of the idea of justice which presupposes this distinction, which does not take every behaviour of men as equal. By defining justice as detachment, Eckhart, in the last analysis, aims at substituting God for justice in the nonmystical sense of this word. For, as we shall see later, he attributes detachment to God as his specific virtue. In the other sermon on justice (Meister Eckhart: Selected Treatises and Sermons, translated by James M. Clark and John V. Skinner, London, 1958, p. 54), he says: "the just man is like God, for God is justice. Hence if someone is in justice he is in God and he is God." "The just man does not seek for anything with his works, for those who seek something with their works are servants and hirelings, or those who work for a Why of a Wherefore" (p. 53). "In the just nothing shall work but God alone. For if it happens that anything outside impels you to work, then the works are certainly dead" (p. 54). If there is anything outside that impels man to work, it is the behavior of other men which impels man to exercise justice. What Eckhart calls "justice" is the mystical union of the individual with God. How this "justice" isolates the mystic from his fellow men becomes manifest in the following statement of the second sermon on justice: "The Father begets His son as the

The idea that human society existing in history has a meaning (especially the meaning of social progress) is entirely foreign to a mystic. His concern is

---

just one, and the just one as His Son. For all the virtue of the just and every work that is wrought by the virtue of the just is nothing but this that the Son is begotten of the Father... Therefore I say that it is the nature of the Father to beget the Son, and that it is the nature of the Son that I should be born in Him and in His image. It is the nature of the Holy Spirit that I should be burnt in Him and should be completely consumed in Him and become entirely love. If anyone is in this way within love [and this means is just] and has become entirely love, he thinks *that God loves no one but him alone,* and he does not know of anyone else who has loved anything else or has been loved by anyone else except by Him alone" (p. 56).

Eckhart says: "Those who understand clearly about justice and the just will understand All I say" (Meister Eckhart, A modern Translation, p. 180). And the essence of his teaching is presented in his tractatus on detachmend (Abgeschiedenheit). He asks: "What is the best and highest virtue, with the aid of which man could be most closely united with God, by which man could become by grace what God is by nature, and by which man would be most like the image of what he was when he was in God, when there was no difference between him and God, before God had created the world." And his answer is: "I just find that pure detachment stands above all things, for all virtues pay some regard to the creatures, yet detachment is free from all creatures" (Meister Eckhart, Selected Treatises, p. 160). Since he considers justice to be a virtue [in his tractatus on the perfection of the soul] detachmend stands also above justice insofar as "justice" is not identified with detachment. Detachment stands above all things because "it separates off the creatures and unites the soul with God" (p. 170). It is incompatible with justice in the proper sense of the word. For "it wishes to stand by itself, neither giving joy nor sorrow to anyone ... Detachment wishes to be nothing. For this reason it is not a burden to anything" (p. 162); therefore even not to injustice. Detachment stands above mercy. "For mercy simply means that man going out of himself, turns to the failings of his fellow-men and for this reason his heart is troubled. Detachment is free from this [turning to the failings of his fellow men] it remains in itself and does not allow itself to be troubled by anything" – therefore also not by the wrongdoing of others – "because as long as anything can trouble a man, it is not well with him." "The man who thus stands in complete detachment is rapt into eternity in such a way that no transient thing can move him ..." (p. 163). Therefore he can not feel approval or disapproval, which is an essential element in the exercise of justice. As mentioned above, Eckhart attributes the virtue of detachment also to God. He says: "that in God there are both detachment and humility, so far as we can speak of virtue in God ... His detachment stood immovable in itself when he became man, just as it has done when He created heaven and earth" (p. 162). He says: "If I consider all virtues I find none so completely without defects and so applicable to God as is detachment" (p. 163). If detachment is "in God" then justice in the proper sense of the word cannot be a virtue of the God of Eckhart's mysticism, if consistently maintained. This mysticism is amoral, ie, morally indifferent. If there can be found something like ethics in the works of Meister Eckhart (cf. Herma Piesch, Meister Eckharts Ethik [Luzern, 1935] and Maria Bindschedler, Meister Eckharts Lehre von der Gerechtigkeit, Studia Philosophica, Vol XIII) it is not compatible with his mystic ideal of detachment. Otto Karrer in his Preface to Piesch's work admits that "ethics" in the traditional sense does not exist in Eckhart's not a redemption of society, but his personal redemption – it is the individual mystic, not society, which is united with God. According to the Christian religion, God is transcendent to this world and, as its creator, at the same time permanently immanent in the objective world and in human society; but according to the mystic experience the transcendent God becomes temporarily, that is, only in the stage of ecstasy, immanent in the individual soul of the mystic subject. Christian religion, in contradistinction to true mysticism, has an eminently social character. The mystic experiences of the monks of Joachim's third age – if their experiences are mystic in the true sense of the term – and Joachim's prediction of this age (his theology of history) are two different facts, mixed up in Voegelin's concept of "immanentization." If Joachim's theology of history is Gnosticism and Gnosticism is mysticism, then Joachim's theology of history is mysticism. But Benz, quite correctly, states (p. 26): "The *spiritualis intelligentia*" – an essential element of Joachim's third age – "does not mean the mystic union with the divine Being, not the 'timeless vision,' but the spiritual cognition of man, endowed with spirit, [*homo spiritualis*] of the third age." The goal of the gnosis is the release of the inner man from the bond of the world, and his return to God, not the reform of this world or any future state of the world.[200] Joachim's prediction of an *ecclesia spiritualis*, a religiously perfect state of the world, is foreign to mystic Gnosticism.

---

writings. In her essay "Meister Eckharts Lehre vom 'Gerechten' (Festschrift der Nationalbibliothek in Wien, Vienna, 1926), Herma Piesch says (p. 624) that Eckhart's justice is "not a purely moral concept [keine rein moralische Größe]; "... the just ... is man in the state of mystic union." And Bindschedler (op. cit., p. 61), speaks of Eckhart's "mystic indifference" as of an attitude, which "transcends ethics," and of a "transgression of morals".

200 Cf. Jonas, Gnosis und spätantiker Geist, p. 214; and Jonas, The Gnostic Religion (Boston, 1958), p. 44. In this work Jonas, one of the outstanding authorities in this field, says about "the soul's way out of the world," that it is achieved after death, when equipped with the knowledge of God the soul "travels upward, leaving behind at each sphere the psychical 'vestment' contributed by it: thus the spirit stripped of foreign accretions reaches the God beyond the world and becomes reunited with the divine substance ... In this life the pneumatics, as the possessors of gnosis called themselves, are set apart from the great mass of mankind. The immediate illumination not only marks the individual sovereign in the sphere of knowledge (hence the limitless variety of gnostic doctrines) but also determines the sphere of action. Generally speaking, the pneumatic morality is determined by hostility toward the world and contempt for all mundane ties" (pp. 45 seq.). From this characterization of the Gnostic religion follows that nothing could be more alien to the individualistic, even antisocial gnosis than a desire to reform this world, to bring about a definite status of human society, such as the *ecclesia spiritualis of Joachim of Flora*. Very characteristic in this respect is Marcion's, one of the most important Gnostics, attitude toward the Messianic Kingdom of God to be established in this world. Marcion, Jonas says (op. cit., p. 140), agreed with the Jews that their promised Messiah, "the earthly one, son of the world-god [not of the true, good God of

Voegelin cannot deny that "in the eighteenth century, with the idea of progress" during the period of Enlightenment "the increase of meaning of history" became "a completely intramundane phenomenon, without transcendental irruptions." In order to show that a philosophy that considers the meaning of history as a completely intramundane phenomenon, that is to say, a process which takes place without any interference of God, Voegelin speaks of "secularized" immanentization. He says: "This second phase of immanentization should be called 'secularization'" (p. 119). This immanentization is the same self-contradiction as Sertillanges's laicized Christian thought, Löwith's secularized theology, Rosenstock's secularized eschaton, Aron's, Talmon's, and Brinton's secular religion. It is an immanentization without immanentization. For, if the process of history is "completely" intramundane, nothing could be "immanentized" in the sense of an irruption of the transcendental. Only a transcendental can be "immanentized" in this sense of the ambiguous term.

Joachim's and his modern followers' Gnostic but fallacious immanentization of the Christian eschaton is not, so we are told, the results of stupidity or dishonesty. It is to be understood as a reaction against feelings of uncertainty and anxiety, and these are caused – by Christianity. Until the new science of politics was established, we believed that an essential function of Christianity

the Gnosis], was really still to come and would establish his earthly kingdom just as the prophets had declared. Only this has nothing to do with the salvation brought by Christ, which is acosmic in its nature and does not change the course of worldly events, not even in the sense of amelioration: in fact it changes only the prospect for the future life of the redeemed soul and, through faith in this future, its present *spiritual* condition, but leaves the world to itself – i. e., to its eventual self-destruction." Marcion's principle of morality was "not to complete but to reduce the world of the creator and to make the least possible use of it" (p. 144). The "world of the creator," that means, *this* world, not created by the true, good God, but by Jehova, the God of the Jews, and human society which is part of this world. Consequently Marcion demands perpetual abstention in matters of food and is against sexual intercourse and marriage.

There is, it is true, a "brotherhood of salvation," of which Jonas (op. cit., p. 264) says: "The self is discovered as incommensurable with all things of nature. This discovery at first makes the self emerge in its utter solitude: the self is discovered by a break with the world. At the same time, this recoil from cosmic alienness leads to a new emphasis on the fellowship of man as the only realm of kinship left, united not only by the community of origin but also by the community of the situation of aliens in the world. But this fellowship *refers not to the natural and social concerns of men,* that is, to man's worldly existence, but only to the acosmic inner self and its concern of salvation. Thus is founded the new brotherhood of the elect, or the believers, or the knowers ... the mutual concern of the brotherhood, thrown together by the common cosmic solitude, is to deepen this very alienation and to further the other's redemption, which to each self becomes a vehicle of his own" (italics mine). It is a brotherhood of individual not of social salvation. The idea of a saved society is foreign to the gnosis. See below pp. 73 seq.

was to give men the feeling of certainty through the belief in an all-powerful, absolutely just, and absolutely merciful God whose will is done in heaven and on earth; and that precisely to this function is due Christianity's victory over Greco-Roman polytheism whose gods, moved by human passions, fought each other so that no human being could be sure of protection by a god who might be defeated or outwitted by another god. Now we learn: "What specific uncertainty was so disturbing that it had to be overcome by the dubious means of fallacious immanentization? One does not have to look far afield for an answer. Uncertainty is the very essence of Christianity. The feeling of security in a 'world full of gods' is lost with the gods themselves; when the world is dedivinized [by the Christian religion], communication with the world-transcendent God is reduced to the tenuous bond of faith ... The more people are drawn or pressured into the Christian orbit, the greater will be the number among them who do not have the spiritual stamina for the heroic adventure of the soul that is Christianity; and the likeliness of a fall from faith will increase when civilizational progress of education, literacy, and intellectual debate will bring the full seriousness of Christianity to the understanding of ever more individuals."[201] How a religion whose essence is "uncertainty" and which consequently results inevitably in a "fall from faith," a religion that is a "heroic adventure" in which only a few persons are able to participate, could become and remain a world religion is difficult to understand, and the new science of politics is far from solving this riddle. It only asserts: "Gnostic speculation" – opposed to orthodox Christian religion and condemned by the Church – "overcame the uncertainty of faith by receding from transcendence and endowing man and his intramundane range of action with the meaning of eschatological fulfilment. In the measure in which this immanentization progressed experientially, civilizational activity became a mystical work of self-salvation."[202]

Gnostic experience brings our knowledge of transcendence into firmer grip with its transcendent God than Christianity because this experience is an "expansion of the soul to the point where God is drawn into the existence of man." In this sense, Gnostic experience is "the core of the re-divinization of society [which is the nature of modernity] for the men who fall into these experiences divinize themselves by substituting more massive modes of participation in divinity for faith in the Christian sense."[203] This "more massive mode of participating in divinity", this "expansion of the soul to the point where God is drawn into the existence of man" which, according to Voegelin, is an essential element of Gnostic experience, can hardly be distinguished from what he, in another connection (pp. 67 f.), describes as the experience of man to be "open toward transcendental reality," the opening of man's "psyche to the

201 Ibid., pp. 122–123.

202 Ibid., p. 129.

203 Ibid., p. 124. As to "Gnostic" self-salvation and self-divinization see below pp. 73 seq.

truth of God,"[204] the fact that man "discovers his own psyche as the instrument for experiencing transcendence."[205] It is "the discovery of a true order of the human psyche,"[206] the discovery of a "new truth,"[207] which can only be the truth of the soul, discovered, as Voegelin asserts, by various religious founders and philosophers in the time between 800 and 300 B.C.[208] If, according to this new truth, the soul is "the region in which transcendence is experienced,"[209] this experience is an immanentization of the transcendental; and, if Gnostic experience consists in "the expansion of the soul to the point where God is drawn into the existence of man," then Gnosticism, too, is in possession of the truth of the soul; and then can be no better guarantee of this truth than Gnosticism. But it is just the Gnosticism of modern civilization which the new science of politics accuses of the "destruction of the truth of the soul."[210] Against this Gnostic destruction of the truth of the soul in modern civilization the new science of politics launches a passionate crusade. This is, indeed, difficult to understand, and even more difficult how a Gnostic divinization of society and a "self-divinization of man," this "firm grip" on God, could be possible within a "secularized" view of the world where no "transcendental irruption" occurs because there is no belief in God, and where even an antireligious tendency prevails.

St. Augustine

The de-divinization of society is, according to Voegelin, the work auf Augustine's dualistic conception of Christian society to which Joachim opposed his trinitarian theology of history.[211] By Augustine's doctrine of a "double representation of man in society through church and empire," "the sphere of power is radically de-divinized, it has become temporal."[212] The dualism of Church and state, of a spiritual and a temporal sphere of society corresponds in Augustine's theology to his distinction between the civitas *dei* and the civitas *terrena* – the City of God and the City of Earth. But there is no complete separation.[213]

204 Ibid., p. 69.
205 Ibid., p. 67.
206 Ibid., p. 62.
207 Ibid., p. 67.
208 Ibid., p. 60.
209 Ibid., p. 67.
210 Ibid., pp. 163 seqq., 166.
211 Voegelin, The New Science of Politics, p. 111.
212 Ibid., p. 106.
213 See Heinrich Scholz, Glaube und Unglaube in der Weltgeschichte (Leipzig, 1911), pp. 127 seqq.

The civitas *dei* does not only exist in the other world but also in this world, side by side with the civitas *terrena*. The civitas *dei* on earth is an image or shadow of the civitas *dei* in heaven, and the civitas *terrena*, an image or shadow of the civitas *dei* on earth.[214] Thus the civitas *dei* forms an essential part of human society, the two communities penetrate each other, one depends on the other. Augustine says: "The two cities are in this world entangled together and intermixed until the last judgment effect their separation."[215] The divine or eternal peace, the peace of the soul, the essential characteristic of the City of God to which the Church corresponds, and the earthly peace, the peace of the body, the essential function of the state, more or less identical with the City of Earth, belong together. The state guarantees the earthly peace which is necessary to the Church, the civitas *dei* on earth. "The whole use, then, of things temporal has a reference to this result of earthly peace in the earthly community, while in the City of God it is connected with eternal peace ... The peace of the body might contribute to the peace of the soul. For if bodily peace be wanting, a bar is put to the peace even of the irrational soul ... [Man] refers all peace, bodily or spiritual or both, to that peace which mortal man has with the immortal God."[216] In other words, the earthly peace (the peace of the temporal sphere) and the eternal peace (the peace of the spiritual sphere) are united in the peace of man with God. "The earthly city, which does not live by faith, seeks an earthly peace ... The heavenly city, or rather the part of it which sojourns on earth and lives by faith, makes use of this peace only because it must, until this mortal condition which necessitates it shall pass away. Consequently, so long as it lives like a captive and a stranger in the earthly city, though it has already received the promise of redemption, and the gift of the Spirit as the earnest of it, it makes no scruple to obey the laws of the earthly city, whereby the things necessary for the maintenance of this mortal life are administered; and thus, as this life is common to both cities, so there is a harmony between them in regard to what belongs to it."[217] Consequently, Augustine is far from conceiving the state – so far as it corresponds to the City of Earth – as a body alienated from God. Voegelin's statement that in Augustine's theology the "sphere of power," that is, the state, is "radically de-divinized," contradicts Augustine's doctrine that the same divine principle, the principle of divine justice, governs the state as well as the Church. It is by justice that the state differs from a band of robbers.[218] "A republic cannot be administered without justice. Where there is no

214 Augustine, City of God, Book XV, chap. 2. See Leisegang, Denkformen, p. 384.

215 Augustine, City of God, Book I, chap. 35. This quotation and those that follow are taken, with slight modifications, from the English edition (translation by Marcus Dodd), published by The Modern Library, New York, 1950).

216 Ibid., Book XIX, chap. 14.

217 Ibid., Book XIX, chap. 17.

218 Ibid., Book IV, chap. 4.

true justice, there can be no right." Where there is no true justice, there can be no assemblage of men which deserves the name of state. "Justice is that virtue which gives every one his due." Hence justice is to give the true God what is his due. Therefore man is just if he serves the true God and not impure demons.[219] Justice is Christianity, and a Christian state is not a godless institution. It is willed by God.[220]

The prevailing view in the Middle Ages of the relationship between the temporal sphere, represented by the state, and the spiritual sphere, represented by the Church, is formulated in the famous doctrine of the two swords: God gave to the emperor one sword to rule man, and another sword to the pope to rule man's soul. Both, the temporal and the spiritual swords, come from God; hence, the temporal rule of the state as well as the spiritual rule of the Church are ordained by God. According to another version of this doctrine, laid down in the papal bull *Unam Sanctam*, issued by Boniface VIII, God gave both swords to the pope who transmitted the temporal one to the emperor. God thus established the supremacy of the pope over the emperor, and the state as a province of the Church, whereby the unity of the two spheres under God and his deputy was still more emphasized. The relationship between state and Church symbolized in the two swords was not only regarded as a religious but also as a political problem – the determination of the jurisdictions of emperor and pope. The latter aspect of the problem becomes manifest in the *Defensor Pacis* of Marsilius of Padua (A.D. 1290–1343) who rejected the claim of the Church to supremacy over the state. His main thesis was "That the Roman or any other bishop or priest, or clergyman, can by virtue of the words of Scripture claim or ascribe to himself no coercive rulership or contentious jurisdiction, let alone the supreme jurisdiction over any clergyman or layman."[221] Even the most radical advocates of the independence of the emperor did not question the teaching of St. Paul (Rom. 13) that "there is no authority except from God, and those that exist have been instituted by God." To conceive of the sphere of power under the emperor as temporal never meant that it was beyond the realm of the divine. Moreover, the separation of state and Church was confined to the Western world; in the East, the Byzantine emperor united in himself the temporal and spiritual leadership of Christian society. There is, then, no reason to assume a de-divinization of the sphere of power or of society or even of the world which "lasted through the Middle Ages."[222]

219 Ibid., Book XIX, chap. 21.

220 See Ernest Barker in his introduction to the edition of John Healey's translation of the City of God, Everyman's Library (London, 1947), pp. XVIII, XIX.

221 Marsilius of Padua, The Defensor Pacis, translated with an introduction by Alan Gewirth, New York, 1956, Vol. II, p. 113.

222 Voegelin, The New Science of Politics, p. 106.

Starting from this erroneous assumption, Voegelin interprets Joachim's trinitarian theology of history as "the first clear and comprehensive expression of the idea" of a "re-divinization of society,"[223] achieved by endowing "the immanent course of history with a meaning that was not provided in the Augustinean conception."[224] It is true that Joachim's periodization of history was different from Augustine's philosophy of history: Augustine rejected, as a ridiculous misinterpretation of St. John's Revelation, the chiliastic dream – the belief in a perfect state of society to be established in the near future in this world, the belief in a future Kingdom of Heaven on earth that will last a thousand years in which "those who then rise again shall enjoy the leisure of immoderate carnal banquets, furnished with ... meat and drink."[225] Joachim's theology of history, however, culminated in the prediction of a future age analogous to the hope of the chiliasts – a hope closely connected with the Jewish idea of the coming Messiah and the Kingdom of God as a second paradise on earth. However, the antagonism between Joachim's prediction of an age of monarchism and Augustine's rejection of chiliasm cannot be interpreted as a re-divinization against a de-divinization of society. For Augustine rejected chiliasm only so far as he taught that the Kingdom of Heaven is not to be expected in the future, but exists already, that this Kingdom is represented by the *civitas dei* on earth: the Church[226] in which Christ is incorporated, the most perfect state which is possible in this world.[227] A world in which the Kingdom of Heaven already exists is certainly not a de-divinized world. The difference between Augustine and Joachim in this respect is only that the latter did not consider the Church as it existed as the most perfect state possible on earth, but that he expected a more perfect state in the near future, a spiritual Church. If this expectation, in contradistinction of Augustine's theology, is to be understood as an immanentization of the Christian transcendental fulfilment, then it is hardly possible to assert, as Voegelin does, that the problem of an eidos in history arises only when such an immanentization takes place and, consequently, not "in orthodox Christianity"[228] as interpreted in Augustine's theology. For Augustine is far from the view that history has no meaning. One of the best authorities, Heinrich Scholz,[229] writes about Augustine's philosophy of his-

223 Ibid., p. 110.

224 Ibid., p. 119.

225 Augustine, The City of God (De civitate Dei), transl. by John Healey (= Everyman's Library; London, 1947), Book XX, chap. 7.

226 Ibid., Book XX, chap. 9: "Therefore the Church even now is the Kingdom of Christ, and the kingdom of heaven. Accordingly, even now His saints reign with Him, though otherwise than as they shall reign hereafter."

227 See Herbert Grundmann, Studien über Joachim von Floris (Leipzig, 1927), p. 86.

228 Voegelin, The New Science of Politics, pp. 119, 120.

229 Scholz, Glaube und Unglaube, p. 140. Also Karl Löwith, Meaning in History, p. 170, writes: "The whole scheme of Augustine's work serves the purpose of vindicating God

tory: "It is a continuously repeated thought of Augustine that history is the expression and vindication of divine providence"; and an indubitable authority on Catholic theology, Father Sertillanges, states: "Augustine lays the foundation of the first philosophy of history which inspired not only Bossuet in his *Discours sur l'Histoire universelle*, but also Vico, Herder, Condorcet, Krause, Hegel, and many others."[230] Augustine, like Hegel, one of the most celebrated philosophers of history of modern times, interprets history as a theodicy. This is the inevitable consequence of the belief in an omnipotent and just God who created this world and who formed man in his own image, so that the existence of mankind can in time be the realization of God's absolutely good will.[231] Only an areligious, antimetaphysical, positivistic view of the world, rejected by the new science of politics, may assert that history has no meaning – that the "meaning of history... is an illusion."[232] A typical representative of this antimetaphysical, positivistic attitude toward history, Theodor Lessing,[233] at the beginning of the twentieth century, published his *Geschichte als Sinngebung des Sinnlosen*. In this book Lessing characterized "the view that history reflects reason and meaning, progress and justice," as a "pious delusion."[234] Against this antimeta-

---

in history." He refers (ibid., pp. 174 seqq.) to a disciple of Augustine, Orosius; who also recognized salvation as the meaning of history. See also: M. C. D'Arcy, S. J., The Sense of History, Secular and Sacred (London, 1959). He says: Augustine "had to spend part of his great work commenting on human history. To him it was a sad spectacle. Man at variance with God and with himself chasing false hopes and dreams. Peoples and civilizations rise and fall, and their distresses are due to sin ... Orosius, his disciple, is in accord with his main ideas, and fills up to the picture of history sketched by Augustine ... Man being what he is there is no reason for looking for better things in the future. The world will always be a place of suffering and sin, and the Christian alone is blessed because he knows, that after the suffering comes the reward, and that in the after-life true peace and happiness can alone be found. No more than in Augustine, therefore, is there a philosophy of human history. There is, however, a moral or theological view of history running through the thought of Augustine and Orosius and it is this theology of history which became the conventional Christian view until the eighteenth century, and even now it remains the uncritical, spontaneous reaction to history of many religious men and women" (p. 87). See also: Jean, Daniélou, "The Conception of History in the Christian Tradition", The Journal of Religion (1950), p. 171 seqq.

230 Sertillanges, Le Christianisme, I, p. 210.

231 Huck, Joachim von Floris und die joachitische Literatur, pp. 244 seqq., says that the eschatological interpretation of history is not Joachim's discovery. It was familiar to Augustine and other Christian thinkers of the past. He rejects as un-christian the view, that history is a product of accident. "Christian philosophy of history seeks and finds the ultimate answer to the questions of the 'why' and the 'what for' of history in the transmundane and transhistoric absolute reason of the divine logos."

232 Voegelin, The New Science of Politics, p. 120.

233 Theodor Lessing, Geschichte als Sinngebung des Sinnlosen, 2nd ed. (München, 1921).

234 Ibid., p. 3. To the question: What is the content of history?, he answers: "Meaningless tragedies of an ant hill which, driven by hunger, sex, vanity, continues in live until it

physical, areligious, "destructive" positivism the new science of politics demands the return to "metaphysical speculation and theological symbolization" under the authority of Augustine. Thomas Aquinas, and other religious thinkers[235] who – if they are consistent – are by their specific view of the world forced to find a meaning in history. If the new science of politics has anything to object against the positivists Comte and Marx, it cannot be their attempt to find a meaning in history; and that the meaning they thought to have found is – in Voegelin's opinion – somehow akin to that discovered by Joachim in his theologico-metaphysical trinitarian eschatology. The new science of politics can only object that the secular philosophy of history tries to find a meaning based on empirical science instead of on faith.

Thus Joachim and Augustine do not, and cannot, disagree on the question whether history has a meaning. These two Christian theologians do not even disagree on the periodization of history into three ages. For Augustine, too, uses a threefold scheme of history – in addition to a sixfold scheme. He distinguishes an epoch of natural religion (*tempus ante legem*), an epoch of the law (*tempus sub lege*), and an epoch of grace (*tempus sub gratia).*[236] As Henry Bett[237] correctly remarks, the conception of three dispensations is "inevitable, in one form or another, to anyone whose thought moves within the range of the Christian religion." Before Joachim, Rupert of Deutz and Hugh of St. Victor applied even the concept of the holy trinity to history. Rupert of Deutz[238] distinguished seven times and works of the Father, seven of the son and seven of the Holy Spirit, as the movement and the work of the Trinity.

Hugh of St. Victor distinguished an age of fear under the dominion of power, which belongs to the Father, an age of truth under the dominion of wisdom, which belongs to the Son, and an age of love under the dominion of benignity, which belongs to the Spirit.[239] The division of history into three periods – the epoch before the fall of man, the time of the first paradise; the time after the fall; and the future time of the Kingdom of God, the second paradise – is already the basis of the Jewish Messianic idea. Hence, it was not Joachim who, as Voegelin asserts,[240] created as a symbol "the conception of history as a sequence of three ages of which the third age is intelligibly the final Third

will perish ... by a cosmic catastrophe" (pp. 17 seq.). His own view of history, he says, "destroys the old belief in natural evolution, progress, immanent world order, God, divine providence in history" (p. 76).

235 Voegelin, The New Science of Politics, p. 6.

236 Augustine, De Trinitate, IV, p. 7; Enchiridion, p. 118; see Scholz, op. cit., p. 164.

237 Henry Bett, Joachim of Flora (London, 1931), p. 52.

238 In his work De S. Trinitate et eius operibus (published about 1117). See R. Rocholl, Rupert von Deutz (Gütersloh, 1886), p. 137.

239 Hugh of St. Victor, Didascalion, VII, 26, 27, as cited by Bett, op. cit., p. 55–56.

240 Voegelin, The New Science of Politics, p. 111.

Realm." Clearly, there is not sufficient reason for Voegelin, following Taubes,[241] to recognize "the humanistic and encyclopedist periodization of history into ancient, medieval, and modern history" as a variation of this Joachite symbol. Joachim's allegedly "Gnostic" symbol and our periodization of history have nothing in common but the division of a whole into three parts, which is a general scheme of articulation or systematization as old as human thinking. The notion of a divine trinity which, as an essential element of Christian religion, is the basis of Joachim's periodization of history, forms an important part also in the Indian and Egyptian religions and in Neoplatonic speculation.[242] To recognize Joachim's three ages in our periodization of history is as justifiable as to recognize the mystic trinity in the distinction between childhood, manhood, and old age. Our rational periodization of history can have nothing to do with Joachim's trinitarian speculation projected into history because there is no probable connection between the two, and because their meaning is totally different. Joachim's three stages represent an order of rank, the third stage being a definite stage of perfection. Its purpose is evidently the glorification of monarchism, and not a scientific analysis of history. Our periodization of history into three stages has never been understood as a definite articulation; but only as a systematization from the point of view of our present knowledge of history, which may be replaced at any time by profounder knowledge. The concept of the third stage (modern times) is far from implying the idea of perfection and is compatible with any value judgment. It certainly does not convey the idea of a definite status of human civilization, incapable of further evolution. It seems, however, that Voegelin himself does not stick to the view that our periodization of history is a Gnostic-Joachite symbol because he asserts in another connection that the problem of periodization of his-

241 Ibid.

242 See W. Fulton, article "Trinity" in Encyclopaedia of Religion and Ethics, XII, 458: "Although the notion of a divine Triad or Trinity is characteristic of the Christian religion, it is by no means peculiar to it. In Indian religion, e. g., we meet with the trinitarian group of Brahma, Siva, and Visnu; and in Egyptian religion with the trinitarian group of Osiris, Isis, and Horus, constituting a divine family, like the Father, Mother, and Son in medieval Christian pictures. Nor is it only in historical religions that we find God viewed as a Trinity. One recalls in particular the Neo-Platonic view of the Supreme or Ultimate Reality (άρχικαί ὑποόтάσεις), which was suggested by Plato in the Timaeus; e. g., in the philosophy of Plotinus the primary or original Realities are triadically represented as the Good or (in numerical symbol) the One, the Intelligence or the One-Many and the World-Soul or the One and Many. The religious Trinity associated, if somewhat loosely, with Comte's philosophy might also be cited here: the cultus of humanity as the Great Being, of space as the Great Medium, and of the Earth as the Great Fetish." As for the attempt to interpret Comte's distinction of a theological, a metaphysical, and a scientific age as a reappearance of Joachim's trinitarian speculation, see below, pp. 150 seqq.

tory "cannot be solved on the level of Gnostic-symbolism. We must descend to the level of existential representation in order to find a motive for periodization."[243] He does not explain what he means by that. But the following passages may be understood to mean that the conventional periodization becomes meaningful when we recognize that "a clear epoch in Western history is marked by the Reformation," and Reformation is "understood as the successful innovation of Western institutions by Gnostic movements."[244] The assumption that a clear epoch of Western history is marked by the Reformation is as good as the assumption that this epoch was inaugurated by the emancipation from a theological interpretation of nature by the birth of modern science in the intellectual movement of the Renaissance. But even if the first assumption is accepted, it has nothing to do with the questionable characterization of the Reformation as a Gnostic revolution (see below, pp. 259 seqq.). And, even if this characterization is accepted, it remains obscure why the fact that a Gnostic movement marked one epoch of Western history, should make the periodization of the history of mankind into three epochs meaningful; and why this periodization should be the application of Joachim's symbol.

243 Voegelin, The New Science of Politics, p. 134.
244 Ibid., p. 134.

Chapter IV Gnosticism

Eric Voegelin's paradoxical interpretation of modern civilization as Gnosticism depends in the first place on his assertion that Joachim is a Gnostic prophet and that his theology of history decisively affected the social philosophy and political ideology of our time. As pointed out, Joachim's Gnosticism manifests itself, according to Voegelin, in a re-divinization of society de-devinized by Augustinian Christianity; and this re-divinization is supposed to be the result of Joachim's trinitarian periodization of history culminating in an age of monarchism, a perfect society of the future, inaugurated by a Gnostic redeemer, the *Dux e Babylone*. Joachim's view – even in Voegelin's interpretation – is historical and social, based on an optimistic evaluation of this world as the possible theatre of redemption.

We have seen that Joachim's theology of history in its relation to orthodox Christianity cannot be understood as a re-divinization because Christianity does not and cannot de-divinize the world. Its God, although transcendent to the world, is, as its creator and ruler, also immanent in the world.[245] The only difference in this respect between Joachim and Augustine is that Joachim emphasizes much more than Augustine God's immanence by predicting, like Jewish Messianism, a fulfilment of the redemption on earth, a fact which Voegelin calls "immanentization." But even if Joachim's theology of history is at least divinization of society, if not re-divinization, it cannot be classified as Gnosticism. For the gnosis is precisely the contrary, according to all author-

245 Sertillanges, a Catholic theologian, at least as competent as Professor Voegelin to interpret the meaning of Christianity, says about the incarnation of God in Jesus Christ: "For the Christian the event par excellence, the point of enlightenment of the entire reality: light upon God, light upon man, light upon their relationship, and what a relationship! light upon destiny which is a divinization of humanity and its ascension to its very source, light upon the universe and civilization ... God irrupts into his creation at the point where matter and spirit join together ("au point de suture de la matière et de l'esprit") in order to transform and, at the same time, to push his work up to the point where it becomes identical with his Principle!" (Le Christianisme, I, p. 16). This means that an essential function of Christianity is the radical divinization of the world in general, and humanity or society in particular.

ities dealing with this religious movement, and especially according to Hans Jonas, the authority to which Voegelin himself refers. The gnosis is an outspoken, nay, the most radical de-divinization of this world and of human society still possible within the framework of a religion. Its main thesis, constituting the decisive conflict with orthodox Christianity, is that this world, as a realm of evil, is the creation of an evil demiurge, the Jehovah of the Old Testament, a demon of revenge or retribution; that Jesus Christ is not and cannot be his son but is the son of the true, the good God, the unknown, foreign God, the God of love who has nothing to do with this world of sin, which, indeed, is an entirely godless, de-divinized world. The divine has no part and no concern in the physical universe.[246] The God of the gnosis, which opposes the New to the Old Testament,[247] is a truly transcendent God.[248] The more the evil of this

246 Jonas (Gnosis und spätantiker Geist, p. 176) states that the result of Gnostic speculation which separates *heimarméne* from prónoia, that is, the destiny of the world from the will of God, is "a de-divinized world" ("eine entgötterte Welt"). This is compatible with the fact that in Gnostic speculations this world is the realm of a satanic demiurge and evil demons. By re-divinization through modern Gnosticism, Voegelin does not mean a denomization of society. In The Gnostic Religion (Boston, 1958, p. 42), Jonas says: "The cardinal feature of Gnostic thought is the radical dualism that governs the relation of God and world, and correspondingly that of man and world. The deity is absolutely transmundane, its nature alien to that of the universe, which it neither created nor governs and to which it is the complete antithesis: to the divine realm of light, self-contained and remote, the cosmos is opposed as the realm of darkness. The world is the work of lowly powers which though they may mediately be descended from Him do not know the true God and obstruct the knowledge of Him in the cosmos over which they rule." On page 236, Jonas speaks of the "antidivine universe" of the Gnostic speculation. On page 250, he says of the Gnostic world: "A world emptied of divine content had its own order: an order empty of divinity." And on page 251, we read: "The Gnostic God is not merely extra-mundane and supra-mundane, but in his ultimate meaning contramundane ... God and world, God and natur, spirit and nature, become divorced, alien to each other, even contraries."

247 This opposition is a main concern to Marcion, the most outstanding theologian of the Christian gnosis. See Adolf von Harnack, Marcion: Das Evangelium vom fremden Gott (Leipzig, 1921, pp. 32 seqq.); and Jonas, Gnosis und spätantiker Geist, pp. 173 seqq. According to Harnack, Marcion is not a typical Gnostic. But most writers on Gnosticism treat him as belonging to this religious movement. R. A. Lipsius, Der Gnosticismus, sein Wesen, Ursprung und Entwicklungsgang (Leipzig, 1860), p. 160, considers him one of "the most prominent representatives of the gnosis in the last phase of its development," and says on page 163, that "the Marcionite system must be recognized as a true Gnostic one." J. P. Steffes, Das Wesen des Gnostizismus und sein Verhältnis zum katholischen Dogma in Forschungen zur Christlichen Literatur- und Dogmengeschichte (Paderborn, 1922, XIV:4, p. 205), speaks of Marcion as of "one fo the most prominent representatives of the Gnostic movement." Cf. also Hans Jonas, The Gnostic Religion, pp. 130 seqq.

248 See Jonas, Gnosis und spätantiker Geist, p. 5.

world is emphasized – in contradistinction to the good of the other world – the greater is man's need for redemption in this world. Thus redemption is an essential element of Gnosticism.[249] But redemption in this religion means emancipation from the world and hence from society, and can be achieved perfectly only after the death of the body, which is regarded as the prison of the soul. But man, while still living in this world, may, in a state of ecstasy, take a first step on the way to redemption. In this state the human soul leaves the human body and makes room for the divine pneuma.[250] This means, indeed, a certain immanentization of the transcendental, a mystic union with God. But emphasis is placed on the transcendence of God, on his transmundane existence, his alienation from the world. He becomes immanent only in the individual soul of the Gnostic, not in a community, in a church. Gnostic redemption is highly individualistic; it is the liberation of the individual soul from its prison; it is not the realization of a social ideal on earth, like the Messianic and Joachite redemption with their belief in a perfect society of the future; it is an asocial and sometimes even antisocial view of the world. The gnosis, in its anticosmic[251] attitude, is pessimistic[252] about this world and the society in it; it is optimistic only about the other world. The idea of social progress or a revolution for the improvement of the social situation is foreign to the gnosis. To call the gnosis "revolutionary" because its order of values is different from or even opposite to the traditional Christian order is a problematical analogy; therefore to characterize on the basis of this analogy the European revolutions in general and the Communist revolution in particular as "Gnostic"[253] is a misuse of terminology. Significant in this respect is the Gnostic doctrine that justice, the central value of a social philosophy, is not a characteristic of the true God, but only of the evil, cruel demon of the Jewish Testament. The true God, the God of the New Testament, the Father of Christ, is not a God of "justice" – which means of law, retribution, judgment, punishment – but a God of love. He is

249 Steffes, Das Wesen des Gnostizismus, p. 2, characterizes Gnosticism as "a religion of revelation and redemption [Offenbarungs- und Erlösungsreligion]". "The world is alienated from God; man, composed of antagonistic elements, needs redemption. Revelation and redemption is offered by a human-divine being: Jesus Christ. He redeems man from the evil and its consequences."

250 See Hans Leisegang, Die Gnosis (Leipzig, 1924), pp. 27, 101. Jonas, Gnosis und spätantiker Geis, pp. 199 seqq., describes this Gnostic experience as "mystic-ecstatic transformation [palingenesis]," "the exchange of the demonic for the pneumatic ego."

251 See Jonas, Gnosis und spätantiker Geist, p. 49.

252 Wilhelm Bousset, Hauptprobleme der Gnosis (Göttingen, 1907, p. 119), speaks of the "absolute and disconsolate pessimism of the gnosis [der absolute und trostlose Pessimismus der Gnosis]".

253 Voegelin, The New Science of Politics, pp. 13 seqq. In Gnosis und spätantiker Geist, p. 214, Jonas speaks of a "revolutionary" element of the gnosis. But he emphasizes that this term, if applied to the gnosis, cannot be used in its modern political sense.

neither a legislator nor a judge, like the demiurge of the Old Testament.[254] Joachim's third stage, however, is the realization of eternal justice.[255] The antisocial character of the gnosis shows itself in a tendency against propagation – human society in this evil world is not worthy of being preserved – and, in some Gnostic sects, even against sexual intercourse as a satanic practice.[256]

From all this follows that the gnosis is a thoroughly ahistoric[257] view of the world. In conflict with this undeniable fact Joachim's theology of history is interpreted by Voegelin as Gnostic because he assumes that gnosis is a speculation about the meaning of history. He says: "In order to lend validity and conviction to the idea of a final Third Realm, the course of history as an intelligible, meaningful whole must be assumed accessible to human knowledge, either through a direct revelation or through speculative gnosis."[258] It is not understandable why the view that history has meaning is possible only on the basis of "a direct revelation or speculative gnosis." This view has been advocated by rationalistic, antimetaphysical, and antireligious positivistic thinkers like Comte and Marx. To find a meaning in history does not necessarily presuppose a metaphysical hypothesis. "Meaning of history" may merely signify that man's social life and its evolution, like nature itself, are determined by laws, and to discover these socio-historical laws is to discover the meaning of history. Whether this view is correct, whether it is possible to discover laws of evolution in history, is another question. Just as natural science in its attempt to describe natural phenomena in accordance with a law of evolution formulated on the basis of facts, so can history, in principle, be interpreted in the same way without any metaphysical hypothesis. This was certainly the intention of Comte's and Marx's philosophies of history. Whatever the basis of these philosophies may be, it is certainly not Gnostic speculation, which is the opposite of any kind of philosophy or theology of history. Such a basis is especially incompatible with Joachim's optimistic hope of the future realization of a perfect society based on belief in God, the omnipotent creator of this world, and the just legislator and judge in conformity with Christian religion. This belief presupposes, at least in principle, a concordance between the Old and New Testaments. Joachim was anxious to confirm this concordance, despite certain differences which he did not deny.[259]

254 This is the teaching of Marcion. See Harnack, Marcion, pp. 28, 86 seqq.

255 Cf. Benz, Ecclesia Spiritualis, p. 24.

256 Harnack, Marcion, p. 97; Leisegang, Die Gnosis, pp. 110, 135, 192.

257 See Jonas, Gnosis und spätantiker Geist, p. 227. Wilhelm Kamlah, Christentum und Geschichtlichkeit (Stuttgart, 1951), p. 101, states that the Gnostic myths do not know a historic but only a cosmic eschatology.

258 Voegelin, The New Science of Politics, p. 112.

259 In his Concordia novi ac veteris testamenti. See Grundmann, Studien über Joachim von Floris, p. 60.

To justify his classification of Joachim's theology of history as Gnosticism, Voegelin stresses Joachim's symbol of the prophet, the "Gnostic prophet."[260] However, Joachim himself was not and did not pretend to be a prophet.[261] He did not justify his prediction of the age of monarchism by a miraculous illumination. He based his theology of history on, so to speak, a scientific analysis of the Scripture. He asserted, it is true that he owed his understanding of the Scripture to the Holy Spirit. But this understanding did not, in his own opinion, have the character of a supernatural vision based on mystic inspiration,[262] but of rational knowledge. The *novus dux*, the Elias of the third age, whom Joachim mentions occasionally, is not an essential element of his theology of history. The representative of Christ in the third age is not a Messianic leader, but the monastic order that constitutes a religiously perfect society of the future. Joachim speaks in very vague terms of the leader, "whosoever it will be."[263]

260 Voegelin, The New Science of Politics, p. 112.

261 Grundmann, Studien über Joachim von Floris, p. 56, rejects the "erroneous opinion that Joachim considered himself as a prophet of the end of the world." He refers (p. 21) to a chronicle of the beginning of the thirteenth century in which it is related that once in Rome Joachim had been asked on what ground he ventured his historic prediction. "Respondit se neque prophetiam neque coniecturam neque revelationem de his habere. Sed Deus, inquit, qui olim dedit prophetis spiritum prophetiae, mihi dedit spiritum intelligentiae, ut in Dei spiritu omnia mysteria sacrae scriptureae clarissime intelligam." To be true, Huck, op. cit., p. 237, says that Joachim considered himself as the prophet and intellectual Elias of the third age. But, referring to Thomas Aquinas' opinion about Joachims prediction, he says (pp. 268–269): "Joachim's prognosis of the future is only human conjecture, some of it correct, some false. He is not a prophet in the narrower sense of the term and never pretended to be a prophet, but, on the contrary, denied it." Thomas criticized the abbot of Flora "but never hereticated him."

262 See Grundmann, Studien über Joachim von Floris, p. 21.

263 See Benz, Ecclesia spiritualis, pp. 43, 45. Benz emphasizes (p. 44) that the *Novus Dux* of Joachim's prediction is the spiritual leader of the spiritual church of the third age. "Dux" is a specifically spiritual title. Benz says it would be incorrect to atribute to this title a political meaning. E. Schott, in "Die Gedanken des Abtes Joachim von Floris" (Zeitschrift für Kirchengeschichte, XXIII [1902]), p. 185, lays stress on the fact that in Joachim's eschatology there is no political train of thought. How, then, is it possible to assert – as Löwith (op. cit., p. 159) does – that "the third dispensation of the Joachites reappeard as a third International and a third *Reich,* inaugurated by a *dux* or a *Führer* who was acclaimed as a savior and greeted by millions with *Heil*!"? The "Third Reich" of Moeller van den Bruck (Das Dritte Reich, 3rd ed. [Hamburg, 1931]), in which not only Löwith but also other writers believe to recognize Joachim's third age, has, in truth nothing to do with this prophecy. Not only because the former designates a specifically political idea, whereas the latter has a purely religous character. Joachim speaks of three periods of time (*tempus:* Concordia novi ac veteris testamenti, lib. II, tract. I, chap. 4), of three conditions of the world (tres mundi status: see op. cit., lib. V, chap. 84), not of three "empires." Joachim's third *status mundi* is a kind of chiliastic hope and Moeller

The "prophet" is certainly not a specifically Gnostic symbol. Where it appears in Gnostic speculation – as in the doctrine that a divine prophet revealed himself first in Adam then in Enoch, Noah, Abraham, Isaac, Jacob, Moses, and Christ,[264] – it is taken over from the Jewish religion. And if an ideology that uses the symbol of the prophet is Gnosticism, then Islam proclaiming Mohammed as the true prophet of God, is Gnosticism, too. If Voegelin means by the "Gnostic prophet" the person of the redeemer, the redeemer of the gnosis has a function totally different from that of the *novus dux* and of any other Messianic leader or prophet of a perfect future society. For he is a messenger of the true God, the God foreign to this world and its society; he descends to the depths of the evil world to liberate the imprisoned souls from the fetters of this world and its society, and to lead them into the spiritual sphere beyond.[265] The Messianic redeemer brings God to society; the Gnostic redeemer brings the individual to God.[266] Consequently Joachim's theology of history has nothing to do with Gnosticism if this term has anything to do with the historic movement of the Christian gnosis.

Since Christian gnosis was a deeply religious movement and Joachim was still a religious thinker whose firm belief in the God of the Bible is beyond any doubt, Voegelin's interpretation of his theology as Gnosticism is not so astonishing as his characterization of outspoken atheistic thinkers like Comte, Marx, and Nietzsche as Gnostics and of antireligious or religiously indifferent political movements such as communism, national socialism, fascism, or liberal democratism as Gnosticism. This is all the more amazing for Voegelin in his recent work emphasizes the religious character of the ancient gnosis. He says the Gnostic experiences this world "as a foreign country into which man has gone astray and from which he must again go home to the other world from

van den Bruck expressly rejects such a hope as Utopian. He says (op. cit., p. 29): "The essence of Utopia is that it is never realized. The essence of all chiliastic hopes is that they are never fulfilled. The essence of the millennium is that it lives always only in prophecies but never lets men share in it." He postulates the "Third Empire" certainly not as a Utopian scheme. Speaking of the Third Empire he says (p. 321): "The German nationalism is fighting for the *possible* empire ["Der deutsche Nationalismus kämpft für das mögliche Reich"]" (Italics mine).

264 See Bousset, Hauptprobleme der Gnosis, pp. 172 seqq.

265 See Jonas, Gnosis und spätantiker Geist, p. 5.

266 One of the authorities to whom Voegelin in his interpretation of modernity as Gnosticism refers is Hans Urs von Balthasar who in his Prometheus (Heidelberg, 1947), p. 25, attributes great importance to the writings of Joachim. But Balthasar is far from classifying Joachim as a Gnostic. On the contrary, he stresses the antagonism between Joachim's chiliasm and the gnosis (p. 26). As a Catholic he rejects both as ideologies which endanger Christian eschatology. The one – chiliasm – "degrades heaven to earth." The other – the gnosis – "raises earth into heaven." This implies that Joachim's theology of history means a deification, where as the gnosis means a de-deification of society.

which he has come."[267] "In the ontology of the old gnosis the redemption from this world is secured by the belief in the 'foreign,' the 'hidden' God who comes to the assistance of men sending his messenger to them and showing them the way out of the prison of the evil God of this world."[268] This is a correct characterization of the gnosis, but hardly compatible with the Gnostic self-divinization and the Gnostic self-salvation of which Voegelin speaks in his *New Science of Politics*, and with his interpretation of Joachim's theology of history as Gnosticism. The belief in the existence of the good transcendent God is an essential element of Gnosticism as a truly religious view of the world. An atheistic, antireligious, antitheological, and antimetaphysical attitude is absolutely foreign to Gnosticism. How, then, can Voegelin's use of this term be justified? In his recent publication he says: "It may surprise the reader to see modern thinkers and movements dealt with under the title of gnosis. Since the result of scientific research in these questions is still very little known to the public, an introductory explanation may be welcome."[269] This statement implies that his use of the term "Gnosticism" corresponds to an opinion generally accepted in the history of religion. "It may seem strange today to say that one of the main trends of European, and particularly of German, thought has Gnostic character; actually, this is not a new statement, for it was a well-known fact until a century ago. In 1835, Ferdinand Christian Baur's monumental work *Die christliche Gnosis; oder, die christliche Religionsphilosophie in ihrer geschichtlichen Entwicklung (The Christian Gnosis or the Christian Philosophy of Religion in its Historical Development)* was published. In the last part of this work, under the title 'The old gnosis and the new philosophy of religion,' the following topics are discussed: (1) the theosophy of Böhme, (2) Schelling's philosophy of nature, (3) Schleiermacher's doctrine of faith, and (4) Hegel's philosophy of religion. The speculation of German Idealism is correctly placed in its connection with the Gnostic movement since antiquity."[270] By this passage Voegelin can only mean that his use of the term "Gnosticism," especially the doctrine that a main trend of European and particularly of German thought has a Gnostic character, can already be found in Baur's work. This, however, is not true. First of all, Baur is dealing – apart from the ancient Christian gnosis – exclusively with *philosophy* of religion. He expressly says in the preface that for him the concept of gnosis is the concept of "philosophy of religion."[271]

He says that the questions which were raised by the gnosis "could never be entirely ignored. They became again and again the subjects of a philosophy of

267 Voegelin, Wissenschaft, Politik und Gnosis, p. 15.

268 Ibid., p. 17.

269 Ibid., p. 9.

270 Ibid.

271 Ferdinand Christian Baur, Die christliche Gnosis; oder, die christliche Religionsphilosophie in ihrer geschichtlichen Entwicklung (Tübingen, 1835), p. VII.

religion that endeavored to realize its idea – a philosophy of religion which, the more decidedly it became aware of its task, the more it seemed to be forced to *return to the viewpoint of the old gnosis*."[272] (Italics mine.) As to this viewpoint of the old gnosis Baur says: "Among all characteristics of the old gnosis none manifests itself more clearly, and we see at first sight none penetrate more deeply into its essence, than the relation it has to religion. Religion is the very object with which it is concerned; but, primarily, not religion in its abstract idea but in its concrete manifestation and positive forms in which it came historically into objective existence at the time Christianity appeared."[273] "If therefore as often happens, the essence of the gnosis is seen in philosophical or theological speculations, this definition must immediately be corrected by the statement, that it is not the speculation in itself, the way philosophy is engaged in it, which may be considered as the object of gnosis, but speculation only so far as it is determined by its content: the positive religions [paganism, Judaism, and Christianity] to which it is keeping";[274] but "Christianity, according to the general opinion of the Gnostics, is ... the religion of absolute truth and knowledge, the return from the world of antagonism and disunion to union with God."[275] "All religions are one in the idea [which the gnosis has] of religion,[276] and the idea of religion coincides with its essential and necessary content, the idea of God."[277] "The Gnostics cannot find enough expressions to designate the in-itself-closed, hidden, nameless, inexpressible essence of divinity, exalted above any imagination and description."[278] From this characterization of the gnosis it is evident that Baur can see Gnosticism only in a true philosophy of religion, that is, a philosophy which presupposes the existence of God; in other words: in a theology. Indeed, the thinkers he considers as representatives of modern Gnosticism are true theologians: the German mystic Jacob Böhme; Friedrich Wilhelm Schelling, whose philosophy of nature was, according to Baur's interpretation, genuine theology;[279] Friedrich Schleiermacher, a leading Protestant theologian; and Hegel of whose philosophy Baur says: "It is characteristic of Hegel's philosophy that it considers philosophy of religion an integral part of the entire philosophy"; and that Hegel insists "on the recognition that the task of philosophy is to bring religion to the true conception of itself and to raise faith to knowledge, since philosophy and religion coincide and the

272 Ibid., p. 544.
273 Ibid., p. 18.
274 Ibid., p. 19.
275 Ibid., p. 27.
276 Ibid., p. 21.
277 Ibid., p. 22.
278 Ibid.
279 Ibid., pp. 611 seqq.

object of religion as well as of philosophy is the eternal truth in its objectivity, the absolute, God."[280]

Baur asserts, it is true, that Schleiermacher's theology is near to Kant's philosophy of religion;[281] that is, however, to Kant's *Religion within the Limits of Reason*, not to Kant's philosophy of nature or Kant's epistemology! But Baur does not characterize Kant as a Gnostic, which in view of Kant's attitude toward God, the immortality of the soul, and freedom of will in his *Critique of Pure Reason* would be impossible. Baur even emphasizes a difference which exists between Schleiermacher's theology and Kant's philosophy of religion. "What, in Kant's doctrine, is the moral consciousness, the moral disposition, of man, which conditions the victory of the good over the evil principle, is, in Schleiermacher's theology, the consciousness of the existence of God, the religious disposition."[282] "Kant's religion is, despite all antipathy to Judaism, only a religion of the law because corresponding to the nature of the law it can never abolish the conflict between the individual and the moral obligation, and does not allow a real union of the divine and the human, since the Savior again and again disappears in the unattainable remoteness of an ideal."[283] These two elements of Kant's philosophy of religion are incompatible with Gnosticism.[284] Baur restricts his analysis to the mentioned four theologians and does not deal with "the speculations of German Idealism" as such. He is far from placing this great intellectual movement, which has only partly the character of philosophy of religion, "in its connection with Gnosticism." What Baur understands by "philosophy of religion," in which alone he looks for Gnostic elements, becomes evident from his judgment of the natural theology of Christian Wolf (1679–1754). Baur says: "It is true that it presents itself as a philosophy of religion; however, its God is only the abstract rational concept of the *ens perfectissimum* [the most perfect being], and the difference placed in the divine being ["*der in das göttliche Wesen gesetzte Unterschied*" meaning probably the two different criteria of the concept of God] is the rigid, nonvivid, abrupt antagonism dividing the nature of God in two different halves: on the one hand a God, recognizable, knowable by reason, with all the evidence of Wolf's logic and metaphysics, on the other hand a God who cannot be reached by human rea-

280 Ibid., p. 669.

281 Ibid., pp. 660–667.

282 Ibid., p. 665.

283 Ibid., pp. 667–668.

284 Leisegang, in his work on the gnosis (Die Gnosis, pp. 14, 18), says of the "rational-scientific thinking" "manifesting itself most clearly in the philosophy of Kant which lastingly has influenced the scientific and philosophical thinking of the nineteenth century because it expressed most appropriately the spirit of this time," that it is "the counterpart" of the "mythical-mystical" view of the world and the ego of the gnosis; and R. A. Lipsius, op. cit., p. 101, asserts "what Fichte, in his rough way, says against *Naturphilosophie*, may be advanced against the Gnostic ..."

son but can be known only by supernatural revelation."[285] Because Wolf's "natural theology" has not the true concept of God, it is – according to Baur – no true philosophy of religion and hence does not come into consideration from the point of view of Gnosticism. Baur says: "There is hardly anything more opposite to the gnosis than Wolf's natural theology," although this theology presupposes the existence of a divine transcendent being. From the point of view of Baur's doctrine of Gnosticism, to which Voegelin refers in order to justify his use of this term, it is absurd to characterize as "Gnostic" a philosophy or science that rejects a transcendent divinity of any kind. The idea of an atheistic gnosis has certainly no basis in Baur's "monumental work" on the gnosis.

In addition to the work of Baur, Voegelin refers also to Mosheim's *Versuch einer unpartheiischen und gründlichen Ketzergeschichte* (1748), and to two works about the ancient gnosis, which were published in the time of Baur: Neander's *Genetische Entwicklung der vornehmsten gnostischen Systeme* (1818), and Matter's *Histoire critique du Gnosticisme et de son influence sur les sectes religieuses et philosophiques de six premiers siècles de l'ère chrétienne* (1828).[286] Immediately after mentioning these works Voegelin says: "It was well understood that the Gnostic movement in the philosophies of Enlightenment and Idealism rose to massive social relevance ["Dass in der Aufklärung und im Idealismus die gnostische Bewegung sich zu massiver Sozialrelevanz erhob, war wohl verstanden"]". This can only mean that three works confirm his opinion of the Gnostic character of a main trend in European and especially in German thought in general and in the philosophies of Enlightenment and Idealism in particular. However, the first-mentioned work of Mosheim,[287] has two parts of which only the first deals with Gnosticism, and only with the doctrine of one Gnostic sect, the so-called Ophites. The second part comprises a history of the "Apostel-Orden," a Gnostic sect of the thirteenth century. This work contains not the slightest hint of Gnosticism in modern European and especially German thinking or in the philosophies of Enlightenment and Idealism.

Neander's work[288] on the development of the principal Gnostic systems discusses exclusively the Gnostic systems of the first Christian centuries. It contains an appendix on the pseudo-Clementine Homilies,[289] as a contribution to the history of the Ebionites, and some incidental remarks on the descend-

285 Baur, Die christliche Gnosis, pp. 555 seq.

286 Voegelin, Wissenschaft, Politik und Gnosis, p. 10.

287 Johann Lorenz von Mosheim, Versuch einer unpartheiischen und gründlichen Ketzergeschichte, 2nd ed. (Helmstaedt, 1748).

288 August Neander, Genetische Entwicklung der vornehmsten gnostischen Systeme (Berlin, 1818).

289 Ibid., pp. 361 seqq.

ants of the Gnostics and Manicheans in the Middle Ages,[290] and on the Cathari of the Middle Ages.[291] In a note[292] Neander speaks of true and false philosophy in general, but without referring to a special philosophical school and without characterizing the one or the other as Gnostic. The philosophies of the Enlightenment or of the Idealism are not mentioned at all; and there is not a word about the Gnostic character of a main trend in European or German thought. The work of Matter,[293] as its title indicates, is restricted to ancient Gnosticism and its influence on the religious and philosophical sects of the first six Christian centuries. But in the last chapter under the heading "Conclusions générales de cet ouvrage"[294] Jacques Matter, an admirer of the gnosis, compares this religion with the philosophy and science of his time. The result of the comparison is that this philosophy and this science are – much to their disadvantage – in strict opposition to the gnosis. He says: "Modern psychology has not progressed one step toward the great questions which Gnosticism has dealt with ... If we ask of science today what the soul is, from whence it comes, where it goes, how it is united with its envelope, how it differs from it [questions to which the gnosis has definite answers] our science, so verbose on the minor questions, is silent on the major ones. [La psychologie moderne n'a pas fait un pas de plus sur les grandes questions dont s'occupait celle des gnostiques ... si nous demandons à la science de nos jours, ce qu'est l'âme, d'où elle vient, où elle va, comment elle est unie à son enveloppe, comment elle en est distincte, notre science, si verbeuse dans les petites questions, est muette dans les grandes.]"[295] "Our philosophy is no philosophy. There is no longer any philosophy; there is only scepticism, and scepticism itself is disfigured today; it no longer leads to faith. [Notre philosophie n'en est pas une ... Il n'y en a plus; il n'y a plus que du scepticisme, et le scepticisme lui-même est altéré aujourd'hui; il ne mène plus a la croyance.]"[296] "How poor is our pneumatology as compared with such a science [the Gnostic pneumatology]! The fact is that no longer have we pneumatology ... Knowing nothing about the good spirits, our science has disembarrassed itself of the evil spirits [which played an important part in the gnosis] and, for us, demonology, which explained to the ancients so many enigmas [and which was an element of gnostic speculation] ceased to exist. [Que notre pneumatologie est pauvre auprès d'une telle science! Le fait

290 Ibid., p. 216.
291 Ibid., p. 336.
292 Ibid., pp. 26–27.
293 Jacques Matter, Histoire critique du gnosticisme et son influence sur les sectes religieuses et philosophiques des six premiers siècles de l'ère chrétienne, 2 vols. (Paris, 1828).
294 Ibid., II, pp. 481 seqq.
295 Ibid., p. 484.
296 Ibid., p. 485.

est que nous n'avons plus de pneumatologie ... Ne sachant rien sur les bons esprits, notre science s'est débarrassée également des esprits mauvais, et, pour nous, la démonologie qui expliquait tant d'énigmes aux anciens, a cessé d'exister.]."[297] "Our philosophers no longer deal with cosmogoy or cosmology. The gnosis, on the contrary, stated precisely, of what, why, how, and when the world was made; it even added very reliable theories concerning the causes and the way of its destruction. [Quant à nos philosophes, il ne s'occupent plus ni de cosmogonie ni de cosmologie. La gnose, au contraire, disait nettement de quoi, pourquoi, comment et jusques à quand le monde était fait; elle y ajoutait même des théories très confantes sur les causes et le mode de sa destruction.]."[298] To the author of *Histoire critique du gnosticisme* nothing could be more questionable than to consider modern philosophy and science as Gnosticism, and especially to regard atheistic thinkers and politicians as Gnostics.

Baur mentions the fact that the Gnostics were condemned by those who formed the Orthodox Church as the first of all heretics;[299] and Voegelin sees a relationship between the work of Baur and the history of heresy. He says: "Baur's work was not an isolated phenomenon. It stands at the end of a centenary dealing with the history of heresy, a branch of science which, not without reason, has grown simultaneously with the Enlightenment."[300] If the Church would consider the antitheological philosophy of the Enlightenment to be a new religion, it would certainly condemn it as heretical; therefore, Voegelin sees in the Enlightenment Gnosticism. (See below, pp. 123 seqq.). The only common denominator between the atheistic, antireligious thinkers, and the politicians whom Voegelin calls "Gnostics" and the adherents of the ancient gnosis is that the formers' "secular religion" is heresy. Since Voegelin shares in principle the view of the Church, his – otherwise incomprehensible – use of the word "Gnosticism" can be explained only if it is assumed that he identifies this word with heresy. When he condemns most modern thinkers and politicians as "Gnostics" he condemns them – without saying so expressly – as heretics. Of course, only a religious view can be a heresy because heresy is a deviation from the orthodox religion. But if an intellectual system, despite its atheistic character is considered a "secular" religion, it may also be called a heresy. In this sense Brinton, who considers the philosophy of the Enlightenment and its various offspring (materialism, rationalism, humanism, scientism, naturalism, secularism, evolutionarism, positivism, democratism, and especially Marxism and communism) to be "religions," characterizes all these intellectual move-

297 Ibid., p. 486.
298 Ibid., p. 487.
299 Baur, Die christliche Gnosis, p. 415.
300 Voegelin, Wissenschaft, Politik und Gnosis, pp. 9–10.

ments as modern heresies.[301] Voegelin's interpretation of modern civilization as Gnosticism amounts to an approval of the attitude of the Catholic Church toward the heretical gnosis and the modern views of the world, which deviate from the teaching of Catholic theology.

301 Brinton, A History of Western Morals, pp. 175, 275 seq., 374. He says that "Marxist socialism" is a "heretic rebellion against democratic nationalism" (p. 322), and that "Russian communism" is "the most successful heresy of othodox Western democracy" (p. 402).

Chapter V Hobbes's Leviathan

If the nature of modernity is Gnosticism, as Voegelin asserts, then Thomas Hobbes, whose philosophy has essentially influenced the political thinking of modern man, must be a Gnostic. To prove this seems to be still less possible than to interpret Joachim's theology of history as Gnosticism. For the philosophy of the atheist Hobbes[302] is outspokenly rationalistic. His *Leviathan* is one of the first and most remarkable attempts to establish a positivistic political and legal theory at a time when theological speculation and natural-law doctrine were prevailing. This does not prevent Voegelin from characterizing Hobbes's philosophy as Gnosticism which – if this word has any meaning at all – can be understood only as a religious-theological speculation.

First, Voegelin says that the theory "which Hobbes developed in the *Leviathan*, to be sure, purchased its impressive consistency at the price of a simplification which itself belongs in the class of Gnostic misdeeds,"[303] as if simplification were a specifically Gnostic characteristic. Further, Voegelin maintains that Hobbes essentially intended to establish "Christianity (understood as identical in substance with the law of nature) as an English *theologia civilis* in the Varronic sense."[304] However, Hobbes did not understand Christian religion as identical with the "law of nature" in the proper sense of the term. For Hobbes taught that a law of nature, in the sense of a normative order of justice valid independently of and above positive law, does not exist. In the state of nature, that is, before the establishment of a "commonwealth" – which is Hobbes's term for state – there is no law but only a state of "war of every man against every man" in which "the notions of right and wrong, justice and injustice have ... no place." There is especially no right of property, "no mine and thine distinct"; only *that* is "to be every man's that he can get; and for so long, as he can keep it."[305]

302 See Fritz Mauthner, Der Atheismus und seine Geschichte im Abendland (Stuttgart and Berlin, 1920–1923), II, pp. 530 seqq. F. A. Lange, Geschichte des Materialismus (7th ed. Leipzig, 1902), says of Hobbes that he was considered "the head and father of atheism" (I, p. 225), and that he "certainly came very near in theory to open atheism" (I, p. 381).

303 Voegelin, The New Science of Politics, p. 152.

304 Ibid., p. 155.

305 Hobbes, Leviathan, edited with an introduction by Michael Oakeshott (Oxford, 1960), chap. XIII, p. 83.

Law comes into existence only within the state, that is to say, as positive law. There are, it is true, certain "dictates of reason [which] men used to call by the name of laws," the so-called laws of nature. But they are called "laws" improperly: for "They are but conclusions, or theorems concerning what conduceth to the conservation and defence of themselves; whereas law, properly, is the word of him, that by right hath command over others."[306] The dictate of reason, the so-called law of nature, is law in the proper sense of the term only if it is incorporated into positive law, the law of the state. "The law of nature, and the civil [that is, positive] law, contain each other, and are of equal extent. For the laws of nature, which consist in equity, justice, gratitude, and other moral virtues on these depending, in the condition of mere nature ... are not properly laws, but qualities that dispose men to peace and obedience. When a commonwealth is once settled, then are they actually laws, and not before; as being then the commands of the commonwealth; and therefore also civil laws; for it is the sovereign power that obliges men to obey them."[307] In other words, there is no natural law beside and above positive law – a dualism characteristic of the natural-law doctrine, but only one law: the positive law. This is the view of legal positivism, and Hobbes's legal philosophy is a theory of legal positivism, although he uses the terminology of the natural-law doctrine of his time.

As for the Christian religion, Hobbes taught that it is a "doctrine" contained in "the books of the New Testament" and as such no law. "Our Saviour, and his apostles, left not new laws to oblige us in this world, but new doctrine to prepare us for the next; the books of the New Testament, which contain that doctrine, until obedience to them was commanded by them that God had given power to on earth to be legislators, were not obligatory canons, that is, laws, but only good and save advice, for the direction of sinners in the way to salvation, which every man might take and refuse at his own peril, without injustice." "That the New Testament should in this sense be canonical, that is to say a law, in any place where the law of the commonwealth had not made it so, is contrary to the nature of a law."[308]

This means the Christian religion can be a law binding upon men only as a positive law, the law of a state, not as the law of nature. But the power of the legislator with respect to the Christian religion is restricted, according to Hobbes; and this restriction is characteristic of Hobbes's personal attitude toward the Christian religion: the sovereign may oblige men to obey the advice of the Christian religion, but he cannot oblige men to believe in that doctrine. "When God speaketh to man, it must be either immediately; or by mediation of another man, to whom he had formerly spoken by himself immediately.

306 Ibid., chap. XV, pp. 104–105.
307 Ibid., chap. XXVI, p. 174.
308 Ibid., chap. XLII, pp. 342–343.

How God speaketh to a man immediately, may be understood by those well enough, to whom he hath so spoken; but how the same should be understood by another, is hard, if not impossible to know. For if a man pretend to me, that God hath spoken to him supernaturally and immediately, and I make doubt of it, I cannot easily perceive what argument he can produce, to oblige me to believe it. It is true, that if he be my sovereign, he may oblige me to obedience, so, as not by act or word to declare I believe him not; *but not to think any otherwise than my reason persuades me.*"[309] – (Italics mine.) There can be little doubt that in the last sentence Hobbes is speaking *pro domo*. That he did not believe shows his definition of religion: "*Fear* of power invisible, feigned by the mind, or imagined from tales publicly allowed, RELIGION; not allowed, SUPERSTITION." Only an atheist can define religion in this way. Hobbes adds, it is true, evidently to avoid prosecution: "And when the powered imagined, is truly such as we imagine, TRUE RELIGION."[310] But he says only "when" the power imagined; he does not say "that" the power which men, in accordance with the doctrine of the Christian religion, imagine, *is* such as they imagine. All this must be mentioned to show how unfounded it is to characterize as a "Gnostic" such a radical rationalist and skeptic as Hobbes.

As we may suppose on the basis of earlier statements,[311] Voegelin understands by theologia *civilis* in the sense of Varro, the Roman historian of the first century B.C., a theology, that is, a doctrine about God, imposed by the authority of the state upon the citizens. Since, according to Hobbes's political doctrine, all teaching should be placed under the control of the state, theology too could be taught only with the permission and authorization of the government. But this extension of state's competence to religious matters has nothing to do with Gnosticism or any other kind of mysticism; it is the rationalistic attempt to use religion as an instrument of politics. Nothing could be more alien to the gnosis than such an attempt. Finally, Voegelin maintains that Hobbes's *Leviathan* was "an instance of the general class of Gnostic attempts at freezing history into an everlasting final realm on this earth"; it shows Hobbes's "own Gnostic intentions."[312] "Freezing history into an everlasting final realm on this earth" is a characteristic element of Jewish Messianism (in its original, not in its later spiritualized version). It is certainly not a Gnostic idea; for in Gnostic speculation the end of the world means the disappearance of the physical world together with its evil creator and mankind on earth.[313] But let us accept, for a moment, Voegelin's identification of Gnosticism with Jewish Messianism

309 Ibid., chap. XXXII, p. 243.
310 Ibid., chap. VI, p. 35.
311 Voegelin, The New Science of Politics, pp. 81 seqq.
312 Ibid., pp. 160 seq.
313 See Harnack, Marcion, p. 179.

(although the one was strictly opposed to the other) and see how Hobbes's political theory can be demonstrated as "Gnostic" Messianism.

To confirm this interpretation, Voegelin refers to a passage in Chapter XXX of *Leviathan*, which he reproduces as follows: "He, therefore, declared it the duty of the sovereign to repair the ignorance of the people by appropriate information. If that were done, there might be hope that his principles would 'make their constitution, excepting by external violence, everlasting.'"[314] The passage, if quoted literally and completely, reads as follows: "So, long time after men have begun to constitute commonwealths, imperfect, and apt to relapse into disorder, there may principles of reason be found out, by industrious meditation, to make their constitution, excepting by external violence, everlasting. And such are those which I have in this discourse set forth: which whether they come not into the sight of those that have power to make use of them, or be neglected by them, or not, concerneth my particular interest, at this day, very little."[315] This passage must be interpreted in the light of preceding statements. At the end of Chapter XXVIII, Hobbes emphasizes that the commonwealth is mortal, and says that he will speak in the following chapter of its "diseases." Chapter XXIX begins with the statement: "Though nothing can be immortal, which mortals make, yet, if men had the use of reason they pretend to, their commonwealths might be secured, at least, from perishing by internal diseases."[316] If interpreted in the light of these statements, it is evident that Hobbes did not predict the inevitable because Godsendt, coming of an everlasting realm – the essential content of "Gnostic" eschatology. He referred only to the possible establishment of a commonwealth that would not perish by internal disease. He did not exclude the possibility that such a commonwealth would never be established, and he expressly admitted that even if it would be established, it might perish by "external violence." Hence the word "everlasting" used in the passage quoted by Voegelin is evidently a typical hyperbole, a slightly exaggerated expression of the idea of an internally stabilized regime. Last but not least: Hobbes did not refer to a final stage of mankind, not even to a worldwide commonwealth, but to commonwealths in the plural form. These commonwealths have nothing to do with that really "everlasting," final realm on this earth: the Kingdom of God of the Judaeo-Christian theology, to which Hobbes frequently refers. But he does so only to reject that interpretation of this belief according to which the Kingdom of God has already come with Jesus Christ. For on this interpretation the Church based her claim to stand above the state. Therefore Hobbes emphasizes that the Kingdom of God will come only at the end of time, after the general resurrection of the dead; and only in this kingdom, which is not of this word, Christ will – accord-

314 Voegelin, The New Science of Politics, p. 160.

315 Leviathan, chap. XXX, p. 220.

316 Ibid., chap. XXIX, p. 209.

ing to his doctrine – reign "everlastingly."[317] Only of this Kingdom of God does Hobbes say that – according to the doctrine of the Christian religion – it will be an "everlasting," final realm on this earth; and that means, from the viewpoint of a man who, like Hobbes, does not believe in this doctrine, that such an everlasting kingdom will never come.

There is no similarity between the realistic picture of Hobbes's *Leviathan* and the Utopian perfection mankind will reach in the realm of a thousand years to come according to the Messianic prophecy.

317 Ibid., chap. XXXVIII, p. 303: "From this that hath been said of the kingdom of God, and of salvation, it is not hard to interpret what is meant by the WORLD TO COME ... Of the present world, our Saviour speaks (John, 18:36) *'My kingdom is not of this world.'* For he came only to teach men the way of salvation, and to renew the kingdom of his Father, by his doctrine. Of the world to come, St. Peter speaks (2 Pet., 3:13) *Nevertheless we according to his promise look for new heavens, and a new earth.* This is that WORLD, wherein Christ coming down from heaven in the clouds, with great power, and glory, shall send his angels, and shall gather together his elect, from the four winds, and from the uttermost parts of the earth, and thenceforth reign over them, under his Father, everlastingly." See also chap. XLII, p. 343.

Chapter VI The Philosophy of the Enlightenment

In his work *Die Philosophie der Aufklärung* Ernst Cassirer (see above, p. 5) tries to show that the "strongest intellectual forces of the Enlightenment do not lie in its rejection of belief but rather in the new form of faith which it proclaims, and in the new form of religion which it embodies."[318] It is not scepticism to which the Enlightenment owes its achievements. For "this era is permeated by genuine creative feeling and an unquestionable faith in the reformation of the world. And just such a reformation is now expected of religion." "The controversy from now on is no longer concerned with particular religious dogmas and their interpretation, but with the nature of religious certainty."[319] It is true that some philosophers of the Enlightenment – unlike the atheists La Mettrie, Diderot, Holbach, Grimm, D'Alembert – were deists, although they rejected the Christian religion. They maintained in their philosophy the idea of God as a supreme being, although this was an almost empty concept. Deism as a "natural" religion was, then, nearer to atheism than to true religion: belief in an omnipotent God who justly rules the world. Orthodox contemporaries of the deists considered them atheists.[320] The political circumstances of their time forced the philosophers to use theological language in their fight against Christian theology.[321] The real content of their "religion" was morality. One of the most important principles of this morality was tolerance, the principle of the freedom of faith and conscience. In this moral principle Cassirer sees the new religion of the Enlightenment. He says: "The principle of freedom of faith and conscience is the expression of a new and positive religious force which uniquely characterizes the century of the Enlightenment. In this principle was embodied a new form of religious awareness which asserts itself thereafter clearly and confidently. The new form was indeed attain-

318 Cassirer, The Philosophy of the Enlightenment, pp. 135–136.

319 Ibid., p. 136.

320 Chr. A. Crusius, Entwurf der notwendigen Vernunft-Wahrheiten, 2nd ed. (Leipzig, 1753), § 236, designates as "deists" or "universalists" "a type of atheists." See "Deismus" in Rudolf Eisler, Wörterbuch der philosophischen Begriffe, 4th ed. (Berlin, 1927).

321 See Fritz Mauthner, Der Atheismus und seine Geschichte im Abendland, II, pp. 376 seq.; III, p. 110.

able only as a result of a complete change of religious aims and sentiment. The decisive transformation took place when a genuine religious ethos superseded the religious pathos which had motivated the preceding centuries of religious controversy." An "ethos" without a religious "pathos," however, is not a "religious," but a secular ethos. "Henceforth," Cassirer says, "religion is not to be a matter of mere receptivity; it is to originate from, and to be chiefly characterized by activity. Man is not merely seized and overwhelmed by this activity as by a strong power, but he in turn influences and shapes the activity from within. It is not supernatural power nor divine grace which produces religious conviction in man; he himself must rise to it and maintain it."[322] But true religious conviction is belief in the existence of a supernatural being, which, in his relation to man, has such an overpowering authority that man can only be seized and overwhelmed; and it is this supernatural power and especially divine grace which – according to true religion – produces religious conviction. It is secular morality to which man can rise by himself and which man can maintain by his own will. The eighteenth century, says Cassirer, "strives for the freedom of an all-comprehensive, a truly universal awareness of God." Probably this "universal awareness of God" is the "new form of religious awareness," the "religious certainty" he mentioned before as characteristic of the Enlightenment. As an example of this universal awareness of God he quotes Diderot. "Diderot in his *Philosophical Thoughts*, gave the most incisive expression of this fundamentals attitude of the epoch: 'Men have banished Divinity from their midst; they have relegated it to a sanctuary; the walls of a temple are the limits of its view; beyond these walls it does not exist. Madmen that you are, destroy these enclosures which obstruct your horizon; liberate God; see Him everywhere where He actually is, or else say that He does not exist at all.'"[323] This invitation to see God everywhere, or to say that he is nowhere, is a rather problematical testimony to a "religious certainty, "a new form of "religious awareness" as a "universal awareness of god." It is a highly ambiguous formula that shows more of Diderot's skepticism in religious matters than of his universal awareness of God. In his *Addition aux pensées philosophiques*, where his skepticism is even more openly manifested, he says: "Doubts in matters of religion, far from being acts of impiety, should be considered to be good works, when they are expressed by a man who humbly recognizes his ignorance, and if they originated in the fear to displease God by misuse of reason."[324] Thus Diderot defends skepticism in matters of religion against religious orthodoxists who condemn skepticism as insulting God. It is against orthodoxy that the skeptic opposes reason to faith when he says: "If reason is

322 Cassirer, The Philosophy of the Enlightenment, p. 164.

323 Ibid., p. 166; Denis Diderot, Pensées philosophiques, in Œuvres complètes (Paris, 1821), I, p. 214.

324 Diderot, Pensées philosophiques, I, pp. 243–244.

a gift of heaven, and if one may say the same of faith, heaven has given us two gifts which are incompatible and contradictory."[325] And: "Going astray in an immense forest by night, I have only a small light to guide me. A stranger comes up to me and says: *My friend, blow out your candle in order the better to find your way.* This stranger is a theologian."[326] These thoughts do not express "universal awareness of God," religious certainty.

Religion in the philosophy of the Enlightenment, according to Cassirer, is "in the last analysis only what it does, and its essential nature can be realized in no other way than through feeling and action. Here we have the touchstone of all true religion: Diderot goes back to this basic argument to prove the advantages of natural over revealed religion."[327] Cassirer refers to Diderot's essay *De la suffisance de la religion naturelle*. In this work Diderot identifies natural religion (*"la religion naturelle"*) with natural law (*"la loi naturelle"*). "The natural religion would be sufficient if God could not demand of me more than what this law prescribed to me."[328] This law, the natural law, establishes our obligations "and" we cannot be obliged beyond its commands."[329] "The revealed law [that is, the revealed religion] does not contain any moral precept which I do not find recommended and practiced under the law of nature."[330] "The religion or the natural law, is of all religions the one that accords best with justice."[331] "Natural religion" means morals. Cassirer refers to Tindal and Kant: for both of whom "religion is the recognition of our duties as divine commands; it consists in starting with generally valid and generally accessible norms and then in relating these to a divine Author and looking at them as expressions of His will!"[332] Since Kant in his *Critique of Pure Reason* declares that the existence of a transcendent being cannot be asserted from the point of view of pure reason, the connection of morals with God can have only the character of a practical fiction.[333] We must look at the norms of morality as if they were the will of God. Tindal, the author of *Christianity* as old as Creation or the Gospel a Republication of the Religion of Nature, did not go so far as Kant. He did not touch the belief in God – probably for reasons of political convenience.[334]

325 Ibid., p. 245.
326 Ibid., p. 246.
327 Cassirer, The Philosophy of the Enlightenment, p. 169.
328 Diderot, Pensées philosophiques, I, pp. 261–262.
329 Ibid., p. 262.
330 Ibid.
331 Ibid., p. 265.
332 Cassirer, The Philosophy of the Enlightenment, p. 174.
333 See Hans Vaihinger, Die Philosophie des Als Ob, 7th and 8th eds. (Leipzig, 1922), pp. 41 seq., 65 seqq., 613 seqq.
334 See Mauthner, Der Atheismus, II, p. 496. Matthew Tindal's *Christianity* as old as Creation or the Gospel a Republication of the Religion of Nature (2nd ed., London, 1731),

Cassirer's view that the Enlightenment incorporates a "new form of religion" is to a certain extent based on his opinion that the problem of theodicy still existed for the philosophers of the Enlightenment. Theodicy in a wider sense of this word is the problem of the evil, especially the moral evil in the world; and the optimistic view that the good will finally triumph over the evil is an attempt to solve it. But in a specifically theological sense theodicy is the problem of how moral evil comes into this world created and governed by an all-good and all-powerful God. It is the problem of the fall of man, the original sin of man created by God in his own image. The fundamental contradiction implied in this theological doctrine constitutes the problem. Its solution must consist in an attempt to deny the existence of the evil as such and to interpret it as something good. The most characteristic solution presented by theology is that God endowed man with free will, which made sin possible. But at the same time divine providence provided for salvation. Sin is, therefore, the condition of salvation; in the last analysis sin is good because it is established by God for a good purpose. The belief in the existence of the all-good and all-powerful God, creator and ruler of the world, is the indispensable presupposition of the problem of theodicy in this theological sense of the term.

It seems that Cassirer speaks of theodicy in the theological sense because he discusses it in a chapter entitled "The Dogma of Original Sin and the Problem of Theodicy."[335] But he admits that the philosophy of the Enlightenment rejected the theological doctrine of original sin. "The concept of original sin is the common opponent against which all the different trends of the philosophy of the Enlightenment join forces."[336] If this is true, the problem of theodicy seems to be deprived of its theological character. But Cassirer asserts: "If it [the philosophy of the Enlightenment] rejected the mystery of original sin, it had to shift the cause and origin of evil to another quarter; it has to recognize and prove the necessity of the source of evil in the eyes of reason. There

has on its title page several mottoes. The first one is Grotius's statement: "Est autem jus naturale adeo immutabile, ut ne quidem a Deo mutari potest"; which means that the moral code is independent of God, so consequently there can be morality without belief in God. Tindal, indicating the content of Chapter II of his work, defines "religion of nature" as follows: "'The Religion of Nature' consists in observing those things which our Reason … demonstrates to be our duty." This shows that he understands by religion of nature morals as a system of norms deducible from reason. The words left out in the quoted sentence are: "by considering the nature of God and Man, and the relation we stand in to him and to one another." If we take into consideration the first motto which he puts at the head of his book, we may assume that the reference to God is not essential, but a concession to the orthodox Church. Tindal closes his book with the statement: "Errare possum, Haereticus esse nolo," evidently to protect himself against attacks from the Church.

335 Cassirer, op. cit., pp. 137 seqq.

336 Ibid., p. 141.

seemed, therefore, no escape at this point from metaphysics as such; for the doubts regarding dogma compel us all the more inexorably toward the riddle of theodicy."[337] This statement is questionable.

For the doubts regarding dogma, especially the dogma that the world and man are created and governed by an all-good and all-powerful God, do not "compel" us toward the riddle of theodicy. These doubts, on the contrary, compel us to consider the evils in this world and in the mind of man as facts which, as all facts, are necessary according to the law of causality as a law of impersonal nature. This is the "necessity of the source of evil in the eyes of reason." This was probably Voltaire's true opinion, to whom Cassirer refers to demonstrate that in view of the riddle of theodicy the philosophy of the Enlightenment could not escape metaphysics. He further says: "This riddle exists too for Voltaire since he looks upon the existence of God as a strictly demonstrable truth. The proposition: 'I exist; therefore a necessary and eternal being exists,' has lost none of its force for Voltaire." Voltaire's opinion about the existence of God is far from clear. His statements are ambiguous and contradictory.[338] The statement quoted by Cassirer certainly does not show that Voltaire looked upon the existence of God as a strictly demonstrable truth. Actually the sentence refers to one by Pascal to the effect that if there is a God he is inconceivable. Voltaire's complete remark runs as follows: "It is very strange that Pascal should have thought we could guess at original sin from reason, and that he should say we cannot know from reason that God exists. It was probably the reading of this thought that made Father Hardouin place Pascal in his ridiculous list of atheists. Pascal had most evidently renounced this notion since he has combated it in several other places. In fact we are under the necessity of admitting several things that we cannot conceive 'I exist, therefore something exists from all eternity' [not, as Cassirer translates: "*ein notwendiges und ewiges Wesen existiert*" – "a necessary and eternal being exists"]. This is an evident proposition; and yet can we say, that we conceive what eternity is?"[339] It is not God as a personal being, but the abstract and impersonal idea of eternity to which Voltaire's remark refers. He did not expressly deny the existence of God. But he emphasized that we cannot know anything about his qualities. In his *Philosophical Dictionary* he says in the article "God – Gods": "We feel that we are under the hand of an invisible being: this is all; we cannot advance one step further. It is mad temerity to seek to divine what this

337 Ibid., p. 146.

338 Mauthner, Der Atheismus III, considers Voltaire to be an atheist who only "was cautiously hiding his last conviction" (p. 43). "The assumption is probably not unjustified that Voltaire was furtively laughing at his dear deism and had only enough self-control to ... suppress his atheistic laughing" (pp. 59–60).

339 Voltaire, "Remarks on M. Pascal's Thoughts," The Works of Voltaire (Paris, London, New York, Chicago, 1901), XXI, p. 262.

being is – whether he is extended or not, whether he is in one place or not, how he exists or how he operates."[340] Since Voltaire does not assume that God is all-good and all-powerful, the problem of theodicy – in the specific theological sense of the term – does not exist for him. One might object that Voltaire, in the same article under the heading "The Necessity of Believing in a Supreme Being," refers to "a rewarding and avenging God." But he says in the following passage: "The great, the interesting object, as it appears to me, is not, to argue metaphysically [that is, to prove the existence of God in metaphysical-theological speculation] but to consider whether for the common good of us miserable and thinking animals, we should admit a rewarding and avenging God, at once our restraint and consolation or should reject this idea, and so abandon ourselves to calamity without hope, and crime without remorse."[341] It is evident from this passage that Voltaire considered the idea of a rewarding and avenging God not as true, but as useful, as a political means for the maintenance of morality in the sense of Hobbes's civil theology.[342]

A Revival of Augustine's City of God

In the same year in which Cassirer's *Philosophie der Aufklärung* appeared, Carl L. Becker published *The Heavenly City of the Eighteenth Century Philosophers*, in which he tried to show that the philosophers of the Enlightenment "demolished the Heavenly City of St. Augustine only to rebuild it with more up-to-date materials." Becker starts by confronting the climate of opinion of the Middle Ages with that of the eighteenth century. He characterizes the former by its specifically Christian view about "intelligence," by which he probably means human reason. "Intelligence was essential, since God had endowed men with it. But the function of intelligence was strictly limited. Useless to inquire curiously into the origin or final state of existence, since both had been divinely determined and sufficiently revealed. Useless, even impious, to inquire into its ultimate meaning, since God alone could fully understand it."[343] This can only mean that the answers to these questions are beyond human reason; that they are reserved to the unrestricted, absolute reason of God who has revealed them to man; and that, consequently, it is impossible through re-

340 Ibid., IX, p. 216.

341 Ibid., IX, p. 240.

342 Alfred Noyes, in Voltaire (3rd ed., London, 1939), tries to show that "the real Voltaire was very different from the traditional protrait, and that his beliefs were nearer to Christianity than was usually supposed" (p. XIV); that Voltaire did retain "belief not only in Almighty God but in a God of love, compassion, justice, eternal life" (p. 638). But Noyes' arguments are not very convincing.

343 Becker, The Heavenly City, p. 7.

stricted human reason to demonstrate their truth, that is, the truth of revealed knowledge.

Belief in divine revelation is faith and as such is different from, even opposed to, human reason. But Becker continues: "The function of intelligence was therefore to demonstrate the truth of revealed knowledge, to reconcile diverse and pragmatic experience with the rational pattern of the world as given in faith." This was the view of medieval theologians. It is a fundamentally erroneous view, for it is impossible to explain by the specific means of human reason what is beyond human reason. But Becker accepts this view and thus obliterates the essential difference between reason and faith. For he says: "the best thought of the time assumed a thoroughly rationalistic form." It is true that the theology of the Middle Ages, as all theology, attempts to rationalize that which, by its nature and as admitted by theology itself, is irrational, that is, beyond human reason. But this attempt is a deception or a self-deception. In medieval theology religion does not – as Becker asserts – assume a "rationalistic," but a pseudorationalistic form. Then he says: "I know it is the custom to call the thirteenth century an age of faith, and to contrast it with the eighteenth century, which is thought to be preeminently the age of reason ... Since eighteenth-century writers employed reason to discredit Christian dogma, a 'rationalist' in common parlance came to mean an 'unbeliever,' one who denied the truth of Christianity. In this sense Voltaire was a rationalist, St. Thomas a man of faith. But this use of the word is unfortunate, since it obscures the fact that reason may be employed to support faith as well as to destroy it." However, it follows from Becker's own statement, quoted above, that human reason cannot be employed to support faith, because, as Becker asserts, in the climate of opinion of the Middle Ages the function of human reason was considered to be "strictly limited"; it was considered to be "useless" for human reason to inquire into the object of faith, to ask questions whose answers were reserved for divine reason and hence to be obtained by man through revelation only – which means through faith and not through his own reason. Becker continues: "There were, certainly, many differences between Voltaire and St. Thomas, but the two men had much in common for all that. What they had in common was the profound conviction that their beliefs could be reasonably demonstrated." But Voltaire and especially such outspoken atheist philosophers of the eighteenth century as Helvetius and Holbach had no "belief" in the sense of faith in God and his revelation. Their confidence in human reason was entirely different from the belief in the supernatural absolute reason of God. On the basis of the confusion of reason and faith Becker comes to the conclusion: "In a very real sense it may be said of the eighteenth century that it was an age of faith as well as of reason, and of the thirteenth century that it was an age of reason as well as of faith."[344]

344 Ibid., pp. 7–8.

This is the problematical starting point of Becker's attempt to show that the ultimate aim of the antitheological philosophers of the Enlightenment was St. Augustine's City of God.

What Becker really proves is that these philosophers did not "objectively," that is, without presupposed values, interpret the natural and social reality, but proclaimed moral-political ideals. They had "a philosophical message to deliver; they were the eager bearers of good tidings to mankind. Disinterested? Objectively detached? By no means."[345] They were "making or dreaming of projects ... for opening all roads available to the pursuit of happiness, for securing the blessings of liberty, equality and fraternity to all mankind."[346] "The amelioration of society was the very thing Philosophers had most at heart,"[347] "A distinction of good and bad! Not a novel idea, certainly; on the contrary, a very old, a most Christian idea;"[348] but certainly not *only* a Christian idea! "The eighteenth-century Philosophers were not primarily interested in stabilizing society; but in changing it,"[349] in accordance with certain ideals. This is true; but without any foundation Becker asserts that the projects of the eighteenth-century philosophers were "inspired by ... the Christian ideal of service the humanitarian impulse to set things right,"[350] as if the ideal of service, the humanitarian ideal, the impulse to set things right were only Christian ideals; as if ascertaining and proclaiming moral-political values were possible only on the basis of the belief in God, and especially in the Christian God! Even if the philosophers of the eighteenth century were inspired by moral ideals identical with those maintained by the Christian religion, their ideals were not imposed upon man by the will of God, but – according to their opinion – derived from human reason. It is this difference that is essential, and not a – questionable – similarity.

The philosophers' assumption that moral and political principles can be found in human reason is certainly an illusion, for these values have their ultimate source in the emotional, not in the rational, component of the human mind. The philosophers' illusion was the result of their overestimation of the faculties of human reason. This overestimating intensifies rather than diminishes the contrast between their philosophy and the Christian religion with its tendency to degrade human reason as compared with divine reason.

Becker attributes to the philosophers of Enlightenment "professions of faith," a "natural religion."[351] He quotes Voltaire's statement:

345 Ibid., p. 36.
346 Ibid., p. 40.
347 Ibid., p. 85.
348 Ibid., p. 86.
349 Ibid., p. 97.
350 Ibid., p. 41.
351 Ibid., p. 44.

"I understand by natural religion the principle of morality common to the human race";[352] and says later:[353] "The atheist Holbach, rejecting all religion, nevertheless holds that 'the morality suitable to man should be founded on the nature of man'."[354] Other philosophers of the eighteenth century also proclaimed principles of morality, which they called "religion."[355] Becker formulates the essential articles of the religion of the Enlightenment as follows: "(1) man is not natively depraved; (2) the end of life is life itself, the good life on earth instead of the beatific life after death; (3) man is capable, guided solely by the light of reason and experience, of perfecting the good life on earth; and (4) the first and essential condition of the good life on earth is the freeing of men's minds from the bonds of ignorance and superstition, and of their bodies from the arbitrary oppression of the constituted social authorities."[356] Hence, what these philosophers called their "religion" was a secular morality emphatically and correctly opposed to the religious morality of Christianism and Christian theology. Holbach expressly opposes the "natural" or "human morality,"[357] described in his work, to the "religious morality" taught by theology. He says: "Instead of seeking on the earth the principles according to which

352 Voltaire, Œuvres Complètes (Paris, 1877–1885), XXII, p. 419.

353 Becker, The Heavenly City, p. 52.

354 P. H. T. Holbach, Système Social; ou Principes Naturels de la Morale et de la Politique (Paris, 1822), I, p. 74.

355 Thus, for example, Helvetius, in Œuvres complettes (Paris, 1795), III, p. 86, wrote: "C'est uniquement du corps législatif qu'on peut attendre une religion bienfaisante ... Que des magistrats éclairés soient revêtus de la puissance temporelle et spirituelle, toute contradiciton entre les préceptes religieux et patriotiques disparoitra: tous les citoyens adopteront les mêmes principes de morale, et se formeront la même idée d'une science, dont il est si important que tous soient également instruits. [It is only from the legislative body that we can expect a beneficent religion ... When enlightened judges are vested with temporal and spiritual power, all contradiction between religious and patriotic duties will disappear: all citizens will accept the same moral principles and will have the same idea of a science in which all should be equally instructed.]" The "religion bienfaisante" is a set of principles of morality and is characterized – evidently in opposition to religion in the proper sense of the term – as "science." In the preface to De l'Esprit, Helvetius says: "J'ai cru qu'on devoit traiter la morale comme toutes les autres sciences, et faire une morale comme une physique expérimentale [I thought that ethics should be treated like all other sciences and presented like experimental physics.]" (I, p. cx). That Helvetius meant morals when he said "religion" becomes evident by his statements: "La morale fondée sur des principes vrais, est la seule vraie religion [Morality based on true principles is the only true religion.]" (III, p. 73). "S'il ne s'agit que de former des citoyens vertueux, qu'est-il besoin à cet effet de recourir à des moyens impossibles et surnaturels?" (IV, p. 238). This means: If the only purpose is to make citizens virtuos, why is it necessary to have recourse to religion in the proper sense of a belief in a supernatural authority?

356 Becker, The Heavenly City, p. 102.

357 Holbach, op. cit., I, p. VII.

men ought to behave, religion sought it in heaven; instead of founding morality on the perceptible relations which exist among men, religion founded it on the relations which allegedly exist between men und unknown forces, which were placed in a sphere inaccessible to experience."[358] If this secular morality is called "religion," it is a religion without God.[359] But a religion without God is a contradiction in terms – it is not religion in the specific sense of this term.

In ideological conflicts it is typical to designate one's own ideal with the same value-pregnant word by which the attacked ideal is represented, and to oppose the former as "true" to the latter as "false." The conscious or unconscious purpose of this terminological device is to disqualify more effectively the attacked idea especially among its adherents. To take a recent example, Russian communism, in its fight against Western democracies, declared true democracy to be the dictatorship of the Communist party – which is the exact opposite of democracy. In the same way have atheistic and antireligious philosophers of the eighteenth century designated as "religion" the secular morality postulated by them, which was in strict opposition to religion as the belief in a transcendent and just God. To characterize in a history of ideas their philosophy as "theology" is as misleading as to characterize dictatorial communism as "democracy."

If the secular morality of the Enlightenment was in truth no religion, how could Augustine's theological idea of the City of God come into the philosophy of the eighteenth-century atheist thinkers, how did they "rebuild" the City of God they were so eager to "demolish," as Becker affirms? He says: "The picture of salvation in the Heavenly City they toned down to a vague impressionistic image of a 'future state,' 'immortality of the soul,' or a more generalized earthly and social *félicité* or *perfectibilité du genre humain.*" "The new heaven had to be located somewhere within the confines of the earthly life, since it was an article of philosophical faith that the end of life is life itself, the perfected temporal life of man" – which is in truth not an article of faith but only a rejection of the faith in the immortality of the soul – "and in the future, since the temporal life was not yet perfected. But if the celestial heaven was to be dismantled in order to be rebuilt on earth [correctly formulated: because the belief in a celestial heaven was rejected and the moral postulates referred only and exclusively to the life on earth] it seemed that the salvation of mankind

358 Ibid., I, p. 28.

359 Becker (The Heavenly City, p. 155) refers to Alexis de Tocqueville, L'Ancien régime et la Révolution (Paris, 1866), p. 19, who characterizes the French Revolution as "a kind of new religion, an imperfect religion, it is true, a religion without God." But Tocqueville uses the term "religion" only by analogy. He says (p. 16): "C'est à des révolutions religieuses qu'il faut comparer la Révolution française, si l'on veut se faire comprendre à l'aide de l'analogie [We must compare the French Revolution with the religious revolutions, if an understanding by analogy is desired.]"

must be attained, not by some outside, miraculous, catastrophic agency (God or the philosopher), but by man himself, by the progressive improvement made by the efforts of successive generations of men; and in this cooperative enterprise posterity had its undeniable uses: posterity would complete what the past and the present had begun."[360]

Is a more radical contrast imaginable than that between this philosophy and Augustine's theology? If this philosophy means rebuilding the City of God, then any secular morality and any optimistic interpretation of history as a progressive evolution – ideas frequently propounded long before Christianity came into existence and afterward independently of it – means to build or rebuild the City of God. But that means to call white black and black white because both are colors.[361]

A Recapitulation of The Theological Interpretation of History

Like Cassirer and Becker, Charles Frankel, in his work on the idea of progress in the French Enlightenment, also tries to show that the antagonism between the philosophy of the Enlightenment and the metaphysical-theological speculation which this philosophy rejected was not so fundamental as the *philosophes* themselves assumed. He does not deny that "the eighteenth century *philosophes* opposed universal reason to special revelation, and man's natural powers and interests to his supernatural salvation and destiny;"[362] he refers to "the attempt of the Enlightenment to disengage itself from the supernatural";[363] but he says: "The *philosophes* could read reason as itself a revelation, and find a support for man's natural interests in the fortuitous – one might say, providential – appropriateness with which human strivings fit the Order of Nature. And they could persist in a separation of the goal or meaning of life from the present character of their experience which was not unlike a more traditional otherworldliness," that is, the Christian dualism of this and a transcendent world. One of the purposes of his work, he says, is "to relate the *philosophes'* ideas on progress to the larger metaphysical prepossessions which they inherited" and "which they unconsciously shared with many of those whom they opposed."[364] He admits, it is true, that "many of the *philosophes*

360 Becker, The Heavenly City, pp. 48, 129.

361 Cf. Carl Becker's Heavenly City Revisited, edited by Raymond O. Rockwood (Ithaca, N. Y., 1958), and especially Peter Gay's excellent criticism of Becker's work in this volume: "Carl Becker's Heavenly City," pp. 27–51.

362 Frankel, The Faith of Reason, p. 1.

363 Ibid., p. 51.

364 Ibid., p. 2.

struggled with their metaphysics, and some of them succeeded in moving beyond it." But finally he says that the enlightened theory of progress "paradoxically recapitulated in a different language the main features of the theological interpretation of history which the *philosophes* were combating. The emergence of science [the instrument of progress] became either the product of a revelation, a sudden discovery without historical antecedents, and carrying its own certificate of validity, or it became the culmination of a process in which all evil was not really or finally evil, and all errors were necessarily steps in the improvement of mankind. The harmonious order of nature emerged as a thinner version of Providence."[365] This means that science, the most characteristic element of the Enlightenment, is revelation, and that the order of nature, discovered by this science, is Providence. It follows, then, that there is no essential difference between the philosophy of the Enlightenment and Christian theology! The attempt of the *philosophes* to emancipate human cognition from theological metaphysics failed.

Frankel explains this failure by the fact that the *philosophes*, or some of them, "placed science in a larger metaphysical context." The reason for this statement is that they "attempted to establish its validity as an instrument of progress unprovisionally by basing it on absolute grounds external to the method of science itself, and defined progress in terms of the movement toward fixed moral goals which were also established absolutely."[366] "The conception of science and enlightenment came to connote not only a habitual attitude of critical inquiry but a set of absolute beliefs upon which inquiry and action must rest, and which are not themselves modifiable by further inquiry ... The *philosophes* tended to think of reason and enlightenment as a system of simple, indubitable, and eternal truths."[367]

It is true that an absolute in general, and absolute truths and absolute moral values in particular (that is to say, truths, or moral values, which exclude the possibility of contrary truths or moral values), can be consistently maintained only under the presupposition of a supernatural authority establishing them. As a matter of fact, however, philosophers frequently claim for some of their propositions absolute truth and for some of their moral values absolute validity, without presupposing a supernatural authority, even expressly rejecting it and emphasizing the empirical character of their philosophy. They may be criticized as inconsistent, their truths and moral values may be declared to be only relative and not absolute, but their doctrine must not be characterized as "metaphysics," this word meaning a speculation about the transcendent supernatural. It is in this sense that Frankel uses the word when he relates the philosophy of the Enlightenment to "metaphysical prepossessions which the *philo-*

365 Ibid., p. 154.
366 Ibid., p. 3.
367 Ibid., p. 154.

sophes inherited" from those "whom they opposed." The "metaphysics" they inherited and "opposed" was the metaphysics of the Christian theology. It may be that the *philosophes*, or some of them, thought that human reason is absolute, that science produces absolute truths, and that science is the source of absolute moral values. But since they opposed human reason to divine revelation, it is incorrect to say that they considered reason itself to be a revelation and considered the emergence of science as the product of a revelation. What may correctly be said is that the *philosophes* attribute to reason and to its product, science, what the Christian's attribute to revelation, namely absolute truth and absolute moral values. It does not follow from this view that the reason of the Enlightenment or its science was a revelation. Even if the emergence of science appears in the philosophy of the Enlightenment as "a sudden discovery without historical antecedents and carrying its own certificate of validity," it is not justifiable to call it "the product of a revelation." For the essence of a revelation is not that it is a sudden discovery without historical antecedents, carrying its own certificate of validity, but that it is the conveyance of a divine truth by a supernatural, superrational act of God. Reason and science do not have this character according to the unmistakable conviction of the *philosophes*. Since they rejected the theological dualism of two worlds, their separation of the goal or meaning of life from the present character of their experiences was in no way like the Christian "otherworldliness." Their idea of the goal or meaning of life was expressly opposed to the Christian idea of the other world. The discrepancy between the social reality of their time and their social ideal shows no more similarity to the Christian dualism of this world and the other world than any dualism of reality and ideal. It was certainly an error of some *philosophes* to believe that science could be based on absolute grounds external to the methods of science itself, and that science could determine absolute moral values to be realized in the progressive evolution of social reality. But since they did not conceive of the ground of science and the absolute moral values as established by a supernatural authority, they did not place science in general and ethics in particular in a "metaphysical" context.

Why should the harmonious order of nature discovered by the science of the Enlightenment be a version of Providence? Because, according to this philosophy, progress was a process in which all evil was not finally evil, and all errors were necessary steps in the improvement of mankind? Even if the *philosophes,* or of some of them, really believed this, it was no "version of Providence" because the essential characteristic of the theological doctrine of divine Providence is not this view but rather the belief that evil originates in the original sin, from which man will be delivered by redemption – the one instituted by God to make the other possible. In this way, as pointed out, theology tries to justify the existence of evil in a world created by a good God and to justify sin in man shaped in the image of God. The philosophers of the Enlightenment reject the belief in original sin. The problem of their doctrine of progress is not how evil and error came into this world, but how progress is possible in spite of the undeniable existence of evil and error. It is true that there is no satisfactory answer to this question in their doctrine of progress. Their assumption that progress takes place in spite of evil and error is merely an optimistic presupposition. They try to prove by historical evidence that evil and error did not and therefore will not prevent progress, but they do not assume that evil and error are conditions of progress in the sense that sin is a condition of redemption. There is not sufficient reason for Frankel's assertion that the enlightened doctrine of progress is a "recapitulation of the main features of the theological interpretation of history." The main feature of this interpretation is that the course of history is determined by the will of God and leads to salvation. The enlightened doctrine of progress shows neither of these features.

Frankel tries to exemplify his interpretation of the enlightened philosophy by referring to F. J. de Chastellux's work *De la Félicité publique* (1772).[368] He speaks of Chastellux's "metaphysical faith in the harmony of nature,"[369] of his idea of "a masterplan" of nature.[370]

He says "Chastellux's theory of progress was strikingly similar to the medieval theory that history was the work of a benevolent Providence." The similarity consists, Frankel asserts, in the fact that in Chastellux's theory of progress "evil and error remained part of a masterplan supporting human strivings," that this philosopher "went far in order to show not only that error had been the precondition of truth but that the workings of a beneficent nature absolutely required error, just as the design of a benevolent God required that man be free, and so provided the necessary condition of sin. The concept of man's perfectibility played a similar role in Chastellux's philosophy to that played by free will in the traditional Augustinian philosophy of history. In his utilitarian theory of progress, as in the supernatural theory of Providence, the problem of evil was solved by showing that the prerequisite of man's salvation was also the condition of his fall."[371]

"Chastellux's account of progress resembles the struggle of the heavenly city with those of this earth."[372] The decisive point in this theological interpretation of Chastellux's doctrine of progress is that in this doctrine the problem of evil played the same role and found the same solution as in the theological doctrine of Providence. To justify this interpretation Frankel refers to Chastellux's view "that man's happiness, like that of other creatures, lay originally in his preserving and reproducing himself. However, just because man was per-

368 Marquis de Chastellux, De la Félicité Publique ou Considerations sur le Sort des Hommes dans les Différentes Epoques de l'Histoire. Nouvelle édition (Paris, 1822).

369 Frankel, The Faith of Reason, p. 65.

370 Ibid., p. 66.

371 Ibid.

372 Ibid., p. 67.

fectible 'he has broken away from this common law, and having soon found it too easy to satisfy his appetites, he has been exposed to boredom and factitious needs.' The law of human perfectibility was inexorable. The fact of error did not disprove the law of human perfectibility any more than sin disproves Providence: in both cases they were results of the very perfection of man. And by recognizing his perfection – which now was possible with the revelation of the true principles of scientific policies – and the part it played in the cosmic plan, man could escape the consequences of his fall. 'In inquiring whether the perfectibility of men was not the source of their ills, we have found that it was their general remedy.'"[373] The passage from which Chastellux's last-quoted statement is taken runs as follows: "The distressing we made about the misery of a certain class of the people in certain countries have led us to the comforting conclusion that the progress of Enlightenment has delivered from slavery not only the lowest classes but even half the human race; so that in inquiring whether man's perfectibility was not the source of their ills, we have found that it was their general remedy. [Les réflexions affligeantes que nous avons faites sur le malheur attaché à certaine classe du peuple dans certain pays, nous ont conduits à ce résultat consolant, que le progrès des lumières avait affranchi de l'esclavage non seulement les dernières classes du peuple, mais même la moitié de l'espèce humaine; de sorte qu'en examinant si la perfectibilité des hommes n'était pas la source de leurs maux, nous avons trouvé qu'elle en était le remède général.]"[374] The reflections on the misery of a certain class of people include also a discussion of the miserable situation of the peasants in France and other countries of Europe. Chastellux concludes: "This is the situation of the peasants in France and some other countries of Europe; but should we consider it a necessary evil, an immediate consequence of the progress of society? Certainly not; it is a relic of barbarism, which arouses our anger and which will not last long." ("Tel est le sort des paysans en France et dans quelques autres pays de l'Europe; mais devons nous le regarder comme un mal nécessaire, comme une conséquence immédiate des progrès de la société? Non assurément; c'est un reste de barbarie qui nous révolte, et qui ne durera pas longtemps.")[375] Here Chastellux categorically denies that the evil is the result of progress or, in other words, of the development of man's perfectibility.[376] Hence the statement quoted by Frankel can only mean that the perfectibility of men is not the source of their ills, for it is the general remedy. Chastellux's theory is: Evil exists and makes progress difficult, but it does not prevent progress, because progress is guaranteed by the fact that the evil is es-

373 Ibid., pp. 66–67.

374 Chastellux, De la Félicité Publique, II, p. 258.

375 Ibid., II, p. 250.

376 The correlation which in Chastellux's theory exists between perfectibility and progress follows from many statements. For instance: II, pp. 227, 237, 234, 240, 244, 248, 257, 258.

sentially connected with its remedy in the same way a cause is connected with its effect. "There took place in the moral order what happened generally in the physical order. From the very excess of evil has come the remedy. [Il est arrivé dans l'ordre moral ce qui arrive assez communément dans l'ordre physique. De l'excès même du mal est sorti le remède.]"[377] There are, it is true, critical situations in which reason is on one side and force on the other ("où les sciences, les arts, la raison même sont d'un coté, et la force de l'autre".) "In this crisis the evil is more violent and the remedy more distant. [Dans cette crise le mal est plus violent, et le remède plus éloigné.]"[378] But also in this situation the remedy is attached to the evil. There is a law of nature according to which pleasure is attached to all the means of conservation and multiplication, which promote progress, and pain to all the means of destruction, which restrain but do not prevent progress. "To subsist and to reproduce is the general law that nature has imposed upon all living beings; and this very simple law is carried out by means that are just as simple: pleasure attached to all the means of conservation and multiplication; pain to all the means of destruction. "Subsister et se reproduire c'est la loi générale qu'elle [nature] leur a imposée; et cette loi si simple s'exécute par des moyens aussi simples qu'elle. Le plaisir et la douleur sont les seuls ministres qui la secondent: le plaisir attaché à tous les moyens de conservation et de multiplication, la douleur annexée à tous le moyens de destruction.]"[379] Since pain is attached to the evil of destruction, and man wants to avoid pain and, when it is not avoided, to terminate it, the evil produces its own remedy. A great, if not the greatest, evil is the inequality of the conditions of men. Inequality is not the consequence of progress, but the consequence of the unequal way in that progress takes place within humanity: "The first reflection that presents itself to our minds is that since the human race, the most perfectible of all, was not able to exercise this faculty in an equal and uniform way, there resulted a great inequality in the situation of the individuals. [La premiere réflexion qui se présente à notre esprit, c'est que l'espèce humaine étant la plus perfectible de toutes, et n'ayant pu exercer cette faculté d'une manière égale et uniforme, il a dû en résulter une grande inégalité dans le sort des individus.]"[380] There is inequality in the condition of different peoples, inequality of property and conditions among men subjected to the same legislation. ("Inégalité dans le sort de differents peuples, inégalité de fortune et de condition parmi les hommes soumis à une même legislation.")[381] Chastellux asks: "What is, then, the remedy for this misfortune of the human race? If you want to find it, remember the origin of the evil. [Quel est donc le remède à ce

377 Chastellux, De la Félicité Publique, II, p. 242.
378 Ibid., II, p. 229.
379 Ibid., II, p. 237.
380 Ibid., II, p. 240.
381 Ibid., II, p. 243.

malheur de l'espèce humaine? Si vous voulez le trouver, rappelez-vous l'origine du mal.]" Here he expressly raises the question of the origin of evil; and his answer is: "Men are perfectible in the highest degree; but the greatest inequality prevails in their progress, and it is only at the end of this progress that they may meet. Strive, therefore, to accelerate their advance, to make the career easy for all. [Les hommes sont perfectibles, ils le sont au plus haut degré; mais la plus grande inégalité règne dans leurs progrès, et ce ne sera jamais qu'au terme de ces progrès qu'ils pourront se rencontrer. Táchez done d'accélérer leur marche, de rendre la carrière facile a tous.]"[382] The origin of evil is not that it is a condition of progress, as sin is a condition of salvation, but that "the greatest inequality prevails in progress." This is a regrettable fact, but it is not instituted by nature as a beneficent power in order to make progress possible. On the contrary: its effect is that it makes progress difficult; it is opposed to progress. Chastellux examines why in the past mankind has not progressed much and says that one of the main reasons is "that despotism and superstition have reigned commonly in the first eras of the world. [... que le despotisme et la superstition avaient régné assez généralement dans ces premiers âges du monde.]"[383] "Under such conditions, the coming into existence and propagation of true morality and sound policy [that is, progress] was difficult. [Dans cet état des choses, la véritable morale et la saine politique pouvaient difficilement naître ou se propager.]"[384] In another connection he says: "Ignorance and error shared in the domination of the world. Ignorance disappeared first, error still remains because only reason can triumph over it. Finally, the time has come when the latter dares to appear. [L'ignorance et l'erreur se partagaient l'empire du monde. L'ignorance fuit la prèmiere; l'erreur reste encore, parce que la raison seule peut en triompher. Enfin, le moment est venu où celle-ci ose se montrer.]"[385]

Reason, the instrument of progress, "triumphs" over the evils of ignorance and error, which means that they are an obstacle, not a condition of progress. Hence his suggestion: try to accelerate progress by abolishing despotism and superstition, by eliminating ignorance and error. Resuming his ideas about progress Chastellux says: "Finally, wherever you look you will see on the surface of the globe only an intense race where some run fast, others drag on wearily, pushed and offended by those who want to pass them; and you will be led to the reflection that if the disproportion in the situation of the individuals is a disadvantage necessarily attached to the perfectibility of the human race, the most effective remedy for this disadvantage is still the greatest acceleration in the march of its progress. [Enfin, de quelque côté qu'on porte ses re-

382 Ibid., II, p. 244.
383 Ibid., II, p. 224.
384 Ibid., II, p. 226.
385 Ibid., II, p. 232.

gards, on ne verra sur la surface du globe qu'une immense carrière, où les uns courent rapidement, et les autres se trainent avec peine, heurtés, froissés par ceux qui veulent les devancer; et l'on sera conduit à cette réflexion, que si la disproportion dans le sort des individus est un inconvénient nécessairement attaché à la perfectibilité de l'espèce humaine, le remède le plus sûre à cet inconvénient est encore la plus grande accélération dans la marche de ses progrès.]"[386] The disproportion, in the situation of men, is a disadvantage "necessarily attached" to the perfectibility of the human race. After all that Chastellux has said about the relationship between this evil and progress, the statement can only mean that this disadvantage necessarily accompanies the perfectibility of men, its progress; it is not a condition of it. The statement has the same meaning as the common phrase that error is necessarily attached to the search for truth – a statement which nobody would interpret to mean that error is a necessary condition for the search for truth.

The other statement by Chastellux, which Frankel quotes to justify his interpretation that "man just because he was perfectible," was exposed to the evil runs as follows: "Que l'homme par sa perfectibilité naturelle s'est derobé à cette loi commune, et qu'ayant bientôt trouvé trop de facilité à contenter ses appétits, il a été exposé à l'ennui et aux besoins factices."[387] This statement is point two in a résumé whose point one is: "Que la nature semble avoir placé le bonheur de tous les êtres dans les principes de leur conservation et de leur multiplication." This statement refers only to one aspect of the general law formulated before – the law that pleasure (that is, happiness) is attached to all means of conservation and multiplication, but pain (that is, unhappiness) to all means of destruction. The second point of the résumé evidently refers to the second aspect of this law. That man too easily satisfies his appetites and thus creates artificial needs causes disproportion in the situation of the individual; it is a means of destruction; hence, "*ennui*" is its effect. *Ennui* in this connec-

386 Ibid., II, pp. 247–248.

387 See the statement on p. 240, quoted above page 106, where Chastellux says that a great inequality in the situation of men is the "result" of the fact that it was not possible to exercise the faculty of perfectibility in an equal and uniform way. Point 4 (p. 284) of the résumé runs as follows: "Qu'une autre conséquence de la perfectibilité de l'espèce humaine a été l'inégalite des progrès, qui a établi une grande difference d'homme à homme, de peuple à peuple, et qui a donné naissance à la guerre et à l'oppression. [That another consequence of the perfectibility of the human race has been the inequality of progress, which has established a great difference between man and man, nation and nation, and which has given birth to war and oppression.]" This point is the recapitulation of the thought expressed in the passage quoted above. It must have the same meaning as this passage. Hence by saying that the inequality is a "consequence of the perfectibility," Chastellux means that the inequality is the consequence of the fact that the perfectibility of man cannot be exercised in an equal and uniform way; he does not mean that the situations of men are inequal *because* men are perfectible.

tion does not mean, as Frankel translates it, "boredom," but worry, annoyance, anxiety, hence something like pain, unhappiness. Points one and two of the résumé recapitulate the "general law" in its two aspects. This is the law which guarantees progress. The formula *par sa perfectibilité naturelle* may indeed, if literally translated, mean "because of his perfectibility." But in connection with previous statements the meaning of point two of the résumé cannot be that man, because he is perfectible, has broken away from the general law, but that man in the process of exercising his faculty of perfectibility not only finds happiness in his activity of conservation and multiplication, but also exposes himself to *ennui* by satisfying too easily his appetites and artificial needs. The formulation of point two is not very fortunate. Not only because of the words *par sa perfectibilité*, but also because of the phrase, *s'est dérobé a cette loi commune*. Man cannot break away from the law which Chastellux has previously formulated: that pleasure is attached to all the means of conservation and multiplication, pain to all the means of destruction. If man satisfies his appetites too easily, and thus adopts a measure of destruction he does not break away from this law; he remains subjected to the law, just by exposing himself to *ennui*.

Concerning Chastellux's "metaphysical faith in the harmony of nature," his idea of a "masterplan" of nature, of nature as a kind of "benevolent providence," Frankel[388] refers to Chastellux's assertion that pleasure is attached to the means of conservation and multiplication, pain to the means of destruction. According to Chastellux this is a causal connection constituted by a law which can be observed in nature. To justify his statement on this "general law" he says: "If you are not satisfied with these general considerations and want to proceed to particular observations, look around you. [Si vous n'êtes pas content de ces considerations générales, et que vous vouliez descendre à des observations particulières, regardez autour de vous.]"[389] Then he presents observable facts which, in his opinion, confirm the existence of the law. Hence the harmony of nature is, according to Chastellux, a fact which can be observed by methods of empirical science. The result of his observation may be wrong, the law which he thinks to have found by his observation of nature may not exist, but the harmony of nature, which manifests itself in this law, is not the object of a metaphysical faith. It is true that Chastellux adds: "Starting from this principle, which cannot be denied, we can easily see that the happiness of everything that exists consists uniquely in fulfilling the wish of nature. [En partant de ce principe, qu'il est impossible de nier, il est aisé de voir que le bonheur de tout se qui existe consiste uniquement à remplir le vœu de la nature.]",[390] and that he also speaks of a "plan which nature seems to have fol-

388 Frankel, The Faith of Reason, p. 65.

389 Chastellux, De la Félicité Publique, II, p. 238.

390 Ibid., II, pp. 237–238.

lowed ["plan que la nature paraît avoir suivi."][391] The phrase "wish of nature" is evidently a figure of speech by which Chastellux in a metaphorical way expresses the idea that there exists a law of nature. He says of this law that nature has "imposed" it on all living beings ["la loi générale qu'elle (nature) leur a imposée"].[392] When Chastellux speaks of nature he always refers to the laws of nature, which are impersonal laws of causality. His idea of nature is totally different from the benevolent Providence of Christian theology. This Providence is not a set of causal laws, but the will of a supernatural, personal being. Frankel admits that Chastellux's "wish of nature" was perhaps a metaphor. But he adds: "Indeed it may not have been intended entirely as a metaphor."[393] This doubt is not justified. Frankel sees some similarity between Chastellux's and Holbach's "faith in progress"; he thinks that Holbach shared "Chastellux's confidence that the infallible principles of social physics had already been discovered,"[394] and he refers to Holbach's emphasis on the beneficence of nature[395] just as he speaks of Chastellux's idea of a beneficent nature, and asserts that "the cult of Reason and Nature ... reached its apotheosis with Holbach's expression of the faith of reason." Then he should not ignore what Holbach says about the concept of "nature" in his *Système de la Nature ou Des Lois du Monde Physique et du Monde moral.*[396] "Nature, therefore, in its most extended signification, is the great whole that results from the assemblage of matter under its various combinations, with that diversity of motions which the universe offers to our view ... Having described the proper definition that should be applied to the word NATURE, I must advise the reader, once and for all, that whenever, in the course of this work, the expression occurs, that 'Nature produces such or such an effect'; there is no intention of personifying that nature, which is purely an abstract being; it merely indicates, that the effect spoken of, necessarily springs from the peculiar properties of those beings which compose the mighty macrocosm. When, therefore, it is said, Nature demands that man should pursue his own happiness, it is to prevent circumlocution, to avoid tautology; it is to be understood that it is the property of a being that feels, that thinks, that wills, that acts, to labour to its own happiness." There is no essential difference between Holbach's and Chastellux's concept of nature. Neither writer conceived nature as a personal being en-

391 Ibid., II, p. 237.

392 Ibid.

393 Frankel, The Faith of Reason, p. 65.

394 Ibid., p. 70; see also pp. 102, 103.

395 Ibid., p. 71.

396 P. H. T. Holbach, Système de la Nature ou Des Lois du Monde Physique et du Monde moral (London, 1771), I, pp. 11–12. English translation by H. D. Robinson, The System of Nature or Laws of the Moral and Physical World (Boston, 1868), I, pp. 15–16.

dowed with will and reason, although the language of both might make this impression.[397]

A New Religion

As pointed out on p. 11 Brinton in his *History of Western Morals*, referring to Becker, interprets the Enlightenment as a "new religion"; by this he means the secular ethics of this philosophy. Discussing the views about human nature Brinton asserts that according to the philosophy of the rationalist Enlightenment – in opposition to the Christian estimate of human nature – "men are by nature good."[398] This is a specifically ethical view – a view which he calls a "heretical belief," that is, a religion. In another connection he speaks of "the Enlightened dogma of the natural goodness of man" and opposes this "dogma" to the Christian "dogma of original sin."[399] Brinton refers to the enlightened opinion "that man is simply an animal who has come out on top after a long course of organic evolution." This view is at the basis of the optimistic ethics of the Enlightenment. Brinton calls this ethical view about human na-

397 In his more recent book, The Case for Modern Man (New York, 1956), which is an excellent defense of modernity against the obscurantism of metaphysical-theological speculation, Frankel does full justice to the philosophy of the Enlightenment. He does not stress the metaphysical elements which this philosophy, according to the opinion expressed in his earlier book, The Faith of Reason, inherited and shared with those whom the philosophes opposed. On the contrary! He emphasizes only the antimetaphysical character of the Enlightenment. He says: "It was the philosophers and historians of the eighteenth century who began the modern custom of tracing ideas back to their origins in ordinary experience. They did so to expose and unmask prevailing ideas, and to show that they rested on accidents or superstitions or mere conventions" (p. 141). To be true, he adds: "But at the basis of this criticism was the assumption that there was an objective truth about the human scene that transcended any age and culture. In exposing the bias and partiality of the inherited ideas of their time, eighteenth-century philosophers and historians were measuring these ideas against what they believed were universal canons of science and reason" (p. 141). But he does not interpret this belief to mean that science is the product of a revelation, that the order of nature discovered by science is a version of Providence. "The progress of science as they [the eighteenth-century liberal philosophers] saw, is not" he says, "the progress of some one creed at the expense of others. It is the progress of a set of rules and procedures which allow men to coordinate their thinking and to cooperate in the search for truth" (p. 143). There is a change in his interpretation of the Enlightenment. Perhaps Frankel has become aware of the argument which a theological interpretation of the philosophy of the Enlightenment furnishes to all those against whom his most meritorious Case for Modern Man is directed.

398 Brinton, A History of Western Morals, p. 175.

399 Ibid., p. 464.

ture "the modern Western secular faith."[400] He says: "The ethics, the world view [a word he substitutes for the word "religion"] of both Christianity and the Enlightenment hold that all men are brothers, and that warfare is an evil. Both religions accept, and even cherish, the cultural and emotional ties that bind men in national groups."[401] Hence he characterizes nationalism – a moral-political attitude – as a religion.

Brinton does not ignore the differences between the ethics of Christianity and that of the Enlightenment. "Christian theology," he says, "condemned suicide as a sin, morally a form of murder, since God alone could rightfully end the sojourn of a soul on this earth." The philosophy of the Enlightenment, however, "denied that there was a soul or a God," hence "suicide was to the fully enlightened neither a sin nor a crime, but entirely a matter for the individual to decide."[402] This example shows clearly that the difference between the Christian and the enlightened ethics is that the one has a religious, the other a secular character. What Brinton has to say about the ethics of the Enlightenment concerning suicide is merely that it was not based – as the Christian ethics – on the belief in God and the immortality of the soul.

Nevertheless it is evidently because of its secular ethics that Brinton presents the philosophy of the Enlightenment as a secular religion. This ethics represents the "new view." It started, Brinton says, from a different cosmogony,"[403] different from that of Christianity; for it considered the universe as a "vast mechanism." There is, however, "the rather mysterious phenomenon of organic life, sentience, a not-quite-mechanical, at least not-quite-predictable, apparently related series of responses to stimuli from the environment. At this point, or somewhere near it, the Enlightened found room for – the Christian, I think, has to say smuggled in – a teleology, in fact an eschatology, an ethics, a religion, one which, like all Western religions, was to proliferate in sects, heresies, and schisms, a religion which, in constant mutual interaction with Christianity, is the new religion of the modern West." To say that the philosophy of the Enlightenment, in order to explain organic life, could not maintain its mechanistic world view and had recourse to a teleology, is, at least as a general statement, not correct. One of Enlightenment's most characteristic representatives, La Mettrie, in his *L'Homme machine* (1748), referred to by Brinton,[404] tried to explain organic life mechanically. It is irrelevant that Brinton, perhaps rightly, does not consider this attempt successful. For the philosophy of the Enlightenment must be understood in conformity with its own intentions. But even if it were correct to say that there is within the philosophy of the En-

400 Ibid., p. 175.
401 Ibid., p. 454.
402 Ibid., p. 325.
403 Ibid., p. 306.
404 Ibid., p. 306.

lightenment in addition to mechanistic a teleological explanation of natural phenomena, it would not follow that a religion entered this philosophy, much less that this philosophy as a whole is a religion. It is true that a teleological interpretation of nature – *if consistent* – presupposes a supernatural will, putting definite purposes to the natural processes, and then it has the character of a religion. But if a philosophy is inconsistent – which frequently happens – and accepts a teleological interpretation of nature (explaining certain phenomena as the realization of certain purposes, without presupposing a supernatural will, even rejecting such an assumption as the mechanistic philosophy of the Enlightenment did), then an objective presentation of this philosophy may accuse it of being inconsistent, but must not ascribe to it, much less call it, a religion.

What induced Brinton to assert that the enlightened philosophers found room for a religion is the fact that, at a certain point, ethics entered this philosophy: a doctrine of morals, that is, a definite system of norms prescribing human behavior. But this ethics has nothing to do with a teleological explanation of organic life. The teleology implied in this system of norms was – according to the view of some leading *philosophes* – not based on the assumption of a supernatural will. The view that the moral norms were immanent in nature was an illusion, but not a religious belief; and that many *philosophes* spoke of a "will of nature" was a mere metaphor. It is true that some of them referred to God as the supreme moral authority. They – or at least some of them – meant by it: people had to be made to believe that the moral norms are issued by a rewarding and punishing deity in order to make these norms effective (see above, p. 96). In Brinton's statement: "the Enlightened found room for ... a teleology, in fact an eschatology, an ethics, a religion" the reference to "eschatology" is superfluous, because "eschatology" is implied in "religion"; and it is not by chance that Brinton does not say: ethics *and* religion. He uses the "religion" as synonymous with the "ethics." By "teleology" the ethics of the Enlightenment is meant; and this ethics is called religion.

The Doctrine of Progress: Condorcet

The Enlightenment and its heirs have been interpreted as religions and especially as eschatologies particularly because an essential element of these intellectual movements is a doctrine of progress. Progress is a moral-political concept. It means a social evolution steadily approaching an ideal social order which from a moral-political point of view ought to be established.

"The concept of progress," Brinton says,[405] "is central to all forms of the new eschatology." The new eschatology is, in the first place, the philosophy

405 Ibid., p. 295.

of the Enlightenment. For "the eighteenth-century Enlightenment sought to substitute – take the word literally, as 'put in place of' – for the *transcendental* God-determined Christian otherworldly heaven a this-world *transformed* by human reason guiding human action into ... 'a heaven on earth.'" This "basic article of faith of the eighteenth-century Enlightenment ... took on intensities worth comparing with early Christian expectance of a Second Coming"; "this eighteenth-century eschatology was a messianic belief," a belief "that for all human beings the 'pursuit of happiness' and the attainment of comfort here on earth are normal and expected aims."[406] "The eighteenth century elevated" a historical process "into an eschatology under the name of Progress."[407] Hence Brinton speaks of the "religion of Progress."[408]

The "heaven on earth," to which in the philosophy of the Enlightenment the historical process called "progress" is leading, is a moral ideal. Brinton speaks of "the new moral concept of heaven on earth;"[409] and of "implications" the "new eschatology" has for "Western moral life."[410] Brinton says of the Enlightenment's "hope of a heaven on earth" that a great number of men had come to believe that "a large proportion of what most men most of the time think and feel as *evil*, wars, physical suffering, poverty, frustrations, above all frustrations clearly assignable to human willing and human power, would cease to be."[411] By "evil" not only material but also moral evil is understood.

"Christianity and Enlightenment were *both*, in their inception, attempts to do away altogether with evil. Both were movements that we may call, without undue semantic worry, 'messianic,' 'millenarian,' 'chiliastic,' 'Utopian'."[412] "The true believers in the religion of progress and humanity at the end of the eighteenth century, like the Christians of the first few generations, were millenarians who believed there would be an immediate and total alteration of man's state."[413] Christianity and Enlightenment are "equally messianic religions, both of which, if we followed their most heroic demands, would make us all saints."[414]

To call the enlightened doctrine of progress an "eschatology" is justified only if this doctrine has such essential elements in common with the eschatology of Christian theology that the differences – if there are any – are considered unimportant. In truth, it is the other way around. The differences be-

406 Ibid., pp. 293, 294.
407 Ibid., p. 296.
408 Ibid., p. 373.
409 Ibid., p. 295.
410 Ibid., pp. 296, 297.
411 Ibid., p. 373.
412 Ibid., pp. 446, 447.
413 Ibid., pp. 373, 374.
414 Ibid., p. 447.

tween the two doctrines are so essential that the elements they have in common – if there are any – are irrelevant.

"Eschatology" is the Christian doctrine of "last things." The term includes everything taught in Scripture about the future life of the individual soul in another world and the final destruction of *this* world by direct interference of God. It is the prediction of a definitive end of this world. The "last state," the *eschaton*, is a supernatural situation. Christian eschatology is essentially connected with the belief in the Second Coming of Christ[415] as the judge in the last judgment by which the sinners will be cruelly punished in hell, the pious rewarded by admittance to the Kingdom of God in heaven. From a moral point of view the principle of retribution is the main content of Christian eschatology. Its psychological effect is primarily deterrence by the threat of supernatural penalties; the promise of reward, the hope for the bliss that pious souls may expect in the Kingdom of Heaven, is of relatively minor importance. The enlightened doctrine of progress also implies the prediction of a future state of man. But this is, indeed, the only element that this doctrine has in common with Christian eschatology. In all other respects it is the opposite of it.

In another connection (see above pp. 40 seq.) attention has been called to the fact that according to the Judaeo-Christian myth the history of mankind has not exactly the character of progress because it starts – like the myth of the Golden Age – from an ideal state; and, after the fall of man, does not show a steady improvement of the situation of men but will suddenly turn again to an ideal state. The prediction of this state is based on belief in the irruption of the supernatural into empirical reality. The prediction implied in the enlightened doctrine of progress is based on rational science, on an observation of the facts of human history. Such prediction is a legitimate scientific operation. According to a generally accepted view the possibility of predicting a future event is the criterion of the truth of a causal law formulated by science. The statement expressing the law that heat expands metallic bodies is true if it is possible to predict that a metallic ball that could pass through a wooden ring will not pass after the ball had been heated. The prediction implied in the doctrine of progress may be proved to be erroneous, as Brinton – perhaps correctly – asserts. Many truly scientific theories have been proved erroneous. But for the scientific character of the doctrine, this is irrelevant. Decisive is that the prediction implied in Christian eschatology is based on divine revelation, and not on science as is the prediction implied in the enlightened doctrine of progress. This difference is so essential that the fact that both doctrines imply predictions is irrelevant. If any prediction regardless of whether it is based on science or on revelation is called "eschatology" then the scientific theory of the so-called *Wärmetod* – according to which a steady decrease of temperature

415 See the article "eschatology" in the Encyclopaedia Britannica.

(entropy) will extinguish all life – is an eschatology, which shows the absurdity of such a terminology.

Therefore, the facts predicted by the enlightened doctrine of progress and those predicted by Christian eschatology are essentially different. According to enlightened doctrine, the future state of mankind, the result of progress, is not to be brought about by divine interference or by any kind of superhuman power, but by man himself, by his own will directed by his own reason. Progress is not a supernatural, but a natural process. It takes place exclusively in this world, without any end of it being predicted. Brinton admits this. He says: "The historical process which the eighteenth century elevated into an eschatology under the name of Progress was, to use another great term of the century, considered a *natural* process."[416] He emphasizes that this term was used in opposition to Christian orthodoxy, and says of this natural process that, according to the philosophy of the Enlightenment, "this process is Progress, world without end."[417] He even admits that according to the enlightened doctrine of progress "Christian orthodoxy had not to be modified, but destroyed root and branch, or it might be a more serious obstacle to inevitable Progress."[418] If the idea of progress does not imply any supernatural element, if, in opposition to the Christian religion, it rejects such an element, and is nevertheless called "eschatology," this terminology amounts to the self-contradictory concept of an eschatology without eschaton.

The enlightened doctrine of progress does not imply the idea of retribution, which is the main concern of the Christian eschatology. The justice of progress is not, like the justice of the Christian eschatology, the principle: to everyone what he deserves, evil for evil, good for good; but the totally different principle: to everyone what he needs. Hence, according to the enlightened doctrine of progress, the future state of mankind is a human society on this earth in which as much happiness as possible is guaranteed to everyone. The "last state" of Christian eschatology, however, is not a state of happiness alone. It is, in the first place, a state of unspeakable misery for a great part of mankind, subjected in hell to tortures that only a sadistic imagination can fancy; and only in the second place a state of bliss for those, who in their earthly life obeyed the commands of God. This state of bliss is entirely different from the happiness that the progress of the enlightened philosophy is bringing to mankind. The former is a purely spiritual or, more exactly formulated, a mystic "happiness," the joy of the direct and immediate show of God in the other world as the result of a union of the human soul with God, a state best characterized be the German term *Seligkeit*. Brinton cannot deny it. He says the happiness that the believer in progress can expect "includes the physical comforts, the material satisfactions, the absence

416 Brinton, A History of Western Morals, p. 296.
417 Ibid., p. 377.
418 Ibid., p. 296.

of preventable physical suffering."[419] And he finally admits: "It is still true that Christian distrust of the flesh in this world has spilled over into Christian ideas of the next world. 'Bliss' is the favorite word of the theologians for the heavenly state of man and it is a very sedate and unsensual word."[420]

It is true that according to the original Jewish idea of the Kingdom of God – not according to the later Christian doctrine – this kingdom will be established on this earth, and there will be in this kingdom a state of material happiness. But this state is not the result of man-made progress, but the miraculous work of God. Therefore, to say – as Brinton repeatedly does – that the enlightened doctrine of progress predicted a "heaven on earth" is a wholly unsuitable figure of speech; or as he himself admits, an "inadequate phrase."[421] (See above, p. 31.)

The human society in which, according to the enlightened doctrine of progress, an entirely worldly happiness will be guaranteed to everyone, is evidently not "heaven" that is a supernatural state, and certainly not a "this-worldly heaven" which is as self-contradictory as the statement that the religion of the Enlightenment makes "otherwordly promises" "for this world."[422] This "heaven on earth" is not, as Brinton says "substituted" for the other-worldly heaven; it is not a "surrogate for the Christian heaven;"[423] it is *opposed* to it. Only by taking a metaphor literally – an intellectual offense and a typical source of errors – can Brinton call the doctrine of progress an eschatology, or "apocalyptic hopes."[424]

The enlightened doctrine of progress has been formulated by Condorcet in his work *Esquisse d'un tableau historique des progrès, de l'esprit humain* (1793).[425] Of this work Brinton says: "With Condorcet we find the religion of the Enlightenment in perhaps its purest form."[426] In Condorcet's work Brinton thinks he finds ideas that justify his calling the philosophy of the Enlightenment a religion and its doctrine of progress an eschatology. First, the idea of an end of history: "From primitive man onward, Condorcet traced in nine epochs the gradual rise of man, his progress toward the immanent goal of history. With his own time began the tenth epoch, the end of history and the beginning of ... shall we call it the attainment of universal happiness?"[427] Then

419 Ibid., p. 294.
420 Ibid., p. 295.
421 Ibid., p. 294.
422 Ibid., p. 467.
423 Ibid., p. 403.
424 Ibid., p. 446.
425 Cited hereafter as published in the edition of Bibliothèque de Philosophie (Paris, 1933). English translation by June Barraclough, Sketch for a Historical Picture of the Progress of the Human Mind (London, 1955).
426 Brinton, A History of Western Morals, p. 314.
427 Ibid., p. 314.

Brinton intimates that Condorcet believed in miracles,[428] and finally asserts that Condorcet's doctrine of progress implies a belief in immortality. Brinton says: "This world has with Condorcet become quite the other world. I owe to the work, as yet unpublished of a graduate student at Harvard, Gerald J. Gruman, M. D., now engaged on a historical study of ideas on what he calls 'prolongevity' a really extraordinary parallel with Christianity: according to Dr. Gruman the full implication of Condorcet's work is nothing less than corporeal individual immortality here on earth, eternal life in this flesh, for everybody, an eschatological concept indeed."[429]

The opinion that Condorcet's tenth epoch means the "end of history" is hardly compatible with Condorcet's own statements. Progress, according to Condorcet, is a historical process, hence by its nature subjected to permanent changes. Condorcet says of his work: "Such a picture is historical, since it is a record of permanent change [*perpétuelle variation*] and is based on the observation of human societies throughout the different stages of their development."[430] The historical process of progress consists in a gradual perfection of man, which is due, in the first place, to the progress of natural and social sciences. The progress of science is indefinite. In the chapter on the tenth epoch, Condorcet asserts that "within the body of the sciences of observation, calculation and experiment, the actual number of truths may always increase."[431] "In the political sciences there are some truths that ... can be of use only if they are widely known and acknowledged. So the influence of these sciences upon the freedom and prosperity of nations must in some degree be measured by the number of truths that, as a result of elementary instruction, are common knowledge; the swelling progress of elementary instruction, connected with the necessary progress of these sciences promises us an improvement in the destiny of the human race, which may be regarded as indefinite, since it can have no other limits than that of the same progress."[432] Consequently the process of human perfection – and this is exactly the historical process of progress – is indefinite. Condorcet emphasizes "that the perfectibility of man is truly indefinite; and that the progress of this perfectibility, from now onwards independent of any power that might wish to halt it [these powers are: religion and political autocracy] has no other limit than the duration of the globe upon which nature has cast us."[433] Since progress is the

428 Ibid., p. 382, n. 10. Comparing Condorcet whith Toynbee, Brinton says of the latter: "He wants a miracle, but unlike Condorcet, he cannot quite believe in miracles – or rather, he has to try to persuade himself to a belief in miracles."

429 Ibid., p. 314, n. 21.

430 Condorcet, Esquisse, p. 2; in the Barraclough-translation the word "perpetuelle" is omitted (p. 4).

431 Ibid., p. 219; transl. p. 186.

432 Ibid., p. 232; transl. pp. 196, 197.

433 Ibid., p. 3; transl. p. 4

meaning of history, and progress is an indefinite process, there can be no end of history, according to Condorcet. If his philosophy is the purest form of the philosophy of the Enlightenment, as Brinton asserts, then this philosophy comes to the same result; Brinton himself says of the enlightened doctrine of progress that the process of progress means a "world without end".[434]

As for Condorcet's belief in miracles it suffices to quote the following passage of his work: "Disdain for the human sciences was one of the first characteristics of Christianity. It had to avenge itself against the outrages of philosophy, and it feared that spirit of doubt and inquiry, that confidence in one's own reason which is the bane of all religious beliefs. The natural sciences were odious and suspect, for they are very dangerous to the success of miracles, and there is no religion that does not force its devotees to swallow a few physical absurdities."[435]

The most important argument for calling Condorcet's philosophy of progress an eschatology is his alleged doctrine of individual immortality! Even if it were true that progress, as predicted by Condorcet, will lead to "corporeal individual immortality here on earth, eternal life in this flesh," his doctrine of progress would not constitute a "parallelism" with Christianity. Two ideas are "parallel" if they have the same direction and not if they are opposed to each other. The idea of corporeal immortality, however, stands in direct opposition to the teaching of the Christian religion that man in his flesh, in his corporeal existence, must die in conformity with the will of God who has inflicted the mortality of the body upon mankind as a punishment for the sin of Adam and Eve. Mortality of the body on this earth is inseparably connected with immortality of the soul, whose purpose is to make divine retribution possible, which is itself exercised on the souls in another world. The corporeal individual immortality, allegedly predicted by Condorcet, is a biological, the Christian immortality of the soul a purely metaphysical-ethical concept. Hence the "immortality" of the body is totally different from the "immortality" of the soul. The former means that man can avoid the death of his body, so that there may be no end to his life; whereas the latter means that the empirical concept of life and death is not applicable to the metaphysical-divine substance of the soul.

However, Condorcet does not at all predict corporeal individual immortality here on earth, eternal life in the flesh! He expressly excludes such an idea. He says in his description of the tenth epoch: "Certainly, man will not become immortal. [Sans doute, l'homme ne deviendra pas immortel.]"[436] Condorcet says only "that the day will come when death will be due only to extraordinary accidents or to the decay of the vital forces [which will operate more and more slowly] and that ultimately the average span between birth and decay will have

434 Brinton, A History of Western Morals, p. 377.

435 Condorcet, Esquisse, p. 84; transl. p. 72.

436 Ibid., p. 237; transl. p. 200.

no assignable value [qu'il doit arriver un temps où la mort ne serait plus que l'effet, ou d'accidents extraordinaire, ou de la destruction de plus en plus lente de forces vitales, et qu'enfin la durée de l'intervalle moyen entre la naissance et cette destruction n'a elle-même aucun terme assignable.]"[437] There will always be decay of the vital forces; only the *increase* of the distance between birth and death will be indefinite. This increase may be indefinite but, becoming steadily smaller, life can never reach immortality. Condorcet says expressly: "In truth, this average span of life which we suppose will *increase indefinitely* as time passes, may grow in conformity either with a law such that it continually approaches a limitless length but *without ever reaching it*, or with a law such that through the centuries it reaches a length greater than any determinate quantity that we may assign to it as its limit. In the latter case such an *increase* is truly indefinite in the strictest sense of the word, since there is no term on this side of which it must of necessity stop. In the former case it is equally indefinite in relation to us, if we cannot fix the limit it always approaches *without ever reaching* and particularly if, knowing only that it will never stop, we are ignorant in which of the two senses the term 'indefinite' can be applied to it. Such is the present condition of our knowledge as far as the perfectibility of the human race is concerned; such is the sense in which we may call it indefinite. [En effet, cette durée moyenne de la vie qui doit *augmenter* sans cesse, à mesure que nous enfonçons dans l'avenir, peut recevoir des accroissements, suivant une loi telle, qu'elle approche continuellement d'une étendue illimitée *sans pouvoir l'atteindre jamais*; ou bien suivant une loi telle, que cette même durée puisse acquérir, dans l'immensité des siècles, une étendue plus grande qu'une quantité determinée quelconque qui lui aurait été assignée pour limite. Dans ce dernier cas, les *accroissements* sont réellement indéfinis dans le sens le plus absolu, puisqu'il n'existe pas de borne, en deçà de la quelle ils doivent s'arrêter. Dans le premier, ils le sont encore par rapport a nous, si nous ne pouvons fixer ce terme, qu'ils *ne peuvent jamais atteindre*, et dont ils doivent toujours s'approcher; surtout si, connaissant seulement qu'ils ne doivent point s'arrêter, nous ignorons même dans lequel de ces deux sens le terme d'indéfini leur doit être appliqué; et tel est précisément le terme de nos connaissances actuelles sur la perfectibilité de l'espèce humaine; tel est le sens dans lequel nous pouvons l'appeler indéfinie.]"[438] (Italics mine.)

Condorcet emphasizes that the duration of life will, by a process of steady increase, approach indefinite extension, but will never reach this goal. What is really indefinite is only this process of increase, not the duration of life. To illustrate Condorcet's idea by a geometrical parallel: a given line may be lengthened indefinitely without its length becoming itself indefinite. What is indef-

437 Ibid., pp. 236, 237; transl. p. 200. The words "de plus en plus lente" are omitted in the translation.

438 Ibid., p. 237; transl. p. 200.

inite is the lengthening, not the line, if the lengthening decreases steadily but continues in this way indefinitely.[439]

Since Brinton considers Condorcet's doctrine of progress the "purest form" of the "religion of the Enlightenment," it is not superfluous to quote some passages of the *Esquisse d'un tableau historique des progrés de l'esprit humain*, which show Condorcet's attitude toward religion in general, and his opinion about the relationship between progress and religion in particular.

Characterizing the "new philosophy," that is, the philosophy of the Enlightenment, Condorcet enumerates certain principles, such as "an understanding of the natural rights of man, the belief that these rights are inalienable and indefeasible" and especially "indifference in all matters of religion, which now were relegated to the status of superstitions and political impostures."[440] His own opinion he formulates as follows: "There is not a religious system nor a supernatural extravagance that is not founded on ignorance of the laws of nature. The inventors, the defenders of these absurdities could not foresee the successful perfection of the human mind."[441] In his prediction of future progress he says: "The time will therefore come when the sun will shine only on free men who know no other master but their reason; when tyrants and slaves, priests and their stupid or hypocritical instruments will exist only in works of history and on the stage; and when we shall think of them only to pity their victims and their dupes; to maintain ourselves in a state of vigilance by thinking on their excesses; and to learn how to recognize and so to destroy, by force of reason, the first seeds of tyranny and superstition, should they ever dare to reappear amongst us."[442] "Superstition" means religion in opposition to science; "tyranny" means autocracy in opposition to democracy. It is evident that Condorcet believed humanity will some time live without religion.

From numerous passages of his work it is clear that he considered progress as the increasingly successful effort of human reason to shake off, with the help of science, the chains of religious superstition and political despotism, the one being essentially connected with the other.[443] This, then, is Condorcet's "religion of progress"!

There are, in fact, two essentially different doctrines of progress. According to the one, it is man himself, who, as the master of his fate, through his own steady increasing knowledge of the facts of nature and social life becomes more able to satisfy his needs. According to this theory, progress is man's own work, and his main instrument is science. According to the other doctrine, progress is the work of God. The will of God manifests itself in that process

439 See Charles Frankel, The Case for Modern Man (New York, 1956), pp. 102 seqq.

440 Condorcet, Esquisse, p. 164; transl. p. 140.

441 Ibid., p. 192; transl. p. 163.

442 Ibid., p. 210; transl. p. 179.

443 Ibid., pp. 10, 18–19, 23, 38, 44, 51, 82, 84, 145.

of a steady amelioration of man's situation on earth, and only with the help of God is man able to improve the conditions of his life. If science plays any part in this process, it is only as a gift of God. Not science, but faith is the specific instrument of progress. This is, indeed, a religious doctrine of progress; but even this doctrine, science it refers to happiness on earth, is essentially different from eschatology. It is therefore incorrect to speak, as Brinton and others do, of a "belief in progress" as if there were only one attitude of men in this respect, and no essential difference between a religious "belief" in and a secular doctrine of progress.[444]

444 Clarke A. Chambers (in "The Belief in Progress in Twentieth-Century America", Journal of the History of Ideas XIX, [April 1958], p. 202), says: "The belief in progress, like other religions, was syncretic." However, twentieth-century America did not have *one* "syncretic" belief in progress, but different doctrines of which Chambers gives characteristic examples, and of which only one was a "religion." The followers of one "rejecting the notion [advocated by the spokesmen for industrial capitalism] that progress would come with the release of man's competitive instincts ... posited instead a faith in man's natural instinct for cooperation and love. They believed, moreover, in the efficacy of man's will. Men were not passive instruments of either divine will or natural processes; they were, potentially at least, masters of their own fate if only they would take thought, apply the methods of science to man and society, and strive purposefully for reform. Through such methods, wrote Walter Lippmann [Drift and Mastery: An Attempt to Diagnose the Current Unrest, New York, 1914, pp. 266–267] just before the First World War, man could come to assert "mastery" over the "drift" of life. All men was need do, he wrote, to deal deliberately with life, "devise its social organizations, alter its tools, formulate its method, educate and control it. In endless ways we put intention where custom has reigned. We break up routines, make decisions, choose our ends, select means." Thus, but always contingent upon man's will to use his social intelligence, was progress assured. Man, if he would, had history in his grasp." Another doctrine of progress referred to by Chambers was presented by William Allen White, in A Theory of Spiritual Progress (Emporia, Kansas, 1910), who, as Chambers states, taught the awareness of human suffering, kindness, concern for the welfare of one's brothers were ever more coming to dominate over baser passions of the human race. Through inventions, life was made easier for all men; through social justice the fruits of technology were more equitably distributed; and as life moved forward "in the way of the Lord," mercy and charity conquered over cruelty. Progress is essentially moral progress; and it is this moral progress that man's nature demands. "The divine spark is in every soul ... This holy spirit is in every heart ... It is the fundamental claim men have upon one another as brothers." (White, Theory, pp. 181, 50, 51.) The way of progress is "the way of the Lord," its main instrument is a "divine spark" in every soul; a "holy spirit in every heart." The fundamental difference between these two doctrines of progress is evident; and it consists exactly in that the one has indeed, whereas the other has definitely not, a religious character.

The French Encyclopedia as a Koran

"Koran" is the name of the sacred scriptures of Islam. The term means literally "reading," just as the name of the sacred scripture of the Judaeo-Christian religion. Bible means literally "book." Spengler uses the word "Koran" for the sacred scriptures of other religions. He suggests: "The John Gospel is the first Christian writing of which the evident purpose is that of a Koran and its unknown author is the originator of the idea that there could be and must be a Christian Koran."[445] "A Koran," he says, "is by its very nature unconditionally right, and therefore unalterable and incapable of improvement."[446] This follows from the fact that Muslims regard the Koran as the word of God communicated to Mohammed through the intermediation of an angel, in the same way as Christians regard the Old and New Testaments as the word of God revealed to Moses and Jesus. Since the Koran is much younger than the Judaeo-Christian Bible, it would be more appropriate to speak of the Bible of Islam than of the Koran of the Judaeo-Christian religion. Spengler considers the author of the gospel "according to John" to be "closely related" to Marcion, the great theologian of the gnosis. Spengler regards the latter as the "real creator of the New Testament."[447] Following this example, Voegelin – without referring to Spengler – uses the term "Gnostic koran" to characterize a definite type of writings which, in his opinion, are typical of modern civilization. "A work of this type would serve the double purpose of a guide to the right reading of Scripture and of an authentic formulation of truth that would make recourse to earlier literature unnecessary. For the designation of this genus of Gnostic literature a technical term is needed; since the study of Gnostic phenomena is too recent to have developed one, the Arabic term *koran* will have to do for the present." Then he calls Calvin's *Institutes,* "the first deliberately created Gnostic koran."[448] If the Gnosis had "a koran" in Spengler's or Voegelin's sense, it could only be Marcion's attempt to restore the true Gospel, by eliminating from the existing gospels the Jewish elements.[449] But Marcion's work has by no means the character of a koran. He did not present his work as the result of divine revelation. Harnack says: "[Marcion] did not appeal to divine revelation, or to a particular [divine] assignment, or a pneumatic assistance: he carried on his work not as an enthusiast, but, relying on inner reasons, only by means of philology." In other words, he presented his work as a critical analysis of the text of the Scripture. Harnack emphasizes that Marcion "could not and actually did not claim for his purifications of the text of the

445 Spengler, The Decline of the West, II, p. 245.
446 Ibid., p. 246.
447 Ibid., p. 226.
448 Voegelin, The New Science of Politics, pp. 138–139.
449 See Harnack, Marcion, pp. 32 seqq.

gospels absolute certainty, a fact which is ordinarily ignored;" that "his pupils have, partly more radically than he himself, partly more conservatively, changed the text, perhaps when he was still alive, certainly after his death."[450] From this it follows that there is no such thing as a "Gnostic" koran.

This is, however, a misunderstanding of minor importance. More serious is Voegelin's use of his invention of a "Gnostic koran." For he characterizes not only Calvin's *Insitutes*, but also the works of Comte and Marx in this way. Voegelin even tries to make us believe that one of the most significant documents of the rationalistic Enlightenment, the French Encyclopedia, is a koran, a sacred scripture. He says: "In the eighteenth century, Diderot and d'Alembert claimed koranic function for the *Encyclopédie française*." Why? Did Diderot and d'Alembert pretend that the articles of the *Encyclopédie* were the word of God? Voegelin could not insist on such an absurdity. But he says they claimed koranic function for the *Encyclopédie francaise* because they considered the *Encyclopédie* "as the comprehensive presentation of all human knowledge worth preserving."[451] Did they pretend that every word written in the dictionary had the value of eternal unchangeable truth? They expressly declared that they presented in the *Encyclopédie* only *"l'état présent des sciences et des arts* [the present status of the sciences and arts]"[452], which implies that this status is not to be regarded as definitive. Voegelin can attribute to the authors only the opinion that "nobody" would have to use any work antedating the *Encyclopédie*, and all future sciences would assume the form of supplements to the great collection of knowledge."[453] This statement can only refer to a passage in d'Alembert's *Discours préliminaires de l'Encyclopédie*, 1805, which runs as follows: "De tout ce qui précède, il s'ensuit que dans l'ouvrage que nous annonçons, on a traité des sciences et des arts, de manière qu'on n'en suppose aucune connaissance préliminaire; qu'on y expose ce qu'il importe de savoir sur chaque matière; que les articles s'expliquent les uns par les autres, et que par conséquent la difficulté de la nomenclature n'embarasse nulle part. [It follows from all that has been said before that in the work we are announcing sciences and arts are dealt with in such a way that no preliminary knowledge is presupposed; that all that is necessary to know about each topic is presented; that the articles explain themselves the one by the others, and that consequently technical terms do not embarrass at all.]"[454] This means the reader can understand the content of the various articles without looking for explanation in other books because for every term used in one article but not explained in

450 Ibid., pp. 39 seq.

451 Voegelin, The New Science of Politics, p. 139.

452 D'Alembert, "Discours préliminaire de l'Encyclopédie," Œuvres Philosophiques, Historiques et Littéraires (Paris, 1805), I, p. 247.

453 Voegelin, The New Science of Politics, p. 140.

454 D'Alembert, Discours, p. 323.

it, there is an explanation in another article. D'Alembert continues: "D'où nous inférons que cet ouvrage pourra, du moins un jour, tenir lieu de bibliothèque dans tous les genres à un homme du monde; et dans tous les genres, excepté le sien, à un savant de profession; qu'il développera les principes de choses; qu'il en marquera les rapports; qu'il contribuera à la certitude et au progrès des connaissances humains. [From this we conclude that this work may, at least some day, take the place of a library in all fields of learning for an educated gentleman, and for a professional scholar in all fields except his own; that it will develop the principles of the things; that it will show their relations; that it will contribute to the progress of human knowledge.]"[455] If that could be interpreted to mean that "nobody would have to use any word antedating the *Encyclopédie*," it should be added that it is said only with respect to the *homme du monde*, that is, a gentleman in the sense of an "educated layman," but that the *savant*, the professional scholar, with respect to his special field is expressly excepted; and that the reference to the progress of knowledge evidently implies that the *Encyclopédie* does not pretend to be the end of this progress. D'Alembert's *Discours préliminaire de l'Encyclopédie* shows clearly that the publication of this work certainly did not intend to impose a "Gnostic koran" on this world.

Lessing's Education of the Human Race

According to Taubes, Gotthold Ephraim Lessing's *Erziehung des Menschengeschlechts* (Education of the Human Race), published in 1780, is the first manifestation of eschatological chiliasm in modern philosophy of history. It is the "magna charta of philosophical chiliasm."[456] "Lessing is one of those who do not see the Kingdom of God realized in the world of rationalism, but predicts it as coming in the future. The constellation of Joachim is reestablished. Lessing expressly refers to the Joachites prophecy of the eternal Gospel."[457] Löwith, similarly, says: "Lessing's famous fragment on the *Education of the Human Race* is based on the idea of a progressive revelation ending in a third age, an idea which Lessing explicitly assimilates to the doctrine of the Joachite, though he undermines the faith in revelation and replaces it by education ... The 'elementary' books of the Christian revelation, or rather education, shall be superseded by a 'new eternal Gospel' ... as promised in the New Testament."[458]

455 Ibid.

456 Taubes, Abendländische Eschatologie, pp. 133, 205.

457 Ibid., p. 86. In his interpretation of Lessing, Taubes refers to Hans Urs von Balthasar, Apokalypse der deutschen Seele (1937–1939) – second edition published under the title Prometheus (Heidelberg, 1947) – who characterizes Lessing's Education of the Human Race as "chiliasm in the long run" but adds: "or perhaps only the verve of chiliasm, transplanted into the temporally infinite evolution" (p. 48).

458 Löwith, Meaning in History, p. 208.

Taubes and Löwith's interpretations of Lessing's philosophy of history go back to Gerlich's study on communism as a chiliastic prophecy.[459] Gerlich was probably the first who tried to recognize in Lessing's *Education of the Human Race* the apocalyptic idea of a future millennium, the coming Kingdom of God, and to trace it back to the Joachites of the thirteenth and fourteenth centuries. This interpretation, however, cannot stand a critical test. Lessing was the most outstanding representative of the German Enlightenment. He stood in strict opposition to Protestant orthodoxy in general and to the idea of supernatural revelation in particular; he believed in human reason, as a faculty innate in man, not in the illumination of man from the outside; he rejected the doctrine of the trinity and, above all, the belief in retribution to be executed on the immortal soul in another life. But he had to be cautious in his fight against Protestant orthodoxy still dominant in his time. By an ordinance of the Duce of Braunschweig of August 17, 1778, he was prohibited from publishing anything on religion without previous approval by the government.[460] This explains why his essay *Education of the Human Race* was published anonymously, so that Lessing's authorship, now firmly established, was doubtful.[461] To avoid persecution by the Protestant church, he presented his ideas in the terminology of his opponents. He does not directly deny some fundamental principles of Christian theology and especially not the existence or authority of revelation, but he reinterprets them by rationalizing the irrational. This, of course, is not possible without ambiguities; and these ambiguities led to the attempt to find irrational elements in his rationalistic philosophy.[462]

Rationalization of the irrational is the essence of Lessing's essay. It begins with the statement: "That which education is to the individual, revelation is to the race" (§ 1).[463] "Education is revelation coming to the individual man; and revelation is education which has come, and is yet coming to the human race" (§ 2). The attempt to identify education with revelation is a doubtful enterprise. Lessing himself does not insist on this identification because he continues: "Whether it can be of any advantage to the science of instruction to contemplate education from this point of view, I will not here inquire, but in theology it may unquestionably be of great advantage, and may remove many

459 Gerlich, Der Kommunismus, pp. 142 seqq., 150.

460 See Gottfried Fittbogen, "Der Streit um Lessings Erziehung des Menschengeschlechts," Preussische Jahrbücher, CLIV (1913), p. 222.

461 Ibid., pp. 218 seqq. See also: Erich Schmidt, Lessing, 3rd ed. (Berlin, 1909), II, pp. 471 seqq.

462 See Martha Waller, Lessings Erziehung des Menschengeschlechtes. Interpretation und Darstellung ihres rationalen und irrationalen Gehaltes, in Germanische Studien, Heft 160 (Berlin, 1935).

463 The English translation follows, by and large, The Education of the Human Race by Gotthold Ephraim Lessing. Translated by the late Rev. Fred. W. Robertson, M. A., 4th ed. (London, 1883).

difficulties, if revelation be conceived of as the educator of humanity" (§ 3). The reinterpretation of irrational revelation as rational education is the main concern of this study. The rationalistic tendency shows clearly in the following statement: "Education gives to man nothing which he might not educe out of himself; it gives him that which he might educe out of himself, only quicker and more easily. In the same way, too, revelation gives nothing to the human species which the human reason left to itself might not attain; only it has given, and still gives to it, the most important of these things earlier" (§ 4). In his way Lessing deprives revelation, which he recognizes of its supernatural character and reduces it to a function of human reason. Progress of mankind is possible without supernatural revelation. People have attained a higher stage without it. It is true that "the most part had remained far behind the chosen people"; but, "a few had got before them" (§ 20). The Old Testament is merely "a primer for a childlike people as well as for children" (§§ 26, 27, 50). "But every primer is only for a certain age" (§ 51). Consequently, "a better instructor must come and tear the exhausted primer from the child's hands. Christ came!" (§ 53) and with Christ "the second, better primer for the race of man," (§ 64) the New Testament. This was "the second step of education" (§ 54).

The decisive progress consists in Christ's teaching of the immortality of the soul and retribution in another life. But now we can dispense with the Old Testament and can begin to dispense with the New Testament. There might be in the Bible some "truths pretended" (*vorgespiegelt*)[464] "which we are to marvel at, as revelations, exactly as long as until the time shall come when reason shall have learned to educe them out of its other demonstrated truths, and bind them up with them" (§ 72). Among these "truths" are "the doctrine of the trinity" (§ 73), "the doctrine of original sin" (§ 74), "the doctrine of the Son's satisfaction" (§ 75), and, above all, the doctrine of retribution to be executed on the immortal soul in another life (§§ 22, 85). This is the core of Christian eschatology! Lessing substitutes for this doctrine the "hypothesis" of metempsychosis. "Why," he asks, "should not every individual man have existed more than once upon this world?" (§ 94). "Why should I not come back as often as I am capable of acquiring fresh knowledge, fresh expertness?" (§ 98). "Is this hypothesis so laughable merely because it is the oldest?" (§ 95). The "hypothesis" is not laughable, but incompatible with Christian eschatology.

The perfection at which the education of the human race aims is "that purity of heart which makes us capable of loving virtue for its own sake alone" (§ 80). About the future "time of perfection" Lessing has to say merely that it will be a time "when man, the more convinced his understanding feels itself of an ever-better future, will nevertheless not be necessitated to borrow motives

464 Robertson translates "vorgespiegelt" with "prefigured, mirrored as it were." This is certainly not correct. A *vorgespiegelte Wahrheit* is something that pretends to be a truth, although it is not a real truth.

of action from this future; for he will do the right because it is right, not because arbitrary rewards are annexed thereto" (§ 85). This statement implies an unambiguous rejection of the Christian eschaton – it is a glorification of human reason. Lessing calls this doctrine the "new eternal gospel, which is promised us in the primer of the New Testament itself" (§ 86). However, it is the opposite of a "gospel," which is the manifestation of supernatural revelation. Lessing's doctrine is based on human reason alone. His intention was to abolish the concept of supernatural revelation and to substitute for it, by a dextrous argumentation, that of education through human reason. But, for tactical reasons, he tried to do it with the very aid of the concept of revelation.[465]

The reference to Joachim and the Joachites may be found in §§ 87–89: "Perhaps even some enthusiasts of the thirteenth and fourteenth centuries had caught a glimpse of a beam of this new eternal gospel, and only erred in that they predicted its outburst as so near to their own time. Perhaps their 'Three Ages of the World' were not so vain a fancy after all, and surely they had no evil intention when they taught that the New Covenant must become as much antiquated as the Old had grown to be. To them it sill remained the self-same administration of the self-same God; ever – to let them use my language – ever the self-same plan of the universal education of the human race. Only they were premature. Only they believed that they could make their contemporaries, who had scarcely outgrown their childhood, at once, without enlightenment, without preparation, men worthy of their Third Age." It is evident that it is not *their* third age, the Kingdom of God on earth, but Lessing's third age, the age of human reason, which the "enthusiasts of the thirteenth and fourteenth centuries" predicted prematurely because it was not yet preceded by the period of "Enlightenment." Lessing did not identify the age of reason with the third age of monarchism predicted by Joachim. For the same tactical reasons that forced Lessing to present his philosophy of history as a reinterpreted history of revelation, he thought it necessary to show some similarity between his idea of the future and the eschatological hopes of the "enthusiasts." He was fully aware of the fundamental difference. This follows from the fact that he speaks of their hopes as *Schwärmerei*, which has a connotation of unreal dream, and that he expressly declares he lets them use his own language when he interprets their theological speculation as a plan for the education of mankind. All this shows how false and misleading it is to interpret Lessing's *Education of the Human Race* as the expression of an apocalyptic idea of a future millennium, or as a manifestation of eschatological chiliasm; or to consider his doctrine of education as "based on the idea of progressive revelation," and to assert that he "assimilates" his idea to the doctrine of the Joachites.

465 Fittbogen, Streit, pp. 235, 242.

Chapter VII Hume's Empiricism and Kant's Transcendental Philosophy

If any philosophy seems beyond the suspicion of being influenced by Christian theology, it is David Hume's skeptical empiricism. Even Sertillanges admits that it is "without references to ontology,"[466] which means to metaphysics. Nevertheless the Dominican theologian asserts that this "perfect empiricism," too, "is not without relationship to Christian tradition."[467] The only argument set forth by Sertillanges to support this thesis is: "Revelation is not rejected."[468] He adds, "the position of the author, to tell the truth, is not clear in this point"; but he says: "What is certain, is the fact that revelation, though only feebly and dubiously affirmed, inspires the thinker in many respects."[469]

As a matter of fact, Hume decidedly rejected revelation as a mediator of truth. In section 10 of his *Enquiry concerning Human Understanding*, entitled "Of Miracles," he says: "What we have said of miracles, may be applied, without any variation, to prophecies; and indeed all prophecies are real miracles, and, as such only, can be admitted as proofs of any revelation."[470] But what has he said of miracles? That the testimony upon which a miracle (which is a "violation of the laws of nature"[471]) is founded cannot claim credibility; "that there never was a miraculous event established on so full an evidence" that "the falsehood of that testimony would be a real prodigy";[472] and only if the falsehood of the testimony would be more miraculous than the event related, "then, and not until then, can he [who testifies to the miracle] pretend to command my belief or opinion."[473] As a special reason "which diminishes the authority of prodigies," Hume refers to the fact "that there is no testimony

466 Sertillanges, Le Christianisme, II, p. 160.

467 Ibid.

468 Ibid., p. 162.

469 Ibid.

470 David Hume, An Enquiry concerning Human Understanding (La Salle, Illinois, 1949), section X, part II.

471 Ibid., section X, part I.

472 Ibid., section X, part II.

473 Ibid., section X, part I.

for any, even those which have not been expressly detected, that is not opposed by an infinite number of witnesses; so that not only the miracle destroys the credit of the testimony, but the testimony destroys itself."[474] Referring to all religions Hume says: "In the infancy of new religions, the wise and learned commonly esteem the matter too inconsiderable to deserve their attention or regard. And when afterwards they would willingly detect the cheat, in order to undeceive the deluded multitude, the season is now past, and the records and witnesses, which might clear up the matter, have perished beyond recovery."[475] Hume stigmatizes every religion based on miracles as a "cheat," which has to be detected by science in order to "undeceive" the "deluded" multitude. For Hume teaches that "no testimony for any kind of miracle has ever amounted to a probability, much less to a proof ... It is experience only, which gives authority to human testimony; and it is the same experience, which assures us of the laws of nature ... therefore we may establish it as a maxim, that no human testimony can have such force as to prove a miracle, and make it a just foundation for any such system of religion."[476]

The political circumstances under which Hume was living forced him to be cautious. Consequently he says that the method of reasoning which he used in the Enquiry "may serve to confound those dangerous friends, or disguised enemies, to the *Christian* Religion, who have undertaken to defend it by the principles of human reason. Our most holy religion is founded on *Faith*, not on reason; and it is a sure method of exposing it to put it to such a trial as it is, by no means, fitted to endure."[477] He characterizes the Christian religion as "most holy," but after what he said before, the ironic connotation of this attribute is evident. Then he examines the miracles of the *Pentateuch* "according to the principles of these pretended Christians, not as the word or testimony of God himself, but as the production of a mere human writer and historian." Hume certainly did not consider the Scripture as the word of God, but as the production of a human writer and historian. Hume expresses his own opinion, when he, after having ridiculed the miracles of the *Pentateuch*, says: "I desire any one to lay his hand upon his heart, and, after a serious consideration, declare, whether he thinks that the falsehood of such a book, supported by such a testimony, would be more extraordinary and miraculous than all the miracles it relates."[478] He concludes the section "Of Miracles," with the statement: "Upon the whole, we may conclude that the *Christian* Religion not only was at first attended with miracles, but even at this day cannot be believed by any reasonable person without one. Mere reason is insufficient to convince us

474 Ibid., section X, part II.
475 Ibid.
476 Ibid.
477 Ibid.
478 Ibid.

of its veracity: and whoever is moved by *Faith* to assent to it, is conscious of a continued miracle in his own person, which subverts all the principles of his understanding, and gives him a determination to believe what is most contrary to custom and experience." Hume therefore, leaves it to the reader to apply to this miracle of faith what his previous arguments of the *Enquiry* have demonstrated: that "it is experience only which gives authority to human testimony," And that "no human testimony can have such force as to prove a miracle, and make it a just foundation for any such system of religion."

It is true that Hume, at the close of the *Enquiry*, says:

"Divinity or Theology ... has a foundation in *reason*, so far as it is supported by experience." Presupposing that its main assertions are not supported by experience, Hume continues: "But its best and most solid foundation is *faith* and divine revelation." According to the previous reasoning, only experience, not faith, can lead to truth. Consequently, he concludes the *Enquiry*: "If we take in our hand any volume of divinity or school metaphysics, for instance; let us ask, *Does it contain any abstract reasoning concerning quantity or number?* No. *Does it contain any experimental reasoning concerning matter of fact and existence?* No. Commit it then to the flames; for it can contain nothing but sophistry and illusion."

Hence Sertillanges is not correct in saying that Hume has not rejected revelation. Rejection is the inevitable consequence of his skeptic empiricism. However, there are passages in some of Hume's other writings which do not seen to be compatible with the principles of his skeptic empiricism, especially in his *Dialogues concerning Natural Religion*, to which Sertillanges refers. The plan of this work had been thought out by Hume as early as 1750 but, in accordance with his wishes, it was published only after his death.[479]

The work presents itself as conversations among three participants: Demea, an orthodox Christian; Cleanthes, a deist; and Philo, a skeptic. The dialogue form allows Hume to refrain from identifying himself with any of the participants. It is therefore difficult to discover Hume's own opinion. However, it certainly is not Demea's orthodox Christianism. Most critics agree that Philo's skepticism is nearest to Hume's own view. Kant, who was deeply impressed by Hume's philosophy, takes it for granted that Hume speaks in the person of Philo against Cleanthes.[480] If this interpretation is correct, a statement made by Philo at the close of the *Dialogues* may be considered as the result intended by Hume: It is the "simple, though somewhat ambiguous, at least undefined

479 David Hume, Dialogues concerning Natural Religion, reprinted with an introduction by Bruce M'Ewen (Edinburgh and London, 1907), p. VII.

480 Immanuel Kant, Prolegomena zu einer jeden künftigen Metaphysik, die als Wissenschaft wird auftreten können, in Kants Gesammelte Schriften (Berlin, 1903), IV, p. 358.

proposition, *That the cause or causes of order in the universe probably bear some remote analogy to human intelligence.*"[481]

Of this proposition Philo says: "What can the most inquisitive, contemplative, and religious man do more than give a plain, philosophical assent to the proposition, as often as it occurs; and believe that the arguments, on which it is established, exceed the objections, which lie against it?"[482] However, in the previous parts of the *Dialogues* Philo has demonstrated that the analogy between a cause of the order in the universe and human intelligence is not only a mere "guess" or "conjecture"[483] but that "to ascertain this reasoning, it were requisite, that we had experience of the origin of worlds."[484] Finally Philo says: "The most natural sentiment, which a well-disposed mind will feel on this occasion, is a longing desire and expectation, that heaven would be pleased to dissipate, at least alleviate, this profound ignorance, by affording some more particular revelation to mankind, and making discoveries of the nature, attributes, and operations of the divine object of our faith. A person seasoned with a just sense of the imperfections of natural reason, will fly to revealed truth with the greatest avidity: While the haughty Dogmatist, persuaded that he can erect a complete system of Theology by the mere help of philosophy, disdains any farther aid, and rejects this adventitious instructor. To be a philosophical Sceptic is, in a man of letters, the first and most essential step towards being a sound, believing Christian."[485] An attentive reader must notice that Philo in this final statement does not proclaim belief in existing revelation but only admits a "longing desire" for a "more particular revelation"; that to this not-yet-existing revelation a person seasoned with a just sense of the imperfections of natural reason will fly; and that to be a philosophical skeptic may be the first, but (because the "most essential") also the last, step toward a goal he will never reach.

However, even an interpretation that tries to reconcile as far as possible the *Dialogues* with the *Enquiry* cannot ignore the serious contradictions between the two works. In the *Dialogues* Hume lets the skeptic say "all the sciences almost lead us insensibly to acknowledge a first intelligent Author."[486] This "Author" he characterizes as "cause" and says: "We … ought to attribute a much higher degree of power and energy to the supreme cause than any we have ever observed in mankind. Here then the existence of a Deity is plainly ascertained by reason."[487] This statement is incompatible with Hume's theory

481 Hume, Dialogues, p. 189.
482 Ibid., p. 190.
483 Ibid., p. 33.
484 Ibid., p. 44.
485 Ibid., pp. 190–191.
486 Ibid., p. 166.
487 Ibid., p. 170.

of causality. In the *Enquiry* we read: "It appears that, in single instances of the operation of bodies, we never can, by our utmost scrutiny, discover anything but one event following another, without being able to comprehend any force or power by which the cause operates, or any connection between it and its supposed effect."[488] Hume emphasizes "that causes and effects are discoverable, not by reason, but by experience."[489] He declares: "The scenes of the universe are continually shifting, and one object follows another in an uninterrupted succession; but the power or force, which actuates the whole machine, is entirely concealed from us; and never discovers itself in any of the sensible qualities of body."[490] In the *Dialogues* the skeptic does not deny the *being* of the deity; he only asserts that we cannot "comprehend the attributes of this divine Being."[491] This means that he conceives God as a substance different from its attributes. This is in opposition to Hume's doctrine of substance, his rejection of a distinction between substance and qualities. "We have therefore no idea of substance, distinct from that of a collection of particular qualities ... The idea of a substance ... is nothing but a collection of simple ideas, that are united by the imagination, and have a particular name assigned them, by which we are able to recall, either to ourselves or to others, that collection: ... the particular qualities which form a substance, are commonly referred to an unknown *something,* in which they are supposed to inhere."[492] The existence of the deity, admitted by the skeptic of the *Dialogues* to be the supreme cause of nature, can only be an external existence beyond ourselves. But Hume says in his *Treatise of Human Nature* that it is impossible for us to conceive or to form an idea of such external existence: "Let us fix our attentions out of ourselves as much as possible; let us chase our imagination to the heavens, or to the utmost limits of the universe; we never really advance a step beyond ourselves, nor can conceive any kind of existence, but those perceptions, which have appeared in that narrow compass."[493] God, as the supreme cause of the universe, can be only an external existence. There is an undeniable contradiction between Philo's admittance of a "revealed truth" (that is, the admittance of the truth of a miracle) and the statements of the *Enquiry* that the testimony of a miracle cannot pretend to command our belief or opinion, and that "the only methods, by which we can ever hope to reach truth, and attain a proper stability and certainty in our determinations" is the "moderate scepticism"[494] whose principles are so convincingly applied in the section on miracles.

488 Hume, Enquiry, section VII, part II.
489 Ibid., section IV, part I.
490 Ibid., section VII, part I.
491 Hume, Dialogues, p. 29.
492 Hume, A Treatise on Human Nature, Book I, part I, section VI.
493 Ibid., Book I, part II, section VI.
494 Hume, Enquiry, section XII, part II.

Various attempts have been made to explain these contradictions. Perhaps Hume in his innermost heart was not quite free from certain religious feelings, which nobody better analyzed than Hume himself in his *Natural History of Religion*. Perhaps regard for his place in society induced him to pose as a deist. Perhaps also he considered it opportune to operate occasionally with the old device of a twofold, that is, a scientific and a religious truth. However this may be, in the history of ideas Hume has his prominent place not as a human being with the weaknesses of his wishes and fears, with his inclination to opportunist compromises, but as the classic representative of skeptic empiricism and consequently of an atheist philosophy[495] whose principles he has developed most brilliantly in his *Enquiry concerning Human Understanding* and in his *Treatise of Human Nature.*

It was Hume's antitheological philosophy that decisively influenced Kant's theory of knowledge, as Kant himself admitted.[496] In view of this influence it is from the first most unlikely that theological implications can be found in this theory. Nevertheless, it is precisely this interpretation of Kant's epistemology which the Swiss essayist Hans Urs von Balthasar[497] tries to advance.

Kant's philosophy attempts to show that human reason is not able to answer questions referring to objects outside the realm of human experience, that is, in the first place, eschatological questions. The preface to the first edition of Kant's *Critique of Pure Reason* begins: "Human reason, in one sphere of its cognition, is called upon to consider questions, which it cannot decline, as they are presented by its own nature, but which it cannot answer, as they transcend every faculty of the mind."[498] That transcendental philosophy is directly opposed to that theologized metaphysics which pretends to answer such questions. It is, as Kant formulates it – and Balthasar is sincere enough to quote it – "a science of the limits of human reason."[499] This "science" shows that the last question that human reason can answer is the very question of the logical conditions of cognition. The question is: How is scientific cognition, that is,

495 Fritz Mauthner, in Der Atheismus, II, pp. 564, 584, characterizes Hume's philosophy as "skeptic atheism." He says: "Hume has released the entire human thinking from every religious fetter"; and J. M. Robertson in A History of Free Thought (4th ed. [London, 1936], II, p. 758), says Hume's "posthumous Dialogues concerning Natural Religion (1779) admit, though indirectly, the untenableness of deism, and fall back decisively upon the atheistic or agnostic position."

496 Immanuel Kant, Prolegomena zu einer jeden künftigen Metaphysik, IV, p. 260: "I frankly avow: It was David Hume's reminder that many years ago interrupted my dogmatic slumber and gave to my research in the field of speculative philosophy an entirely new direction."

497 Hans Urs von Balthasar, Prometheus, pp. 91 seqq.

498 Immanuel Kant, Critique of Pure Reason, (= Everyman's Library, No. 909; New York, 1934), p. 1.

499 Balthasar, Prometheus, p. 93.

experience, possible? This is the "transcendental" question that Kant distinguished from the "transcendent" question, that is, the question which transcends the realm of human experience, the metaphysical question in the traditional sense of the term, implying the question of the *eschaton*. Kant's transcendental philosophy is a theory of cognition, an epistemology that has nothing to do with problems such as God, the immortality of the soul, its fate after death, the end of the world – in other words, with eschatology. If, as Balthasar says, "apocalypse of the soul" is but a concrete term for "eschatology,"[500] Kant's transcendental philosophy explicitly excludes any kind of apocalypse or eschatology from its own sphere. Nevertheless, Balthasar speaks of "Kant's transcendental eschatology" and characterizes Kant's theory of cognition, his determination of the condition of the possibility of cognition, as "self-apocalypse," as "method of the inner apocalypse."[501] This, however, is possible only by changing the meaning of *eschaton*. Balthasar says: "[Kant's] last things are no longer God and world things, but the conditions of his intellectual existence [*Geistsein*]. The 'metaphysical' eschatology is replaced by the 'transcendental' eschatology."[502] However, a "transcendental eschatology" – if "transcendental" is used in its Kantian meaning – is a self-contradiction; for "eschatology" is, by its very nature and in its only admissible sense, the answer to those questions which Kant's transcendental philosophy refuses to answer because they "transcend" human experience and belong, therefore, to metaphysics which Kant's transcendental philosophy has destroyed.[503] To interpret Kant's epistemology as eschatology is an unfortunate distortion of the clearly expressed intentions of this thinker.

500 Ibid., p. 3.

501 Ibid., p. 92.

502 Ibid.

503 It is true that Kant in his moral philosophy has abandoned the antimetaphysical tendency and tried to justify from the point of view of "practical reason" the theological dogmas of the existence of God, the immortality of the soul, and the freedom of will, all of which he rejected from the point of "pure reason." But only Kant's epistemology is here in question.

Chapter VIII Saint-Simon's "New Religion" and Proudhon's Social Theory

Saint-Simon's Philosophy of History

Henri de Saint-Simon's philosophy of history and his plans for the reformation of society are essentially determined by the conflict between empirical science and metaphysical religion. The meaning of history is the emancipation of human nature from the superstitious beliefs in transcendent forces, and a future society will be founded on an encyclopedia of scientific knowledge. It will be an industrial society whose leaders will be scientific and industrial captains.[504] The *leitmotif* of his philosophy is the anti-Christian truth: "Man must believe only in facts recognized by reason and confirmed by experience."[505] Despite this antireligious and especially anti-Christian attitude, Etienne Gilson interprets Saint-Simon's philosophy as "a new Christianism of science."[506] To justify this interpretation he refers to statements in Saint-Simon's *Lettres d'un habitant de Genève*, which, according to Gilson, mean the establishment of a "new religion." "By the side of God sits Newton. The council, representing God on earth, will be called the Council of Newton; it will create others, of which each will erect a mausoleum to Newton, surrounded by colleges, laboratories, workshops – in a word by all institutions necessary for the scientific organization of human society. But let us not hesitate to say that this social reformer considered himself at the same time a religious chief. 'It is God who has spoken to me, he calmly declares in the second *Lettre*. Can a man invent a religion superior to all those which have existed?'"[507] However, the first statement quoted by Gilson is taken from a passage of the second letter, which is

504 See F. M. H. Markham (ed.), Introduction to Henri Comte de Saint-Simon, Selected Writings (Oxford, 1952).

505 "L'homme ne doit croire que les choses avouées par la raison et confirmées par l'expérience." Saint-Simon refers to this "vérité antichrétienne" as proclaimed by Bacon and Descartes in his work: Introduction aux Travaux Scientificques du Dixneuviéme Siécle in Œuvres Choisies (Brussels, 1859), I, p. 209.

506 Gilson, Les Metamorphoses, p. 252.

507 Ibid., p. 250.

introduced by the following sentences: "Is it an apparition? Is it only a dream? I do not know, but I am sure that I had the sensation of which I shall now give you a report. Last night I heard the following words."[508] Then Saint-Simon lets God speak, the God of the Bible who has forbidden Adam to eat from the tree of knowledge. But the words that he puts in God's mouth are so obviously incompatible with the God of the Bible that without a doubt Saint-Simon is consciously using a fiction, and is referring to a fiction when he, at the beginning of the third letter, says: "God has spoken to me." For in the same letter he says in a postscript: "I intend to write you a letter in which I shall consider religion as a human invention; I shall consider it as the only kind of political institution [*la seule nature d'institution politique*] which aims at a general organization of humanity."[509] Moreover, Saint-Simon in his writings speaks not only as the "voice of God" but also, frequently, as the "voice" of Bacon, Socrates, or Charlemagne.[510] His statement: "God has spoken to me" cannot be understood without taking into consideration what he says in his *Introduction aux Travaux Scientifiques du Dixneuvième Siècle*. In the chapter "Sur l'Unité de Cause" we read: "The idea of God being invalid [*vicieuse*] all applications of this idea must be invalid ... I say that I have demonstrated that the idea of God must not be applied in the sciences of physics; but I do not say that it should not serve in political combinations, at least during a long time. This idea is the best method of motivating higher legislation."[511] It is especially important to note Saint-Simon's statements in the chapter "Sur la Religion." "My opinion: I believe in the necessity of a religion for the maintenance of the social order." But opposing "physicism" (that is, natural science) to religion, he says: "I think that the facts force us to distinguish two doctrines: Physicism for the instructed people, and deism for the ignorant class."[512] "I say, that there will be necessarily two different doctrines: that of the scholars, they will be *physicists*; that of the people, it will remain *deist*."[513]

It is not possible to understand Saint-Simon's philosophy without considering his adoption of the device of the "twofold truth" – not, indeed, in its original sense that what is true according to reason (*secundum rationem*) may be untrue according to faith (*secundum fidem*); but in the sense that what is true (that is, useful) in politics, may be untrue in science. Saint-Simon's "twofold truth" is the Platonic principle of truthful (meaning politically useful) lies.[514] Saint- Simon believed in religion, but only as an instrument of politics.

508 Saint-Simon, Introduction, I, p. 32.
509 Ibid., p. 41.
510 Markham (ed.), Introduction, p. XVIII.
511 Saint-Simon, Introduction, I, pp. 218 seq.
512 Ibid., p. 214.
513 Ibid., p. 229.
514 Plato, Laws, 662b.

It is from this point of view that the following statements in his last work (*Nouveau Christianisme; Dialogues entre un Conservateur et un Novateur*) may be interpreted. "The Conservative: Do you believe in God? The Reformer: Yes, I believe in God. The Conservative: Do you believe that the Christian religion has a divine origin? The Reformer: Yes, I do."[515] If it is not assumed, however, that the answers of the Reformer are given with the mental reservation of a twofold truth, the confession of the Christian faith in the work Saint-Simon wrote shortly before his death can hardly be considered as anything but a deathbed conversion[516] that must not influence the interpretation of his previous works.

Proudhon's Social Theory

If we are to believe that the philosophers of the Enlightenment and Comte, the passionate opponent of theology, rebuilt Augustine's City of God; that the French *Encyclopedia* was "a koran"; that Lessing, the defender of human reason against metaphysical obscurantism, was a Joachite apocalyptic; that in the writings of Hume, the protagonist of skeptic empiricism, belief in revelation was implied, then we must not be astonished to learn from Löwith that Proudhon, the most radical atheist, was a "religious soul" and "the theologian of progress."[517]

Before examining Löwith's interpretation, some statements by Proudhon should be quoted, made in chapter VIII of his *Système des Contradictions Eco-*

515 Markham (ed.), Introduction, p. 83.

516 Markham (ed.), Introduction, rejects this interpretation: "There is no essential change in St. Simon's ideas from the earliest to the last writings" (p. XX). How is it possible to reconcile the statements that religion is a human invention and that the Christian religion has a divine origin, without assuming that mental reservation of twofold truth? After Saint-Simon's death his doctrine assumed – under the influence of Enfantin – a more or less religious form. But F. A. Hayek, in The Counter-Revolution of Science (Glencoe, Illinois, 1952, p. 152), perhaps exaggerates when he says that the doctrine "was turned into a religion." The Hegelian Eduard Gans, who made the acquaintanance of the Saint-Simonians in Paris in 1830, reports in his Rückblicke auf Personen und Zustände (Berlin, 1836), p. 92, that Benjamin Constant told him the Saint-Simonians had asked Constant, about a year before, how they could spread their principles; and that his answer was: transform them into a religion (quoted by Hayek, The Counter-Revolution, p. 234). But Gans got the impression that the "religion" of the Saint-Simonians was not more than a "superfluous disguise" and that only their social and economic principles deserved serious consideration ("Wenn wir somit uns von dem religiösen Kleide abwenden, das die St. Simonisten überflüssigerweise umwarfen, so wird doch ein ernsteres Eingehen in ihre gesellschaftlichen und nationalökonomischen Grundsätze nicht entbehrt werden können" [Gans, Rückblicke, pp. 94–95]).

517 Löwith, Meaning in History, pp. 61, 65.

nomiques ou Philosophie de la Misère.[518] Referring to Voltaire's famous word: "If God did not exist it would be necessary to invent him," Proudhon stigmatizes it as a "strange aberration of a great mind." "For my part I say: The first duty of man, on becoming intelligent and free, is to continually hunt the idea of God out of his mind and conscience. For God, if he exists, is essentially hostile to our nature, and we do not depend at all upon his authority. We arrive at knowledge in spite of him, at comfort in spite of him, at society in spite of him; every step we take in advance is a victory in which we crush Divinity" (pp. 447–448). "Your name [the name "God"], so long the last word of the *savant*, the sanction of the judge, the force of the prince, the hope of the poor, the refuge of the repentant sinner, – this incommunicable name, I say, henceforth an object of contempt and curses, shall be a hissing among men. For God is stupidity and cowardice, God is hypocricy and falsehood; God is tyranny and misery; God is evil." "I swear with hand extend to heaven, that you are only the tormentor of my reason, the spectre of my conscience" (p. 450). It is evidently not God as a really existing being, but the idea of or the belief in God, a "spectre," to which Proudhon refers. At the end of this chapter Proudhon says: "What solution will result later from these data? Will God, in the end, be found a reality? – I do not know whether I shall ever know. If it is true, on the one hand, that I have today no more reason for affirming the reality of man, an illogical and contradictory being, than the reality of God, an inconceivable and unmanifested being, I know at least, from the radical opposition of these two natures, that I have nothing to hope or to fear from the mysterious author whom my consciousness involuntarily supposes; I know that my most authentic tendencies separate me daily from the contemplation of this idea; that practical *atheism* must be henceforth the law of my heart and my reason; that from observable necessity I must continually learn the rule of my conduct; that any mystical commandment, any divine right, which should be proposed to me, must be rejected and combated by me; that a return to God through religion, idleness, ignorance, or submission, is an outrage upon myself; and that if I must sometimes be reconciled with God, this reconciliation, impossible *as long as I live* and in which I should have everything to gain and nothing to lose, can be accomplished only by my destruction."[519]

---

518 Œuvres Complètes de P.-J. Proudhon, Vol. IV (Paris, 1867). English translation: The Works of P. J. Proudhon. System of Economic Contradictions (Boston, 1888). The following quotations are taken from the English translation.

519 Ibid., p. 468. Italics mine. George Woodcock in (his biography) Pierre-Joseph Proudhon (New York, 1956), says quite correctly of this chapter in Proudhon's work: "here Proudhon issues a passionate call to liberation from the reactionary idea of deity" (p. 98). But later, after quoting Proudhon's statements: "I affirm that God, if there is a God, bears no resemblance to the effigies which the philosophers and the priests have made of him; that he neither thinks nor acts according to the law of analysis, foresight and progress, which is the distinctive characteristic of man; that on the contrary, he

This is the unreserved avowal of an atheist; but of an atheist who is well aware of the limitations of his rational cognition. In view of these statements it is hardly possible to consider Proudhon as a "religious" soul and "theologian" of progress. Löwith, of course, cannot deny that Proudhon declared God or the absolute the one great obstacle to human progress, the "ghost of our conscience," and that "all the attributes of divine providence ... are nothing else than a caricature of humanity, incompatible with autonomous civilization"; nevertheless Löwith asserts that Proudhon "was deeply marked by Christianity in his blasphemies," and that "his language, imagination, and turn of mind were decidedly theological."[520] The method by which Löwith achieves his conclusion is characteristic. He frankly admits that Proudhon teaches: "Man has to replace God, and the belief in human progress has to supplant the faith in providence."[521] But Löwith adds: "At first, however, it seems impossible to reduce the working of God to the labor of men; for all traditional understanding of history depends on the distinction between the will of God and the will of man, between hidden designs and visible agencies, between prompting necessity and personal freedom of choice." This statement presupposes the ex-

---

seems to follow an inverse retrograde path; that intelligence, liberty, personality are constituted otherwise in God than in us, and that this originality of nature ... makes of God a being who is essentially anti-civilised, anti-liberal, anti-human," Woodcock says: "These are not the statements of an atheist ... Rather we are in the presence of the final contradiction – God and Man. And whether we regard God as an objective reality or as a projection of human beliefs and traditions does not matter a great deal. The important thing is that a principle of evil and a principle of good appear as active and rival entities, in Proudhon's world." An atheist from the point of view of the Christian religion – and this *is* the religion from the point of view of which the question arises as to whether Proudhon was an atheist – is the one who denies the existence of God as he is presented in dogmas of the Christian religion: as a supernatural being whose essential qualities are to be absolutely powerful and, above all, absolutely good and just, who created man in his own image. That Proudhon denied the existence of *this* God and consequently declared himself expressly to be an atheist, is shown in the quoted statements and even in the statement quoted by Woodcock. Proudhon, when speaking of "God," frequently means the "idea" of God. When he speaks of God as an existing being, he adds "if there is a God." That seems to mean that he does not exclude the possibility of the existence of a God, but of a God who is certainly not the God of the Christian religion. And what Proudhon has to say about the former is hardly compatible with the nature of a being who deserves the name of "God." Woodcock thinks he can support his second interpretation by two extracts from Proudhon's diary during the year 1864: (1) "God and man, neither is more than the other; they are two incomplete realities, which have no fulness of existence." (2) "God is necessary to reason but rejected by reason." These statements, however, may be used rather against Woodcock's interpretation. An "existence" which is not full existence, is no existence at all, and a God "rejected by reason" can only be an *idea* of God, not God as an existing being.

520 Löwith, Meaning in History, pp. 63, 64, 65.

521 Ibid., p. 62.

istence of God and his "hidden designs." Only under this presupposition does it seem "at first" impossible to reduce the working of God to the labor of man. Löwith presents Proudhon's doctrine as if it accepted this presupposition, and as if Proudhon attempted to solve the antagonism between the working of God and the labor of man. Löwith says: "Proudhon tried to solve this antagonism by a sociological transposition." However, Proudhon did not at all try to "solve" this antagonism because it did not exist for him. He denied it. According to Löwith, Proudhon thought: "The providence of God is nothing else than the 'collective instinct' or 'universal reason' of man as a social being. The God of history is but man's own creation and 'atheism (that is, humanism) the foundation of every theodicy.'"[522] Löwith's statements: The providence of God "*is*...," the God of history "*is*..." convey the impression that Proudhon did not teach that the providence of God *is not*, that the God of history *is not*, that there is *no* providence of God or a God of history; that the doctrine of Proudhon is merely a particular interpretation of the providence of God whose existence this allegedly only "apparent" atheist presupposes – not explicitly and consciously, but implicitly and unconsciously, that theodicy is to Proudhon a real and not a merely sham problem. By this method an atheist can be transformed into a theologian, and his fight against the belief in God and providence into his "faith in a coming Kingdom of God."[523]

Characteristically Löwith's interpretation of Proudhon's atheistic social philosophy follows, in principle, a study by the French Jesuit Henri de Lubac,[524] who asserts, "that our anti-clerical Proudhon deserves in his own way, and under more than one heading, the name of a theologian."[525] Lubac gives a whole chapter, entitled "Proudhon the Theologian,"[526] to this thesis, which he tries to defend with remarkable objectivity by referring also to antitheological declarations of Proudhon; and these are, if not more numerous, certainly more convincing than the symptoms that Lubac is able to produce for Proudhon's alleged theology.

Lubac says that Proudhon "constantly quoted, criticized and commented upon" many theologians, that he offered his services to the editor of a Catholic encyclopedia,[527] that "he gave a delicate and very apposite criticism" of a theological work,[528] and that he expressed his opinions on the Jansenist quarrel;

---

522 Ibid., p. 62.

523 Ibid., p. 66.

524 Henry de Lubac, S. J., Proudhon et le Christianisme (Paris, 1945). English translation by R. E. Scantlebury, The Un-Marxian Socialist. A Study of Proudhon (New York, 1948). See above, Introduction, note 23.

525 Ibid. (English translation), p. 102. Lubac quotes André Rousseau's *Proudhon et nous*: "This frantic anticlerical is an unsatiated theologian."

526 Ibid., pp. 102–126.

527 Ibid., p. 104.

528 Ibid., p. 105.

that he pronounced special interests in theology; and that he studied this discipline intensively. Lubac quotes Proudhon's statement: "[Theology] is a study I have never abandoned and which still seems to me the most beautiful and most fruitful of all."[529] In order to criticize theology and to show its futility, as Proudhon did, it is, of course, essential to study it carefully; but studying theology for this purpose does not turn a scholar into a theologian. Lubac does not deny that "Proudhon's theological readings and studies, however great the part they played in his life, were undertaken more from a political and social than from a really religious point of view."[530] Lubac admits that Proudhon "affected to have a great contempt for classical theology; it pleased him to see in it only a distortion of Christ's teaching, as regrettable from the intellectual as from the moral point of view. He said, for instance, that it was 'the science of the infinitely ridiculous.'"[531] Undoubtedly some of the theologians Proudhon studied were brilliant polemicists whose technique of arguing was highly effective. But this technique is not specifically theological and can be applied to the discussion of any problem. Proudhon may have learned much in this respect useful in his own fight against theology. This is hardly a reason to call him a theologian or to assume that he has been "molded"[532] by theology. Lubac quotes Proudhon's statement "I have been thinking of God since I began to exist";[533] but in the mouth of a declared antitheist this does not mean he was thinking of God as an existing being, but that he was contemplating the idea of God as presented in the theology he tried to destroy.

Lubac says further that Proudhon had Catholic friends; that, as a printer and proofreader, he had to deal with works of theology; that in his application for an award to be granted by the Academy of Besançon he declared that he "learned the laws of reasoning and of style from those great masters [Bossuet, Bergier, etc.]."[534] However, he did not declare that he shared their theological views. Lubac mentions that Proudhon as a printer had helped in printing the works of theologians;[535] but printing a theological work does not mean being a theologian. Lubac notes that Proudhon "outlined for a while a quasi-system of apologetics, after the style of Joseph de Maistre," but he adds "an ambiguous system which could equally well be turned into Naturalism," but admits: "These leanings to apologetics, however, already rather complicated, were not long in giving way to anti-religious tendencies."[536] He mentions that

529 Ibid., p. 106.
530 Ibid., p. 108.
531 Ibid., p. 105.
532 Ibid., p. 115.
533 Ibid., p. 106.
534 Ibid., p. 107.
535 Ibid., p. 108.
536 Ibid., p. 110.

Proudhon, as a youth, was "led astray for a while ... by Deism," but adds that "he was not long in seizing upon the inconsistency of this 'would-be philosophical Theism'." He reproduces extensively Proudhon's criticism of that theological doctrine.[537] Showing Proudhon's opposition to Protestantism, Lubac, as a Catholic priest, emphasizes that Proudhon's criticism was in some respects favorable to Catholicism; that he, for example, "had less reluctance than many of the faithful of his day in sharing the point of view of those who upheld infallibility."[538] Rejection of Protestantism does not mean being a Catholic, and even the most radical adversary of religion and theology may recognize the excellence of the organization of the Catholic Church, without becoming – for this reason – a theologian.

Lubac particularly stresses the argument that Proudhon had a profound knowledge of the Bible;[539] that he again and again quoted the Scripture and interpreted it – most frequently, in opposition to theological interpretation; that he was especially interested in the problem of justice as presented in the Old and the New Testaments. However, Proudhon was interested in the Bible not from a theological, that is, a religious, but from a historical point of view – not as a theologian who has to accept its content as a revelation of divine truth, but as a scientific critic. Lubac's statement that Proudhon had a "Biblical turn of mind"[540] is without foundation. In view of the extraordinary influence of the Bible on Western civilization, familiarity with this book is indispensable for any study of that civilization. It is absurd to assume that a scholar who meets this requirement has a Biblical mind.

Lubac attaches importance to Proudhon's disagreement with Renan's *Vie de Jésus*.[541] This disagreement was not caused by Renan's rejection of the theological interpretation of the New Testament. Proudhon's hostile reaction to Renan's work can be explained entirely – not only partly, as Lubac suggests – by Proudhon's jealousy. Lubac, with admirable objectivity, reports that Proudhon, "for over twenty years had been collecting notes hoping one day to deal thoroughly with the subject himself, when the *Vie de Jésus* appeared. Renan had got in ahead of him, and it was only natural that he should feel 'a certain resentment',"[542] as Proudhon himself frankly confessed.[543] The fact stressed by Lubac that Proudhon expressed greatest admiration for the figure of Christ[544] does not make this atheist a theologian; he admired Jesus not as a

537 Ibid., p. 112.
538 Ibid., p. 114.
539 Ibid., pp. 115 seqq.
540 Ibid., p. 115.
541 Ibid., pp. 99, 119.
542 Ibid., p. 100.
543 In a letter to J. Buzon, quoted by Lubac, ibid., p. 100.
544 Ibid., p. 122.

deity, not even as a religious founder, but as "a moralist, a social reformer, *in fine* a lover of justice."[545] Proudhon declared: "The teaching of Christ was entirely social, it was neither political nor theological."[546] It was not as a theologian, but as a social reformer that Proudhon appreciated the teaching of Christ.

545 In a letter to Defontaine, quoted by Lubac, ibid., p. 120.
546 Quoted by Lubac, ibid., p. 122.

Chapter IX Comte's Positive Philosophy

The Catholic theologian Sertillanges considers Comte's positive philosophy "derived from Catholicism";[547] but the Catholic philosopher Maritain sees in it a religious ideology to which Catholicism is opposed, namely Gnosticism.[548]

547 Sertillanges, Le Christianisme, II, p. 240.

548 Jacques Maritain, On the Philosophy of History (New York, 1957), p. 31: "The Gnosticism of history... which was carried by Hegel to supreme metaphysical heights ... is to be found also, at quite another level, in a system as completely fascinated by positive sciences and as decidedly anti-metaphysical as Comte's system is." How an antimetaphysical "Gnosticism" is possible, is difficult to understand inview of the highly metaphysical character of the gnosis. Maritain says (pp. 22–23): "The Hegelian metaphysics and the Hegelian philosophy of history are modern Gnosticism – they are pure Gnosticism." But "Gnosticism of history" is a "spurious" philosophy of history. "Spurious philosophy of history," Maritain says, "is Gnosticism in the most general sense of this expression and insofar as it is characterized by the four 'capital sins'" (p. 31). These "capital sins" of a spurious philosophy of history are: "First, its almost inevitably oversimplyfied, arbitrary and wanton approach in regard to the choice of materials, the historical value of which is assumed for the sake of the cause; secondly, its self-deceptive ambition to get an *a priori* explanation of the course of human historiy; thirdly, its self-deceptive ambition to get an *all-inclusive* explanation of the meaning of human history; and fourthly, its self-deceptive ambition to get at a so-called *scientific* explanation of history" (p. 30). Comte's philosophy may be guilty of these "capital sins"; but why should a philosophy of history guilty of these sins be "Gnosticism," which is an entirely ahistoric view of the world? The answer to this question may perhaps be found in Maritain's definition of a "genuine" philosophy of history: "No philosophy of history can be genuine," he says, "if the general philosophy it presupposes and of which it is a part, does not recognize the existence of human free will (together with the other properties of the human person) and the existence of God: the consequence of these two truths being that human history implies a double kind of contingency, on the one hand with respect to the transcendent freedom of God, and on the other hand with respect to human free will as well as to natural accidents and vicissitudes" (p. 34). This means: Only Catholic theology of history is "genuine" philosophy of history. Since neither Hegel's nor Cormte's philosophy of history conform to Catholic theology of history they are "Gnostic," meaning: heretic. Since Maritain is a faithful son of the Catholic Church, it is perhaps not superfluous to quote what the Catholic Dictionary *Der Grosse Herder*, 5th ed. (Freiburg, 1954), IV, p. 200, says about "Gnosticism": "In seiner gedankliche In-

Löwith goes so far as to interpret Comte's antitheological philosophy of history as a theodicy, an attempt to "reconcile the world to God."[549] Löwith asserts that "the revolution which had been proclaimed [by Joachim] within the framework of an eschatological faith and with reference to a perfect monastic life was taken over five centuries later by a philosophical priesthood," especially by Comte, whose scientific age is a "'spiritual' realization of the Kingdom of God on earth";[550] Voegelin asserts that Comte's theory of a sequence of theological, metaphysical, and scientific phases is a variation of Joachim's "conception of history as a sequence of three ages of which the third is intelligibly the final Third Realm";[551] and declares Comte a "revolutionary activist," in whose doctrine – just as in those of Marx and Hitler – "volitional" gnosis assumes "the form of activist redemption of man and society."[552] This misinterpretation of Comte's philosophy is based on the assumption formulated by Voegelin,[553] that Comte had "religious experiences"; but Voegelin admits that the "religious experiences" of the antireligious Comte "prohibit the asking of metaphysical questions."[554] Here again appears the inevitable logical fallacy of

---

tuition und visionäre Schau verbindenden Denkart behauptet der *Gnostiker* die gegenseitige Durchdringung von Makro- und Mikrokosmos, die Durchbeseeltheit beider auf Grund der erlebten Harmonie zwischen dem eigenen Sein und der Welt … Die Entrückung Gottes ist meist vom metaphysischen Dualismus bestimmt, wonach Gott, der reine Geist, als das absolut Gute der in sich bösen Materie gegenübersteht … Der Mensch ist, indem er der Materie unterworfen ist, von Gott gänzlich getrennt. Der Logos aber lehrt den Menschen den Weg des Aufstieges. [The Gnostic, combining in his thinking intellectual intuition with visionary view, asserts on the basis of the experienced harmony between his own being and the world that macro- and microcosmos penetrate each other, that both are animated … The remoteness of God is mostly determined by the metaphysical dualism according to which God, the pure spirit, is opposed as the absolute Good to the evil matter… Man as subjected to matter is totally separated from God. But the logos shows man the way of ascent.]" If this is a correct characterization of a Gnostic world view, it is hardly possible to interpret Comte's positivism as Gnosticism.

549 Löwith, Meaning in History, p. 67.

550 Ibid., p. 159.

551 Voegelin, New Science of Politics, p. 111.

552 Ibid., p. 124.

553 Ibid., p. 24.

554 In his Wissenschaft, Politik und Gnosis, Voegelin asserts that Comte's philosophy contains the above-mentioned *"Frageverbot,"* the prohibition of questions about the origin of man and nature, aiming at God as the creator and ruler of the world. According to Voegelin Comte teaches: "The one who asks questions about essence, vocation, and destiny of man is, for the time being, ignored: later, when the system of Positivism will be carried through on the social level, he must be silenced by appropriate measures [Wer Fragen nach Wesen, Beruf und Schicksal des Menschen stellt, werde vorläufig ignoriert; später, wenn sich das System des Positivismus sozial durchgesetzt habe, müsse er durch geeignete Massnahmen zum Schweigen gebracht werden.]" (p. 37). Voegelin refers to

a contradiction in terms, for the essence of a religious experience is to ask metaphysical questions and to find the answers in the wishful imagination that is

the first lecture of Comte's Cours de Philosophie Positive, without quoting a specific passage of this work and without indicating the page on which Comte's thought is to be found. There is a passage on page 9 of the first lecture which deals with the question concerned. It runs as follows: "Enfin, dans l'état positif, l'esprit humain reconnaissant l'impossibilité d'obtenir des notions absolues, renonce à chercher l'origine et la destination de l'universe, et à connaître les causes intimes des phénomènes, pour s'attacher uniquement a découvrir, par l'usage bien combiné du raisonnement et de l'observation, leurs lois effectives, c'est-à-dire leurs relations invariables de succession et de similitude. [Finally, in the positive state, the human mind, recognizing the impossibility of obtaining absolute notions, renounces the search after the origin and destination of the universe and the cognition of the inner causes of phenomena in order to apply itself to discover, by the combined means of reasoning and observation, their real laws, that is, their invariable relations of succession and resemblance.]" This is certainly not a "prohibition" of the question about the origin and the destiny of the universe; it is simply the renunciation of a question which human reason cannot answer. There is, however, another passage (page 13) that Voegelin probably had in mind when he attributed to Comte's positive philosophy the "Frageverbot". Comte says of the positive philosophy: "... dont la plus haute ambition est de découvrir les lois des phénomènes, et dont le premier caractère propre est précisément de regarder comme nècessairement interdits à la raison humaine tous ces sublimes mystères, que la philosophie theologique explique, au contraire, avec une si admirable facilité jusque dans leurs moindres details [... whose highest ambition is to discover the laws of phenomena and whose first characteristic is exactly to regard as necessarily interdicted to human reason the sublime mysteries which theological philosophy explains with such an admirable facility in their minutest details]". Taking the word "interdits" literally, this passage seems indeed to express a prohibition. But that which is "interdicted," is not a question, but the "mysteries" that theology pretends to explain; and these mysteries are "interdicted" "à la raison humaine," to human reason. In the statement that certain mysteries are "interdicted" to human reason, the term "interdicted" must not be taken literally. A mystery cannot be "interdicted." In the literal sense of the word only an action can be interdicted, for an interdiction is directed at human will, not at cognition as the function of human reason. By stating that these mysteries are interdicted to human reason Comte means, merely, that these mysteries are not a possible object of human cognition, that they are suprahuman and that therefore the positive philosophy renaunces dealing with them. The statement means exactly the same as the first quoted sentence: "L'esprit humain ... renonce a chercher l'origine et la destination de l'univers." That Voegelin imputes to Comte's philosophy a "prohibition" in the literal sense of the term, a command, a "ukase," as he says in another connection (see op. cit., p. 36), is evident from his statement that according to this philosophy the man who asks the question concerned must be silenced by appropriate measures. In the passage of the first lecture which alone could be the basis of Voegelin's assertion of Comte's "Frageverbot," there is not the slightest hint of measures to be taken against a man who asks questions whose answers are beyond human reason. What Voegelin misinterprets as a "Frageverbot" is not the interdiction of a question, but the resigned recognition of the impossibility of an answer.

the specific product of this experience. A religious experience which prohibits the asking of metaphysical questions is like a Christian who does not believe in God, or an atheist who does.

The view that Comte's positivistic philosophy is only a hidden eschatological speculation about history is based on the assumption the he – like the Judeao-Christian prophets, relying on a belief in progress – predicts a final state of perfection in the future, implying the end of history. Löwith says of this kind of philosophy in general that the leading idea of progress is "as Christian by derivation as it is anti-Christian by implication," that its starting point "is an eschatological anticipation of a future salvation."[555] Comte, he asserts, "blames Christianity for having barred its own progressive tendency by its claim to being the final stage of man's progression; and yet he attributes the self-same ultimacy to the scientific stage,"[556] which he predicts. "The leading idea of a temporal progression toward a final goal in the future reflects the derivation of positive philosophy from the theological interpretation of history as a history of fulfillment and salvation."[557] However, as pointed out on pp. 39 seq., even if the idea of progress were specifically Christian, there is a fundamental difference between the Christian and the positivistic values to be realized by this progress, and the ideological bases on which the values are assumed and the future course of their realization foreseen. Any attempt to conceive of the relation between Christian theology and positive philosophy as anything but as an unsumountable antagonism is without foundation.

Christian theology interprets history as the realization of the personal and inscrutable will of an omnipotent God directed at the salvation of the individual soul of man, that is, a deliverance from sin through the atoning and redemptive work of his son, Jesus Christ. To foresee this fulfillment in the future is the privilege of prophets endowed by the grace of God with the faculty of supernatural vision; and the state of the redeemed soul is indeed an ultimate state of absolute perfection, the union with God, which does not allow any further progress. Comte's positive philosophy interprets history as a progressive evolution determined by impersonal laws that are learned by observation of facts controlled by human reason. The meaning of this evolution is the realization of values that have an emphatically accentuated social character; the welfare of society which, in the first place, is material, but also intellectual. But intellectual progress is the progress of rational science and has nothing to do with salvation, that is, redemption from sin. Salvation is a process that refers to the individual human soul, not to society. Comte's positive philosophy is directed precisely against this individualistic attitude of the theological doctrine of salvation. "It is necessary," he says, "to strip away the last metaphysic-

555 Löwith, Meaning in History, p. 61.
556 Ibid., p. 83.
557 Ibid., p. 68.

al illusions, and show what is the true human point of view, – that is not individual but social; for under either the statical or the dynamical aspect, Man is a mere abstraction, and there is nothing real but Humanity, regarded intellectually or, yet more, morally."[558]

A collectivistic philosophy that considers the individual human being as a mere "abstraction", not as a real entity, has no room for salvation. The state of society, in the scientific age predicted by Comte, is the very opposite – indeed the direct negation – of Christian salvation. By progress as the effect of social evolution, Comte understands "improvement," "amelioration" subject to limits, general and special. "Taking the human race as a whole, and not any one people, it appears that human development brings after it, in two ways, an ever-growing amelioration, first, in the radical condition of Man, which no one disputes; and next, in his corresponding faculties, which is a view much less attended to. There is no need to dwell upon the improvement in the condition of human existence, both by the increasing action of Man on his environment through the advancement of the sciences and arts, and by the constant amelioration of his customs and manners; and again, by the gradual improvement in social organization."[559] Progress refers to the external circumstances of man (*"système extérieur de nos Conditions d'existence"*), to the habits and mores, and especially to social organization. Nothing could be more alien to the fulfillment of the Christian *eschaton* than this progress of positive philosophy. Positive philosophy, Comte emphasizes, is "confining research to the invariable relations which constitute natural laws." He repeats Bacon's statement "that observed facts are the only basis of sound speculation"; he stresses the principle "that no proposition that is not finally reducible to the enunciation of a fact, particular or general, can offer any real and intelligible meaning."[560] He characterizes the logical and scientific method of his positive philosophy as follows: "The first consist in the preponderance of observation over imagination, contrary to the earliest mode of proceeding. We have no longer anything to fear from theological appeals to the imagination ... It is still necessary to point out that laws are the true subject of investigation, and that the function of imagination in philosophizing is to create or perfect the means of connection between established facts, but not, in any case, to meddle with the point of departure or the direction of the inquiry ... *To see in order to foresee is the business of science: to foresee everything without having seen anything is only an absurd metaphysical Utopia* which still obtains too much favor. The scienti-

558 Auguste Comte, Cours de Philosophie Positive [1830–1842] 4th ed. (Paris, 1877), VI, p. 590. English translation, The Positive Philosophy of Auguste Comte, freely translated and condensed by Harriet Martineau (New York, 1858), p. 797.

559 Comte, Cours de Philosophie Positive, IV, p. 275; Martineau, transl. p. 467.

560 Comte, Cours de Philosophie Positive, VI, p. 600; Martineau, transl. p. 799.

fic view which corresponds with this logical one is, that the positive philosophy substitutes the relative for the absolute in the study of qualities."[561]

Is this the creed of a "religion" of progress, "the eschatological anticipation of a future salvation?" What can a scientific attempt to foresee future events on the basis of observation of facts have in common with an eschatological anticipation of a future salvation, especially if, as Löwith admits, "Comte understood only the obvious antagonism between progress and providence but not the hidden dependence of the secular religion of progress on the Christian faith, hope, and expectation of progressing toward a final fulfillment of history by judgment and salvation"?[562] And "hidden", indeed, is this "dependence."

A theological interpretation conceives history as the realization of an absolute value. But Comte emphasizes the relativistic character of his philosophy. The "inevitable passage from the absolute to the relative is one of the most important philosophical results of each of the intellectual revolutions which has carried on every kind of speculation from theological or metaphysical to the scientific state. In a scientific view, this contrast between the relative and the absolute may be regarded as the most decisive manifestation of the antipathy between the modern philosophy and the ancient. All investigation into the nature of beings and their first and final causes, must always be absolute; whereas the study of the laws of phenomena must be relative, since it supposes a continuous progress of speculation subject to the gradual improvement of observation, without the precise reality being ever fully disclosed; so that the relative character of scientific conceptions is inseparable from the true idea of natural laws, just as the chimerical inclination for absolute knowledge accompanies every use of theological fictions and metaphysical entities."[563]

Löwith cannot deny Comte's opposition to theological absolutism, but he tries to interpret his relativism as absolutism. Comte, he says,[564] "had to conceive relativity itself as an absolute principle, connecting all phenomena by the one and supreme law of progressive evolution." Relativism cannot be reduced *ad absurdum* by the cheap argument that its thesis (of all judgments being relative) presupposes the absoluteness of the very thesis. Relativism remains true, if all judgments except for this thesis are relative. Löwith would prove right if Comte excluded the law of evolution from the principle of relativity. But there is no good reason to assume that he refuses the application of the principle of relativity to his own "study of the laws of phenomena," or that he pretends that his philosophy has "fully disclosed the precise reality." He says: "Adhering to our relative, in opposition to the absolute view, we must conclude the

561 Comte, Cours de Philosophie Positive, IV, pp. 616, 618; Martineau, transl. p. 803. Italics mine.

562 Löwith, Meaning in History, p. 83.

563 Comte, Cours de Philosophie Positive, IV, p. 216; Martineau, transl. p. 453.

564 Löwith, Meaning in History, p. 68

social state, regarded as a whole, to have been as perfect, in each period, as the co-existing condition of humanity and of its environment would allow. Without this view, history would be incomprehensible."[565] There is no reason to assume that Comte considered the future scientific state of humanity as absolutely perfect; that, in predicting a scientific state, he had the illusion of proclaiming an absolute truth. He was fully conscious of the limitations of human cognition, of the "feebleness of the speculative faculties in the human being," "the very weakness of our understandings,"[566] his own included. "Our intellectual resources are too narrow, and the universe is too complex, to leave any hope that it will ever be within our power to carry scientific perfection to its last degree of simplicity."[567] This consciousness was the basis of his relativism. The relativistic philosophy requires "faithful subordination of conceptions to reality," and if this is secured, "we may depend upon being as near the truth as the corresponding state of things allows."[568] We may be near the truth, but not fully possess it.

This relativism prevents the positive philosophy from conceiving the scientific state of the future as the absolute end of evolution. It is true that Comte refers to the third (scientific) state as a "definitive" or final epoch. This does not mean, however, that the law of evolution, which enables us to foresee this future, will cease to apply in the future – an assumption incompatible with the essence of this law; nor does it mean that progress will stand still when evolution has reached the scientific stage, that then the end of history has come. Comte says of the third epoch: "It can never again change its character [as a scientific stage] though it will be forever [*indéfiniment*] in course of development by additions of new knowledge."[569] This means that the progress of *science* – and that is the hallmark of progress – is indefinite. Science aims not only at increasing the knowledge of facts, but also at decreasing as much as possible the number of laws necessary to explain the facts. "While pursuing the philosophical aim of all science, the lessening of the number of general laws requisite for the explanation of natural phenomena, we shall regard as presumptuous every attempt, in all future time, to reduce them rigorously to one."[570] In this respect, too, the progress of science is an indefinite approximation to its ideal.[571] Comte says: "Our historical survey has shown us that,

565 Comte, Cours de Philosophie Positive, IV, p. 279; Martineau, transl. p. 468.
566 Comte, Cours de Philosophie Positive, VI, p. 629; Martineau, transl. p. 807.
567 Comte, Cours de Philosophie Positive, I, p. 44; Martineau, transl. p. 37.
568 Comte, Cours de Philosophie Positive,VI, p. 628; Martineau, transl. p. 806.
569 Comte, Cours de Philosophie Positive, I, p. 22; Martineau, transl. p. 30.
570 Comte, Cours de Philosophie Positive, I, p. 46; Martineau, transl. p. 38.
571 J. B. Bury, The Idea of Progress (New York, 1932, pp. 304–305) shares the view that Comte's positive stage means the end of history: "For Comte the coming society whose organization he adumbrated was the final state of humanity beyond which there would be no further movement. It would take time to perfect the organization, and the period

through successive phases, the human race was advancing toward the fundamental truth to which we ourselves are only approximating, without any hope

would witness a continuous increase of knowledge, but the main characteristics were definitely fixed. Comte did not conceive that the distant future, could he survive to experience it, could contain any surprise for him." He did not contemplate an "indefinite" progress. "He expressly repudiated this notion of *indefinite* progress; the data, he said, justify only the inference of *continuous* progress, which is a different thing." It is true that Comte (Cours de Philosophie Positive, IV, pp. 274–275; Martineau, transl. p. 467) speaks of the "chimerical notion of unlimited perfectability" [la chimérique conception d'une perfectibilité illimitée]"). But by this statement he rejects, from the point of view of his relativism, the metaphysical idea of a state of *absolute* perfection of the human soul. The statement is made in connection with his rejection of the "metaphysical controversy about the absolute happiness of Man" (Martineau, Cours de Philosophie Positive, transl. p. 467); and this part begins: "L'esprit essentiellement relatif dans lequel doivent être désormais conçues toutes les notions quelconques de la politique positive, doit d'abord nous faire ici écarter irrévocablement, comme aussi vaine que oiseuse, la vague controverse métaphysique sur l'accroissment du bonheur de l'homme aux divers âges de la civiliation [The essentially relativistic approach to a theory of positive politics requires from the very beginning to eliminate irrevocably the vague metaphysical controversy of the growth of human happiness.]" (Comte, Cours de Philosophie Positive, IV, 272 seqq.).

The statement excluding the chimerical notion of unlimited perfectibility is a conclusion from the immediately preceding answer to the question whether the development (which is one aspect of progress) is necessarily accompanied by a corresponding amelioration (the other aspect of progress). The answer reads as follows: "Je ne dois pas cependant hesiter à déclarer ici, de la manière la plus explicite, que cette amélioration continue, ce progrès constant, me semblent aussi irrécusables que le développement même d'où ils dérivent: pourvu toutefois qu'on ne cesse de les concevoir, ainsi que ce développement, comme inévitablement assujettis, sous chaque aspect quelconque, à des limites fundamentals, les unes générales, les autres spéciales, que la science pourra ultérieurement caractériser, au moins dans les cas les plus importants; ce qui élimine aussitôt la chimêrique conception d'une perfectibilité illimitée ... le développement humain me semble, en effet, entraîner constamment, sous tous le divers aspects principaux de notre nature, une double amélioration croissante, non seulement dans la condition fondamentale de l'homme, ce qui serait aujourd'hui difficilement contestable, mais même aussi, ce qui est beaucoup moins apprécié, dans nos facultés correspondantes: le terme propre de *perfectionnement* convient surtout à ce second attribut du progrès [I must not hesitate to declare in the most explicit way that this continuous amelioration, this constant progress, seem to me as unquestionable as the development from which it proceeds, provided we regard it as subject, like the development itself, to fundamental limitations, general and special, which the science will be found to prescribe, at least in the most important cases. The chimerical notion of unlimited perfectibility is thus at once excluded ... it appears to me that human development brings after it, in view of all the principal aspects of our nature, in two ways an evergrowing amelioration, not only in the radical condition of man, which would be difficult to contest today; but also even in our corresponding faculties, which is a view much less attended to. The term *perfectionnement* [not *perfectibilité,* meaning perfectibility] properly refers to this second attribute of proof attaining it."[572] This constitutes an essential difference between the positive and the Christian idea of progress, and hence between the scientific and the theological-eschatological interpretation of history. For, according to the latter, the future state predicted by the prophets, the Kingdom of God, signifies the absolute end of progress in history, provided that, from the point of view of this interpretation, there is "progress" in the specific sense of this word. If salvation (that is, deliverance of the soul from sin) is achieved, if the last obstacle of a union of the individual soul with God is removed, then a stage of absolute perfection is reached, which means that no further evolution is possible. Only by ignoring this fundamental difference, can an analogy be construed between Comte's scientific stage of the future and the Kingdom of God to come.

Löwith says: "Comte's dependence on the Christian tradition is more obvious in his insistence on a spiritual order independent of the temporal than it is with regard to the leading idea of progress." Löwith thinks "the theological derivation of this basic distinction ... is already indicated by the terms 'spiritual' and 'temporal.'"[573] However, this derivation is only terminological because the meaning of the terms in Comte's positive philosophy is entirely different from that in theology, where they imply the antagonism of God and man, heaven and earth. When Comte insists on a separation of spiritual and temporal authority, he says, in order to stress the difference between his use of the terms and their theological significance: "The Catholic division was instituted on the ground of a mystical opposition between heavenly and earthly interests, as is shown by the terms spiritual and temporal, and not at all from any sound intellectual and social appreciation, which was not then possible, nor is possible even yet," but will be possible in the future scientific age. "The positive polity must ... reestablish it [the division of the two authorities] on evidence afforded by the whole human evolution."[574] In this connection Comte does not use the words "spiritual" and "temporal," but "intellectual" and "material." With respect to the "new spiritual authority," he says: "There will be no organization like that of the Catholic priesthood, for the benefit of any existing class."[575] "If we resort to the Catholic organization as to a sort of pattern of spiritual government, we must remember that we have now nothing to do

---

gress.]" It is evident from these statements that Comte assumes – also in the third, scientific stage – a "continuous improvement," a "constant progress," or, as Bury formulates it, a "continuous progress." There is no difference between an "indefinite" and a "continuous progress." If progress continues in the third age, it will not end, and hence there will be no end to history.

572 Comte, Cours de Philosophie Positive, VI, 625; Martineau, transl. p. 805.

573 Löwith, Meaning in History, pp. 84 seq.

574 Comte, Cours de Philosophie Positive, VI, pp. 747–748; Martineau, transl. p. 834; the French text of the last phrase reads: "l'avenir positif en accomplira d'abord la rectification essentielle, d'après une juste appreciation du cours entier de l'évolution humaine."

575 Comte, Cours de Philosophie Positive, VI, p. 438; Martineau, transl. p. 765.

with the religious element."[576] Comte identifies the distinction between spiritual and temporal not only with that of intellectual and material, but also with that of morality and polity,[577] education and action,[578] theory and practice. The separation of the two authorities "will arise from that distinction between theory and practice which is indispensable to the common destination of both."[579] Comte uses "spiritual" authority as synonymous with "theoretical" or "speculative" authority and insists, with respect to the theoretical authority, on the "irrevocable elimination of religious influences."[580] His postulate of a separation of the two authorities or powers implies also the principle of independence of science from politics. He speaks of a "just independence of the theory (from practice) without which its proper development and consequently that of the practice, would be fundamentally checked."[581] In view of these statements, the assumption of Comte's dependence on Christian theology proves to be unfounded.

Löwith summarizes his analysis of Comte's philosophy as follows: "The whole scheme of Comte's philosophy of history is thus as much theological as it is positive, the first by its universal claim and indefinite eschatology, the second by disowning the individual, who is the ultimate concern of the gospel – however 'social' it might be."[582] Löwith correctly states: "Political history can never adopt the Christian scheme of the history of salvation, since salvation refers to the individual soul – to each of us – but not to mankind. Humanity cannot be saved." How, then, can Comte's political and consequently entirely secular theory of history be 'theological'"? Löwith's answer, "By its universal claim and indefinite eschatology," is anything but convincing. For the universal claim is not specifically Christian – only eschatology is. But how can Comte's philosophy be eschatological if he does not and cannot accept the Christian idea of salvation of the individual soul? The only element that positive philosophy and the Christian scheme of salvation have in common is the idea of improvement, which is certainly not a monopoly of the Christian religion. The improvement of the state of society in Comte's scientific age has nothing in common with the improvement of the state of fulfillment in the Kingdom of God. Nevertheless, Löwith recognizes in the former a "relative Kingdom of God,"[583] which means the realization of a relative absolute value –

576 Comte, Cours de Philosophie Positive, VI, p. 456; Martineau, transl. p. 769.
577 Comte, Cours de Philosophie Positive, V, p. 749; Martineau, transl. p. 834.
578 Comte, Cours de Philosophie Positive, VI, pp. 457–458; Martineau, transl. p. 770. See also: Comte, Systéme de Politique Positive, (Paris, 1851), I, p. 89.
579 Comte, Cours de Philosophie Positive, VI, p. 749; Martineau, transl. p. 834.
580 Comte, Cours de Philosophie Positive, VI, p. 750 (not translated by Martineau).
581 Ibid., VI, p. 751 (not translated by Martineau).
582 Löwith, Meaning in History, pp. 88–89.
583 Ibid., p. 90.

the usual contradiction in terms with whose aid this attempt to discover theological implications in antitheological doctrines is undertaken.

Löwith's and Voegelin's reinterpretation of Comte's positive philosophy is in principle the same as its Catholic version presented by Gilson. The only difference is that Löwith sees in Comte's scientific age the Kingdom of God and Voegelin discovers in it Joachim's age of the Holy Spirit, whereas Gilson affirms that it is one of the many metamorphoses of Augustine's City of God. Comte, according to Gilson, is even the most striking witness of this Christian ideal.[584] But what do Augustine, the Christian saint, and Comte, the atheist philosopher, have in common? Gilson says: After the model of Augustine who distinguishes three degrees of social reality, *domus, urbs, orbis*, Comte distinguishes family, state, humanity.[585] But this distinction is not a specific element of Augustine's theology. It is a sociological commonplace and has nothing to do with the metaphysical speculation leading to the City of God. This city is a universal society united by a common truth and by the love of God. True, Comte's positive philosophy, also, aims at a universal society based on truth generally accepted by all men;[586] he, too, recognizes love as a fundamental principle of the future universal society;[587] the motto of his *Catéchisme positiviste (Catechism of Positivism)* was indeed: "Love as our principle, Order as our basis, Progress as our end." But – as Gilson[588] admits – "in the Christian City of Augustine the object of this love was furnished by a supernatural faith" because the object of this love was God. However, the "love," which is a principle of Comte's future society, is not the love of God, but the love of mankind. "Humanity, destined by sociological laws to constant development under the preponderating influence of biological and cosmological necessities. This, the real Great Being, on whom all, whether individuals or societies, depend as the prime mover of their existence, becomes the center of our affections."[589] The object of this love is not furnished by a supernatural faith but – in Comte's opinion – by laws of nature known by science. Whether this opinion is right or wrong is irrelevant from the point of view of an objective interpretation of Comte's philosophy, just as it is irrelevant from the point of view of an objective interpretation of Augustine's theology whether its fundamental assumption of God's existence is right or wrong. Gilson sees a common feature in Comte's positive philosophy and Augustine's theology, namely, that Comte's

584 Gilson, Les Métamorphoses, p. 248: "Pour nous, Comte est un témoin sanspareil et, si l'on peut dire, une expérience parfaite."

585 Ibid., p. 255.

586 Ibid., p. 248.

587 Ibid., p. 258: "Comte, lui aussi, pose 'l'amour pour principe' à l'origine de la société universelle de demain."

588 Gilson, Les Métamorphoses, p. 258.

589 Auguste Comte, The Catechism of Positive Religion. Translated by Richard Congreve (London, 1858), pp. 63–64.

society of the future is based on faith like Augustine's City of God. But Gilson admits that Augustine's was a "supernatural faith," a "theological faith," whereas Comte's was a "natural faith," a "demonstrable faith" [*foi demonstrable*], a "positive faith;" and this faith, "which without an effort embraces really the entire human existence, will be sufficient to unite the different cities of earth."[590] But "faith" by its nature refers to the supernatural, and a "faith" which refers to something natural and is demonstrable is no faith in the only proper sense of the word. In this respect, Comte has nothing in common with Augustine.

Comte's positivism, too, says Gilson, "has a dogma, but it is a demonstrated dogma, not less certain than the science from which it borrows its content."[591] But a "dogma" that can be demonstrated, that takes its content from empirical science, is not a dogma in the correct sense of the word. In this respect also, Comte and Augustine have nothing in common. The idea of a universal society comprising all mankind is not a specific element of Augustine's theology – it is, for example a characteristic idea of Stoic philosophy, which is certainly not a metamorphosis of the City of God.[592] On the other hand, there are essential differences between Comte's *cité des savants* and Augustine's City of God. Gilson admits that the "common truth" on which the former is founded is scientific truth, not the theological truth on which the latter is based. Comte's aim "was a universal society based on a truth generally accepted by all men; and since he did not recognize any other truth but that of science, he relied upon science in order to accomplish his work."[593] A City of God without God, is, to use Gilson's expression, a "parody"[594] rather than an avatar of St. Augustine's idea. Moreover, Comte envisages only one unique universal society, whereas Augustine develops the idea of two,[595] the City of God and the City of Men. Finally, Augustine's City of God reaches its ultimate state in the other world, whereas Comte's *cité des savants* is to be firmly established in this world. Thus, on the one hand, what Comte's society of the future has in common with Augustine's City of God it can also have in common with other ethi-

---

590 Comte, Système de Politique Positive (Paris, 1852), II, p. 306. Gilson, Les Métamorphoses, pp. 257–258.

591 Gilson, Les Métamorphoses, p. 258.

592 Max Mühl, Die antike Menschheitsidee in ihrer geschichtlichen Entwicklung (Leipzig, 1928, pp. 46–48), shows the Stoic idea of a "world state" uniting entire mankind and based on the "mutual love of men." He says: "The spirit of antique culture culminates in the idea of humanity as the idea of a universal community comprising the entire mankind" (p. 113); and: "The antique idea of universality falls into the Christian idea and is replaced by the conception of catholicity, based on the principle of authority. This principle, however, separates by a deep abyss the new from the old time" (p. 115).

593 Gilson, Les Métamorphoses, p. 248.

594 Ibid., p. 258.

595 Gilson does not ignore this fact. See ibid., p. 49.

copolitical systems; and, on the other hand, the differences between the two ideals are so profound that the interpretation of the one as a metamorphosis, or even a parody, of the other has no foundation. Gilson says of Comte's positive philosophy: "In order to serve as a social bond science had to become philosophy and then religion."[596] This is not correct. Comte's positive philosophy was from the beginning intended as a scientific philosophy, and he never abandoned it by transforming it into a religion. From the point of view of an unbiased presentation of Comte's idea, it is correct to say only that he *called* his scientific atheist philosophy a "religion," precisely in the same way as several philosophers in the eighteenth century – for reasons already indicated on pp. 92 seqq. – presented their secular ethicopolitical systems as religions. The subtitle of his *Catechism of Positivism* is "Summary Exposition of the Universal Religion." It is in the form of conversations between a woman and a "priest of humanity," and in these conversations the "faith" of his universal religion is frequently referred to. But what does Comte mean by his "religion" and "faith"? In the first conversation the priest explains *religion* as follows: "In itself it expresses the state of perfect *unity* which is the distinctive mark of man's existence, both as an individual and in society, when all the constituent parts of his nature, moral as well as physical, are made habitually to converge towards one common purpose. Thus the term religion would be equivalent to *synthesis*, were it not that this last, not by force of its composition, but by nearly universal custom, is now limited entirely to the domain of the intellect, whilst the other embraces all the attributes of man. Religion, then, consists in regulating each one's individual nature, and forms the rallying point for all the separate individuals."[597] Therefore, by "religion" Comte means a social order without any meta-physico-theological implication – a secular moral order whose *anti*theological character is emphasized.[598] This meaning of "religion" is clear from many other statements. In the preface to the *Catechism*, Comte refers approvingly to "the noblest philosophers and statesmen of the Roman world" who rejected "as the enemy of the human race, a provisional religion which considered perfection as consisting in an entire concentration upon heavenly objects." He asserts: "Our modern instinct condemns still more strongly a morality which proclaims that the benevolent sentiments are foreign to our nature; which so little understands the dignity of labor as to refer its origin to a Divine curse."[599] "Positive Philosophy places morals at the summit of its encyclopedic construction."[600] "Everything, in that religion, is subordinate to

596 Ibid., p. 248: "Pour que la science devînt un lien social, elle a dû se faire philosophie, puis religion."
597 Comte, The Catechism of Positive Religion, p. 46.
598 Ibid., pp. 9, 10, 48, 399, 417.
599 Ibid., p. 10.
600 Ibid., pp. 32–33.

morals, be it the free play of our feelings, the development of our knowledge, or the course of our actions; so that morality is our constant guide in our threefold research after the beautiful, the true, the good."[601] "By the universal adoption of an exclusively human point of view, it was possible for a subjective synthesis to construct a philosophy which should be proof against all objections. The next step after the synthesis was to found the final religion. To this I was led as soon as the renovation of the intellect had been followed by a regeneration of the moral nature ... The relative finally takes the place of the absolute; altruism tends to control egoism; systematic progress is substituted for spontaneous growth. In a word, Humanity definitely occupies the place of God, but she does not forget the services which the idea of God provisionally rendered."[602] The service which the idea of God (that is, religion in the proper sense of the term) "provisionally" rendered was to guarantee morality to a certain extent, but not to the extent of which positive religion is capable.[603]

As indicated in the quoted passage, the secular morality, presented by Comte as "positive religion," has an altruistic character. Its problem is "to secure the gradual predominance of sociability over personality."[604] Positive religion guarantees moral unity or "moral harmony."[605] There are, according to Comte, "two opposite forms which our moral unity might naturally take, according as its internal basis should be egoistic or altruistic ... Moral unity, then, is impossible even in a solitary existence, in the case of any being absolutely under the dominion of personal affections, which prevent his living for others."[606] The moral unity that positive religion guarantees is a "unity in the altruistic sense, [which] does not as the egoistic unity does, require the entire

601 Ibid., p. 68.

602 Ibid., p. 427.

603 If – as may be assumed – the third volume of Saint-Simon's work, L'Industrie, was written by Comte in his capacity as secretary of Saint-Simon (See F. A. Hayek, The Counter-Revolution of Science, p. 130), the following statements may be attributed to Comte: "Il faut passer de la morale celeste à la morale terrestre ... le temps de la théologie est passé sans retour... L'ère des idées positives commence: on ne peut plus donner à la morale d'autres motifs que des intérêts palpables, certains et présentes. Tel est l'esprit du siècle et tel sera, pour jamais, de plus en plus, l'esprit des générations futures. Voilà le grand pas que va faire la civilization; il consistera dans l'établissement de la moral terrestre et positive. [It is necessary to pass from the celestial to the terrestrial morality... the time of theology has passed without return ... The era of the positive ideas has begun: one can no longer attribute to morality other motives than obvious, certain, and actual interests. Such is the spirit of the century and such will be, more and more, the spirit of the future generations. This is the big step that civilization will make; it will consist in the establishment of a terrestrial and positive morality.]" Œuvres de Saint-Simon et D'Enfantin (Paris, 1869), XIX, pp. 37–38.

604 Comte, The Catechism of Positive Religion, p. 52.

605 Ibid., p. 51.

606 Ibid., pp. 52–53.

sacrifice to itself of the inclinations which are contrary to it in principle. All it asks is, what they shall be wisely subordinate to the predominant affection. When it condenses the whole of sound morality in its law of *Live for others*, Positivism allows and consecrates the constant satisfaction of our several personal instincts."[607] "To constitute a complete and durable harmony, what is wanted is really to *bind together* man's inner nature by love, and then to *bind* the man to the outer world by faith."[608] But what does Comte mean by the "faith" that binds man to the outer world? Comte lets the priest say: "The faith of man never had but one object, if you press to the root of the matter. This was, to form a conception of the order under which man lives, with the view to determining our relation generally to that order. Man might ascribe that order to fictitious causes" – this is religion in the true sense of the word; "or he might study its real laws"[609] – this is positive religion. "Faith in the Positive sense has for its proper office the setting forth of the real *laws* of the different phenomena that are open to observation, whether internal or external. By the laws of phenomena I mean, their unvarying relations of succession and resemblance, by which we are able to foresee some by virtue of our knowledge of others."[610] This means the object of "positive faith" are the laws of nature. Comte emphatically opposes this "positive faith" to metaphysical speculation about first or final causes. "Such faith puts aside, as absolutely beyond our reach and essentially conducive to no useful result, every inquiry into the *causes*, properly so called, either first causes or final, of any events whatever."[611] "Positive faith" is the empirical science on which Comte tries to found the secular morality which he calls "positive religion." In the preface Comte says, with reference to his "new religion": "The intellectual discipline instituted by Positive Philosophy rests on logical and scientific foundations of the utmost solidity."[612] This "positive faith" is the opposite of faith in the proper sense of the word. It is irrelevant – from the point of view of an objective presentation of Comte's philosophy – whether it is possible to found principles of morality on empirical science. The only thing that is relevant is: that the "positive faith" of Comte's "positive religion" has not the slightest similarity to the faith of St. Augustine's Christian religion.

Gilson particularly stresses that the organization of Comte's society of the future is an imitation of that of the Catholic Church.[613] But the organization of the Church and the Christian religion are two different things. The one is a so-

607 Ibid., p. 54.
608 Ibid., p. 51.
609 Ibid., pp. 56–57.
610 Ibid.
611 Ibid., p. 57.
612 Ibid., p. 14.
613 Gilson, Les Metamorphoses, pp. 258 seqq.

cial reality; the other is its ideology. Since Comte considered the organization of the Catholic Church highly efficient, he accepted it as a model, but he did not accept its ideology.[614] If a social organization is called "church" in contradistinction to "state" because of its theologico-metaphysical ideology, Gilson does not use "church" [*église*] in its proper sense when he characterizes Comte's, *cité des savants* as a "positivist church" [*église positiviste*].[615] The hierarchically organized humanity predicted by Comte is not a "church now on earth," which according to Augustine is "both the Kingdom of Christ and the Kingdom of Heaven."

"Religion," "faith," "church": The ambiguity of these words abets the misinterpretation of Comte's ideas. In his *Leviathan*, Hobbes says there are "abuses of speech": "First, when men register their thoughts wrong, by the inconstancy of the signification of their words; by which they register for their conceptions, that which they never conceived, and so deceive themselves. Secondly, when they use words metaphorically; that is, in other sense than that they are ordained for, and thereby deceive others."[616]

614 Comte, Cours de Philosophie Positive, V, p. 344; Martineau, transl. p. 636: "The only possible solution of this great historical problem is that the part of Catholicism which was thus destined to expire was the doctrine, and not its organization, which was only transiently spoiled through its adherence to the theological philosophy; while, reconstructed upon a sounder and broader intellectual basis, the same constitution must superintend the spiritual reorganization of modern society, except for such differences as must be occasioned by diversity of doctrine." Referring to this passage, Thomas Huxley, "Scientific Aspects of Positivism," in Lay Sermons, Addresses and Reviews, 5th ed., (London, 1874, p. 152), says: "Comte's philosophy, in practice, might be described as Catholicism *minus* Christianity." But if Christianity is substracted from Catholicism, what remains cannot be Catholicism; for Christianity is an integral element of Catholicism; and Comte's philosophy did not accept Catholicism, but the organization of the Catholic Church.

615 Gilson, Les Metamorphoses, p. 260.

616 Hobbes, Leviathan, Part I, chap. 4.

Chapter X Marx's Economic Interpretation of History

A Secular Religion

The first attempt to show theological implications in Marx's economic interpretation of history was made, as pointed out earlier, by Fritz Gerlich (see above, p. 5) who tried to demonstrate that communism is a secularized religion of redemption,[617] and, especially, a chiliastic movement. "Marxism," he says, "implies a corrupted Christian idea."[618]

Raymond Aron[619] – as pointed out – characterizes Marxian socialism as "secular religion" (see pp. 22, 25 seqq.); but he admits that this doctrine, because of its "secularization of human thought and ambition" is "essentially directed against religion."[620] He refers expressly to the antireligious tendencies of the young Marx. Nevertheless Aron asserts that "socialism is religion to the same extent as it is antireligion." "If it denies another world it brings back to this world some of the hopes which, until now, only transcendent faiths were able to rouse." This is incorrect: Marxian socialism does not transfer from the other to this world the hopes, which religion, and especially Christian religion, arouses. The hopes of a Christian and the hopes of a socialist are entirely different. The former hopes for spiritual bliss in heaven, the latter for material happiness on earth.

Aron recognizes the scientific character of the Marxian doctrine and is aware of the antagonism between science and religion. He says: "There will certainly be objection to these analogies [here he assumes only an "analogy" between Marxism and religion, whereas, according to his main thesis, there is identity: "socialism *is* religion"] in that they ignore the scientific character of Marxian socialism. But nobody thinks of denying the scientific character of a great number of statements contained in this doctrine. The historic materialism

617 Gerlich, Der Kommunismus, pp. 9 seqq.
618 Ibid., p. 19.
619 Aron probably did knot know Gerlich's work.
620 Raymond Aron, L'Avenir, pp. 210 – 211.

in the ingeniously simplified form presented in the Communist *Manifesto*, is a landmark in the development of sociological theory." But how does Aron meet this serious objection? By the statement that "the influence of *Capital* is to a great extent independent of the truth or untruth of the theories presented in the work. These abstract theories, understandable only to specialists, have become convictions in the minds of many hundreds of thousands of men, for the only reason that they justified, with apparent rigor, the feeling which stirred up the socialist masses: the moral condemnation of the system of wages, the hope that capitalism, by its periodic crises, has the immanent tendency to abolish itself, and so forth. Whatever scientific merit is attributed to the Marxian ideas concerning the value of labor and wages, they were, above all, the demonstration of value judgments, the assurance of success given to the wills of men. They were, so to speak, the intelligence of the socialist faith; *fides quaerens intellectum*"[621]. From the fact that a scientific theory is taken by those who do not understand it as a justification of certain emotional evaluations, nothing follows with respect to the character of this theory, especially not that this theory has the character of a religion. Even if Marxian socialism does not only describe and explain social reality in an objective, scientific way, but actually implies moral value judgments, there is not the slightest reason to consider it a religion; for moral value judgments are possible without any religious basis. Behind this logical fallacy is the idea that morality is not possible without religion, that is, without the belief in God as the only moral authority. It is precisely this idea that Aron – unintentionally we may assume – is supporting.

The fundamental contradiction in which Aron's interpretation of Marxism is entangled manifests itself most clearly in the following statement: "Of all secular religions socialism was and remains the most rationalistic. It has elaborated in intellectual terms the faith it nurtured. It aims less at exploiting the blind passions than at enlightening men on legitimate revolts, it looks forward to salvation in the way of an intelligible history, by the deliberate will of men armed with science and mastering nature."[622] It is hardly possible to define socialism more decidedly as nonreligious than by emphasizing its rationalistic character: If socialism elaborates its object in "intellectual" terms, that means by means of reason, this object cannot be faith, because faith cannot be based on reason. By not exploiting blind passions socialism opposes religion which it accuses of just such exploitation; if the "salvation" at which socialism is aiming has to be achieved in an intelligible history – and not, as the salvation of religion, in a history ruled by inscrutable divine providence; if the "salvation" of socialism is the liberation of society from capitalism – and not the redemption of sin by a divine Saviour, and if "salvation" is to be reached by the deliberate (that is, reasonable) will of men, by their "legitimate revolt," by the work of

621 Ibid., p. 212.
622 Ibid., p. 214.

men armed with science – not with belief in God and not by the will of God the only master of nature: then socialism is the perfect counterpart of religion.[623]

Christian Eschatology

Brinton's interpretation of Marxism as a secular religion is influenced by Aron to whom he refers.[624] (See above p. 11) He tries to bolster this interpretation by showing parallelisms between Marx's social theory and theological doctrines. He compares the relationship between Marxist socialism and the original philosophy of the Enlightenment, the "enlightened orthodoxy," with the relationship between Protestantism and Catholicism. He says: "Socialism and its allies are all efforts to preserve, even to increase, the extreme, the violent, the Utopian effort of the Enlightenment to bring heaven to earth, to end moral evil and achieve moral good, here, now, completely. The socialists and the other radicals are the protestants of the new faith in the principles of 1776 and 1789, principles tarnished, compromised, in the eyes of the protestants by the new Rome of nationalist popular governments and semi-democracies, of societies without the fundamental equality of the new religion – equality of income, 'material' equality. Like the Protestants of the sixteenth and seventeenth centuries, the socialists show a marked tendency towards sectarianism. Out of Marx's life and work develops as the nineteenth Century comes to an end

623 It is true that Friedrich Engels in an article "On the History of Early Christianity," published in Die Neue Zeit, XIII (1894–1895), pp. 4–13, 36–43 (English translation in Marx and Engels: Basic Writings on Politics and Philosophy, edited by Lewis S. Feuer [Garden City, N. Y., 1959]), says: "The history of early Christianity has notable points of resemblance with the modern working-class movement. Like the latter, Christianity was originally a movement of oppressed people ... Both Christianity and the workers' socialism preach forthcoming salvation from bondage and misery" (pp. 168 seqq.). But he adds: "Christianity places the salvation in a life beyond, after death, in heaven; socialism places it in this world, in a transformation of society. Both are persecuted and baited, their adherents are despised and made the objects of exclusive laws, the former as enemies of the human race, the latter as enemies of the state, *enemies of religion*, the family, social order ... The parallel between the two historic phenomena forces itself upon our intention as early as the Middle Ages, in the first risings of the oppressed peasants and particularly of the town plebeians. These risings, like all mass movements of the Middle Ages, were bound to wear the *mask of religion*." And in a footnote (p. 170) he says: "In the popular risings of the Christian West ... the *religious disguise* is only a flag and a *mask* for attacks on an economic order which is becoming antiquated." (Italics mine.) Thus Engels clearly distinguished between the "salvation" at which the Christian religion and the "salvation" at which socialism is aiming.

624 Brinton, A History of Western Morals, p. 29.

what begins to look like a church, not merely a sect."[625] By this "church" Brinton means the socialist Soviet state. This comparison of the relationship between socialism and the original philosophy of the Enlightenment on the one hand, and the relationship of the Protestant and the Roman Catholic religion on the other, is superficial; but even if there were more fundamental similarities it would not follow that socialism and the Enlightenment are religions; nor would it follow from the fact that the socialists, like the Protestants, show a tendency toward "sectarianism," that is, toward splitting into different parties; that the socialists are "Protestants," that is, followers of a kind of religion in opposition to another religion.

The same false conclusion lies behind the conscious or unconscious argument that Marxism is a religion because it is – like Calvinism – determinism. "The Marxist," says Brinton, "like the Calvinist, is a determinist determined to follow what his conscience (a word the Marxist would not use) tells him is right, and to avoid in fear and trembling what that God- or Dialectical Materialism-implanted voice tells him is wrong. This is an old and cherished solution of the insoluble problem of free will, perhaps a necessary one."[626] This is a self-contradictory interpretation of Marxism which a Marxist may justifiably reject. If it is his own conscience which tells him what is right, it cannot be the voice implanted (into him?) in a mysterious way by dialectical materialism which tells him what is wrong, because what is right implies what is wrong. If dialectic materialism tells the Marxist what is wrong, the Marxist certainly does not avoid it in fear and trembling, because to the atheist Marxist dialectic materialism is certainly not the voice of God, even if it has an ethical implication; the ethical implication has no religious character. It is true that dialectic materialism, which according to its own intention is a causal explanation of social reality, implies a moral-political element, that it is, at the same time, a kind of natural-law doctrine according to which a moral value is immanent in social reality. It is the idea that the social evolution has the immanent tendency to lead to a situation which corresponds to a social ideal. And it is a justifiable criticism of Marxism to ascertain that this natural-law doctrine is without foundation, that the mixture of causal explanation of social reality with value judgments is logically inadmissible. This projection of moral-political values into social reality is characteristic of all natural-law doctrines including those which refuse to consider the norms of natural law as the will of God in nature. But it goes far beyond legitimate criticism to interpret the moral-political element projected into social reality as the voice of God and hence Marxism as a religion which "passionately justifies the ways of the god Dialectical Materialism to man – that is, a theodicy."[627]

625 Ibid., pp. 365–366.
626 Ibid., pp. 404–405.
627 Ibid., p. 61.

It is also true that Marx took his "dialectic" from Hegel's philosophy of history which, indeed, was a theodicy, or, as Brinton puts it: The "class struggle works itself out (the reflexive verb is important) along the lines of Hegelian dialectic, rescued by Marx and Engels from Hegel's silly idealism about 'spirit' and put squarely on the solid ground of 'matter.'"[628] But just because Marx substituted for Hegel's idealism a strictly antimetaphysical, atheistic materialism his dialectic materialism does not make it a theodicy, that is, the justification of God's will in history. Whether it is consistent to accept Hegel's dialectic of the spirit and, at the same time, reject his idealism is another matter. In any case, Marx did it; therefore, his dialectic materialism has to be taken as it presents itself, not as a Hegelian theology of history.

So far as dialectic materialism is a causal explanation of social reality – and this is its main concern – it is certainly a scientific theory. Brinton's interpretation of Marxism exceeds all bounds of an objective criticism when he places Marx's claim to a scientific theory on a level with Christian Science. After asserting that Russian communism is a "successful heresy of orthodox Western democracy" (admitting that "these terms taken from the Western religious vocabulary are repudiated with great vigor by all Marxists") Brinton says the Marxists "share with the followers of a very different prophet, Mary Baker Eddy, the conviction that they are scientists, that they understand the universe and man's fate as scientists in the past understood somewhat more limited, or, at least, more specific, more concrete, matters. Yet, the religious parallel seems obvious. The part of God as designer and ever-present cause is, for the Marxist, played by a 'theory' of the structure and dynamics of society known as Dialectical Materialism. The good Marxist considers dialectical materialism as a 'scientific' theory."[629] This means: just as Christian Science is a religion but pretends to be a science, so Marxism pretends to be science but is a religion. This "religious parallel" is wrong in every respect. For Christian Science is – by its own definition – true knowledge of God and of Christ his son, the belief that sickness may be dispelled by faith in supernatural, divine power. Consequently Christian Science is a genuine religion. No scientist considers Christian "science" as anything but illusion, perhaps *bona fide* illusion; whereas Marx's materialistic interpretation of social reality, which may have some moral-political implications but emphatically rejects any recourse to supernatural powers and is directly opposed to any kind of religion, is recognized by many social scientists – even by those who do not share its moral-political implications – as a serious contribution to social science.

Brinton views the Enlightenment, because of its "eschatological doctrine of progress," as a religion and in the same way sees its descendant, Marxism, as a religion because of its specific doctrine of progress, the eschatological predic-

628 Ibid., p. 403.
629 Ibid., pp. 402–403.

tion of a classless society. "Marxism-Lenini is the child or grandchild, not only of the Utopian faith in human perfectibility of the Enlightenment, but also of the nineteenth-century feeling for process, for change, for an unending dynamics of Progress."[630] The Marxian doctrine of progress is "eschatology," for "the classless society is heaven, a universalist heaven, unbalanced in the end by any hell, a heaven-to-be in a certain if not quite unpostponable future here on earth."[631] "The whole Marxist eschatology is an attempt to imagine a set of human relations *on this earth* in which there will be change, indeed Progress, rivalry (or emulation, about the nicest word available), in short, some kind of conflict but no wounds, no cruelties, no suffering, no defeat, not even any maladjustments, merely victory for all, and no tie games, either."[632] Whether this picture of the Marxian idea of progress is correct is a question in which we are not interested here. The important point to be noted is that Brinton admits in this connection that "the Marxist- Leninist world view rejects all notions of a supernatural being or beings, of an immaterial soul, and of an afterlife; good Marxists are infuriated even by the Freudian concept of a psyche, and an unconscious, as violations of the 'principles' of materialism."[633] If this is true, how can the prediction of a classless society of men living on this earth be an "eschatology," a doctrine of "last things" which will happen in another world? The only possible answer to this question is Brinton's statement: "As to the nature of the classless society once it is attained, the Marxists, and in particular their more subtle theorists, are reticent. They feel, I think, that the concept embodies a lofty ethical ideal, that it is in some sense a surrogate for the Christian heaven; but their whole moral and intellectual background turns them away from the admission that they harbor any such concepts."[634] The classless society is an ethical ideal. Brinton, as pointed out, simply identifies ethics with theology, morals with religion, and, on the basis of this erroneous identification, characterizes the prediction of the classless society as an eschatology and Marxism as a religion. Not only a Marxist but any objective historian of ideas, even an anti-Marxist must reject any suggestion that Marxism "harbors such concepts."

Fulfillment and Salvation

Without referring to Gerlich or Aron, Löwith states: "Historical materialism is essentially, though secretly, a history of fulfillment and salvation in terms of economy ... from the first to the last sentence inspired by an eschatological

630 Ibid., p. 404.
631 Ibid., p. 403.
632 Ibid., p. 404.
633 Ibid.
634 Ibid., pp. 403–404.

faith,"[635] a "pseudomorphosis of Jewish-Christian messianism."[636] He asserts that the antagonism between bourgeoisie (the representative of capitalism) and proletariat (the representative of communism) has only a moral connotation. He says: "The fundamental premise of the *Communist Manifesto* is not the antagonism between bourgeoisie and proletariat as two opposite facts; for what makes them antagonistic is that the one class is the children of darkness and the other the children of light."[637] The premise of Marx's description of the class struggle is the undeniable fact of a fundamental antagonism between the economic interests of the bourgeoisie and the proletariat, which can be ascertained without any value judgment. If we grant that such a value judgment influenced Marx's prediction of the future Communist society it does not follow that "the real driving force behind this conception is a transparent messianism which has its unconscious root in Marx's own being, even in his race. He was a Jew of Old Testament stature, though an emancipated Jew of the nineteenth Century who felt strongly antireligious and even anti-Semitic. It is the old Jewish messianism and prophetism – unaltered by two thousand years of economic history from handicraft to large-scale industry – and Jewish insistence on absolute righteousness which explain the idealistic basis of Marx's materialism."[638] It is difficult to understand how "a Jew of Old Testament stature" can be an "emancipated Jew" and why an antireligious and especially an anti-Semitic thinker was so completely under the influence of Jewish religion that he, as Löwith assumes, could see the future only in the light of the Messianic Kingdom of God. That he was of Jewish parentage is certainly not a sufficient explanation, because the prediction of the scientific age by Comte, who did not belong to the Chosen people, contains, according to Löwith, as much of Jewish Messianism and prophetism as Marx's prediction of the Communist society.

At first sight, the reader may be impressed by Löwith's attempt to compare the way in which Marx and Engels criticize the capitalistic system with the religious myth of the fall of man and the theological doctrine of original sin; together with the emancipation of human society from capitalism by a revolutionary action of the proletariat with the redemption through the Messiah. But the comparison is superficial. In the economic Interpretation of history capitalism is by no means considered an absolute evil. Until a certain point in economic evolution is reached, Marx recognizes capitalism as a necessary, even a progressive factor. It is true that moral condemnation of capitalist exploitation plays an important part in Marxian socialism. However, this condemnation does not imply individual responsibility and is therefore very different from the religious rejection of sin. Exploitation is the inevitable

635 Löwith, Meaning in History, p. 45.
636 Ibid., p. 46.
637 Ibid., p. 44.
638 Ibid.

consequence of an economic system, which itself results from the impersonal forces of production – a wrong not committed by the individual capitalist. The concept of redemption, therefore, cannot apply, not even in a metaphorical sense. The overthrow of capitalism and the establishment of communism are totally different from, indeed, directly opposite to, the redemption of the soul, that is, its purification from sin committed by the individual in whose body it has dwelled. Marx's materialistic interpretation of history – like Comte's positive philosophy – is based on the idea of progressive evolution that is foreign to the Messianic belief. The Kingdom of God is not the result of such an evolution. It will come suddenly after a cosmic catastrophe and the last judgment. There is no reason to assume that the last judgment of Judaeo-Christian Messianism, this divine intervention in the history of mankind, was the model after which Marx and Engels formed their idea of the proletarian revolution, as Löwith[639] suggests. It was rather the French Revolution, an entirely human action, the self-liberation of a people, which inspired their conception of the future. To identify the materialistic interpretation of history with the Messianic belief in the coming of God is in flagrant contradiction to its spirit, which Engels formulated in one of his earliest writings: "We do not doubt or despise the 'revelation of history' [he puts this term between quotation marks in order to indicate that he does not use it in its theological sense], history is our one and all, and it is more highly appreciated by us than by any other philosophical school, even by Hegel ... The non-recognition of the evolution of mankind is entirely on the other side. It is the Christians who, by presenting a peculiar 'History of the Kingdom of God, 'deprive real history of its very essence and claim this essence solely for their transcendental, abstract and merely invented history, who have history arrive at an imaginary end in their Christ as the perfection of the human race; who interrupt history in the midst of its course; and consequently are compelled to declare the eighteen hundred years following Christ as absurd nonsense and void of content. *We* reclaim the content of history; but we see in history not the revelation of 'God' but of man and only of man. We do not need to have recourse to the abstraction of a 'God,' and to ascribe to it everything which is beautiful, great, sublime, and really human; we do not need this detour in order to see the excellence of human nature, to recognize ... the irresistible progress of the human race in history, its certain victory over the unreason of the single individual, its overcoming of everything apparently superhuman ... its achieving the free human self-consciousness, its understanding of the unity of man and nature and of the free, autonomous creation of a new world based on purely human moral conditions of life."[640] Is this belief in a final disappearance of religion a Messianic

639 Ibid., p. 41.

640 Friedrich Engels, "Die Lage Englands," in: Karl Marx-Friedrich Engels, Historisch-Kritische Gesamtausgabe (Berlin, 1930), Erste Abteilung, II, p. 427, Löwith, Meaning

faith? Is this radical atheism the basis of an eschatological theology? Is this the expression of the hope for a Kingdom of God? If this philosophy of history aims at the Kingdom of God, it is – as Löwith puts it using a contradiction in terms – a "Kingdom of God without God."[641]

Chiliasm

Talmon shows that the totalitarian democracy of Marxism, which he calls a "secular religion," has its roots in the common stock of eighteenth-century ideas, especially in the doctrines of the Jacobins and Babeuf. He points out that the most important change that occurred in the eighteenth century was "a peculiar state of mind" which was, in the first place, the result of the fact that "religion lost its intellectual as well as its emotional hold ... The rationalist idea substituted social utility for tradition as the main criterion of social institutions and values."[642] How could a political movement, which, according to Talmon, is a religion, be rooted in an intellectual atmosphere, which is areligious and rationalist? The answer is that which Talmon, like Aron, calls "secular religion"; but this is *not* religion in the proper sense of the word, i. e., belief in God or a God-like supernatural authority, but simply social morality. He says: "The decline of religious authority implied the liberation of man's conscience, but it also implied something else. Religious ethics had to be speedily replaced by secular, social morality. With the rejection of the Church, and of transcendental justice, the State remained the sole source and sanction of morality."[643] "Nothing was left to stand between man and the State ... Man was to be sovereign."[644] Talmon says that "preeighteenth-century chiliasm" could not play the part of modern political Messianism because of its "religious essence." Its driving power "was the Word of God and the hope of achieving salvation by facing God alone and directly." Its "sovereign was not man, but God," its aim was "personal salvation,"[645] whereas the sovereign of political Messianism is man, not God, its aim not personal but "social salvation."[646] Talmon means by "secular religion" simply "secular morality" as shown by his description of the antagonism between the Church and the secular philosophy of the eighteenth century. The Church accused the proponents of this philosophy of de-

in History, p. 48, cannot help quoting, at least in part, this passage, which he erroneously ascribed to Marx.

641 Löwith, Meaning in History, p. 42

642 Talmon, The Rise of Totalitarian Democracy, pp. 3, 249.

643 Ibid., p. 4.

644 Ibid., p. 250

645 Ibid., pp. 9 seq.

646 Ibid., p. 5.

stroying the essential conditions of morality. "If there is no God, and no transcendental sanction, why should men act virtuously?" But the philosophers were aware of the challenge "to redefine the guarantees of social cohesion and morality."[647] They were anxious to oppose to the religious morality a secular morality. Even to those of them who were not atheists "the vital consideration was not really the existence of a Divine Being, but guarantees for social ethics."[648] Talmon admits that there is only "superficial similarity"[649] between religious chiliasm and the secular political system which he calls modern Messianism.

To save his contradictory terminology of "secular religion," Talmon says: "The concrete elements of history, the acts of politicians, the aspirations of people, the ideas, values, preferences and prejudices of an age, are the outward manifestations of its religion in the widest sense."[650] Then, politics – any politics – is "religion in the widest sense." But in this widest sense, deprived of its metaphysical implication, the term "religion" has lost its specific meaning.[651]

---

647 Ibid., pp. 21 seq.

648 Ibid., p. 23.

649 Ibid., p. 10.

650 Ibid., p. 11.

651 As pointed out p. 92, some philosophers of the eighteenth century presented as "religion" the secular morality, which they tried to establish in opposition to the Church and theology. In characterizing the political system of communism (which is a dictatorship) as totalitarian "democracy," Talmon uses the same misleading terminology. See my "Foundations of Democracy," Ethics, LXVI:1, part II (1955), p. 95.
Under the title *Religion civile*, meaning the same as "secular religion," Rousseau suggests in his Contrat Social (Book IV, chap. 8) principles of morality to be ordained by the government. This "civil religion" is not Christianism which he considers to be "true" religion [religion veritable]; for he declares this "true" religion to be "destructive to the social spirit [contraire a l'esprit social]". The principles of this civil religion concern the "important point" which is the law. "The right which the social contract gives the sovereign over the subjects extends no further than necessary for the public welfare." "It is important to the state that each citizen has a religion which makes him love his duties." "But the dogmas of this religion interest neither the state nor its members except as far as they refer to morality and the duties which the professor of it is required to discharge toward others." No reference to God is made. The religion of the citizens comes into consideration only as far as it is morality. For, the sovereign has no right to control men's ideas about another world and life after death; he is not interested in these ideas, provided that they do not prevent man from being a good citizen in this world. "There is therefore a profession of faith merely civil the articles of which it is the business of the sovereign to arrange, not precisely as dogmas of religion but as sentiments of sociability, without which it is impossible to be either a good citizen or a faithful subject." "A man who does not believe in these articles may be banished by the sovereign, not as godless but as unsocial, as incapable of being sincerely attached to law and justice and of sacrificing, if necessary, his life to his duty." This means that Rousseau defines "civil religion" as secular morality. But the positive dogmas of this civil religion to be proclaimed by the sovereign,

The Twentieth-Century Islam

The French sociologist Jules Monnerot, also, characterizes Marx's economic interpretation of history as "Messianism"[652] or "eschatology"[653] and Marxian communism a "secular religion";[654] but, according to him, this doctrine is not a heretical Christian religion – as Gerlich, Löwith, and other reinterpreters of Marxism try to make us believe – but a Mohammedan religion, the "twentieth-century 'Islam'"![655] He says: "There is, moreover, a resemblance between the use made of Marxism by the present masters of the totalitarian world and the conversion of nomadic barbarians, such as the Goths of Alaric and the Turkish mercenaries of Mahmud of Ghazna, Togrul Beg, and Alp Arslan, to the universal religion of the civilizations they threatened, namely Christianity in the first case and Islam in the second. Like Stalin's Marxism, their conversion gave them the pretext for disrupting civilization *from within*; as converts they were

are the following: "The existence of the divinity, powerful, wise and benevolent, beholding all and providing for all, life after death, happiness of the just, punishment of the wicked, sanctity of the social contract and the laws." This is a flat contradiction – not the only one in his theory of the social contract. It may be explained by the fact that Rousseau considered the belief in God and in the immortality of the soul to be a guarantee of the obedience to the law, even if this belief is a mere illusion; and that the legislator may use it as a political instrument to make the law effective. The "religion" that he proclaims is "civil" because it is not its metaphysical implication but its moral function that counts.
This is the view that Robespierre, as a disciple of Rousseau, expounded in the report justifying the decree that recognized the existence of God and the immortality of the soul. "The various hypotheses by which certain philosophers explain the phenomena of nature are of no importance to you, as legislators. You may leave all these subjects to their everlasting disputes; it is neither as metaphysicians nor as theologians that you have to envisage them. From the viewpoint of the legislator all that is useful to the people and good in practice is true. The idea of the Supreme Being and of the immortality of the soul is a continual appeal to justice; this idea is, then, social and republican." See Charles Vellay, Discours et Rapports de Robespierre (Paris, 1908), p. 361. Robespierre seriously takes into consideration the possibility that these ideas are mere fictions. "Why, these ideas are not true? I cannot imagine how nature could inspire man with fictions more useful than all realities; and if the existence of God, if the immortality of the soul were dreams only, they would still be the most beautiful conceptions of the human mind" (op. cit., p. 360). Referring to the legislators of the past, he says: "Even the wisest among them have taken the liberty of mingling some fictions with the truth, either to impress the imagination of ignorant people or to tie them more firmly to their institutions" (op. cit., p. 361). Talmon's attempt to defend Robespierre against "the charge of Opportunist social utilitarianism" (Talmon, The Rise of Totalitarian Democracy, p. 148) is not convincing.

652 J. Monnerot, Sociology and Psychology of Communism (Engl. transl.), pp. 39 seqq., 156.

653 Ibid., p. 35.

654 Ibid., pp. 133 seqq.

655 Ibid., pp. 9 seqq.

able to attack in the name of the true Faith the very societies which had brought the Faith to them."[656] It is true that the Bolsheviks have taken over Marxism from the Western world. But to interpret this fact as a "conversion" already presupposes that Marxian communism is a religion and, as Monnerot assumes, a special religion, namely, Islam. The main thesis that communism is the "twentieth-century 'Islam'" (the last word Monnerot puts between quotation marks) and not a heretic Christian religion, is justified by Monnerot: "Communism takes the field both as a *secular* religion and as a *universal State*; it is therefore more comparable to Islam than to the Universal Religion which began by opposing the universal State in the Hellenistic and Roman worlds, and which can be said to have drawn men's hearts away from the State to itself."[657] By "universal State" he means the Soviet Union. But communism, as a specific theory, cannot be a state; it can only be a theory used by the government of a state as its political ideology. The Soviet Union, as a matter of fact, is far from being a "universal" state. If it ever had the intent to become a *state* – that is, a most centralized community – including the entire earth, it certainly has now given up this intention. Moreover, in the same way as the government of the Soviet Union uses the theory of communism as its political ideology in its fight against capitalist states and for the establishment of a Communist regime in all states of the world, the governments of the capitalist states use the doctrine of democratic liberalism as political ideology in their fight against the Soviet Union – a fight for the destruction of Communist rule and its replacement by an economic-political regime corresponding to democratic liberalism. Therefore, this doctrine of liberalism could with the same justification as the doctrine of communism be called twentieth-century "Islam." As a matter of fact Brinton sees the same spiritual elan, by which the Russians are moved, in the Christian crusades and in the Moslem jihads.[658]

"As secular religion," Monnerot continues, "[communism] canalizes discontent, organizes and reinforces every impulse that sets men against their native society, and works pertinaciously to aid, abet, and accelerate the self-division and secession of part of their own vital force which plunge societies into dissolution and ruin."[659] It may be true that communism, or rather the policy of the government of the Soviet Union, has these destructive effects. But from the fact that the policy of a government which used Islam as its political ideology had these destructive effects it does not follow that communism or the policy of the Soviet government is a religion and especially not that it is the "Islam" of the twentieth century. Two different causes may have similar effects.

656 Ibid., p. 15.
657 Ibid., p. 18.
658 Brinton, A History of Western Morals, p. 412; see above p. 32.
659 Monnerot, Sociology and Psychology of Communism, p. 19.

Monnerot's main reason for interpreting communism as "Islam" seems to be that "merging of religion and politics was a major characteristic of the Islamic world in its victorious period."[660] It may be true that merging of religion and politics was a major characteristic of Islam, or rather of the governments using Islam as their political ideology. But this merging of politics and religion was also – and still is – characteristic of the policy of the Christian governments of the capitalist states. But the Communist government of the Soviet Union, in opposition to the Christian governments of the capitalist states, is not merging religion and politics, because its atheistic ideology is free from religion in any proper sense of this term. Monnerot's statement that communism makes no distinction between politics and religion, presupposes that communism is a religion. This, however, is still a question.

To the question why communism has to be considered a religion, Monnerot tries to give an answer in the paragraph following the just quoted statement. He says: "Communism is on its way. A religion is seen as such only by those outside it. For its adherents it is simply the highest form of truth. For the true believer Russia no longer exists as such; but he does not believe that he is a believer; he believes he possesses the truth. In fact he is *possessed* by something which he believes to be the truth; and for this truth he feels an active attachment of a kind which truth (at least scientific truth) does not usually inspire or demand.

Communism is a faith ..."[661] That a religion is seen as such only by those outside it, that a Christian is not aware that his belief (i. e., Christianity) is a religion, and that the truth, he possesses is a religious truth does not hold. Monnerot is misled to utter this unfounded statement by the fact that the Communists do not see in communism a religion, which only Monnerot as an outsider sees in this doctrine; and he sees a religion in this doctrine because the attachment the Communists feel for communism resembles the attachment that a religious man feels for his religion. He assumes that a scientific truth *usually* does not inspire or demand the feeling of attachment a religious truth inspires or demands. This is a psychological problem. If there is a difference, it could only be in the intensity of the feeling by which men are attached to the two kinds of truths. Such a difference may – usually – exist. But exceptionally a man may – rightly or wrongly – be as intensely convinced of a scientific truth as a Christian of the existence of God, without the scientific truth being transformed by the intensity of the conviction into a religious truth. But so far as a political truth, that is, the justice of a political system, is concerned – and communism is for the Communists in general and for the Communist government of the Soviet Union in particular a political system – there is, from a psychological point of view, certainly no essential difference between the possible intensity

660 Ibid.

661 Ibid., p. 20.

of feelings with which men may be attached to it and the intensity of feelings of attachment which a religion may inspire.

Later Monnerot says: "The communist Campaign could not exist if it were not religious; it could not exist if it were not pervaded by religion through and through. The leaders and strategists of the contemporary world will ignore this fact at their risk and peril. The Campaign is what it is solely because it has proved capable of mobilising and energising a deep and powerful fund of affective impulses."[662]

Communism is a religion because it mobilizes feelings of attachment – powerful affective impulses such as a religion inspires. Thus, the amazing view that communism is the twentieth-century "Islam" is based on the same logical fallacy as the other theological interpretations of modern philosophy, science, and politics.

Monnerot's study contains still another argument for this view: "When an entire category of events and people and ideas becomes *immune from criticism*, we are in the presence of a religious phenomenon; a distinction being established between a sacred sphere and a profane sphere. In secular religion (and also in the totalitarian State, for the two are connected) this phenomenon is recognizable by the active presence of a *faith*, and of *myths* and *dogmas*".[663] "Marxists claim to be scientific, but if Marxism were science it could not be Marxism, for in that case it would meet criticism more than half-way and would thrive upon it instead of fleeing it like the plague. Science takes note of errors, but dogma only takes note of crimes."[664] If "Marxism" means the theory Marx presented in his writings, the statement is unfounded. But Monnerot now uses this term to designate the policy of the Soviet government. He says: "The reign of dogma implies the existence of fanatics to enforce it; and a pitiless *militia* of the faith is indispensable to the totalitarian party which enforces its dogma *manu militari* in the twentieth century … [This dogma] issues imperatives and *watchwords*, which are rules for action in the task of transforming the world."[665] He even tries to differentiate between the theory presented by Marx and what he here calls "Marxism."[666] "The Marxist dogma in its compulsive aspect makes it unlawful to follow Marx's own example in sifting the treasures of human knowledge and separating gold from dross (I refer to Marxism in its positive aspect and not to the negative aspect, the *system*, in which the error becomes irreparable)." It is not the theory presented by Marx, or "Marxism in its positive aspect," as Monnerot calls it, that is a religion issuing dogmas and rejecting criticism, but the *activity* of the Bolshevik party or

662 Ibid., pp. 21–22.
663 Ibid., p. 146.
664 Ibid., p. 154.
665 Ibid., pp. 154–155.
666 Ibid.

the policy of the government of the Soviet Union: "The communist campaign is a religious campaign."[667] If by "Marxism" or "Marxist communism" the activity of the Bolshevik party or the policy of the Soviet government is to be understood, then Marxism or Marxist communism cannot be a religion because, as pointed out, religion is something spiritual, some specific ideas men have in their mind, not their actions, even if they are motivated by religious ideas. Hence the statement that the Communist campaign is a religious campaign means that the doctrine that motivates this campaign is a religion; and it is – according to Monnerot – a religion because those who conduct this campaign or participate in it reject criticism of this doctrine, and enforce it – or what they consider it to be – in their fanatical attempt to transform the world. But from this fact it does not follow that the doctrine is a religion, that its propositions are dogmas, and that the campaign is a religious campaign. It is simply not true that when ideas become immune from criticism we are always in the presence of a religious phenomenon. Rejection of criticism may have totally different reasons. Nor is it true that "a philosophy lived collectively cannot remain philosophy but is transformed into religion."[668] What may happen is merely that the feelings which tie men to this philosophy become as intense as the feelings which tie men to a religion. Again the well-known logical fallacy; and behind this interpretation of an atheist doctrine as a religion, the conscious or unconscious tendency to disqualify it as a false, heretical religion in comparison with which Christianity is preferable. Monnerot says of the Communist party: "The very purpose of the party is totalitarian, and religion is the only

667 Ibid., p. 124. Monnerot says: "Marx may be regarded as a professional revolutionary, but *bound* within the realm of theory. History imposed upon him his specialization as a technological prophet" (p. 43). "In order to arouse the masses, Marxism is transformed from a philosophy into a religion, from a doctrine of the élite into an ideology for the masses; and thanks to a series of distortions and simplifications, it is made more easily assimilable and more acceptable to those whom it is intended to exalt. But precisely to the extent that this is achieved, it departs from the definition of Marxism which an historian of philosophy, if no one else, would arrive at through the rational Interpretation of Marx's texts" (p. 112). However, in this respect Monnerot is not consistent. In other connections he interprets the theory presented by Marx in his writings as Messianism and "eschatology," hence as theology of a religion. To give some examples: He says of Marx that "he simplifies the Hegelian scheme down to an archetypal eschatological dualism of the type of which manicheism is historically the most illustrious example" (p. 39). Monnerot interprets Marx's theory of evolution as follows: "Evolution becomes revolution, the evolution of capitalism culminates in the revolutionary transition to socialism. Such is the elaborately intellectual formulation of the process by which the last become first and the first last. Observe how the Hegelian dialectic is used to *clothe* a messianic archetype and eschatological theme ... It is an apocalypse, an *end of the world.* The revolution is the great ordeal – a sort of spontaneous last judgment, without a judge or a judgment seat." (p. 297)

668 Ibid., p. 123.

known historical framework that can embrace the sum total of human activities."[669] This is not true even from a historical point of view. To give only one example: the Greek states of antiquity had an outspoken totalitarian tendency. The state was considered competent to prescribe a certain religion; the state order *embraced* religion but was not itself religion. Even if it were true that from a historical point of view religion was the only framework that embraced the sum total of human activities, it does not follow that a totalitarian order must always and, especially in our time, be a religion. A totalitarian order may prohibit religion. The legal order of the Soviet Union does not even prohibit religion but leaves it within the private sphere of the individual and is therefore not entirely totalitarian.

Then Monnerot says: "For its members, the Party takes the place both of civilization and of society (though there are conflicts and the Party's supremacy is not unchallenged); and it is the secular religion (the Party) which provides the model, or pattern, to be conformed to. When such a substitution has taken place within it a civilization is really threatened with scission (to use Sorel's term) or schism (to use Arnold Toynbee's). An increasing part of the civilization's human energies, which constituted its historic force, is diverted to a different purpose. Christianity effected this kind of displacement of psychological force in the classic civilization and turned the force against the civilization. It must be said that the communist 'Islam' is an historical form much less well equipped for bringing about a similar general disintegration and *re-integration*."[670] The difference between Christianity and "Communist Islam" is that the former, after it has disintegrated the antique civilization, brought about a general integration, whereas the Communist "religion," the "Islam of the twentieth Century," is not able to have this effect; it is – though not to the same extent as Christianity was in relation to antique civilization – only a disintegration of modern civilization. Christianity is a constructive, communism a merely destructive religion. Now the reader knows how to make his choice.

A Myth

In the recently published study *Philosophy and Myth in Karl Marx*, Robert C. Tucker, professor of government at Indiana University,[671] expounds the view that Marx is "a religious kind of thinker,"[672] that his "scientific socialism" is "a

669 Ibid., p. 144.

670 Ibid., p. 145; the italicization of the last word provided.

671 Robert C. Tucker, Philosophy and Myth in Karl Marx (Cambridge, The University Press, 1961).

672 Ibid., p. 12.

religious system," "inspired by fundamentally religious impulses."[673] Tucker does not quote one of the authors who try to interpret Marxism in the same way, but he is, of course, familiar with this literature, for he says: "We now frequently read that Marxism is essentially a moralistic System, that it stands or falls as ethical, that *Capital* is a moral or even metaphysical treatise in economic disguise, that the Materialist Conception of History is a form of eschatology, that Marxism is a religion of the age of industrialism, and so on."[674] The main concern of his study is to define this view, but he does not ignore the fact that Marx presented himself as an atheist and developed his doctrine in vigorously stressed opposition to religion and metaphysical theology. Tucker says: "The religious essence of Marxism is superficially obscured by Marx's rejection of the traditional religions. This took the form of a repudiation of 'religion' as such and an espousal of 'atheism'. Marx's atheism, however, meant only a negation of the transmundane God of traditional Western religion."[675] Now we expect Tucker will show us the particular God in whom Marx, the disguised theist, really believed. And this, indeed, Tucker seriously thinks he is doing in the following passage, continuing the just quoted statement: "It [Marx's atheism] did not mean the denial of a supreme being." If Marx was not an atheist – as he claims to be – but a religious thinker, the "supreme being," whose existence he believed in, must be a god, a supernatural being. The word "supreme being" must have a religious meaning, not the meaning used in "supreme court" or in "the king is the 'supreme being' in an absolute monarchy." The king is "supreme" in an empirical world, as a natural, not as a supernatural being, even as a "supreme" value in a nonreligious sense is a value established by the will of man as a natural being, whereas a "supreme" value in a religious sense is a value established by the will of God as a supernatural being. Not only the God of traditional Western religion, but the God of all religions is a "transmundane" – that is, a supernatural – being, even the fetish worshipped by a primitive tribe as its god. For, what they worship is the supernatural power they believe to be represented by the fetish. Besides, the God of traditional Western religion is not only transmundane, but also intramundane; he is conceived of as existent not only outside but also inside the empirical world; and even within the empirical world he exists as a supernatural being. It is exactly his supernaturalness that makes him a god, an object of religion. Since Tucker asserts that Marxism is a "religion" because it expresses the belief in a "supreme being," he must show the supernatural being whose existence this doctrine affirms or presupposes. But what does he really show? Referring to a statement made by Marx in his essay *Zur Kritik der Hegelschen Rechtsphilosophie*[676], Tucker says: "Denial of

673 Ibid.
674 Ibid., p. 13.
675 Ibid., p. 22.
676 Karl Marx, Die Frühschriften, ed. by Siegfried Landshut (Stuttgart, 1953), p. 216.

the transmundane God was merely a negative way of asserting that 'man' should be regarded as the supreme being or object of ultimate concern. Thus his atheism was a positive religious proposition."[677] The passage to which Tucker refers, runs as follows: "The criticism of religion ends with the doctrine that man is the supreme being for man." It is evident that Marx uses the term "supreme being" not in a religious, but in an antireligious sense, that he opposes man as a natural being of empirical reality to God as a supernatural being, as the specific object of a religious worship. Man as the "supreme being" for man is anything but the object of a religion. Besides, Marx explains what he means by the phrase that "man is the supreme being for man." The sentence quoted by Tucker continues: "therefore [*also*] with the categorical imperative to overthrow all relations in which man is a debased, enslaved, forsaken, contemptible being." That means that the dignity of man destroyed by the capitalistic regime ought to be restored – a moral postulate, but not a religious belief. Tucker falls into the trap of confusing morals with religion. That religion usually – not always – implies a system of morals does not justify the identification of morals with religion. There are systems of morals which have no religious character. The one implied in Marxian socialism is of this type.

Another argument advanced by Tucker for his characterization of Marxism as a "religious System" is the fact that this doctrine – as Tucker assumes – "follows in certain ways the pattern of the great religious conceptions in Western culture,"[678] for instance "the aspiration to totality of scope,"[679] the view of "all existence under the aspect of history," the scheme of history: "communism lost – communism regained" in analogy to "paradise lost – paradise regained,"[680] the idea of a "radical transformation of human nature."[681] However, some of these patterns, for example, the aspiration of totality of scope, are not specifically Christian-religious, as pointed out. The Marxian scheme of history is, as Tucker himself says, that of a "temporalized" prehistory and a "temporalized" posthistory,[682] and this simply means that his scheme of history is not religious. The radical change of human nature in Marx's doctrine – as Tucker cannot deny – is the change from a condition of servitude to a condition of freedom and not, as in Christian religion, the change of a state of sin into a state of salvation. Even if such analogies exist they do not justify the interpretation of the antireligious, materialistic conception of history as a religion. Tucker characterizes Marx's description of the warfare between labor and capital as "myth" because Marx in his work *Capital* occasionally personifies the two so-

677 Tucker, Philosophy and Myth in Karl Marx, p. 22.
678 Ibid., p. 22.
679 Ibid.
680 Ibid., p. 23.
681 Ibid., p. 24.
682 Ibid., p. 23.

cial phenomena, speaking of "Monsieur Capital" or "My Lord Capital" and of a collective labor personality, "The Collective Worker", and because his description of the relation between capital and labor is not objective, but influenced by subjective value judgments. For Marx presents it as a conflict between "The monstrously greedy My Lord Capital and the enslaved and exploited Collective Worker."[683] As for these personifications, they are hardly more than a not very tasteful way of speaking of social relations. That Marx's description of these relations is influenced by his subjective value judgments, is true. But this defect does not degrade his work to a "myth," especially if this term has a religious connotation as it is used in general and especially by Tucker, who misinterpretes Marxism as religion.

Gnosticism

Even less founded than the characterization of Marxism as chiliasm, Messianism, Islam, or secular religion are Taubes's and Voegelin's attempts to qualify it as mystic Gnosticism, to call Marx a "speculative Gnostic,"[684] a "Gnostic magician."[685] What makes Marx a Gnostic for Taubes is his dialectic. This view is based on Taubes's assumption that the dialectical logic, as opposed to the Aristotelian logic, has its origin in the gnosis.[686] This assumption is wrong because

683 Ibid., p. 234.

684 Voegelin, Wissenschaft, Politik und Gnosis, pp. 33, 39, 51.

685 Ibid., p. 79.

686 Taubes, Abendländische Eschatologie, pp. 34 seqq. Taubes speaks of the "Marxian apocalyptic," and asserts that "the gospel of the remote and unknown, even non-existent God, which the gnosis proclaims" could become "the generally inflammatory catchword for the nihilistic-revolutionary desire" (p. 10). What the gnosis proclaims is the gospel of a remote, unknown God, who does not exist in *this* world, but all the more beyond this world; not the gospel of a nonexistent God. Taubes says: "the 'new God' is according to [the Gnostic] Basilides the nonexistent God [der nichtseiende Gott]" (p. 9). But Wilhelm Bousset, Hauptprobleme der Gnosis (Göttingen, 1907, p. 19), asserts that in the system of Basilides the last of the 365 emanations of the supreme God are the world-creating angels; and Hans Leisegang, Die Gnosis (Leipzig, 1924, p. 215), interprets the Basilidean formula of the "nonexistent God," reported by Hippolytus, not to mean that God does not exist, but that God is to be considered as beyond the antagonism of Being and Non-Being ("über den Gegensatz von Sein und Nichtsein erhaben"). This "nonexistent God" creates, according to the report of Hippolytus on the doctrine of Basilides, the sperm out of which the cosmos develops. Hence this "nonexistent God" exists, and cannot be the catchword of a nihilistic-revolutionary, that is, essentially atheistic doctrine. Taubes admits that "the 'non-existent God' is an enormous power [*eine ungeheure Mächtigkeit*]".
As for the "Marxian apocalyptic" it must be noted that "apocalyptic" means "unveiling," and in its original and proper sense: unveiling the secret of God. It is a collective term for specifically religious, namely prophetic writings about the end of the world

in Gnostic speculation the antagonism between good and evil does not lead to a synthesis as does the antagonism between thesis and antithesis in the dialectical logic. The dynamic of the gnosis starts from the good God, proceeds to the evil world and its satanic creator, and culminates in the return of the fallen *aion* to the good God. It is a circular movement,[687] just as the history of redemption, according to the belief in the Kingdom of God, is the return to the lost paradise. As such it is essentially different from the rectilinear dynamic of the Marxian dialectic. The future state of perfect communism is not the return to an original state of mankind. The idea of progress, which is at the base of Marx's interpretation of history, is incompatible with such a return that would undo any progress previously achieved. The communism of the society of the future is not a return to the communism which – according to Engels' study *The Origin of the Family*, the Private Property and the State – existed in primitive society. It is communism of a much higher level. Marxian dialectic is the logic of history conceived of as a continual progress from lower to higher stages of civilization. The gnosis, however, as pointed out, is by its nature an ahistoric speculation. Hegel created the dialectical logic for his theology of history,[688] based on a belief in the immanence of God (as reason) in the world.

decided upon by a transcendent god. Cf. Der Grosse Herder, 1952, l, 463, and The New Schaff-Herzog Encyclopedia of Religious Knowledge (1928), I, p. 208 seq. The "nihilistic" – that is, atheistic and revolutionary – desire leads to the view that there is no secret of God to unveil. To characterize the prediction of a future state of human society made by an atheistic, antireligious philosophy of history as "apocalyptic" is the typical misuse of terminology here frequently stigmatized.

687 See Leisegang, Article "Gnosis" in Die Religion in Geschichte und Gegenwart (Tübingen, 1927–1931), II, 1273.

688 Leisegang, Denkformen, pp. 143 seqq., 438 seqq., says that Hegel constructed history as the system of "a circle of circles." "The oriental state is for Hegel the first really historic phenomenon." It represents "a unity of Religion, State, Law and Morality. The temporal government is at the same time theocracy, the ruler is at the same time high priest or a God; the constitution is based on divine law; religious orders and customs are at the same time legal norms. At the end of world history, in the era in which Hegel himself lives, the same unity of religion, Weltanschauung and law of the State is again achieved from within" (p. 439). Hegel did not completely identify the Prussian monarchy with the oriental state of antiquity. He did not deny essential differences between the two forms of government. Hence, history, in his conception, does not return at its end to its beginning, and thus its course is not exactly a circle. It could be compared, at best, with a spiral which only apparently returns to its starting point, since the distance from the center is steadily increasing. Moreover, the relationship between Hegel's dialectical logic and his construction of a "circle of circles" is not very clear in Leisegang's analysis of Hegel's philosophy. However this may be, Marx has taken over Hegel's dialectic not without essential changes (see Ernst Troeltsch, Der Historismus und seine Probleme, in Ernst Troeltsch, Gesammelte Schriften [Tübingen, 1922], III, pp. 315 seqq.); and history is, according to its economic interpretation, certainly not a circle where the end point coincides with the starting point.

Therefore, Hans Jonas characterizes him as the last representative of an interpretation of the reality diametrically opposed to the gnosis,[689] which is based on the belief in a complete transcendence of God to the world.

According to Voegelin, gnosis, as a "volitional" force, assumes "the form of activist redemption of man and society" in Marx as a "revolutionary activist."[690] To reject this fantastic notion of a volitional gnosis or Gnostic activism, it is sufficient to quote Jonas's study of the gnosis, which is one of Voegelin's sources for the interpretation of this religious system. Jonas states that "the existential basis of any 'ethics' possible within the gnosis requires the radical *negation,* not the development of, the naturalhuman element. As a consequence of the radical dualism there is no relationship between the starting point and the goal. There is, then, no possibility of an active subject continuously realizing himself [*kein tätiges Subjekt kontinuierlicher Selbstvollziehung*]", there is only a passive subject of 'dying' and 'regenerating,' a subject of discontinuous transformation."[691] About the allegedly "revolutionary" character of the gnosis, Jonas says: "If we understand by 'revolutionary' an attitude which aims at substituting for the existing *conditions* of social existence others, likewise objective ones, and hence at transforming by force the *world* after a model which, too, is shaped after the world, and the active arrangements for the realization of this aim" – and this is exactly the meaning of "revolution" within Marxian socialism – "the gnosis is indeed everything else but revolutionary in this modern and political sense of the term."[692]

The gnosis – as Voegelin in his recent publication admits – aims at the redemption of man from this world through the good God of love, who, through his chosen messenger, comes to the assistance of man.[693] Hence Gnostic redemption is – by its very nature – not self-redemption.[694] Marxism pre-

689 Jonas, Gnosis und spätantiker Geist, p. 170. He speaks (p. 227) of the "ahistoric timeless idea of redemption" of the gnosis, and states that its "ahistorism" was the main reason of its necessary decline. See above, p. 74.

690 Voegelin, The New Science of Politics, p. 124.

691 Jonas, Gnosis und spätantiker Geist, p. 200.

692 Ibid., p. 214.

693 Voegelin, Wissenschaft, Politik und Gnosis, p. 17.

694 R. McL. Wilson, The Gnostic Problem (London, 1958), pp. 218–219, characterizes the Gnostic doctrine of redemption as follows: "Man is essentially a divine being, imprisoned in the body, and of himself he is powerless to escape. He therefore requires the assistance of a higher power, greater than those who hold him in subjection, a being who can rouse him from his stupor und impart to him the knowledge and the power which he needs." Hence "in most Gnostic systems there appears the figure of a Redeemer, who is usually in some way associated with Jesus of orthodox Christianity if not identified with him, and who performs similar functions." Cf. also: Walther Köhler-Zürich, Die Gnosis (Tübingen, 1911), p. 28: "Man on his way to salvation is not dependent on himself. God is assisting him by special means: the mysteries, the consecrations, the sacraments."

dicts the liberation of man in this world by man's own work. Marx says – quoted by Voegelin himself – "for the socialist man the entire so-called world history is nothing else but the creation of man through the work of man."[695]

In his New Science of Politics (pp. 124, 129) Voegelin speaks of Gnostic ... self-divinization and self-salvation (see above, p. 77); and, in contradistinction to his admission (Wissenschaft, Politik und Gnosis, p. 17), that according to the gnosis, redemption requires the assistance of God, Voegelin says: "The Gnostic man has himself to accomplish the work of redemption." "The Instrument of redemption is the Gnosis itself, the knowledge." He refers to a Statement of lrenaeus concerning the meaning of "gnosis" in the doctrine of the Valentinians which — in the English translation by John Keble (Five Books of S. Irenaeus Against Heresies. Oxford, 1872, I, 21, 4, p. 66) – runs as follows: "... that it is perfect Redemption, simply to know well the unspeakable Greatness. For that defect and passion having been caused by ignorance, the whole that is framed out of this ignorance is done away by knowledge. And that so knowledge is the redemption of the inner man ... For that by knowledge the inner or spiritual man is redeemed, and that they are content with the right knowledge of all things; and that this is real Redemption" (Wissenschaft, Politik und Gnosis, pp. 18, 19). This he interprets as "self-redemption"; and since Marxism proclaims the redemption of man by his own work, he sees Gnosticism in Marxism. The passage quoted by Voegelin refers only to the teaching of some Gnostics, not of the Valentinians in general. It is preceded by the sentence, not quoted by Voegelin: "Others ... affirm that the mystery of the unspeakable and invisible Power must not be wrought by visible and corruptible creatures, nor that of the things unconceivable and incorporeal and remote from sense, by sensible and bodily things." The "unspeakable and invisible Power," the "unspeakable Greatness" is the foreign, the unknown God; and gnosis is just the knowledge of this God. If redemption is the work of this gnosis, it is, in the last analysis, the vision of God who redeems men by being known, in a mystic way, by those who need and are capable of redemption. Gnosis as knowledge in general and especially the Valentinian gnosis is the knowledge of God. Baur, in his "monumental" work referring to Irenaeus I, 6, 1, says with respect to the Valentinian System: "The perfection is reached, when the mind is formed and finished by knowledge, i. e., when all pneumatic men have the perfect knowledge of God, and, as the Valentinians boast, are initiated into the mysteries of Achamoth [the mother of the demiurge who created the world]." Something must be divine in the nature of man if his redemption shall be possible. But it is the work of the redeemer, to awaken this spiritual element, to bring to full consciousness what is sleeping in the soul of the pneumatic natures. (Baur, Die christliche Gnosis, pp. 137, 264.) It is true that Harnack (Marcion, p. 3), speaks of a "self-redemption" of the Gnostics, but he does not deny that there is a "saving action [rettende Tat]" of a redeemer, without which no redemption was possible. Baur emphasizes that "the Gnostic idea of redemption is taken directly from Christianity or is a copy of the Christian model" (ibid., p. 27). It is, therefore, essentially redemption through a divine redeemer and not man's self-redemption. Moreover, the redemption of the Gnostics – as Voegelin is forced to admit – is the redemption of the "inner" man, whereas the so-called "redemption" of man through the socialist revolution is the liberation of man (living with his body in this material world) from a definite economic-political System, and therefore has nothing in common with the redemption of the gnosis.

695 Karl Marx, "Nationalökonomie und Philosophie", in Marx, Die Frühschriften, p. 247.

Voegelin, correctly, says: "The purpose of this speculation is to isolate the process of [empirical] being from the transcendent being and to have man create himself."[696] In his polemic against the theological dogma of the creation of man by God Marx says: "An individual being presents itself as independent only when it stands on its own feet; and it stands on its own feet only, if it owes its existence to itself. A man who lives by the grace of another, considers himself as a dependent being. I am living completely by the grace of another if I owe to him not only the subsistence of my life, but if he in addition has created my life, if he is the source of my life; and my life has necessarily such a reason outside itself if it is not my own creation." He admits that it is very difficult to push away from the popular consciousness the idea of a creation of man by God. The "being-through-itself of nature and man ["das Durchsichselbstsein der Natur und des Menschen"] is uncomprehensible because it contradicts all the perceptible facts [Handgreiflichkeiten] of practical life."[697] This statement is interpreted by Voegelin to mean: "Marx does not deny that the 'perceptible facts' support the idea of the dependence of man. But the reality must be destroyed – the great concern of the gnosis. Reality is replaced by the Gnostic who produces the independence of his existence by speculation."[698] It is not the "concern of the gnosis" to destroy the reality but to escape a reality which is evil because it is created by an evil deity.[699] The Gnostic tries to escape this reality and to flee to another, imaginary, transcendent reality. On the other hand, Marx, by his rejection of the belief in creation of man and nature by God, does not destroy reality. What he destroys is an ideology hiding reality, a primitive myth. The passage in Marx's essay *Nationalökonomie und Philosophie* which Voegelin quotes as proof of Marx's Gnosticism is the expression of an idea which, in direct opposition to Gnostic speculation, is the radical rejection of any such speculation transgressing the realm of rational empirical cognition.

In his earlier writings Marx speaks of man's self-alienation as the effect of the exploitation by the capitalist system under which man is enslaved by powers alien to him. By these powers Marx means the forces of production, controlled by a minority, the private owners of the means of production. There is a conflict between the nature of man and his situation in the capitalist world,

696 Voegelin, Wissenschaft, Politik und Gnosis, p. 34.

697 Marx, "Nationalökonomie und Philosophie", p. 246.

698 Voegelin, Wissenschaft, Politik und Gnosis, p. 46.

699 Harnack, Marcion, p. 3, says of the Gnostic doctrine, that the world must become worthless if not considered to be created by the true, good God. The true reality must be sought in the realm of this foreign, unknown God. This world "becomes a prison, a hell, something senseless, a disgusting appearance, even a nothing." But he adds: "All these judgments are, in the last analysis, identical; [this world] has been deprived of the right to exist; hence its existence perceptible by man's senses, causes all imaginable displeasure and condemnation."

between man's essence and his existence. Communism will resolve this conflict; for under this economic system, when the means of production are under the control of the entire society, man will master the forces of production and thus again be free. Man will "return to himself."[700] This view presupposes, indeed, a natural-law-doctrine – the doctrine that man is by his nature free, which means that man originally is what he, according to this doctrine, ought to be; the view also presupposes that justice, that is, freedom (and thereby the original nature of man), will be reestablished by communism. This reestablishment is in accordance with nature, whereas capitalism is contrary to it.[701]

The natural-law doctrine that prevailed during the Enlightenment has not necessarily a religious implication. The nonreligious version of the doctrine had a radically rationalistic basis; it proclaimed human reason, and not the will of God, as its source. The belief in reason as the basis of natural law was certainly an illusion; but it was another illusion than the one on which the religious version was based. The rationalistic, not the religious, natural-law-doctrine was the – probably unconscious – background of Marx's view of man's self-alienation under the capitalist system. It is true that the idea of self-alienation of man and his return to his original divine self, as the image of God, is an essential element of the theological doctrine of redemption. But the self-alienation in the theological doctrine has a meaning different from, even opposite to, that which Marx has in mind when he speaks of man's self-alienation: namely, the slavery of the Proletariat under the system of capitalist exploitation. For, according to Christian religion, man is or ought to be a slave of God, and if he actually is a slave of man his social status is ordained by God. Christian theology has justified this institution as in conformity with divine law, since Paul wrote his letter to the Ephesians and his letter to Timothy.[702] In theology the self-alienation of man does not mean that man has become a slave. It means that he has deserted God and God has withdrawn from him.[703]

According to Marx, religion had the effect that man "sought in the fantastic reality of heaven a superman, but found only the reflexion of himself." The ef-

700 Karl Marx, "Nationalökonomie und Philosophie", p. 235.

701 See my The Communist Theory of Law (New York, 1955), p. 22. Recently also the Marxist Ernst Bloch, Naturrecht und menschliche Würde, in Ernst Bloch, Gesamtausgabe, VI, p. 237, recognizes a relationship between Marxism and the natural-law-doctrine.

702 "Slaves, be obedient to those who are your earthly masters, with fear and trembling, in singleness of heart, as to Christ; not in the way of eye-service, as men-pleasers, but as servants of Christ, doing the will of God from the heart, rendering service with a good will as to the Lord and not to men." Ephesians, 6:5. The Holy Bible, Revised Standard Version (London, 1952).

703 Lewis Feuer, "What is Alienation?" in New Politics, I (1962), p. 117, traces the concept of "alienation ... to Calvin who saw man alienated through all time from God by his original sin" (John Calvin, Commentaries on the Epistles of Paul to the Galatians and Ephesians, transl. by Rev. William Pringle [Grand Rapids, 1948], p. 219).

fect of critique of religion will be that man will no longer be inclined "to find only the appearance of himself, only the non-man [*den Unmenschen*], where he is seeking and must seek his true reality." In religion man has "lost himself." "It is the first task of philosophy which is serving history, after having unmasked the halo of human self-alienation, to unmask the self-alienation in its secular form. The critique of heaven is thereby transformed into the critique of the earth, the critique of religion into the critique of the law, the critique of theology into the critique of politics." What Marx means by the unmasking of the self-alienation in the secular form becomes clear in his statements that the Proletariat is the sphere of society characterized by "the complete loss of man"; and that the "complete recovery of man" is possible only by the emancipation of the proletariat, which implies the emancipation of the entire society.[704]

The Marxian idea of man's self-alienation does not contain a trace of theological implication. In the quoted essay dealing with economic-philosophical problems, first published in 1932,[705] Marx identifies the self-alienation of man with private property. He says: "Communism is the positive abolition of private property as human self-alienation and therefore the real appropriation of human nature." He expressly opposes the "economic alienation [die ökonomische Entfremdung]" to the "religious alienation [die religiöse Entfrem-

704 Marx, "Zur Kritik der Hegelschen Rechtsphilosophie" in: Die Frühschriften, pp. 207, 209, 222–223. As for Marx's view of man's self-alienation, see Hans Barth, Wahrheit und Ideologie (Zürich, 1945), pp. 112 seqq., and Heinrich Popitz, Der entfremdete Mensch, in Philosophische Forschungen (Basel, 1953), II, 109 seqq. Popitz, probably under the influence of Löwith, assumes that Marx's view of man's self-alienation has, in the last analysis, an "irrational origin" (p. 82), and characterizes Marx as an "eschatological utopist" (p. 165).
Tucker in his study referred to above, calls attention to the doctrine of "self-alienation" in Hegel's Phenomenology of Mind, and asserts that under the influence of Hegel "the main subject of Marx's first system is just this self-alienation of man" (Philosophy and Myth in Karl Marx, p. 97). This is true. But in Hegel's philosophy "self-alienation" has a theological character. Marx divests the Hegelian self-alienation of the theological character. Cf. the statement of his essay "Zur Kritik der Hegelschen Rechtsphilosophie" quoted above. His "self-alienation" is a moral-political relation of a purely secular character. He uses the same term as Hegel, but with a totally different meaning. Besides, Marx and Engels, as Feuer says ("What is Alienation?", p. 118) "came to reject emphatically the use of the concept 'alienation' as the foundation for their socialism. Their Communist Manifesto ridiculed in scathing terms the German True Socialists who refurbished the economic sense of the French Socialists with their metaphysical nonsense of 'alienation': They wrote their philosophical nonsense beneath the French original. For instance, beneath the French criticism of the economic functions of money they wrote Alienation of Humanity ...'" (Manifest der Kommunistischen Partei in: Die Frühschriften, p. 552). Cf. also: Julius Kraft, "Die Selbstentfremdung des Menschen," Geist und Tat XI, (March 1956), 71 seqq., especially p. 78.

705 Marx, "Nationalökonomie and Philosophie", in Die Frühschriften, pp. 225, 235–236.

dung]" and asserts: "The economic alienation is the alienation of real life." Nor is there, as Löwith assumes, a theological implication in Marx's statement, quoted by Löwith as follows: "We know that the new form of social production, to achieve the good life, needs only [!] *new men.*" Referring to this statement Löwith says: "One may wonder if Marx ever realized the human, moral, and religious implications of his postulate: to create a new world by creating new men, a new kind of man."[706]

The quoted sentence is an English translation of the statement: "Wir wissen, dass die neuen Kräfte der Gesellschaft, um gutes Werk zu verrichten, nur *neue Menschen* brauchen, – *und dieses sind die Arbeiter.*" The translation quoted by Löwith is not correct. A correct translation would run as follows: "We know that the new forces of society [not: "the new form of social production"] in order to work satisfactorily [not: "to achieve the good life"] need only *new men – and such are the working men.*" The last words which are essential to understand what Marx meant by the "new men" are not quoted by Löwith. They show that the "new men" already exist. "They are," says Marx, "a product of the present time just as the machine." The workers of modern industry are "new" just as the machines are "new," and there is, in these "new men," as little a religious implication as in the new tools, the machines. In his speech Marx characterizes the nineteenth century [in the translation quoted by Löwith] as follows: "Mankind became master of nature, but man the slave of man ... The result of all our inventions and progress seems to be that material powers become invested with spiritual life, while human life deteriorates into a material force. This antagonism between modern industry and science on the one side, modern misery and corruption on the other side, this antagonism between the forces of production and the social conditions of our epoch is a tangible, overwhelming and undeniable fact." Löwith interprets these statements as the description of the "alienation of man from himself." But Marx did not speak in his address of "self-alienation," for, as mentioned above, he had long ago rejected the use of this phrase.

There is no reason to assume that the "new man" of the materialistic interpretation of history has anything to do with that element of religious redemption which consists in the radical change of human nature, in man's regeneration – an idea that goes back to the saying of Jesus, "unless one is born anew, he cannot see the Kingdom of God" (John, 3:3). In the Gnosis this regeneration,

706 Löwith, Meaning in History, p. 36. The statement is taken from Marx, "Die Revolution von 1848 und das Proletariat," in Karl Marx als Denker, Mensch und Revolutionär, edited by D. Ryazanoff (Berlin, 1928), pp. 41 seqq. This is a speech Marx delivered on the occasion of the fourth anniversary of "The People's Paper" in London, first published in this review in 1856, later in Karl Marx, Man, Thinker and Revolutionist. A Symposium, edited by D. Ryazanoff (New York, 1927). The German edition was published a year later by the same editor.

by which a new man replaces the old man, means the return of the soul to God, the mystic experience of a union with God, achieved in a state of ecstasy.[707] It is precisely this "radical immanentization of the [Christian] eschaton," this mystic "transfiguration," this "divinization" of man, which Voegelin considers an essential element of Marxism; he characterizes Marxism as "active mysticism of a state of perfection, to be achieved through a revolutionary transfiguration of the nature of man." "Feuerbach and Marx" says Voegelin, "interpreted the transcendent God as the projection of what is best in man into a hypostatic beyond; for them the great turning point of history, therefore, would come when man draws his projection back into himself, when he becomes conscious that he himself is God, when, as a consequence, man is transfigured into superman. This Marxian transfiguration does, indeed, carry to its extreme a less radical medieval experience which draws the spirit of God into man, while leaving God himself in his transcendence."[708] In *Wissenschaft, Politik und Gnosis* Voegelin says: "The [Marxian] new man is, indeed, like Nietzsche's superman, the man who makes himself God."[709] He considers this self-divinization of man a consequence of Marx' atheism; and he call his atheism a "revolt against God." A revolt against God is possible only if God exists. Thus Voegelin suppositiously attributes to Marx a belief in God, whereas Marx, as an atheist, simply denies the existence of God, and therefore does not and cannot "revolt" against him but attacks only the belief in a non-existing transcendent being. Since God – in Marx's opinion – does not exist, Marx's "new man" does not and cannot make himself God; but can and shall – as Marx in the above-quoted sentence says – make himself a real man. It is true that Marx in *Zur Kritik der Hegelschen Rechtsphilosophie* turns from a theoretical to a political approach, that he proclaims the critique of religion as means in the revolutionary movement directed against a social situation maintained by religion. He says: "The object of this critique is its enemy whom it wishes not to refute but to destroy."

707 A. M. J. Festugière, O. P., La Révélation d'Hermès Trismégiste, IV: Le Dieu inconnu et la Gnose (Paris, 1954), pp. 264 seqq., and Jonas, Gnosis und spätantiker Geist, pp. 200 seqq.

708 Voegelin, The New Science of Politics, pp. 121, 125, 188.

709 Voegelin, Wissenschaft, Politik und Gnosis, p. 78; but on page 67 he says: "In the Marxian gnosis the decisive point is man's 'being through himself' [das *'Durchsichselbstsein des Menschen'*]; this idea finds its speculative support in the interpretation of nature and history as a process in which man produces himself his perfect stature [*in der Auslegung der Natur und Geschichte als des Prozesses, in dem der Mensch sich selbst zu seiner vollen Statur schafft*]." This means that man does not make himself God, but that he makes himself man. Besides, if there is a doctrine according to which man is making or should make himself God, it is the one presented in the Old Testament: "And God created man in his own image, in the image of God he created him" (Gen., 1:27), and the teaching of Jesus who said to men: "You, therefore, must be perfect, as your heavenly Father is perfect" (Matt., 5:48).

Quoting this sentence Voegelin says: "This is the expression of a Gnostic magician's will of murder (*"Hier spricht der Mordwille des gnostischen Magiers"*)."[710] It is superfluous to object that murder is not a specific element of the gnosis. The question remains why Voegelin calls the challenge of revolution against social conditions – considered to be unbearable – an instigation to murder. The idea implied in this interpretation of Marx's critique of religion is that atheism is leading to crime, as if religion, the belief in a specific God, and especially the belief in the Christian God had not led to bloody wars, as if in the name of this God thousands of man believing in another God had not been burned alive on the stakes of the Christian inquisition![711]

710 Voegelin, Wissenschaft, Politik und Gnosis, p. 79.

711 Voegelin (ibid., pp. 46 seqq.), sees a "revolt against God" also in Marx's doctoral dissertation, published in 1841. In the preface Marx says of a really independent philosophy: "The confession of Prometheus: 'In plain truth, I hate all the Gods' is its own confession, its own maxim against all heavenly and earthly Gods who do not recognize the human self-consciousness as the supreme deity. There shall be no God beside it" (Karl Marx, Zur Differenz der demokritischen und epikureischen Naturphilosophie, in Marx-Engels, Gesamtausgabe, Erste Abteilung, I, p. 10). Marx takes the mythical personality of Prometheus as symbol of an independent philosophy, that is, a philosophy independent of the belief in a transcendent God beyond any possible human cognition. But Voegelin accuses Marx of consciously cheating the reader by pretending that the words of Prometheus express the meaning of Aeschylus's tragedy. This disgraceful reproach is based on the fact that Marx did not quote the answer that Hermes gives to Prometheus in the tragedy of Aeschylus: "I hear you raving with no slight disorder." Voegelin says: "What has Marx to say to this consideration of the messenger of the Gods? He says nothing. Who does not know 'Prometheus Bound' must conclude from the confession that the verse quoted expresses the meaning of the tragedy, not that Aeschylus stigmatized the hate of Gods as madness." Voegelin speaks of a "deception of the reader by isolating the quotation," of a "fraud [*Schwindel*]", "for, we assume that Marx has read the tragedy." In other connections (see above, p. 52) he calls Marx an "intellectual swindler" (pp. 38, 39). However, not a single word in Marx's preface to his doctoral dissertation permits the assumption, that Marx tried to make the reader believe, that hatred of Gods was the meaning of Aeschylus's tragedy, the opinion of the poet. Marx in no way refers to the meaning of the tragedy. No unprejudiced reader can doubt that the atheist Marx identified himself with the opinion of Prometheus, with the antireligious attitude which this hero manifests in tragedy, whereas Voegelin, in his passionate fight against atheism, identifies himself with Hermes, the messenger of the Gods, whose opinion he – rightly or wrongly – considers to be the opinion of Aeschylus. Marx evidently assumes that the educated reader knows the tragedy; he is far from isolating the saying of Prometheus from the rejoinder of Hermes. He refers to a passage in which Hermes accuses Prometheus of "self-will," by quoting the answer that Prometheus gives to this "lackey of the Gods" (as Prometheus calls Hermes in the tragedy): "Be well assured that I would not barter my wretched plight for thy drudgery, for better do I deem it to be a lackey of this rock, than to be born the confidential courier of father Jove" (The Tragedies of Aeschylos, transl. by T. A. Buckley [London, 1863], pp. 31–32). Marx closes the preface with the words: "Prometheus is the principal saint

and martyr in the calendar of philosophy." Marx speaks of the *hero* Prometheus, not of the tragedy by Aeschylus called "Prometheus" – Marx does not even mention the name of Aeschylus. This new interpretation of the Prometheus symbol in Marx's doctoral dissertation is astonishing; but even more astonishing is the fact that Voegelin sees in Marx's "revolt against God" a Gnostic element. He says (p. 48 seq.): "The dethronization of the Gods and the victory of Prometheus … are the work of the gnosis. Only in the Gnostic revolt of Roman times do Prometheus, Cain, Eve, and the serpent become symbols of the emancipation of man from the rule of the tyrannical God of the world." But the gnosis attempted to emancipate man from the evil God of this world in order to subject him to the good God of love, the God unknown to the Jews of the Old Testament, with its Jehovah, the God of revenge. The gnostic's attitude toward God was not – as Marx's "revolt against God" – an atheist's denial of the existence of God, but the emphatic assertion of the existence of God, namely, of the true God of love.

In connection with his misinterpretation of Marx's Prometheus-symbol Voegelin refers to the *"Frageverbot"* which he asserts to have found in Marx's essay "Nationaloekonomie und Philosophie," and to the *"Schwindel"* implied in this *"Frageverbot."* In this essay Marx discusses the theological doctrine of the creation of the world by God, that is, the creation of the world by a transcendent being outside the world, as answer to the question of the origin of the world. To this theological answer he opposes the doctrine of self-creation, a *generatio aequivoca* Marx does not "forbid" the question aiming at a creator of the world outside the world; he simply declares the question to be wrong, not answerable. The decisive passage runs as follows: "I can only answer: Your question is itself a product of abstraction. Ask yourself how you arrive at this question, ask yourself whether your question is not propounded from a point of view, to which I cannot answer because it is wrong [*verkehrt*]. Ask yourself whether that progress as such exists from the point of view of reasonable thinking? When you ask about the creation of nature and man, you abstract from man and nature. You consider them *nonexistent,* yet you ask that I demonstrate them as *existent.* I tell you: if you abandon your abstraction, you abandon also your question; or, if you want maintain your abstraction, be consistent; and if you think of nature and man as nonexistent, then think of yourself as nonexistent, since you, too, are nature and man. Do not think, do not ask me, for when you are thinking and asking, your abstraction from the being of nature and man has no sense … Since the essence of man in nature, since man for man as existence of nature, in nature for man as existence of man has become practically, sensually perceptible, the question about a foreign being, about a being above nature and man – a question implying the admission of the irrelevance of nature and man – has become practically impossible" (Marx, "Nationaloekonomie und Philosophie," Die Frühschriften, pp. 247–248). The first part of the last sentence is not clear. The German text runs as follows: "Indem die *Wesenhaftigkeit* des Menschen in der Natur, indem der Mensch für den Menschen als Dasein der Natur, in der Natur für den Menschen als Dasein des Menschen praktisch, sinnlich anschaubar geworden ist, ist die Frage nach einem *fremden* Wesen, nach einem Wesen über der Natur und dem Menschen – eine Frage, welche das Geständnis von der Unwesentlichkeit der Natur und des Menschen einschliesst – praktisch unmöglich geworden." Decisive is the meaning of the second part of the sentence: The question about God has become practically impossible. Of the whole pas-

Laicized Mysticism

The view that Marx's doctrine of man's self-alienation is a Christian scheme and that his critique of religion aims at man's self-divinization, was expounded long before Voegelin by the Dominican theologian Sertillanges. Since he considers Marxism an essentially Christian scheme,[712] he illustrates this view by referring to Marx's doctrine of man's self-alienation and man's return to himself by his emancipation from capitalism. Sertillanges interprets this doctrine to mean an "internal liberation, the liberation of man from his criminal selfishness [*la libération du criminel attachement que l'homme a pour soi*]"; which means that Marx has in mind what the Christian mystics call the 'freedom of the Children of God.'" This interpretation is based on a misunderstanding. The liberation of the workers from the status of capitalist chattels does not mean an "internal liberation," the liberation of the worker from his selfishness (or – as Sertillanges formulated it in another connection – "from inhuman which is in himself") because he does not benefit from the institution of private property. Capitalism is in the egoistic interest of the capitalists; and the capitalist's "internal" liberation is not in question. According to Marx, the evil from which the working class is to be liberated is not within man but in the external circumstances, in the social system of capitalism. If the abolition of man's self-alienation in the sense of Christian theology leads to the "freedom of the Children of God," this "freedom" is very different from the social freedom which, according to Marx, follows the abolition of capitalism. The "freedom of the Children of God" is a mystic-religious freedom that even a slave may enjoy. The abolishment of man's self-alienation in the theological sense of the term is characterized by Sertillanges as follows: "The Christian, in surrendering to God, intends to free himself from himself, from the slavery of nature, from social constraint, merging in the universe [*s'universalisant*] by adhering to the first Principle which unites all, men and things."[713] It is evident that the process by which man's self-alienation in the theological sense is undone has nothing in common with the self-alienation of man and his return to himself in the Marxian doctrine. The only difference that Sertillanges can see between the

sage Voegelin quotes only the sentences "When you ask about the creation of nature and man, you abstract from man and nature ... If you abandon your abstraction you abandon also your question ... Don't think, don't ask me. Evidently it is on the last sentence that Voegelin bases his assertion that Marx issues a "*Frageverbot.*" He says: "The question of the individual man are cut off by the ukase of the speculatist who does not want to have his construction be disturbed" (p. 36). But from the whole passage it is evident, that the linguistic imperative "don't ask me" has not the meaning of a moral-political command, of a "ukase," but means only that the question is from a reasonable point of view senseless and therefore practically impossible.

712 Sertillanges, Le Christianisme, II, p. 222.

713 Ibid.

theologian and the Marxian self-alienation of man is the fact that, according to Marx, "God is man himself [*Il n'y a qu'une différence, c'est qu'ici Dieu c'est l'homme lui-même*]." "The humanism of Marx ... is precisely an apotheosis. But what does this substitution of one God by another matter?"[714] Hence, according to Sertillanges, Marxism is a "laicized mysticism [*mysticisme laicisé*]."[715] This view, like Voegelin's analogous assertion, is the most obvious misinterpretation of Marx's and Feuerbach's critique of religion. According to these antireligious thinkers, what man should draw back to himself is not and cannot be God – whose existence they denied – but all that is best in man and which the Christian religion has projected into an imaginary beyond. By drawing back what is best in man to himself, man does not and cannot become God because this process means the dissolution of the hypostatization of his own qualities, called God. By drawing back what is best in man to himself, man abolishes the religious self-alienation, in the same way as by the proletarian revolution he abolishes his economic self-alienation. By undoing the projection of his self, man returns to himself and thus becomes not a superman but *man* in the restored sense of this term. This is neither an "apotheosis" nor a "transfiguration," but the recovery of man's nature. It does not carry to its extreme the mystic union with God, but is the most radical negation of this Gnostic experience.

The Messianic Kingdom of God means, indeed, the definite end of history; but to assert that the future Communist society of historic materialism means the same, "an ultimate end, as both *finis* and *telos*" (in Löwith's words[716]), is as unjustified as the analogous misinterpretation of the scientific age of Comte's positive philosophy. It contradicts clear statements made by Marx and Engels. In his *Contribution to the Critique of Politiclal Economy*,[717] Marx says that the bourgeois-capitalist society constitutes "the closing chapter of the *pre*-historic stage of human society," which implies that history begins – and does not end – with the postcapitalist, that is, the Communist, society. In *The German Ideology*,[718] Marx and Engels declare that only in the period after the capitalist society, that is, in the period of communism, "history becomes transformed into world-history," which is contrary to the idea that this period constitutes the *end* of history. In *The Development of Socialism from Utopia to Science*, Engels characterizes the situation under a Communist system of economy

714 Ibid. The idea behind this interpretation of Marx's atheism is evidently: If man does not believe in God as different from man he must consider himself to be God, since belief in God is inevitable, atheism impossible.

715 Sertillanges, Le Christianisme, II, p. 223.

716 Löwith, Meaning in History, p. 18.

717 Karl Marx, A Contribution to the Critique of Political Economy, translated by N. J. Stone (Chicago, 1904), p. 13.

718 Karl Marx and Friedrich Engels, The German Ideology (New York, 1939), p. 27.

thus: "Then for the first time, man, in a certain sense, is finally marked off from the rest of the animal kingdom, and emerges from mere animal conditions of existence into really human ones ... Man's own social organization, hitherto confronting him as a necessity imposed by Nature and history, now becomes the result of his own free action. The extraneous objective forces that have hitherto governed history pass under the control of man himself. *Only from that time will man himself, more and more consciously, make his own history* – only from that time will the social causes set in movement by him have, in the main and in a constantly growing measure, the results intended by him. It is the ascent of man from the kingdom of necessity to the kingdom of freedom."[719] It is hardly possible to express more clearly the idea that the establishment of communism will be the beginning of a history in the sense of a really human history. Whether this prediction is true or false, is unimportant in the connection. What is important, is how Marx and Engels visualized the period which they expected to follow the capitalist age within the whole of history. This vision certainly does not imply that this period will be the end of history. History will continue – but will be the result of man's conscious action. If one objects that such a prediction was impossible on a scientific basis, then one cannot object that Marx and Engels did not extend their prediction to the course of the historic movement under the conscious direction by man. From the fact that they were silent about an evolution after the establishment of the Communist system of economy – and nothing else can be said about their prediction – it does not follow that they excluded the possibility of progress beyond communism.

Sertillanges concludes his theological interpretation of Marxism as follows: "Marx evidently depends on the Christian ideology. The fact that he combats faith does not change a thing. From our point of view, anti-Christianism is still Christianism."[720] This is the point of view of a Christian theologian who cannot admit that in a world created and ruled by an all-powerful God atheism can really exist. From this point of view atheism is only an unconscious belief in God. It is the only point of view from which an antireligious ideology can be interpreted as a religion. If writers who are not professional theologians accept such an interpretation they either have to admit that this is also their own point of view, or they have to bear the reproach of an inadmissible self-contradictory misinterpretation.

719 Socialism, Utopian and Scientific, translated by E. Aveling (New York, 1901), pp. 52 seq. (Italics mine).

720 Sertillanges, Le Christianisme, II, p. 224.

The Political Metaphysics of Marxism

Even T. D. Weldon, in his most meritorious work *The Vocabulary of Politics*,[721] speaks of "Marx the Communist theologian,"[722] and characterizes the foundation of Marxism as a metaphysics.[723] There is a conviction, he says, that these foundations "must be maintained at all cost against heretics and unbelievers,"[724] that they are regarded as "sacred, unalterable and timeless truths about the nature of the world."[725]

The metaphysical element of Marxism is – according to Weldon – the dialectical materialism.[726] But Weldon admits that Marx's dialectic is not at all identical with Hegel's dialectic which, indeed, is metaphysics. Nevertheless Weldon asserts: "Marx might have attacked Hegelianism by empirical arguments," but "he did not do so. He chose to set a metaphysics to catch a metaphysics and he attacked Hegel wit his own favorite weapon."[727] This is hardly compatible with what Weldon says about the meaning of Marxianism in general and especially about the difference between Hegel's and Marx's dialectic. "What Marx said," Weldon writes, "was quite simple. Poverty is unnecessary. It is not the result of the will of God but of special economic and political conditions. It can be got rid of by changing those conditions."[728] This is an empirical scientific – in open opposition to a metaphysical – interpretation of social reality. As to the importance of economic circumstances Weldon says: "Marx did not discover it. Aristotle, Machiavelli, Hobbes and Adam Smith had all of them taken it for granted. What Marx did was to convert it from a vague to a fairly precise statement by concentrating attention on the means of production, for this gave his answer to the question, 'Why are the rich rich and the poor poor?' The rich are rich because they control the means of production, the poor are poor because they do not. There is nothing mysteriously or divinely ordained about it and the mechanics of the process are easily explained."[729] If this is the meaning of the process Marx calls "dialectic materialism," then "dialectic" is indeed "materialistic" in the sense of *anti*-metaphysical. What Marx had in mind when he said he, as Weldon formulates it, "maintained that Hegel's version [of dialectic] was upside down and what he [Marx] had done was to turn it right way up," Weldon says, was "that Hegel had conceived dialectical development as some-

721 T. D. Weldon, The Vocabulary of Politics (Harmondsworth, Middlesex, 1955).
722 Ibid., p. 126.
723 Ibid., p. 137.
724 Ibid., p. 127.
725 Ibid., p. 137.
726 Ibid., pp. 128, 137.
727 Ibid., pp. 129–130.
728 Ibid., p. 118.
729 Ibid., p. 121.

thing essential mental or spiritual and had thus been led to ignore or minimize the importance of economic factors in political developments. Marx wanted to reverse this and, largely under the influence of Feuerbach's materialism, to make mental operations of all sorts *causally* dependent on physical changes. Probably what he really wanted was something very like the Physicalist theory developed by the Vienna circle in the nineteen-thirties, but he was in no position to achieve this type of view because the scientific methodology of his time was largely mistaken and because his own knowledge of what was going on in contemporary science was rudimentary."[730] Feuerbach's materialism and the philosophy of the Vienna circle are outspoken antimetaphysical; and if what Marx had in mind with *his* "dialectic" was influenced by Feuerbach and something similar to the Viennese school of philosophy, it was certainly something else but metaphysics at which he was aiming; and we have to understand this "dialectic" in conformity with that which Marx had in his mind when he opposed *his* dialectic to that of Hegel. Weldon admits that Marx "transformed the dialectic [Hegel's] from a theory of the development of spirit to a theory of the development of the means of production and attempt to demonstrate as a necessary and not an empirical truth that feudalism *had* to be succeeded by capitalism and that capitalism *had* to yield to communism."[731]

But Weldon admits: "Marx believed that sociology was a science, that is to say he held that the behavior of human beings in State and other associations was capable of being explained and *predicted*, and the key to such explanation and prediction was given by knowledge of the conditions of economic production."[732] This is an outspoken antimetaphysical approach to the social problems, and if Marx's dialectic materialism was the foundation of this approach, it could not have a metaphysical character. Marx's dialectic materialism was – according to his own intention – a sociological concept, and if sociology was according to Marx a science, and that means not a metaphysical speculation, his "dialectic" was directed against the metaphysical dialectic of Hegel. And when Marx taught that feudalism had to be succeeded by capitalism and predicted that capitalism had to yield to communism, he certainly thought that the relationship of these states of society was that of cause and effect, that is to say, that their succession is determined by the law of causality, which has nothing to do with metaphysics. We quoted Weldon's statement that the foundations of Marxism, that is, the general metaphysic of dialectical materialism are regarded "as sacred, unalterable, and timeless truths about the nature of the world."[733] They may be considered in this way by some people who consider themselves to be Marxists. But they have not been presented in this way by the

730 Ibid., p. 128 (Italics mine).

731 Ibid., p. 130.

732 Ibid., pp. 119, 120. (Italics mine).

733 Ibid., p. 137.

founders of Marxism. Weldon even admits that "Marx, Engels, and Lenin themselves frequently inveigh against doctrinaire adherence to abstract principles as contrasted with empirical study of facts or, as they prefer to call it, objective assessment of the concrete situation."[734] Weldon says: "Marxist foundations are worthless."[735] This may be true. But he continues: "Either they are metaphysical and empty... *or* they are shortcuts, half-truths, and first approximations of a semi-scientific kind which in themselves have little or no predictive value except for a short time and in special circumstances." Hence Weldon, in contradiction to his earlier statements about the metaphysical character of the dialectical materialism, does not exclude the possibility of interpreting the foundations of Marxism as *not* metaphysical. He even says:[736] "His [Marx's] foundations are logically worthless, are not metaphysical and harmless in the sense in which those of the democrats and Hegelians are." But they are also *not* metaphysical in the sense Weldon himself uses the term "metaphysics" when he characterizes a metaphysical view as "to be beyond the range of empirical confirmation."[737]

That Marx was not of the opinion that his dialectic materialism was beyond the range of empirical confirmation is shown by the way in which Weldon himself presents Marx's doctrine. It may be true that – as Weldon asserts – "the dialectic, whether manipulated by Hegel or Marx, is incapable of providing good reasons for any political action or inaction." But that "Marx did not hold this view"[738] is no reason to call *his* dialectic a metaphysics.

734 Ibid., p. 127.
735 Ibid., pp. 137–138.
736 Ibid., p. 129. (Italics mine).
737 Ibid., p. 94.
738 Ibid., p. 129.

Chapter XI Nietzsche the Christian

Friedrich Nietzsche wrote in his *Antichrist*: "I *condemn* Christianity and confront it with the most terrible accusation that an accuser has ever had in his mouth. To my mind it is the greatest of all conceivable corruptions."[739] If we have to accept the paradox that there can be a theology, that is, a doctrine of God, without a belief in God, then we have also to accept the paradox that Nietzsche, this "anti-Christ," is a Christian – as Sertillanges asserts. The German philosopher Karl Jaspers tells us that Nietzsche's passionate fight against Christianity "springs from his own Christianness."[740] Jaspers refers to some contradictions in Nietzsche's evaluation of Christian religion.[741] However, most of the statements quoted by Jaspers are compatible with Nietzsche's *Antichrist*. For instance, the statement: "The way in which, on the whole, the reverence for the *Bible* has hitherto been maintained in Europe, is perhaps the best example of discipline and refinement of manners which Europe owes to Christianity."[742] To condemn Christianity because of its bad effects on civilization is not imcompatible with recognizing that it has not only bad but also good effects. Besides, it is the reverence for the *Bible* which Nietzsche appreciates, and he distinguishes carefully between the Christianity which he opposes and the Scripture, especially the teachings of Christ. Nietzsche, who was the son of a Protestant clergyman, sees "the most distinguished type of man" he has met in a perfect Christian. He says, "I consider it an honor to descend from a family which in every respect has taken seriously its Christianity."[743] This is an esteem with which everyone may be regarded who takes seriously

739 Friedrich Nietzsche, The Antichrist, translated by Anthony M. Ludovici, in: Dr. Oscar Levy, ed., The Complete Works of Friedrich Nietzsche (Edinburgh and London, 1903–1913), XVI, p. 230.

740 Karl Jaspers, Nietzsche und das Christentum (Hameln, n. d.). This essay was the basis of a lecture Professor Jaspers delivered on May 12, 1938, before an association of Protestant clergyman in Hannover.

741 Ibid., pp. 5 seqq.

742 Friedrich Nietzsche, Beyond Good and Evil, transl. by Helen Zimmern, in: Complete Works (London and Edingburgh 1909), XII, p. 238 (§ 263).

743 Nietzsches Werke (Leipzig, 1904), XIV (Nachgelassene Werke), p. 358 (§ 223).

the view he professes, religious or nonreligious. Nietzsche expresses high respect for some types of priests, "namely, the gentle, serious, simple, chaste, priestly natures";[744] he recognizes that Christianity "has perhaps chiselled and shaped the most subtle individualities which have everexisted in human society: the individualities of the higher ranks of the Catholic clergy, especially when these priests have sprung from a noble family, and have brought to their work, from the very beginning, the innate grace of gesture, the dominating glance of the eye, and beautiful hands and feet. Here the human face acquires that spiritualization brought about by the continual ebb and flow of two kinds of happiness (the feeling of power and the feeling of submission) after a carefully-planned manner of living has conquered the beast in man ... here we find that noble contempt concerning the perishable nature of the body, of well-being and of happiness, peculiar to born soldiers ... The surpassing beauty and subtleties of these princes of the Church have always proved to the people the truth of the Church."[745] The approbation expressed in these statements is not bestowed to the Christianity of these priests but to qualities which may be acquired also by persons who are not priests of a Christian church. But Nietzsche expressed also a certain esteem for the Church as such. He says: "The Church is under all circumstances a *nobler* institution than the State."[746] This statement is preceded by the sentence: "A Church is above all an authoritative organization [*"ein Herrschaftsgebilde"*] which secures to the *most spiritual* men the highest rank, and *believes* in the power of spirituality so far as to forbid all grosser appliances of authority." It is the Church, as an organization of power, not the Christian religion that Nietzsche appreciates. He admits frankly that "the struggle against the Church is certainly (among other things – for it has a manifold significance) the struggle of the more ordinary, cheerful, confiding, superficial natures against the rule of the graver, profounder, more contemplative natures, that is to say, the more malign and suspicious man, who with long continued distrust in the worth of life, brood also over their own worth."[747] Nietzsche's fight against *Christianity* is entirely compatible with the view that not every fight against the *Church* is justifiable.

Jaspers's main theses are that Nietzsche was bound to Christianity, that some essential elements of Nietzsche's philosophy sprang from "Christian impulses," and that Nietzsche was aware of the fact that his thinking and especially the "boundless will to truth" had its origin in Christianity.[748] Jaspers re-

744 Friedrich Nietzsche, The Joyful Wisdom, transl. by Thomas Common, in: Complete Works (London and Edinburgh 1910), X, p. 292 (§ 351).

745 Friedrich Nietzsche, The Dawn of Day, transl. by J. M. Kennedy, in: Complete Works (London and Edinburgh 1911), IX, pp. 61 seqq. (§ 60).

746 Nietzsche, The Joyful Wisdom, p. 314 (§ 358).

747 Ibid., pp. 290 seq. (§ 350).

748 Jaspers, Nietzsche und das Christentum, p. 9.

fers to a passage in section 344 of *The Joyful Wisdom*[749] entitled: "To what Extent even We are still Pious": "Even we knowing ones of today, the godless and anti-metaphysical, still take *our* fire from the conflagration kindled by a belief a millennium old"; but the passage continues – and this part is not quoted by Jaspers – "the Christian belief, which was also the belief of Plato, that God is truth, that the truth is divine." It is evident from these passages that Nietzsche correctly considered the belief in truth as in a divine value not exclusively Christian. He refers to Plato's idea of the absolute good which implies the value of absolute truth. If he considered truth as a divine value, his opinion could be traced to Plato rather than to the Christian religion, which he rejected. Since the divine truth of the Christian religion and Plato's idea of the absolute truth are placed in the same category, it is not the belief in the Christian God, but the belief in an absolute, metaphysical truth that Nietzsche has in mind. The passage quoted by Jaspers is preceded by the words: "What I have in view will now be understood, namely, that it is always a *metaphysical belief* on which our belief in science rests." Because our belief in science implies the belief in an absolute metaphysical truth, we are still pious. This piety which is "more severe and more refined" than the Christian piety "forbids us to be still Christians."[750]

This, however, is not Nietzsche's last word about the belief in absolute truth. He is aiming at the fact that the assumption of an absolute, metaphysical value is incompatible with an antimetaphysical philosophy. The passage quoted above (that "truth is divine") continues: "But what if this itself always becomes more untrustworthy, what if nothing any longer proves itself divine, except it be error, blindness, and falsehood; what if God himself turns out to be our most persistent lie?" The answer to this question is that an antimetaphysical philosophy like Nietzsche's can recognize only relative values, and that even the value of truth cannot be presented as an absolute one; and not, as Jaspers assumes, that Nietzsche's antimetaphysical philosophy is "the negation of all morals and all truth."[751]

Even more questionable than the assertion that Nietzsche was aware of the Christian origin of his thinking is the view that essential elements of his philosophy sprang from "Christian impulses." What are these "impulses"?

749 Nietzsche, The Joyful Wisdom p. 279 (§ 344). Jaspers quotes Nietzsches Werke, VII, p. 275; but the passage is in V, p. 275.

750 Nietzsches Werke, XIII (Nachgelassene Werke), p. 318 (§ 777), quoted by Jaspers, Nietzsche und das Christentum, p. 10.

751 Jaspers, Nietzsche und das Christentum, p. 67. In his work Nietzsche (Berlin, 1950), Jaspers characterizes Nietzsche's doctrine of values as follows: "Because man is estimating, measuring, evaluating and thereby creating, there are no absolute values which exist like a reality [*ein Sein*] and are only to be detected; values ... are never final, they are to be created each time. It is from this fact that for Nietzsche in the actual moment of world history the task of a 'transvaluation of all values' arises" (p. 153).

The first "impulse" is the belief in "the possibility of a total vision of world history," presupposed by Nietzsche, that is, the possibility of "obtaining knowledge of the course of human history in its totality," which, according to Jaspers, is of "Christian origin."[752] Jaspers says that the concept of the history of mankind as a series of events that happen but once, beginning with the creation, proceeding to the fall of man, then to appearance of Christ, and eventually to the last judgment and the end of the world, is specifically Christian. "The Christian has an idea of the whole, he considers the empirical history not as arbitrary happening, a mere change, but as included in the one transcendental history. Thereby the empirical history is impregnated with a deep meaning. In addition, the salvation of every individual soul is decided upon in it."[753] "Philosophy of history, as a secular total knowledge [*Totalwissen*], has arisen from Christian historical thinking through a transformation. Herder, Kant, Fichte, Hegel, Marx, and together with them, Nietzsche, too, descend from Christian thinking. What is decisive is the vision of the whole ..."[754]

Neither the assumption that it is possible to gain knowledge of the entire history of the human race visualized as a unit – that is, the idea of a universal or world history – nor the concept of history as a succession of events that happen but once, is specifically Christian. M. Büdinger, in his profound study *Die Universalhistorie im Alterthume*,[755] has shown that the idea of the human race as an organic unit was known in antiquity and that long before Christianity came into existence serious attempts were made to consider the history of mankind in the same way as the history of an individual being. He refers, among others, to Diodorus, who, in the introduction to his work, markedly connected "universal history [*κοιναί* ἱστορίαι]" with "human society" as a whole, assumed that "all men are united to one another by their kinship although separated by space and time," and declared that "we must look upon history... as the benefactor of the entire human race."[756] Diodorus was influenced by Stoic philosophy, which had a tendency toward a universal view of history because it regarded the human race as an organic whole. This tendency manifested itself most clearly in the Stoic concept of world citizenship and in Zeno's ideal of a world state. Clearly, then, the concept of mankind as a unit is not of Christian origin. The Christian idea of the Kingdom of God as a community of all Christian mankind "cannot deny," as von Arnim emphasizes, "its descent from Stoic cosmopolitism."[757]

752 Jaspers, Nietzsche und das Christentum, pp. 42, 43.

753 Ibid., p. 44.

754 Ibid.

755 Max Büdinger, Die Universalhistorie im Alterthume (Wien, 1895), pp. 1, 112 seqq.

756 Diodorus of Sicily, Books I and II, pp. 1–34, with an English translation by C. H. Oldfather (= The Loeb Classical Library; London and New York, 1933), Book I, pp. 1–2.

757 Hans von Arnim, Die europäische Philosophie des Altertums. Kultur der Gegenwart (Berlin and Leipzig, 1909), Teil I, Abt. 5, p. 249.

The concept of history as a succession of events that happen but once was not only implied in the more or less scientific works of Polybius, Diodorus, and other writers, but also in some myths, such as the story of the four (or five) ages, described by Hesiod, Herototus, and Ovid. According to this story, the history of men – of all men – begins with a golden age of peace and justice under which men live as godlike beings in perfect happiness. But the historic process has the character of a steady degeneration from the golden to a silver, a brass, and finally an iron age of moral depravation and misery which represents the counterpart of the golden age. It is a pessimistic view of the world and its history. In the Judaeo-Christian myth history also begins with a golden age, the paradise, and then degenerates into a period of sin and misery. But the difference between the Greek and the Judaeo-Christian myth is not so great as to justify a view that considers only the latter but not the former as the prototype of modern philosophy of history. According to the Judaeo-Christian myth the end of history, the golden age, the lost paradise, will return in the Kingdom of God. Therefore, if it is essential for modern philosophy of history to conceive of history as a succession of events that happen but once, then the Judaeo-Christian myth is certainly a less suitable model than the Greek myth. The hope for the return of the paradise brings the Judaeo-Christian myth dangerously near to the opposite type of historic speculation, the doctrine of eternal recurrence. According to the Judaeo-Christian myth, God Jehovah created the world in six days and rested on the seventh day from his work; formed the first man of dust from the ground and the first female of the rib of the male, but nevertheless in his own image; put them in the Garden Eden, where they lived in happiness until God expelled them as a punishment for their disobedience, cursing them and their descendants; but, according to the myth, the curse will be lifted by Jehova's son Jesus Christ, who will reign in the Kingdom of God to come on earth. The "transformation" through which a secular philosophy of history such as Marx's and especially Nietzsche's could arise from *this* Judaeo-Christian myth had, indeed, to be so radical that the assumption of a derivation of modern philosophy of history from this source would become meaningless.

The doctrine of eternal recurrence, too, has its origin in Greek antiquity. Those initiated in the Orphic mysteries believed that the soul, after the miserable life of the body in this world is terminated, returns to the other world, its divine home, but it must be reborn in a new body. Only initiation in the mysteries can redeem man from this fatal cycle. In close connection with the doctrine of metempsychosis, the view of an eternal recurrence appears in the speculations of the Pythagoreans.[758]

It is understandable that Christian theology rejected this doctrine, though its own interpretation of history culminates in the belief of a return of the beginning. In his work *The City of God* Augustine says: "For what godly ears

758 See Hans Eibl, Metaphysik und Geschichte (Leipzig, Wien, 1913), pp. 105, 107 seqq.

can endure to hear, that after the passage of this life in such misery (if I may call it a life, being rather so offensive a death, and yet we love it rather than death that frees us from it), after so many intolerable mischiefs, ended all at length by true zeal and piety, we should be admitted to the sight of God, and be placed in the fruition and participation of that incorporeal light and unchangeable immortal essence with love of which we burn, all upon this condition – to leave it again at length, and be re-enfolded in mortal misery and infernal mortality, where God is lost, where truth is sought by hate, where blessedness is sought by uncleanness, and be cast from all enjoying of eternity, truth, or felicity; and this not once but often, being eternally revolved by the course of the times from the first to the latter: and all this, because by means of these revolutions, transforming us and our false beatitudes into true miseries (successively, but yet eternally), God might come to know His own works, for otherwise He should neither be able to rest from working, nor know aught that is infinite? Who can hear or endure this? Which were it true, there were not only more wit in conceiling it, but also (to speak my mind as I can) more wisdom in not knowing it."[759] Augustine rejects the Greek doctrine of eternal recurrence, not because it fails to see in history a succession of events happening but once, or because recurrence takes place at all, but because this recurrence is eternal and thus, in its application to the fate of the human soul, conflicts with the Christian doctrine of redemption: The recurrence of the first stage, the union of the soul with God, is not considered by the Phythagoreans to be definitive. Augustine's decisive motive for rejection is not that the heathen doctrine is untrue – if it were true we should "conceal" it or even "not know" it at all – but that we cannot "endure" it. However, one of the essential qualities of Nietzsche's superman is to endure the idea of eternal recurrence, the "most *oppressive* thought"; and "the means of enduring it" is "the transvaluation of all values," "freedom from morality," "*greatest elevation* of man's *consciousness of strength* as that which creates superman."[760] This idea of eternal recurrence, the direct opposite of the uniqueness of historic happening – according to Jaspers an essential element of Christian theology of history – is the essence of Nietzsche's philosophy of history. Therefore, if there is an "impulse" from which this philosophy sprang, it is classical, not Christian.

The second "Christian impulse" of Nietzsche's philosophy, as seen by Jaspers,[761] is the allegedly pessimistic evaluation of man's nature. Jaspers refers to a passage in *The Antichrist* where Nietzsche says: "There are days when I am visited by a feeling blacker than the blackest melancholy – the *contempt of*

759 Augustine, The City of God, Vol. I, Book XII, chap. 20. See Eibl, Metaphysik und Geschichte, p. 5.

760 Friedrich Nietzsche, The Will to Power, II, transl. by Anthony M. Ludovici, in: Complete Works (London and Edingburgh 1910), XV, pp. 424, 425 (§ 1059, 1060).

761 Jaspers, Nietzsche und das Christentum, pp. 52 seq.

man."[762] Jaspers quotes the statement: "There is something fundamentally wrong in man"[763], which he interprets as a transformation of the Christian thought of hereditary sin. However, the passage in *The Antichrist* does not express a judgment about man's nature in general. It is restricted, as the subsequent statements show, to "the man of today", to Nietzsche's contemporaries. Nietzsche is so contemptuous because his contemporaries, though the "truths" of Christianity have been revealed as lies, still pretend to be Christians. He despises their hypocrisy; and this hypocrisy can hardly be compared with the weakness of man from which the evil results called "hereditary sin" by theology. What Nietzsche means by the "fundamentally wrong in man" is even less comparable with this theological concept. The sentence concerned continues – and these words are not quoted by Jaspers – "he [man] is to be surpassed. Try!" The same idea is expressed in *Zarathustra:*[764] *"I teach you the superman.* Man is something that is to be surpassed. What have ye done to surpass man? – All beings hitherto have created something beyond themselves: and ye want to be the ebb of that great tide, and would rather go back to the beast than surpass man? – What is the ape to man? A laughing-stock, a thing of shame. And just the same shall man be to the Superman: a laughing-stock, and a thing of shame." This is not a pessimistic evaluation of the nature of man; it is, on the contrary, a most optimistic belief in the possibility of man's surpassing himself, of becoming superman. The ape has created something beyond himself: man; so, too, man may create something beyond itself: superman. In *Human, All-too-Human*, Nietzsche speaks of "man as the super-animal."[765] Jaspers himself refers to Nietzsche's statement: "man is the animal not definitively settled [*das noch nicht festgestellte Tier*],"[766] and interprets it as the philosopher's belief in man's ability to surpass himself. The statement interpreted by Jaspers as a transformation of the Christian thought of hereditary sin thus proves to be precisely the contrary. For, hereditary sin is a deterioration of man originally created in the image of God; it marks the descent from a godlike being to sinful man. Contrariwise, Nietzsche's belief is in an ascent from animal to man and from man to superman.

762 Nietzsche, The Antichrist, p. 176 (§ 38).

763 Nietzsches Werke, XIV (Nachgelassene Werke), p. 204 (§ 405).

764 Friedrich Nietzsche, Thus Spake Zarathustra, transl. by Thomas Common, in: Complete Works (London and Edingburgh, 1909), XI, p. 6 (§ 3).

765 Friedrich Nietzsche, Human, All-too-Human, transl. by Helen Zimmern, in: Complete Works (London and Edingburgh, 1900–1911), VI, p. 61(§ 40).

766 Jaspers, Nietzsche und das Christentum, p. 52; Nietzsche, Jenseits von Gut und Böse, in: Nietzsches Werke, VII, p. 76 (§ 62). The translation: "the animal not yet properly adapted to his environment" (Complete Works, XII, p. 82) seems to me not quite correct.

The third alleged "Christian impulse" of Nietzsche's philosophy is his "will to truth and science."[767] Jaspers asserts that "it is Christianity which first has called forth the boundlessness of the will to truth, and that Nietzsche was aware of it."[768] That can only mean that unconditioned, boundless search for truth and the absolute freedom to proclaim its results is a postulate of Christian religion. This assertion contradicts the undeniable fact, confirmed a thousand times by the history of the Christian Church, that according to the precepts of Christian religion truth may be searched for and proclaimed only within the boundaries of the Christian faith – only so far as this truth does not conflict with the Old and New Testaments, which must be recognized as divine revelations, as "holy scriptures". Jaspers's assertion openly conflicts with the fact that the Church in the name of Christianity has rigorously and by all means at its disposal attacked all results of science contradicting Scripture; that the Church, as Nietzsche said,[769] is the "mortal enemy of science." If truth is a value recognized by Christianity, it is not truth in the sense of science, that is, a truth accessible to human reason. It is a superhuman, a divine truth, not, or not entirely, accessible to human reason. It is the "truth" of which Jesus declared before Pilate that he has come into the world to bear witness to it, the truth that he was the Son of God and the King of the Jews and as such the ruler of the Kingdom of God to come from heaven to earth. It is a "truth" identical with the social value of the absolute justice of God; it is not the truth of science which, as a function of human cognition, is independent of any social value.

Jaspers sees an "abyss" between modern science and the science of the ancient Greeks because, although the Greeks are, as he admits, "the founders of science," they "do not know the indefinitely progressing science, within which all things are related to one another and are brought to cognition in this correlation, that is, a universal science."[770] The assumption of an essential difference between those who founded science and those who continued their efforts for an objective cognition of reality is paradoxical, until one learns Jaspers's view of the nature of that science which, he asserts, "only the Christian man is able to create out of his Christianess." "The Greek," he says, "recognizes ... what is in conformity with reason and law; everything else is to him nothing, is matter, μή όν, not knowable and not worth knowing. If, however, the world is created by God, then everything which exists, as created by God, is worth knowing."[771] "The idea of creation, which makes everything created as created by

767 Jaspers, Nietzsche und das Christentum, p. 55.

768 Ibid., p. 9.

769 Nietzsche, The Antichrist, p. 196 (§ 47).

770 Jaspers, Nietzsche und das Christentum, pp. 57 seq. The words: "are brought to cognition in this correlation," are the translation of a phrase that is difficult to understand: *"alles auf alles zur Erkenntniswirkung bringende [Wissenschaft]."*

771 Ibid., p. 58.

God worthy of love ... then the struggle for the image of the deity, nay for the concept of God itself, then the claim of truth ordered by God ... these three motives must cooperate to make possible the real, high science."[772] "If in view of the admired results of science God is struck out [*gestrichen*], the creation remains without a creator. However, this creation continues to exist for science in that form which it assumed in accordance with the belief in the creator."[773] This is a "science" which, indeed, is separated by an "abyss" from the science founded by the Greeks. It is not a science that corresponds to the postulate of a boundless search for truth because it is confined to very narrow bounds: to the belief in God as the creator of the world. This is a "science" controlled by theology – the "science," as understood by the theologian Sertillanges who frequently refers to Jaspers.[774]

772 Ibid., p. 61.

773 Ibid., p. 64.

774 Sertillanges, Le Christianisme, II, pp. 433, 439, 537. It is understandable that the Catholic theologian refers to Jaspers, because the latter's philosophy is a welcome support to theology. Jaspers says, in his work *Der philosophische Glaube* (München und Zürich, 1948), Englisch edition: The Perennial Scope of Philsophy, translated by Ralph Manheim (New York, 1949): "The ultimate answer is that authentic being is transcendence (or God), a proposition the true understanding of which embraces all philosophical faith and all elucidating philosophical thought" (p. 28). Under the heading: "Contents of [philosophical] faith" he says: "*God is*: Transcendence beyond the world or before the world is called God" (p. 31). There is no reason to use the word "God" for transcendence if by "God" nothing but transcendence is meant, that is, the idea that something, not nothing, exists beyond the limits of rational-empirical cognition. As a matter of fact, Jaspers's "God" is much more than mere transcendence. He speaks (p. 2) of the "God-given responsibility" of people; his God is "God-creator." Jaspers says: "God without creation is an idea in which everything vanishes. As the world becomes not only vain, but void, we are led to reduce transcendence also to nothingness, as it were, and so nothing is left" (pp. 40–41). His God is the object of the proofs for the existence of God, of which transcendence is a quality, but which is not identical with mere transcendence. After the statement: "Transcendence beyond the world or before the world is called God," Jaspers says: "We have the proofs for the existence of God." He says: "Since Kant honest thinkers are agreed that such proofs are impossible"; but only "if they aim to compel the intellect, as one can compel it to realize the earth revolves around the sun and that the moon has a reverse side." They furnish a certainty much stronger than that established by a scientific proof. As such a proof they are "impossible." "But the arguments for the existence of God do not lose their validity as ideas because they have lost their power to prove. They amount to a confirmation of faith by intellectual operations. When they are original, the thinker struck by their evidence experiences them as the profoundest event of life. When they are reflected upon with understanding, they make possible a repetition of this experience. The idea as such effects a transformation in man, it opens our eyes, in a sense. More than that, it becomes a fundament of ourselves, by enhancing our awareness of being, it becomes the source of personal depth" (p. 31). That Jaspers does not recognize the proofs for the existence of God as "scientifically cogent" (p. 32), does not mean that his philosophy renounces to ascer-

It is the idea of a "science" under the authority of theology, which – to justify itself – tries in vain to find itself in the works of the great thinkers of modern times.

In the wake of Sertillanges and Jaspers, Löwith writes: "Too deeply marked by a Christian conscience, he [Nietzsche] was unable to achieve that 'transvaluation of all values' which Christianity once has effected against paganism; for, though he intended to revert modern man to the ancient values of classical paganism, he was to thoroughly Christian and modern that only one thing preoccupied him: the thought of the *future* and the *will* to create it."[775] It is rather difficult to prove that only a Christian can think of the future and can will to create it. A philosophy, according to which the future is not a state of redemption in the Kingdom of Heaven and thus is not the work of God, but is to be created by man without any intervention by a nonexisting God, is certainly anything but Christian. Löwith admits, it is true, that Nietzsche's *Thus Spake Zarathustra* "is the most elaborate countergospel to the Christian gospel and its theological presuppositions, for the doctrine of eternal recurrence" – the main idea of Nietzsche's interpretation of history – "counteracts the doctrine of creation with all its moral consequences."[776] The last sentence is not wholly correct.

The doctrine of eternal recurrence is not absolutely opposed to the Judaeo-Christian myth of creation according to which human history returns to its starting point – the end of history, the Kingdom of God, being identical with its beginning, the paradise. This myth differs from the classical doctrine of eternal recurrence in that the recurrence is not eternal – it happens only once, at the second advent of Christ. Further, Nietzsche's "eternal recurrence" does not mean that history ends by returning to the paradise lost by the fall of man. There may be, as Löwith asserts, similarities between the *contra gentiles* of the

tain the existence of God; on the contrary. He declares: "A proved God is no God. Accordingly: only he who starts from God, can seek him. A certainty of the existence of God, however rudimentary and intangible it may be, is a premise, not a result of philosophical activity" (p. 32). As to the relationship between philosophy and religion Jaspers says: "Philosophy takes up the cause of the Biblical religion... it, at least, leaves the field open for religion... Philosophy can scarcely hold its position in the world if the human collectivity does not live in the people through religious faith" (p. 112). "With regard to religion philosophy will in practice approve the following propositions: In order to participate in Biblical religion, one must grow up in the tradition of a definite denomination. Every denomination is good to the extent that the people living in it take possession of the Biblical religion as a whole in spite of the special and finite historical degenerations of the particular historical form. Loyalty and historical consciousness bind me to the denomination in which I awakened. A change of religion is difficult without a breach in the soul." (p. 114)

775 Löwith, Meaning in History, p. 221.

776 Ibid., p. 219.

Fathers of the Church and Nietzsche's critique of Christianity and even closer similarities between the latter and the arguments Celsus and Porphyry advanced against the Christians.[777] These similarities may easily be explained by the fact that the writings concerned were directed against a definite religion, and those of Celsus and Prophyry specifically against the same religion that Nietzsche intended to destroy. However, to proceed from these similitarities to the statement that "Nietzsche's neopaganism is ... essentially Christian, by being anti-Christian"[778] is absurd. This "method" of reasoning is based on complete disregard of the logical law excluding contradictions, and therefore further discussion is meaningless.

"Like all Messiahs, true or false," Sertillanges writes, "Nietzsche is haunted [*hanté*] by the idea of redemption."[779] According to Löwith, Nietzsche's Christian faith manifests itself in his "will to a future redemption," which conflicts with his pagan doctrine of eternal recurrence.[780] Is there really in his philosophy an idea that has anything in common with the Christian belief in a future redemption, the expectation of a last judgment, the purification of immortal soul from sin, and the complete change of the old into a new man in the future Kingdom of God? This decisive question must be answered in the affirmative if the statement is to be taken seriously that Nietzsche's philosophy is essentially Christian. Such an answer, however, is impossible unless we ignore some statements Nietzsche made on the immortality of the soul and eternal justice – fundamental conditions of the theological doctrine of redemption. Some of these statements are: "the 'life after death' has no further interest for us! An indescribable blessing, which is yet too recent to be considered as such throughout the world"[781]; "there is no 'eternal justice' which requires that every fault shall be atoned and paid for, – the belief that such a justice existed was a terrible delusion and useful only to a limited extent";[782] and, his statement on redemption by the love of God, the kingdom of grace: "Love yourself through grace, and then you will no longer find your God necessary, and the entire drama of the Fall and Redemption of mankind will reach its last act in yourself."[783] But how does Löwith demonstrate Nietzsches "will to a future redemption"? Löwith says: "To the Greeks the eternal recurrence of generations and corruption explained temporal changes in nature as in history; to Nietzsche the willed acceptance of eternal recurrence requires a standpoint 'beyond man and time.' The Greeks felt awe and reverence for fate. Nietzsche

777 Ibid., p. 220.
778 Ibid.
779 Sertillanges, Le Christianisme, II, p. 432.
780 Löwith, Meaning in History, p. 221.
781 Nietzsche, The Dawn of Day, p. 75 (§ 72).
782 Ibid., p. 390 (§ 563).
783 Ibid., p. 83 (§ 79).

makes the superhuman effort to will and love it. Thus he was unable to develop his vision as a supreme and objective order, as the Greeks did, but introduced it as a subjective ethical imperative. The theory of eternal recurrence becomes with him a practical device and a 'hammer' to pound into man the idea of an absolute responsibility, substituting that sense of responsibility which was alive as long as man lived in the presence of God and in the expectation of a last judgment."[784] That Nietzsche's philosophy establishes an ethical imperative constituting individual responsibility means that it has only moral implication, and not a theological one. A sense of responsibility may be alive in man even if he does not live in the presence of God and in the expectation of a last judgment. One of the main tendencies of Nietzsche's philosophy is, precisely, to emancipate morality from religion. Nietzsche's ethical imperative has nothing to do with a "will to future redemption." However, Löwith continues: "But, since the will does not move in a circle but in a straight line and in an irrevesible direction, the crucial problem of Zarathustra becomes the 'redemption' of the will form its one-dimensional structure. Yet how can the will integrate itself with the cyclic law of the cosmos, where every movement of advance is, at the same time, one of return? Nietzsche's answer is: The will must redeem itself from itself by also willing backward, i. e., by accepting voluntarily what it did not will, the whole past of all that is already done and existent – in particular, the fact of our own existence, which nobody had produced by his will." If this interpretation of the chapter "Redemption"[785] is correct, it means that what Löwith presents as Nietzsche's "will to a future redemption" is not directed at the future but at the past, and that the self-redemption of the will is totally different from Christian redemption. It does not mean the total change of man's existence, but its radical confirmation. The decisive passage reads: "To redeem what is past, and to transform every 'It was' into 'Thus would I have it!' – that only do I call redemption!" It is a "willing backwards." Zarathustra's "redemption" is "reconciliation with time." The will redeems itself by accepting the past – in direct opposition to the Christian idea of redemption which implies the condemnation of the past, the atonement for the sinful past by the last judgment of the future, the principle of retribution which is the essence of this divine justice. "*The spirit of revenge*: my friends that hath hitherto been man's best contemplation; and where there was suffering it was claimed there was always penalty." "'Penalty,' so calleth itself revenge … 'Morally are things ordered according to justice and penalty. Oh, where is there deliverance from the flux of things and from the 'existance of penalty?'[786] Thus did madness preach. 'Can there be deliverance when there is

784 Löwith, Meaning in History, p. 221.

785 Nietzsches, Thus Spake Zarathustra, pp. 165 seqq.

786 The German text of this sentence runs as follows: "Sittlich sind die Dinge geordnet nach Recht und Strafe. Oh wo ist die Erlösung vom Fluss der Dinge und der Strafe 'Dasein'?

eternal justice? ... eternal must also be all penalties!' Thus did madness preach." It is evident that all this is directed against the doctrine of redemption by the last judgment. The entire chapter "Redemption" is a passionate rejection of the Christian idea of redemption. That true redemption is "reconciliation with time" is not even Zarathustra's last word. There is something higher than all reconciliation. "Something higher than all reconciliation must the Will will which, is the Will to Power." There is nothing more incompatible with the Christian idea of redemption than this "Will to Power"!

It is absurd, then, to see in Nietzsche's Zarathustra God who became man, as Sertillanges suggests: "Nietzsche invoked the intervention of a superior individual consciousness, of a superman, a 'solitary being, the summit of mankind' and his folly made him eventually believe that he himself was this being. However, Zarathustra-G did not need to be invented; he was only rediscovered. This concentration and, then, this enlightenment of all through an individual consciousness: it is the Incarnation that realizes it."[787] By "Incarnation" Sertillanges understands the mystery referred to in St. John, 1:1–14: "In the beginning was the Word and the Word was with God, and the Word was God ... And the Word became flesh and dwelt among us." It is the "irruption of God into His creation."[788]

In the same spirit Balthasar takes Nietzsche for an apocalyptic prophet[789] and sees in Zarathustra an "eschatological double [*eschatolologischen Doppelgänger*]".[790] Zarathustra, Balthasar says, "appears messianically adorned," he "has 'his Hazar, his realm of thousand years,' he conducts 'the new supper,' sings the 'song of the seven seals,' he solemnly sets out on his journey of salvation 'down into the world.'" Where does Balthasar take the quotation: Zarathustra has "his Hazar, his realm of thousand years"? Not from Nietzsche's *Thus spake Zarathustra;* probably from a statement made by Nietzsche's sister, Elisabeth Förster-Nietzsche, in an essay "Die Entstehung von 'Also sprach Zarathustra.'"[791] "My brother had the figure of Zarathustra in his mind from very earliest youth: he once told me that even as a child he had dreamt of him. At different periods in his life, he would call this haunter of his dreams by different names; 'but in the end', he declares in a note to the subject, 'I had to do a *Persian* the honour of identifying him with this creature of my fancy. Persians were the first to take a broad and comprehensive view of history. Every series

Also predigt der Wahnsinn." It is not – as in the English translation by Thomas Common – "the 'existence' of penalty" but "the penalty 'existence' [die Strafe 'Dasein']", which means 'existence' *as* a penalty, to which Nietzsche refers.

787 Sertillanges, Le Christianisme, I, p. 17.

788 Seratillanges, Le Christianisme, I, p. 16.

789 Balthasar, Prometheus, p. 704.

790 Ibid., p. 716.

791 Nietzsches Werke, VI, Anhang, p. III.

of evolutions, according to them, was presided over by a prophet; and every prophet had his *'Hazar'* – his dynasty of a thousand years."[792]

This statement is certainly not sufficient to assume that Nietzsche visualized the hero of his main work as a Messiah, inaugurating a realm of thousand years. Nothing of this kind can he found in this work. Such a concept is incompatible with the central idea of the eternal recurrence. The chapter "The Supper"[793] is evidently a persiflage of the Lord's Supper of the Gospel. It ends with the words, "At this [during that meal] there was nothing else spoken of but the *higher man*," not of God, as at the Lord's Supper. In the following chapter, "The Higher Man," we read: "Now however this God hath died! Ye higher men, this God was your greatest danger." The "Song of the Seven Seals" expresses Zarathustra's love of eternity; but Zarathustra's eternity is not the realm of a thousand years. It is "the marriage-ring of rings, the ring of the return."[794] If Zarathustra sets out on a journey of redemption, this redemption, as pointed out, is directly opposed to the Christian *eschaton*. This is the truth about Zarathustra, the "eschatological double."

When Nietzsche worked on *Zarathustra*, he formulated the following aphorism: "Who no longer finds greatness in God, does not find it at all – he must deny or create it."[795] The meaning is evident: If a man – like Nietzsche or his Zarathustra – does not believe in God, he must himself create the values which the believers attribute to God. The values are not created by God, and hence must be created by man. It is an outspoken antitheistic pronouncement: Man against God. Sertillanges, who considers this statement most revealing, distorts it into the opposite. "The principle of values is in God. Whoever denies God abolishes all values. Consequently, man must recreate these values; but how can he succeed without making himself God, without substituting the arbitrary *fiat* and frantic imagination of an anti-God for that which God has done, the truth and goodness of his creation?"[796]

Sertillanges quotes the following sentence by Zarathustra[797] as proof of the "Christian filiation" of Nietzsche's philosophy: "Here are priests: but although they are mine enemies, pass them quietly and with sleeping swords! Even among them there are heroes ... my blood is related to theirs, and I want withal to see my blood honoured in theirs." In order to make his interpretation plausible, Sertillanges has to omit the following words between the two sentences he quotes: "Many of them have suffered too much –: so they want to make others suffer. Bad enemies are they: nothing is more revengeful

792 Translated by Thomas Common in his introduction to Thus Spake Zarathustra, p. IX.
793 Nietzsche, Thus Spake Zarathustra, pp. 347 seqq.
794 Ibid., p. 280.
795 Nietzsche, Gesammelte Werke (München, 1920–1929), XIV, Aus dem Nachlass, p. 80.
796 Sertillanges, Le Christianisme II, p. 439.
797 Ibid., p. 437; Nietzsche, Thus Spake Zarathustra, pp. 105 seqq.

than their meekness. And readily doth he soil himself who toucheth them." Nor does Sertillanges quote the following passage: "And when they had passed, a pain attacked Zarathustra; but not long had he struggled with the pain, when he began to speak thus: It moveth my heart for those priests. They also go against my taste; but that is the smallest matter unto me, since I am among men. But I suffer and have suffered with them: prisoners are they unto me, and stigmatised ones. He whom they call Savior put them in fetters: – in fetters of false values and fatuous words! Oh, that someone would save them from their Savior!" These words certainly prove the opposite of a "Christian filiation."

Nietzsche's philosophy of the superman and Marx's historic materialism are characteristic symptoms of modern civilization. When Voegelin interprets modernity as Gnosticism, he must classify not only Marx but also Nietzsche as a Gnostic. Indeed, in his recent publication he says of Nietzsche that he was, like Marx, "a speculative Gnostic."[798] How does he justify this statement? He refers to section 230 of *Beyond Good and Evil*[799] where Nietzsche tries to explain what he said immediately before (section 229) of the "fundamental will of the spirit," namely that it "instinctively aims at appearance and superficiality." Now he says that the fundamental will of the spirit" which "wishes to be master internally and externally" and which is "the power of the spirit to appropriate foreign elements," "reveals itself in a strong tendency to assimilate the new to the old, to simplify the manifold." It "has at its service an apparently opposed impulse of the spirit, a suddenly adopted preference of ignorance, of arbitrary shutting out ... a sort of defensive attitude against much that is knowable." "Here also belong an occasional propensity of the spirit to let itself be deceived (perhaps with a waggish suspicion that it is *not* so and so, but is only allowed to pass as such) a delight in uncertainty and ambiguity, an exulting enjoyment of out-of-the-way narrowness and mystery ... an enjoyment of the arbitrariness of all these manifestations of power. Finally, in this connection, there is the not unscrupulous readiness of the spirit to deceive other spirits and dissemble before them ... The spirit enjoys therein its craftiness and its variety of disguises." "Voegelin, after quoting these statements, presents Nietzsche's thought as follows: "The *libido dominandi* has, however, a force and cruelty which goes beyond the enjoyment of masquerade and deception of the other. It turns against the thinker himself and unmasks his thinking as a cunning will to power. 'A kind of cruelty of the intellectual conscience,' 'an extravagant honesty' dissolves the deception, but – and this is the decisive point – not in order to advance to the truth beyond the deception, but to substitute a new deception for the old one. The masquerade goes on and the other remains

798 Voegelin, Wissenschaft, Politik und Gnosis, p. 39.

799 Nietzsche, Beyond Good and Evil, pp. 178 seqq.

deceived, if he let himself to be deceived."[800] The passage of which Voegelin quotes only the two phrases "cruelty of intellectual conscience" and "extravagant honesty" runs as follows: "*Counter to this* propensity for appearance, for simplification, for a disguise, for a cloak, in short for an outside – for every outside is a cloak – there operates the sublime tendency of the man of knowledge, which takes and *insists* on taking things profoundly, variously and thoroughly; as a kind of cruelty of the intellectual conscience and taste, which every courageous thinker will acknowledge in himself, provided, as it ought to be, that he has sharpened and hardened his eye sufficiently long for introspection, and is accustomed to severe discipline and even severe words. He will say: There is something cruel in the tendency of my spirit: let the virtuous and amiable try to convince him that it is not so. In fact, it would sound nicer, if instead of our cruelty, perhaps our 'extravagant honesty' were talked about, whispered about and glorified – we free, *very* free spirits – and some day perhaps *such* will actually be our – posthumous glory! Meanwhile – for there is plenty of time until then – we should be least inclined to deck ourselves out in such florid and fringed moral verbiage ..." What these free thinkers decline is not "the sublime tendency of the man of knowledge" of "taking things profoundly, variously and thoroughly," that is to say: the will to truth, but only to qualify it as moral virtue. It is precisely the sincere will to advance beyond deception to the truth, which Nietzsche here finally declares as "the fundamental will of the spirit"; and the "deceptions" against which the man "hardened by the discipline of science" shall stand "with fearless Oedipus eyes, and stopped Ulysses ears," are "the enticements of old metaphysical birdcatchers, who have piped to him far too long: Thou art more! Thou art higher! Thou hast a different origin!" – that is, the theological deception that man is created by God in his own image. In spite of his statement that the deceiving masquerade goes on, Voegelin says: "We recognize in the 'cruelty of the intellectual conscience' the spiritual movement which in Nietzsche's gnosis functionally corresponds to the Platonic *periagoge*, to the turning back, the opening of the soul." But in the next sentence Voegelin says: "In the Gnostic movement, however, man remains closed to the transcendent being. The will to power strikes against the wall of existence, which has become a prison. It forces the spirit into the rhythm of deception and self-torment." The will to power is the will to rule. "To rule means to be God. In order to be God the Gnostic man accepts the suffering of deception and self-torment."[801] In a note to this statement[802] Voegelin refers to Nietzsche's sentence "Herrschen – und nicht mehr Knecht eines Gottes sein: – dies Mittel blieb zurück, den Menschen zu veredeln. [To rule – and to be no longer the servant of a God – this is the

800 Voegelin, Wissenschaft, Politik und Gnosis, p. 40.
801 Ibid., p. 41.
802 Ibid., p. 89 (note 12).

means that is left to ennoble man.]"[803] "Nothing in this statement justifies Voegelin's interpretation. If, by the "Gnostic movement," the original gnosis is meant, the statement conflicts with the historic truth about the Gnostic religion, which more than any other religion tried to open the soul of man to the transcendent being. If by "Gnostic movement" Nietzsche's philosophy is meant, nothing can be more opposite to the gnosis than this philosophy. If the "Gnostic man" is the follower of the original gnosis, the statement that he accepts deceptions and self-torment, in order to rule has no foundation; that he wants to be God is an incorrect description of his mystic experience of a union with God; that Nietzsche's superman has such an experience is evidently not true; that he wants to be God or, as Voegelin says, that "he *must* be God" contradicts Nietzsche's statements. Voegelin[804] refers to a passage in "The Night Song" of *Thus Spake Zarathustra*: "Nacht ist es: ach dass ich Licht sein muss. ['Tis night, alas, that I have to be light!]".[805] "To be light" means here to be someone who has knowledge among those who have none. Nothing justifies the interpretation "to be God." For other passages in *Zarathustra* expressly say that the superman does not want to be God: "Ah, ye brethren, that God whom I created was human work and human madness, like all the Gods!"[806] But man cannot really create a God. "God is a conjecture; but I do not wich your conjecturing to reach beyond your creating will. Could you *create* God? – Then I pray you be silent about all Gods! But ye could well create the Superman." "God is a conjecture: but I should like your conjecturing restricted to the conceivable. – Could ye *conceive* a God? ... But that I may reveal my heart entirely unto you, my friends: *if* there were Gods, how could I endure to be no God! *Therefore* there are no Gods."[807] I *endure to be no God*; because (and therefore) there are no Gods.

The attempt to interpret Nietzsche's philosophy as Gnosticism – and that means, if the term be taken in its only admissible significane, as a kind of religion, though a heretic religion – must founder because of the radically antireligious, atheistic character of the philosophy. But it is exactly Nietzsche's atheism that Voegelin calls "Gnostic." One of the more drastic expressions of this atheism is a chapter of *Joyful Wisdom*, wherein Nietzsche speaks of the madman – "madman" in the eyes of his fellowmen, not in Nietzsche's – who "on a bright morning lighted a lantern and ran to the market place calling out unceasingly: 'I seek God'"; and then called out: "Where is God gone? I mean to tell you! *We have killed him* – you and I! We are all his murderers! ... God is dead! God remains dead! And we have killed him! ... There never was a

803 Nietzsches Werke, XII, p. 282, sentence 250.
804 Voegelin, Wissenschaft, Politik und Gnosis, pp. 41 seqq.
805 Nietzsche, Thus Spake Zarathustra, p. 126.
806 Ibid., p. 32.
807 Ibid., p. 99.

greater event – and on account of it, all who are born after us belong to a higher history than any history hitherto."[808] The expression "death of God" is, indeed, used in Christian theology. There it refers to the death of Christ on the cross,[809] and hence does not mean a real death because Christ continued to live after his "death." Nietzsche, however, uses the phrase in order to express, in a poetical form, the negation of God's existence, the emancipation of man from the belief in God. What he means by the phrase "God is dead" is explained clearly in *The Joyful Wisdom*: "The most important of more recent events – that 'God is dead,' that the belief in the Christian God has become unworthy of belief – already begins to cast its first shadows over Europe."[810] Nietzsche speaks here only of the Christian God, because he refers to Europe of his time. But there can be no doubt that when he says "God is dead", he does not think that other gods are worthy of belief. In *Thus Spake Zarathustra* he says: "Dead are all the gods: now do we desire the Superman to live."[811] According to Voegelin, the phrase means "Gnostic murder."[812] But how can the

808 Nietzsche, The Joyful Wisdom, pp. 167 seq.

809 See Henri de Lubac, The Drama of Atheist Humanism, translated by Edith M. Riley (London, 1949), p. 20. As for Nietzsche's use of this expression, Lubac says: "Whatever its antecedents may have been, the meaning which Nietzsche attaches to this phrase, 'the death of God,' is new. On his lips it is not a mere statement of fact. Nor is it a lament or a piece of sarcasm. It expresses a choice. 'Now,' says Nietzsche, 'it is our preference that decides against Christianity – not arguments'" (p. 22).

810 Nietzsche, The Joyful Wisdom, p. 275.

811 Nietzsche, Thus Spake Zarathustra, p. 91.

812 Voegelin, The New Science of Politics, p. 131. Jonas ("Gnosticism and Modern Nihilism," Social Research, XIX [1952], pp. 441 seqq.) following Martin Heidegger, interprets Nietzsche's saying "God is dead," to mean "that the transcendental world is without effective force." This would imply that the transcendental world exists. But the phrase means that God and, consequently, the transcendental world does not exist at all. Jonas sees in Nietzsche's phrase the expression of nihilism such as apparent especially in modern existentialism; and tries to show an analogy between this nihilism and the gnosis which, he asserts, has a nihilistic character. This analogy is – even according to Jonas's own characterization of modern nihilism and the gnosis – more than doubtful. From the point of view ot nihilism "there is no longer the *cosmos* with whose immanent *logos* my own can feel kinship, no longer the order of the whole which gives meaning to man's part in it, and therefore to his place in it." Nature is indifferent to man, it "has no reference to ends. With the ejection of teleology from the system of natural causes, nature, herself purposeless, ceased to provide any sanction to possible human purposes. A universe without an intrinsic hierarchy of being, as the Copernican universe is, leaves values ontologically unsupported, and the self is thrown back entirely upon itself in its quest for meaning and value. Meaning is no longer found, but is 'given.' Values are no longer beheld in the vision of objective reality, but are posited as feats of valuation. As functions of the will they are solely my own responsibility (pp. 431–432)." However, the gnosis, as a religious doctrine – and Jonas stresses its religious character – is far from being nihilistic in this sense of the term. What Jonas pre-

negation of God's existence be Gnostic, if Gnostic speculation presupposes the most intense belief in the existence of a transcendent God? Very simply: God's

sents as nihilism is incompatible with a religion – the belief in a transcendental God, even if this God has no relation to this world. The Gnostic belief in this God implies the belief in a transcendental world of goodness in opposition to this empirical world of evil; it implies the dualism of two worlds of which the one, so far as it is qualified as good, is placed above the other, disqualified as evil; both worlds are parts of the universe which, consequently, shows a definite hierarchy. "The salient feature to be emphasized here is the radically dualistic mood which underlies the whole gnostic attitude ... The dualism is between man and the world, and concurrently between the world and God." The gnosis teaches "that the Divine has no part and no concern in the physical universe; that the true God, strictly transmundane, is not revealed or even indicated by the world, and is therefore the Unknown, the totally Other, unknowable in terms of any worldly analogies" (p. 435). But this God, in the belief of the Gnostics, exists within a transcendental sphere. He is knowable, though not in terms of worldly analogies, yet by a mystic experience, the typical experience of the Gnostic. "Gnosis" means this mystic knowledge of God. "Gnosticism", says Jonas, "in its cosmological aspect ... states that the world is the creature not of God but of some inferior principle" (p. 435). "Since the true God cannot be the creator of that to which selfhood feels so utterly a stranger, nature must have been created by a lowly demiurge, a power far removed from the supreme source of Being, a perversion of the Divine ... he created the world out of ignorance and passion," he is considered to be a "malignant force" (p. 436). This antagonism between the "true" God, the "supreme" source of being, and a "lowly" demiurge who, as "a malignant force," creates an evil world out of ignorance and passion, is evidently the antagonism between an absolute good and an absolute evil. This positive and negative value are objective values ontologically supported, because imagined as immanent in the two worlds, and independent of the will of man who in his quest for meaning and value is thus not thrown back upon himself. If the physical world is created by an evil demon, teleology cannot be ejected from it, in the way teleology is ejected from the world of modern science, a world not created by a good God or an evil demon. The world created by the demiurge of Gnostic speculation has a definite purpose, not a good one, of course, but a bad one: the realization of the evil. Jonas says of the Gnostic view of the universe: "Yet it is still *cosmos*, an order – but order with a vengeance ... Far from being chaos, the creation of the demiurge, that antitype of knowing, is a comprehensive system, governed by law" (pp. 436–437); but this rule "is tyranny and not providence" (p. 437). If the world is created by a demiurge, and if this world is governed by laws that constitute a tyrannical rule, these laws must be the expression of the evil will of the demiurge, in the same way as the laws of nature created, according to Christian theology, by the good God, are the expression of the good will of this God. This idea is the basis of a teleological view of the world. Man, according to Gnosticism, is a stranger to this world, "man's inner self – called the pneuma – is not part of the world" (p. 435); but man is not a stranger to the true God; and man's *pneuma* is definitely part of the other transcendental world.

If modern nihilism is expressed in Nietzsche's phrase "God is dead," and if God means transcendence, then Gnosticism, is the opposite of nihlism. Referring to his quoted interpretation of Nietzsche's phrase, Jonas says: "In a modified, rather paradoxical way this statement applies also to the gnostic position." This is, indeed, paradoxical! For, death is the death of the spirit. There is no other spirit than God's; and "the death of the spirit is the price of progress" – "progress," of course, only as in-

the center of the Gnostic religion is the "true God." Jonas admits that the "extreme dualism" of the Gnostic religion "is of itself the very opposite of an abandonment of transcendence. The transmundane God represents transcendence in the most radical form ... But this transcendence ... does not stand in any positive relation to the sensible world" (p. 442). This element of the Gnostic religion, however, does not weaken its opposition to atheistic nihilism, it even strengthens it. For the doctrine that God has no relation to this world, is the consequence of his transcendence. Gnostic theology offers the most consistent doctrine of divine transcendence, and is as such more opposed to atheistic nihilism than a religion in which God is not only transcendent to this world, but at the same time immanent in it.

Since modern nihilism is in the first place moral nihilism, as Jonas seems to think, then an analogy to Gnosticism can be assumed only if this religion is nihilistic in a moral sense. This, however, is not very likely, if the Christian gnosis – as Baur has shown (Die christliche Gnosis, p. 27) – was essentialy related to the teaching of Christ, and the Gnostics considered Christianity the absolute religion. But Jonas says: "For all purposes of man's relation to existing reality, this hidden God is a nihilistic conception: no *nomos* emanates from him, no law for nature and thus also no law for human conduct as a part of the natural order" (p. 442). But this does not mean moral nihilism. The moral law does not "emanate" from the true God, but is immanent in the idea of a God whose essential quality is goodness, which is a moral principle; and it is from this idea that the Gnostics deduced the moral postulate to disengage themselves from the evil world. "In Gnostic reasoning," says Jonas, "we sometimes meet the merely subjectivist form of the antinomistic argument: nothing is naturally bad or good, things in themselves are indifferent, and only by human opinion are actions good or bad" (p. 443). But since Gnostic reasoning always presupposes the existence of a God who, by his very nature, is good, the "subjectivist form of the antinomistic argument" can refer only to the values constituted by the *nomos* emanating from the demiurge; and this theory of values must not necessarily imply that the Gnostics, who did not consider themselves bound by this *nomos*, refused to recognize any order regulating their behavior in this world. It can only mean that the values constituted by this order – which does not emanate from the true God but from the demiurge – are only relative; just as modern moral and legal positivism does not mean the negation of moral or legal values, but only that the values generally recognized are relative, not absolute values immanent in nature. Gnostic antinomism can only mean that the values constituted by the *nomos* of the demiurge are inferior to the moral value represented by the true God. Jonas rejects this interpretation by referring to the metaphysical background of the subjectivist view. Its "ultimate source turns out to be not human but demiurgical." The moral Code as well as the physical *nomos* "emanate from the lord of the world as agencies of his power, unified in the double aspect of the Jewish God as creator and legislator" (p. 443). But Ptolemaeus, a Gnostic of the Valentianian sect, taught that the demiurge, the creator of the world, whose function is to establish justice, cannot be absolutely evil, that he must be in the midst between good and evil, that his justice is inferior to that of the true God (Baur, Die christliche Gnosis, p. 205). "Insofar as the principle of the moral law [emanating from the lord of the world, the demiurge] is justice," says Jonas, "it has the same character of constraint on the psychical side that cosmic fate has on the physical side." The tended by atheists. "Nietzsche revealed this mystery of the Western apocalypse when he announced that God was dead and that He had been murdered. This Gnostic murder is constantly committed by the men who sacrificed God to civilization. The more fervently all human energies are thrown into the great enterprise of salvation through world-immanent action, the farther the human beings who engage in this enterprise move away from the life of the spirit [which means: God]. And, since the life of the spirit is the source of order in man and society [which implies that without belief in God there can be no order in man and society], the very success of Gnostic civilization is the cause of its decline." But the decline of the religious movement of the gnosis was not due to atheism, but to its ahistorism (see above, p. 74), which was the consequence of its fanatic theism, its belief in the existence of a transcendent God.

---

man who obeys the law "has abandoned the authority of his self" (p. 444). This attitude has "anarchical and sometimes libertinistic consequences." But Jonas adds: "The consequences can be either libertinistic or ascetic, and actually, except for a brief period of revolutionary extremism, they have probably more often been the latter than the former" (p. 444). Ascetism can only be the consequence of a moral view, but this view may differ from that of Christian orthodoxy. This difference may explain the fact that Irenaeus stigmatized the Gnostic doctrine as immoral and accused the followers of some sects of sexual licentiousness. What is stigmatized as libertinism, for instance, the communism of women advocated by the followers of Basileides and Ephiphanes, was based on the idea of communism, conceived of by the Gnostics as a moral principle (see Leisegang, Die Gnosis, pp. 208, 244, 258, 261). Marcion, it is true, rejected without reservation the retributive justice of the demiurge; but only to oppose to it another moral principle: the love of the true God, because his main concern was to restore the genuine teaching of Christ. Marcion's doctrine, like that of all or at least the more important Gnostics, has a thoroughly moral character, which is the inevitable consequence of the fact that the starting point of the religious movement of the gnosis was the question of the origin of evil (see Baur, Die christliche Gnosis, pp. 19 seq.). If the Gnostics considered the world evil and, consequently, not created by the good God, it was above all the moral evil they saw in this world and passionately condemned. The Gnostic dualism between the good God and the evil demiurge is evidently – in the first place at least – a moral dualism; and in this moral dualism of the gnosis the moral dualism of the Manichean religion is rooted. There is, then, no good reason to interpret Gnosticism as moral nihilism.

Jonas does not ignore the existence of a "cardinal difference" between the gnostic and the existential-nihilistic dualism: "Gnostic man is thrown into an antagonistic, anti-divine, and therefore anti-human nature, modern man into an indifferent one. And only the latter case represents the absolute vacuum, the really bottomless pit" (p. 450). However, Gnostic man is not only thrown in an anti-divine sensible world, but, at the same time, is essentially related, through his *pneuma*, to a transcendental divine world of the absolute good which is the moral basis of his existence. Therefore it is not enough that Jonas admits: "this makes modern nihilism infinitely more radical and more desperate than Gnostic nihilism ever could be, for all its panic terror of the world and its defiant contempt of its laws" (p. 451). It is not enough because the Gnostic religion is not merely less nihilistic than modern nihilism, it is not nihilistic at all.

How can modern civilization be Gnostic if its decline will be the effect of its Nietzschean atheism? According to Voegelin, the very cause of its decline is the belief in self-salvation, and self-salvation is specifically Gnostic, although the gnosis was anything but atheistic. "Gnostic speculation overcame the uncertainty of faith by receding from transcendence and endowing man and his intramundane range of action with the meaning of eschatological fulfillment. In the measure in which this immanentization progressed experientially, civilizational activity became a mystical work of self-salvation."[813] Nietzsche is a Gnostic, his murder of God is a Gnostic murder, because he believed like the Gnostics in the "miracle of self-salvation." "Self-salvation, the tragedy of Gnosticism which Nietzsche experienced to the full until it broke his soul, is a fulfillment of life that will come to every man with the feeling that he is making his contribution to society according to his ability, compensated by a weekly pay check."[814]

If Nietzsche believed in salvation at all, it was certainly self-salvation. But this self-salvation consists in man's emancipation from the belief in God; and it is through this self-salvation – which stands in direct opposition to the Christians salvation through Jesus Christ, the divine redeemer – that man becomes superman. In this respect, Voegelin's interpretation of Nietzsche's philosophy is correct. But Voegelin's hint that the belief in self-salvation shattered Nietzsche's soul is without foundation. Physical and mental illness shattered Nietzsche's soul. To ridicule, from the height of theological speculation, the feeling of a man who seeks the fulfilment of his life in making his contribution to society according to his ability, by assuming that his motive is compensation "by a weekly pay check" (probably referring to the socialist principle: "to everybody according to his needs"), is a matter of taste, which hardly deserves mention. However, one cannot accept Voegelin's assumption that self-salvation is an element of the gnosis – an assumption that is one of the roots of his classification of modernity as Gnosticism and his interpretation of Nietzsche's atheism as a "Gnostic" murder of God. This assumption is a fundamental error. Gnostic redemption is the work of God. This redemption cannot be an autonomous action of the individual to be redeemed – like the proletarian revolution of Marx's interpretation of history or the murder of God in Nietzsche's philosophy of the superman. For, as pointed out on page 73, the Gnostic is not an active subject, not a superman in Nietzsche's sense,[815] and he

813 Voegelin, The New Science of Politics, p. 129.

814 Ibid., pp. 129, 174–175.

815 Harnack (Marcion, p. 188), refers to "supermen" in the Gnostic theology of Marcion. But this word has here a meaning entirely different from that which Nietzsche has in mind. Men who conforming to the Gnostic doctrine reduce eating and drinking to a minimum, abstain from sexual intercourse, and thus destroy their bodies and – in the last analysis – mankind, become "supermen" in the Gnostic sense, "for they consider

is not able to bring about his redemption by himself. He is the passive object of this process that consists in his union with God, a process by which he is reborn. This rebirth is the effect of a mystic operation by which God enters the individual in a state of ecstasy. By this "immanentization", to use the word Voegelin prefers, the divine pneuma is substituted for the human soul. This metamorphosis by which the Gnostic mystic becomes a new man is the Gnostic salvation; it cannot be self-salvation because it is achieved by the complete loss of his human self.[816] If Nietzsche's idea of redemption is the mystic work of Gnostic self-salvation, as Voegelin asserts, then Nietzsche is a mystic; and this could hardly be assumed when Nietzsche's view on mysticism is considered: "Mystical explanations are regarded as profound; the truth is that they do not even go the length of being superficial."[817]

In his recent publication Voegelin again refers to Nietzsche's phrase "God is dead." He says: "The murder of God is, like the Promethean hate of the Gods, a general possibility of man's relation to God. [Der Gottesmord ist, ebenso wie der prometheische Götterhass, eine generelle Möglichkeit menschlichen Verhaltens zu Gott.]".[818] Thus Nietzsche's atheism, like Marx's atheism, is interpreted as theism. A relation of man to God is possible only if God exists. The interpretation is based on the assumption that God exists also in the relation to the atheist – the assumption of one who believes in the existence of God. But atheism is the rejection of this assumption, and its interpretation as theism is based on the supposititious attribution *pi* this assumption to the atheist. "The one who murdered God becomes himself God. [Wer Gott mordet,

the man in themselves [that is, the body] as enemy." Only the soul can be redeemed; there is nothing specifically human in the body (p. 175). To become a superman in the Nietzschean sense man must consider the man in himself as his best friend and as the highest being. Of the "despisers of the body" Zarathustra says: "'Body am I, and soul' – so saith the child ... But the awakended one, the knowing one saith: Body am I entirely, and nothing more; and soul is only the name of something in the body." "I go not your way, ye despisers of the body! Ye are no bridges for me to the Superman!" (Thus Spake Zarathustra, pp. 35 seqq.).

816 Festugière, La Révélation (Paris, 1954), IV, p. 264, describes this process as follows: "Pour voir Dieu, il faut renaître un homme nouveau qui remplace entièrement l'homme ancien ... c'est maintenant le Dieu Noûs luimême qui, substantiellement et personnellement, habite en l'homme. A ce stade, les dispositions à l'union mystique sont portées à leur comble. Homme et Dieu ne s'unissent plus comme deux entités distinctes. L'homme ayant été remplacé par Dieu, on peut presque parler d'identité. Le cercle se ferme: Dieu loue Dieu." Jonas (Gnostis und spätantiker Geist, p. 201), characterizes this Gnostic rebirth as an "extinction of one's own personality" and "its replacement by a totally heterogeneous one." The result is a new self. For the alleged self-alienation in the religion of the gnosis, see above, p. 73.

817 Nietzsche, The Joyful Wisdom, p. 169.

818 Voegelin, Wissenschaft, Politik und Gnosis, p. 68. A similar interpretation has been presented before Voegelin by Martin Heidegger. See below, pp. 225 seqq.

wird selbst zum Gott.]".[819] Hence Voegelin says that Nietzsche's superman is "the man, who makes himself a God [Nietzsches Übermensch, der Mensch, der sich selbst zum Gott macht.]".[820] But since Nietzsche's "murder of God" is only the expression of man's emancipation from the theological doctrine of God as the transcendent cause of reality, it cannot – and certainly does not in Nietzsche's philosophy – mean that man becomes God, that the superman denies the existence of God in order to become God himself. Voegelin refers to the statement of the madman in *Joyful Wisdom*: "Shall we not ourselves have to become Gods, merely to seem worthy of it [that is, of the murder of God]?"[821] It is a question, and the answer to it – according to Nietzsche's intention – is certainly not in the affirmative. It is preceded by the statement: "Is not the magnitude of this deed too great for us?" It is followed by the sentence: "There never was a greater event – and on account of it, all who are born after us belong to a higher history than any history hitherto!" Then we read: "Here the madman was silent and looked again at his hearers, they also were silent and looked at him in surprise. At last he threw his lantern on the ground, so that it broke in pieces and was extinguished. 'I come too early' he said, 'I am not yet at the right time. This prodigious event is still on its way, and is traveling – it has not yet reached men's ears.'" The meaning is clear: The "murder of God," that is, the emancipation from the belief in God, is a deed too great for men of this generation, but not for men of coming generations. They will not have to become gods merely to seem worthy of this deed. An atheist who is convinced that there is not and cannot be such a being as God, cannot think of being a God himself. The statement to which Voegelin refers has evidently the same meaning as the statement in *Zarathustra* quoted above: "*If* there were Gods, how could I endure it to be no God! Therefore there are no Gods." Voegelin distorts the meaning of Nietzsche's words into its opposite. But this is scarcely the worst example of his Nietzsche's interpretations. Voegelin imputes to Nietzsche's philosophy – as to the doctrine of Marx – to bring about murder: "The murder of God is followed in the historic process not by superman but by the murder of men – the *deicidium* of the Gnostic theoreticians is followed by the *homicidium* of the revolutionary practical men [Auf den Gottesmord folgt im geschichtlichen Prozess nicht der Übermensch, sondern der Menschenmord – auf das *deicidium* der gnostischen Theoretiker das *homicidium* der revolutionären Praktiker.]".[822]

Nietzsche's philosophy clearly, incontestably, passionately rejects Christian metaphysics. Nevertheless, the attempt has been made to construct a close affinity between Nietzsche and Kierkegaard, this super-Christian, who consid-

819 Ibid., p. 75.

820 Ibid., p. 78.

821 Nietzsche, The Joyful Wisdom, p. 168.

822 Voegelin, Wissenschaft, Politik und Gnosis, pp. 76, 77.

ered himself a "missionary within Christendom itself, aiming to introduce Christianity into Christendom."[823] Balthasar calls the two anatagonistic thinkers "twin brothers of fate," "companions in arms."[824] How does he demonstrate this companionship in arms of the one who fights against, and the other who fights for Christianity? He quotes[825] a passage from Nietzsche's *Joyful Wisdom*: "There is a lake which one day refused to flow away, and threw up a dam at the place where it had hitherto discharged: since then this lake has always risen higher and higher. Perhaps the very renunciation will also furnish us with the strength with which the renunciation itself can be borne; perhaps man will ever rise higher and higher from that point onward, when he no longer *flows out* into a God."[826] Balthasar, then, confronts this passage with a quotation from Kierkegaard's *Works of Love*:[827] "As the peaceful lake is grounded deep in the hidden spring which no eye can see, so a man's love is grounded even deeper in the love of God. If there were at bottom no wellspring, if God were not love, then there would be no quiet lake or human love." Balthasar exclaims: "How mysteriously close and, at the same time, remote are these two metaphors!" However, the two passages show only how remote from each other the two thinkers are. Kierkegaard thinks that man cannot love, that is, cannot live, without God. Nietzsche thinks the contrary: man can and should live without God. Nietzsche's passage is the end of a chapter in which he says: "Thou wilt never more pray, never more worship ... thou hast no constant guardian and friend ... there is no longer any reason in that which happens, or any love in that which will happen to thee." It is the renunciation of the Christian belief in the love of God that Nietzsche expresses in the poetical figure, whereas Kierkegaard's metaphor confirms and strengthens this belief. As far as the decisive point is concerned, the two similes expressing these opposite thoughts differ essentially. The main feature of Kierkegaard's symbol is a flowing *to* the lake, meaning that there is God; the essential feature of Nietzsche's symbol is that there is no flow *from* the lake, meaning that there is no God. Even in their poetical language, Nietzsche and Kierkegaard are anything but brethren. Of course, even brothers may be enemies, and Balthasar admits enmity between Nietzsche and Kierkegaard by saying: "They are enemies as only relatives can be."[828] But from the fact of their being enemies does not follow that they are relatives.

---

823 Søren Kierkegaard, The Point of View, transl. by Walter Lowrie (London and New York, 1939), p. 138.

824 Balthasar, Prometheus, p. 697.

825 Ibid., p. 724.

826 Nietzsche, The Joyful Wisdom, p. 221.

827 Søren Kierkegaard, Works of Love, transl. by David F. Swenson and Lillian Marvin Swenson (Princeton, N. J., 1946), p. 8.

828 Balthasar, Prometheus, p. 705.

Chapter XII Nietzsche the Metaphysician

In the same way as Nietzsche's anti-Christian attitude has been misinterpreted as Christian, so his outspoken antimetaphysical and especially anti-Platonic philosophy has been presented as metaphysics. Martin Heidegger, in a work of two volumes, recently published,[829] is propounding the thesis that Nietzsche is a metaphysician,[830] that "the thinking of Nietzsche is, as all occidental thinking since Plato, metaphysics."[831]

In order to judge this interpretation it is neccessary to quote at least some of the numerous statements in which Nietzsche, this skeptic and relativist, this heir of the Enlightenment, formulates his opinion about metaphysics in general and Platonic philosophy in particular. In *The Joyful Wisdom* he calls himself "anti-metaphysical"; he rejects even the "belief in science" so far it rests on "a metaphysical belief."[832] He questions the value of truth because it is a metaphysical value. He says in *The Genealogy of Morals*: "What forces it [the repudiation of the senses] into that unqualified will for truth is the faith ... in a *metaphysical* value."[833] His thoughts about truth are very complex and at first sight contradictory. There are statements in which he seems to deny unconditionally the existence of truth. An aphorism written at the time of *The Dawn of the Day* runs as follows: "What is new in our present attitude towards philosophy is a conviction which no age had before: that we have not the truth; all earlier men 'had the truth': even the sceptics."[834] In *The Joyful Wisdom* we read: "But what after all are man's truths? – They are his *irrefutable* errors;"[835] and

829 Martin Heidegger, Nietzsche, 2 vols. (Pfullingen, 1961). The work is a collection of lectures held at the University of Freiburg i. B. from 1936 to 1940 and of essays written between 1940 and 1946 about Nietzsche's philosophy.

830 Ibid., I, pp. 255 seqq.

831 Ibid., II, p. 257.

832 Nietzsche, The Joyful Wisdom, p. 279.

833 Friedrich Nietzsche, The Genealogy of Morals, transl. by Horace B. Samuel, in: Complete Works (London and Edingburgh 1910), XIII, p. 196.

834 Friedrich Nietzsche, Die Unschuld des Werdens, in: Der Nachlass, selected and edited by Alfred Baeumler (Stuttgart, 1956), I, p. 225.

835 Nietzsche, The Joyful Wisdom, p. 208.

in *The Will to Power*: "Truth is that kind of error without which a certain species of living being cannot exist."[836] But if there is error there must be also truth, and Nietzsche is certainly far from ignoring the logical correlation of these two notions. There are many sentences in which he speaks of truth as of a positive value. In *The Antichrist* he says: "Every inch of truth has been conquered only after a struggle, almost everything to which our heart, our love and our trust in life cleaves, has had to be sacrificed for it. Greatness of soul is necessary for this: the service of truth is the hardest of all services."[837]

In an aphorism written at the time of *The Joyful Wisdom* he says: "The passion for that which in spite of all regard for persons, in spite of all 'agreeable' and disagreeable is 'true,' is the highest – therefore, until now, the rarest passion."[838] Zarathustra is a teacher and he presents his thoughts as 'true': "This, however, is my teaching," he says, and: "By diverse ways and wendings did I arrive at my truth."[839] A sentence found in Nietzsche's papers after his death runs: "Our last love ... our love for truth – let us watch that this love, too, does not deceive us."[840] There is a tendency in his thinking to identify truth wih usefulness. An aphorism, written at the time of *The Dawn of the Day*, runs as follows: "To be true means: to be suitable for the existence of man."[841] Nietzsche recognizes truth in science. He says in *The Will to Power*: "Truth, that is to say, the scientific method, was grasped and favoured by such as recognized that it was a useful weapon of war – an instrument of *destruction* ..."[842] His radical negation of truth refers evidently to the idea of an absolute, that is, divine and a-priori truth. In *The Genealogy of Morals* we read: "From the minute that the belief in the God of the ascetic ideal is repudiated, there exists a *new problem*: the problem of the value of truth. The Will for Truth needed a critique – let us define by these words our own task – the value of truth is tentatively *to be called in question*."[843] "To be called in question," not denied! And in another connection: "These thinkers are not at all free spirits, for they still believe in truth [Das sind noch lange keine freien Geister: denn sie glauben noch an die Wahrheit.]." The following passage shows that it is absolute truth Nietzsche had in mind: "Nothing is more really alien to these *so-called* 'free spirits,' whose belief in the one thing is absolute, than freedom and unfettering in that sense; in no respect are they more closely tied; their belief in truth is as firm and absolute as that of nobody else [Nichts ist diesen Unbe-

836 Nietzsche, The Will to Power, II, p. 20.
837 Nietzsche, The Antichrist, p. 202.
838 Nietzsches Gesammelte Werke (München, 1924), XI, p. 240.
839 Nietzsche, Thus Spake Zarathustra, p. 238.
840 Nietzsches Gesammelte Werke, XVI, p. 407.
841 Nietzsches Gesammelte Werke, XI, p. 28.
842 Nietzsche, The Will to Power, I, p. 374.
843 Nietzsche, The Genealogy of Morals, p. 198.

dingten in Einem, diesen *sogenannten* 'freien Geistern' gerade fremder als Freiheit und Entfesselung in jenem Sinne, in keiner Hinsicht sind sie gerade fester gebunden, im Glauben gerade an die Wahrheit sind sie, wie Niemand anders sonst, fest und unbedingt.]".[844] In *Thus Spake Zarathustra* Nietzsche says: "Never yet did truth cling to the arm of an absolute one."[845] In *The Will to Power* he says: "The new kind of courage – no a-priori truths (those who were accustomed to believe in something sought such truths!) but *free* submission to a ruling thought, which has its time."[846] That means: which is only relatively true. That same idea is expresed in the sentence: "The most strongly credit a-priori 'truths' are, to my mind, *mere assumptions pending further investigation*."[847] An aphorism written at the time of *The Dawn of the Day*: "As soon as one speaks of 'truths' which are not absolute [and that means: relative] all visionaries ask again to be admitted."[848] In *The Will to Power* Nietzsche says: "There must be many kinds of 'truths' and consequently there can be no truth."[849] It is evident that "no truth" means: no absolute truth because "many kinds of 'truths'" means: many relative truths. In *Beyond Good and Evil* he says: "It is nothing more than a moral prejudice that truth is worth more than semblance ... what is it that forces us in general to the supposition that there is an essential opposition of 'true' and 'false'? Is it not enough to suppose degrees of seemingness ...?"[850] Since truth is only a relative value, there is only a relative difference between truth and error. And finally, a remark in *Human, All-too-Human*: "Of the Tree of Knowledge: Probalility, but no truth."[851] "Absolute" truth is a metaphysical idea. Nietzsche opposes to this idea the concept of a relative truth. He is a relativist. In *The Will to Power* we read: "The world of appearence, i. e., a world regarded in this light of values ... It is *the point of view*, then, which accounts for the character of 'appearance.' As if a world could remain over, when the point of view is cancelled! By such means *relativity* would also be cancelled!"[852] Relativism is incompatible with metaphysics, which is essentially directed toward the absolute.

In *Human, All-too-Human* Nietzsche says about "metaphysical suppositions": "What has produced them is passion, error, and self-deception; the very worst methods of knowledge, not the best, have taught belief therein. When these methods have been discovered as the foundation of all existing re-

844 Nietzsche, Zur Genealogie der Moral, in: Nietzsches Gesammelte Werke, XV, p. 435.
845 Nietzsche, Thus Spake Zarathustra, p. 58.
846 Nietzsche, The Will to Power, II, p. 298.
847 Ibid., p. 21.
848 Nietzsches Gesammelte Werke, XI, p. 29.
849 Nietzsche, The Will to Power, II, p. 50.
850 Nietzsche, Beyond Good and Evil, p. 50.
851 Nietzsche, Human, All-too-Human, II, p. 184.
852 Nietzsche, The Will to Power, II, p. 70.

ligions and metaphysics, they have been refuted."[853] "Metaphysics ... may be designated as the science which treats of fundamental errors of mankind, but treats of them as if they were fundamental truths."[854]

One of the main features of *Thus Spake Zarathustra* is the polemic against the assumption of a "backworld" splendidly presented in the First Part, chapter 3: "Backsworldsmen" and in chapter 4: "The Despisers of the Body." In the former Nietzsche rejects the metaphysical dualism of this world and another world; "Weariness which seeketh to get to the ultimate with one leap, with a death-leap; a poor ignorant weariness, unwilling even to will any longer: that created all Gods and backworlds."[855] In the latter Nietzsche refuses the metaphysical dualism of a mortal body and an immortal soul. "'Body am I, and soul' – so saith the child ... But the awakened one, the knowing one, saith: 'Body am I entirely, and nothing more; and soul is only the name of something in the body.' – The body is a big sagacity [eine große Vernunft], a plurality with one sense, a war and a peace, a flock and a sheperd. An instrument of thy body is also thy little sagacity [deine kleine Vernunft], my brother, which thou callest 'spirit' – a little instrument and plaything of thy big sagacitiy."[856] It might seem that Nietzsche only replaces the dualism of body and soul by another dualism, that of the 'little' and the 'big reason,' which he identifies with the 'ego' and the 'Self.' For he lets Zarathustra say: "Behind thy thoughts and feelings, my brother, there is a mighty lord, an unknown sage – it is called Self;" and: "Thy Self laugheth at thine ego, and its proud prancings. 'What are these prancings and flights of thought unto me?' it saith to itself. 'A byway to my purpose. I am the leading-string of the ego, and the prompter of its notions!'"[857] This is not a metaphysical dualism like that of mortal body and immortal soul, but the psychological distinction between a conscious and unconscious layer within that which is called man's psyche, a distinction which later played an important part in modern psychoanalysis. In Nietzsche's doctrine it has even a certain physiological-biological touch. For the second of the quoted sentence continues: "It [the Self] dwelleth in thy body, it is thy body."[858] That means, that even the dualistic character of the distinction is dropped.

Finally, in answering the question as to whether Nietzsche is a metaphysician one must not ignore what he says about himself in his autobiographical work *Ecce Homo*. In the preface he declares: "I do not set up any new idols;

853 Nietzsche, Human, All-too-Human, I, p. 20.

854 Ibid., p. 33.

855 Nietzsche, Thus Spake Zarathustra, p. 32.

856 Ibid., pp. 35 seqq. Thomas Common's translation of the German "Vernunft" as "sagacitiy" seems not to be adequate; "reason" is perferable.

857 Ibid.

858 Ibid.

my old idols only learn what it costs to have legs of clay. To overthrow idols (idols is the name I give to all ideals) is much more like my business. In proportion as an ideal world has been falsely assumed, reality has been robbbed of its value, its meaning, and its truthfulness ... The 'True World' and the 'Apparent World' – in plain English, the fictitious world and reality."[859] In the chapter "Why I Am So Clever" he says about the main ideas of metaphysics: "'God,' 'the immortality of the soul,' 'salvation,' a 'beyond' – to all these notions, even as a child, I never paid any attention whatsoever, nor did I waste any time upon them – maybe I was never *naif* enough for that? – I am quite unacquainted with atheism as a result, and still less as an event in my life: In me it is inborn, instinctive ... God is a too palpably clumsy solution of things; a solution which shows a lack of delicacy towards us thinkers – at bottom He is really no more than a coarse and rude *prohibition* of us: you shall not think!"[860]

In the chapter "Why I Am A Fatality" he asks: "Have you understood me?" and says about the fundamental concepts of metaphysics: "The concept of 'God' was invented as the opposite of the concept life – everything detrimental, poisonous, and slanderous, and all deadly hostility to life, was bound together in one horrible unit in Him. The concepts 'beyond' and 'true world' were invented in order to depreciate the only world that exists – in order that no goal or aim, no sense or task, might be left to earthly reality."[861] And in the chapter "Why I Wrote Such Excellent Books" he says: "The fact that a voice which speaks in my works is that of a psychologist who has not his peer, is perhaps the first conclusion at which a good reader will arrive – a reader such as I deserve."[862] That means that Nietzsche wants to be understood as a psychologist – not as a metaphysician.

About Plato's philosophy Nietzsche says in *The Dawn of the Day*: "Plato fled from reality and wished to contemplate things only in their pale creations of fancy; he was full of feeling and knew how easily the waves of feeling would close over his reason. Ought therefore the sage to impress upon himself the following: 'I will honor reality, but, at the same time, turn my back upon it, because I know and dread it'? Ought he to behave as certain African tribes do in presence of their princes: whom they approach only backwards, thus showing their reverence with their dread?"[863] By the last sentence he evidently wants to turn into ridicule Plato's doctrine of ideas. In *The Twilight of the Idols* we read in the chapter "Things I Owe to the Ancients": "Do not let anyone suggest

859 Friedrich Nietzsche, Ecce Homo, transl. by Anthony M. Ludovici, in: Complete Works (London and Edinburgh, 1911), XVII, p. 2.

860 Ibid., pp. 28 seqq.

861 Ibid., pp. 141 seqq.

862 Ibid., p. 64.

863 Nietzsche, Morgenröthe [The Dawn of Day], V, par. 448; Kennedy's translation, Nietzsche, The Dawn of Day, Complete Works, IX, p. 321, slightly changed.

Plato to me. In regard to Plato I am a thorough sceptic, and have never been able to agree to the admiration of Plato the *artist*, which is traditional among scholars … Im my opinion Plato bundles all the forms of style pell-mell together, in this respect he is one of the first decadents of style … the Platonic dialogue – this revoltingly self-complacent and childish kind of dialectics – to exercise any charm over you, you must never have read any good French authors – Fontenelle for instance. Plato is boring. In reality my distrust of Plato is fundamental. I find him so very much astray from all the deepest instincts of the Hellenes, so steeped in moral prejudices, so pre-existently Christian – the concept of 'good' is already the highest value with him – that rather than use any other expression I would prefer to designate the whole phenomenon Plato with the hard word 'superior swindle' or, if you would like it better, 'idealism.'"[864] A sentence written at the time of *The Dawn of the Day* and *The Joyful Wisdom* runs: "Nobody should believe that Plato, if he lived in our time and had Platonic views, would be a philosopher; he would be a religious madman."[865]

Now, where in Nietzsche's works can his metaphysics be found? Heidegger asserts that "Nietzsche's metaphysical basic postion [*die metaphysische Gundstellung*]" manifests itself in his doctrine of the eternal recurrence and that the doctrine of eternal recurrence is necessarily included in the doctrine of the will to power.[866] And what is, according to Heidegger, the essence of this metaphysics or, as he formulates it, "the essence of a metaphysical basic position [*das Wesen einer metaphysischen Grundstellung*]"?[867]

In modern philosophical literature the term "metaphysics" is used in a wider and in a narrower sense. In the wider sense "metaphysics" means any kind of ontology and epistemology, and thus coincides – more or less – with "philosophy." In the narrower and specific sense "metaphysics" designates speculation about a sphere beyond the world of our senses, a transcendental world behind the empirical world, a "backworld" to use a Nietzeschean word. Plato's doctrine of ideas is the model of this kind of philosophy which fundamentally differs from any other philosophy that does not refer to transcendency. This narrower concept of "metaphysics" is the original one, and it is this concept that Nietzsche has in mind when he rejects "metaphysics" and opposes to it his own philosophy. To use the term "metaphysics" in a wider sense, comprising two fundamentally different types of philosophy is – if at all – admissible only if one distinguishes clearly between "critical" and "dogmatic"

864 Friedrich Nietzsche, The Twilight of the Idols, transl. by Anthony M. Ludovici, in: Complete Works (London and Edingburgh, 1911), XVI, pp. 113 seqq.

865 Nietzsche, Die Unschuld des Werdens, I, p. 225.

866 Heidegger, Nietzsche, I, pp. 255, 481.

867 Ibid., p. 258.

metaphysics,[868] the latter term designating a philosophy transcending empirical reality, the former a philosophy strictly abstaining from such intellectual excess. Using the word "metaphysics" without making this distinction is an ambiguous and misleading terminology, obscuring a fundamental antagonism in the history of philosophy. This antagonism is so radical that it is doubtful whether the word "metaphysics" should be used for anything but speculation about transcendency. Metaphysics in the specific sense of the term is in close connection with religion, and terminologically the case of both is the same. Just as "religion" without the belief in God, "metaphysics," without the assumption of transcendency, is a dangerous extension of a concept beyond the limits determined by the object to be conceived.

In view of the fact that Nietzsche expounds his philosophy in sharp opposition to "metaphysics," a conscientious interpretation should, in its answer to the question as to whether "metaphysics" appears in his work, take this word as it is used by Nietzsche himself, namely as a speculation that goes beyond empirical reality, assuming a "backworld." If the interpreter thinks that he can find another kind of metaphysics in Nietzsche's works he should call attention to this terminological difference;[869] otherwise he evokes the impression that Nietzsche's philosophy, in one of his main concerns, was a failure; that this gigantic attempt of establishing a view of the world without any reference to a transcendental sphere was in vain.

Heidegger is building up his concept of metaphysics in the chapter of the first volume entitled: "Die ewige Wiederkehr des Gleichen [The Eternal Recurrence]" under the heading: "Das Wesen einer metaphysischen Grundstellung [The Essence of a Metaphysical Basic Position]",[870] without emphasizing that it is not the one Nietzsche is using. "Metaphysics," Heidegger

868 Cf. Rudolf Eisler, Wörterbuch der philosophischen Begriffe, 4th ed., 1929, II, pp. 126 seqq.

869 As e. g., Rudolf Eisler, Nietzsches Erkenntnistheorie und Metaphysik (Leipzig, 1902) p. IV. To justify the title of his book Eisler says: "Many readers will be surprised that there is a 'metaphysics' of Nietzsche; because metaphysics, as is well known, has no greater adversary than Nietzsche. It is true that he abhorred all metaphysics ignoring reality, aiming at a beyond of 'things in themselves.' Nevertheless, we can find in his works tendencies directed at an 'immanent' [in opposition to a transcendental] metaphysics, at a general view of the world summerizing and uniformly interpreting the facts of experience. His metaphysics differs from preceding froms of this kind of philosophy only by the fact that the latter transcends all experience, whereas the former wants to restore the 'pure' experience by eliminating all hypothetical additions. In so doing, however, it cannot help completing the 'external' experience, which only shows us objects, by an 'inner' experience, which lets us find ourselves as subjects. In this way it finally transcends the external experience, but without advancing to the obscure realm of the absolute." The "inner" experience is the psychological experience which, indeed, plays a very important part in Nietzsche's philosophy. But it is human experience, nothing beyond it.

870 Heidegger, Nietzsche, I, pp. 255 seqq., 448.

states, "is that asking and searching which is always directed by one question: What is that what is? [Metaphysik ist dasjenige Fragen und Suchen, das immer geleitet bleibt von der einen Frage: Was ist das Seiende?"]". "Therefore we call this question the leading question of metaphysics" ("Wir nennen diese Frage deshalb die Leitfrage der Metaphysik").[871] This definition does not contain any reference to a transcendental sphere existing beyond empirical reality. If the word is used in this sense, if any attempt to answer the question: What is the *Seiende?*, even when the answer does not refer to another reality, but only to "that what is" in *this* world, then, of course, Nietzsche's philosophy is "metaphysics." But then this statement says nothing specific about Nietzsche's philosophy. According to Heidegger every true philosophy is metaphysics: "Metaphysics is therefore the title for the true philosophy and consequently concerns at any given time the fundamental thought of a philosophy" ("Metaphysik ist daher der Titel für die eigentliche Philosophie und betrifft deshalb jeweils den Grundgedanken einer Philosophie").[872]

That means that every true philosophy is an attempt to answer the question as to what the *Seiende* is. Hence an interpretation of Nietzsche's philosophy as metaphysics would amount to the empty tautology that Nietzsche's philosophy is – philosophy.

However, Heidegger does not stick to this definition. Even before he defines metaphysics without reference to a transcendental sphere, he says – speaking of the common use of this term –: "It designates something in the background, something that goes beyond us, something incomprehensible [Mit der Benennung 'metaphysisch' bezeichnet man das Hintergründige, irgendwie über uns Hinausgehende, Unfassliche]".[873] "Das Hintergründige" is exactly what Nietzsche calls "die Hinterwelt," the transcendental sphere. Then Heidegger continues: "The word is used sometimes in a degrading sense, according to which the background is only imaginary and, at the bottom, nonsense; sometimes in a highly appreciating sense, according to which the metaphysical is the unattainable ultimate and decisive [Man gebraucht das Wort bald im abwertenden Sinne – wonach dises Hintergründige nur ein Eingebildetes ist und im Grunde Unsinn – bald in einem hochwertenden Sinne, wonach das Metaphy-

871 Ibid., p. 454. There is no word in English that corresponds to Heidegger's "das Seiende." "Seiend" is the present participle of "Sein" (being). "That wich is" is a literal translation, but not quite adequate. Ralph Manheim in his translation of Martin Heidegger, An Introduction to Metaphysics (New Haven, 1959), p. IV, suggests: "The essent," "based on the fiction that essens, essentis is the present participle of *sum*" (p. IV). It is almost impossible to translate Heidegger's language, since it is full of newly created words whose special meaning – if they have such a meaning – is difficult to understand even for German readers. Therefore the following translations of Heidegger's statement are accompanied by the original German text.

872 Ibid., p. 449.

873 Ibid.

sische das unerreichbare Letzte und Entscheidende ist]". But he adds: "*Always* the thinking moves in the realm of the undefinite, uncertain, and obscure [*Jedesmal* bewegt sich aber das Denken im Unbestimmten, Unsicheren und Dunkeln]".[874] The sphere of the "undefinite, uncertain, and obscure" is precisely that which is in the background, which goes beyond us, the uncomprehensible – in other words the backworld, the transcendental sphere. Metaphysics is "moving" in this sphere; and "moving" in the transcendental sphere is an essential element of Metaphysics. Even a philosophy which rejects the assumption of a transcendental sphere as imaginary and nonsense is metaphysics in the sense of "moving" in the transcendental sphere. By this kind of argumentation the most radically antimetaphysical philosophy may be interpreted as metaphysics.

Later Heidegger's view of the essence of metaphysics which he pretends to have discovered in Nietzsche's work becomes still more explicit. He says: "In order to be truly metaphysical the leading question: What is the *Seiende?* must be expanded out of itself and beyond itself into a more original question [die Leitfrage: was ist das Seinende, muss *aus* ihr selbst heraus und *über* sich selbst hinaus in ein ursprünglicheres Fragen entfaltet werden]".[875] "The thinker is asking after the *Seiende* as a whole as such, after the world as such. In this way he is thinking with his first step already of a sphere beyond the world, and thus also back to the world. He is thinking beyond the world after that *around* which a world becomes a world [Der Denker fragt nach dem Seienden im Ganzen als solchem, nach der Welt als solcher. Auf diese Weise denkt er immer mit dem ersten Schritt schon über die Welt hinaus und so zugleich auf sie zurück. Er denkt hinaus auf Jenes, *worum* herum eine Welt zur Welt wird]".[876] This is also the definition of metaphysics formulated by Heidegger in his pamphlet *Was ist Metaphysik?* "Metaphysics is the questioning beyond the *Seiende*, in order to get it back *as such and as a whole* for comprehension [Metaphysik ist das Hinausfragen über das Seiende, um es *als ein solches* und *im Ganzen* für das Begreifen zurückzuerhalten]".[877] This means, translated into plain language: metaphysics is an attempt to answer the question: what is around the world and therefore *beyond* this world – the question after a backworld. In his work *Holzwege*, Heidegger says: "... that we mean by the word 'metaphysics' not a doctrine, much less a special discipline of philosophy, but we are thinking of the fundamental structure of the *Seiende* as a whole, in so far

874 Ibid., p. 450. Italics mine.

875 Ibid., p. 470.

876 Ibid., p. 471.

877 Martin Heidegger, Was ist Metaphysik? (Bonn, 1930), p. 24. In his work *An Introduction to Metaphysics* we read, p. 19: "If for the treatment of the 'question of being' in the indeterminate sense we choose the name 'metaphysics,' then the title of the present work is ambigous. For a first sight the questioning seems to remain within the sphere of the essent as such, yet at the very first sentence it strives to depart form this sphere in order to consider and inquire into another realm."

as the *Seiende* is divided into a material (empirical) and a transcendental world, the former being supported and determined by the latter" ("dass wir bei diesem Namen [Metaphysik] nicht eine Lehre oder gar nur eine Sonderdisziplin der Philosophie meinen, sondern an das Grundgefüge des Seienden im Ganzen denken, sofern dieses in eine sinnliche und übersinnliche Welt unterschieden und jene von dieser getragen und bestimmt wird").[878] Therefore, Heidegger's

878 Martin Heidegger, Holzwege (Frankfurt a. M., 1950), p. 204. In this work Heidegger says (p. 193) of Nietzsche's radical rejection of metaphysics that "metaphysics, through Nietzsche, deprives itself, in a certain sense, of its essential contents [als die Metaphysik durch Nietzsche, in gewisser Weise, sich selbst ihrer eigenen Wesensmöglichkeit beraubt]". That means: Heidegger applies the word "metaphysics" to a philosophy which deprives metaphysics of its esssential contents, namely, to a philosophy which shows that the assumption of a transcendental world behind the empirical world is impossible, that such an assumption is nonsense, and which, therefore, by its very nature is no metaphysics at all but the contrary of metaphysics. This is a trick of language. By using it, Heidegger tries to obscure the fact that what he says amounts to the same as saying white is black, an abstinent is a drunkard, an atheist is a theist, an antimetaphysician is a metaphysician. He recognizes (p. 200) that Nietzsche understands his own philosophy as a reaction against metaphysics, i. e., to him, against Platonism [Nietzsche versteht seine eigene Philosophie als die Gegenbewegung gegen die Metaphysik, d. h. für ihn gegen den Platonismus]." This, however, is to Heidegger a sufficient reason to consider Nietzsche as a Platonic metaphysician. He says: "As a mere reaction it [Nietzsche's philosophy], as all 'anti-,' necessarily is imprisoned in the essence of that against which is directed. [Als blosse Gegenbewegung bleibt sie jedoch notwendig wie alles Anti- im Wesen dessen verhaftet, wogegen sie angeht.]" And on page 193: "What is left to metaphysics after its reversion by Nietzsche is only the conversion into that what is not its essence. [Der Metaphysik bleibt durch die von Nietzsche vollzogene Umkehrung nur noch die Verkehrung in ihr Unwesen.]" And later, page 214: "Nietzsche considers this conversion to be the victory over metaphysics. However, every conversion of this kind remains, deceiving itself, still entangled in that what is conversed and has become irrecognizable. [Nietzsche hält diese Umkehrung fuer die Überwindung der Metaphysik. Allein jede Umkehrung dieser Art bleibt nur die sich selber blendende Verstrickung in das unkennbar gewordene Selbe.]" That means: Nietzsche's antimetaphysical philosophy remains metaphysics – a "reversed metaphysics." But Nietzsche does not "reverse" metaphysics; he emphatically *rejects* metaphysics; and a "reversed" metaphysics is no metaphysics at all. Only in its linguistic expression – not in its thought necessarily expressed in words – does a philosophy which rejects metaphysics remain "entangled" in that what is rejected. Heidegger says on page 193: "The transcendental becomes an objectless product of the material [as the opposite of the transcendental]. The material, however, by such degradation of its opposite, disavows its own essence. The dismissal of the transcendental eliminates also the material and thus the difference between the two ... The dismissal of the transcendental ends in senselessness. [Das Übersinnliche wird zu einem bestandlosen Produkt des Sinnlichen. Dieses aber verleugnet mit solcher Herabsetzung seines Gegensatzes das eigene Wesen. Die Absetzung des Übersinnlichen beseitigt auch das bloss Sinnliche und damit den Unterschied beider ... Die Absetzung endet im Sinnlosen.]" In Nietzsche's

assertion that Nietzsche's thinking is metaphysics, means: Nietzsche's thinking is metaphysics precisely in the sense of the term in which Nietzsche rejects metaphysics.

Nietzsche's doctrine of eternal recurrence, where Heidegger claims to have found his metaphysics, is presented in the last chapter of *The Will to Power* and in a special essay entitled *The Eternal Recurrence*.[879] How Nietzsche wants the doctrine to be understood is clearly expressed in the first chapter of the first part of the essay entitled: "The Doctrine Expunded and Substantiated [Darstellung und Begründung der Lehre]". There we read: "The extent of universal energy is limited, it is not 'infinite': we should beware of such excesses in our concepts! Consequently the number of states, changes, combinations, and evolutions of this energy, although it may be enormous and practically incalculable, is at any rate definite and not unlimited. The time, however, in which this universal energy works its changes is infinite – that is to say, energy remains eternally the same and *is* eternally active: – at this moment an infinity has already elapsed, that is to say, every possible evolution must already have taken place. Consequently the present process of evolution must be a repetition, as was also the one before it, as will also be the one which will follow. And so on forwards and backwards! Inasmuch as the entire state of all forces continually returns, everything has existed an infinite number of times."[880] This is evidently a scientific argumentation from the point of view of physics. The "eternity" of recurrence is clearly explained as the infinity of time, a strictly scientific assumption and not, as it has been misunderstood, as a metaphysical element of this doctrine.[881] That its central concept, "energy [Kraft]", is a concept of the science of physics results unambiguously from the statements: "First principles. – The last physical state of energy which we can imagine must necessarily be the first also. The absorption of energy in latent energy must be the cause of the production of the most vital energy. For a highly positive state must follow a negative state. Space like matter is a subjective form, time is not. The notion of space first arose from the assumption that space could be empty. But there is no such thing as empty space. Everything is energy."[882] And: "Physics supposes that energy may be di-

philosophy, however, the "dismissal of the transcendental" does not at all eliminate the "material," that is, the empirical reality. On the contrary: it restores it in opposition to metaphysics, which tries to degrade it to a mere appearance; and it is precisely this metaphysics that, according to Nietzsche's philosophy, ends in senselessness. What Heidegger says about the transcendental and its relation to empirical reality is not Nietzsche's, it is Heidegger's philosophy, that is exactly that type of metaphysical speculation which Nietzsche stigmatizes as nonsense.

879 Nietzsche, The Twilight of the Idols, pp. 237 seqq.

880 Ibid.

881 For instance by R. Willy, Friedrich Nietzsche: Eine Gesamtdarstellung (Zürich, 1904), p. 102.

882 Nietzsche, The Eternal Recurrence, p. 240.

vided up: but every one of its possibilities must first be adjusted to reality. There can therefore be no question of dividing energy into equal parts; in every one of its states it manifests a certain quality, and qualities cannot be subdivided: hence a state of equilibrium in energy is impossible."[883] Nietzsche stresses the scientific antimetaphysical tendency of his doctrine: "In what principle and belief is that decisive turning point in philosophical thought best expressed, which has come into being thanks to the preponderance of the scientific spirit over the religious and God-creating one? We insist upon the fact that the world as a sum of energy must not be a regarded as unlimited – we forbid ouselves the concept of infinite energy, because it seems incompatible with the concept of energy."[884] And: "He who does not believe in the circular process of the universe must pin his faith to an arbitrary God – thus my doctrine becomes necessary as opposed to all that has been said hitherto in matter of Theism."[885]

In the second part of the essay entitled "The Effects of the Doctrine upon Mankind" Nietzsche characterizes his doctrine as follows: "We must not strive after distant and unknown states of bliss and blessings and acts of grace, but we must live so that we would fain live again and live for ever so, to all eternity… This life is thy eternal life."[886] He says about the downfall of the Alexandrinian culture:

"With all its useful discoveries and its desire to investigate the nature of this world, it did not know how to lend this life its ultimate importance, the thought of a Beyond was more important to it!"[887]

The scientific-physical character of the doctrines comes forth still more clearly in the last chapter of *The Will to Power*, where Nietzsche says: "The principle of the conservation of energy inevitably involves *eternal recurrence*."[888] In this work too Nietzsche emphasizes the antimetaphysical character of his doctrine. He says under the heading *The principal innovations*: "In the place of 'metaphysics' and religion the doctrine of *Eternal Recurrence* (this being regarded as a means to the breeding and selection of men)."[889] Metaphysics and religion stand for speculation about the absolute. The doctrine of eternal recurrence is no such speculation. It is not in conflict with Nietzsche's relativism, expressed again and again and most emphatically in *The Will to Power*: "The absolute is even an absurd concept: an 'absolute' mode of existence is nonsense, the concept 'being,' 'thing' is always *relative* to us";[890] and in *Beyond*

883 Ibid., p. 241.
884 Ibid., p. 239.
885 Ibid., p. 244.
886 Ibid., p. 254.
887 Ibid., p. 255.
888 Nietzsche, The Will to Power, II, p. 427.
889 Ibid., I, p. 381.
890 Ibid., II, p. 82.

Good and Evil: "Everything absolute belongs to pathology."[891] Hence the doctrine of the eternal recurrence is not – at least not as understood by Nietzsche himself – a doctrine of the absolute; and Heidegger's identification of the eternal recurrence with the absolute in the statement: "The superman goes ... beyond himself into his absolute, and that means especially in the totality of the *Seiende*, the eternal recurrence [Der Übermensch geht über sich selbst in sein Unbedingtes hinaus, und d. h. zumal: in die Gänze des Seienden, die ewige Wiederkunft des Gleichen, hinein].",[892] is without any foundation.

Heidegger's main argument for his interpretation of Nietzsche's doctrine of eternal recurrence as metaphysics is that Nietzsch does not conceive of the basic concept of his doctrine, the concept of energy, in the sense of physics. He says: "What Nietzsche calls and understands by 'energy' is not that which is called so in physics [Was Nietzsche mit 'Kraft' bezeichnet und meint, ist nicht das, was die Physik so nennt]." [893] Even if it were true that the meaning of "energy" in the science of physics is different from the meaning of this word in Nietzsche's doctrine, it would be irrelevant in view of the fact that Nietzsche's clearly expressed intention was to use "energy" in the sense of the science of physics, that means, in the sense of natural science and not in a metaphysical sense. Decisive to an interpretation is only that Nietzsche uses the concept of "energy" in his doctrine of eternal recurrence to explain the empirical reality without any reference to a sphere beyond this reality, to a backworld. A conscientious interpretation of an author must always be determined by his recognizable intentions; and about Nietzsche's intentions there can be no doubt.

Heidegger foresees this objection. To meet it he asserts: "Nietzsche does not intend to bring about a perfect understanding of his doctrine of eternal recurrence by the little he himself communicates about it; he is *veiling* his thought; he wants only to initiate a change of the frame of mind from which his doctrine may become comprehensible and effective [Nietzsche will mit dem wenigen und *Verhüllenden*, was er über seine Wiederkunftslehre selbst mitteilte, nicht ein vollendetes Begreifen erwirken, sondern einen Wandel der Grundstimmung anbahnen, aus der heraus seine Lehre erst fassbar und wirksam werden kann]."[894] Thus the metaphysical element of Nietzsche's doctrine is to be found not in what he is saying, but in what he is veiling. The assumption that a philosopher, in order to be understood, not only is veiling his

891 Nietzsche, Beyond Good and Evil, p. 98.

892 Heidegger, Nietzsche, II, p. 303. Walter Kaufmann, Nietzsche, Philosopher, Psychologist, Antichrist (New York, 1959), p. 275, calls attention to the fact that in one of Heinrich Heine's books which Nietzsche owned, we find a passage concerning eternal recurrence which is similar to Nietzsche's presentation of the doctrine. Heine was certainly anything but a metaphysician and Nietzsche was a great admirer of this German poet.

893 Heidegger, Nietzsche, I, p. 343.

894 Ibid., p. 269. Italics mine.

thoughts, but even asserts just the opposite to what he is thinking is indeed a strange basis for an interpretation of his writings.[895] In accordance with this assumption Heidegger continues his quoted characterization of metaphysical thinking as thinking beyond the world toward that around which the world becomes a world, as follows: "This 'around which' is thought most deeply and most purely where it is not permanently and expressly referred to, but concealed within the questioning. For that which is concealed is the truly preserved one and as the most preserved one the nearest and most real one [Dort, wo dieses Worumherum nicht ständig und laut genannt, sondern im innersten Fragen verschwiegen wird, ist es am tiefsten und reinsten gedacht. Denn das Verschwiegene ist das eigentlich Bewahrte und als das Bewahrteste das Nächste und Wirklichste]".[896]

On the assumption that the true thought of a philosopher is not the one he is expressing but the one he is veiling, Heidegger adds to the just-quoted sentence: "What to the reason of an ordinary man seems to be and must seem to be 'atheism' is, at the bottom, the contrary [Was für den gemeinen Verstand wie 'Atheismus' aussieht und so aussehen muss, ist im Grunde das Gegenteil]." Now, it is not an ordinary man, but Nietzsche, a great philosopher, to whom his philosophy seems to be atheism, and not only "seems" to be atheism, but is emphatically presented as atheism. But how does Heidegger reinterpret as theism what Nietzsche considered to be atheism? Referring to Nietzsche's saying: "Around the hero everything becomes a tragedy; around the demigod everything becomes a satyr-play; around God everything becomes – what? perhaps a 'world'."[897] Heidegger rejects the interpretation of the last statement to mean "pantheism" because Nietzsche, at the end of a passage in which he says he has opened his eyes to the idea of eternal recurrence, says: "What? And this would not be – *circulus vitiosus deus* [vitious circle God]?"[898] Heidegger says:

895 In the chapter: "Nietzsches Metaphysik" in the second volume of his work (p. 257) Heidegger defines "metaphysics" as "the truth of the Seiende as such, as a whole. [Die Metaphysik ist die Wahrheit des Seienden als eines solchen im Ganzen.]" The following sentence cannot be translated: "Die Wahrheit bringt das, was das Seiende ist (essentia, die Seiendheit), dass es und wie es im Ganzen ist, in das Unverborgene der ἰδέα, der perceptio, des Vorstellens, Bewusstseins ... Die Wahrheit bestimmt sich als solche Unverborgenheit in ihrem Wesen, dem Entbergen, aus dem von ihr zugelassenen Seienden selbst ..." This means in plain English (if it means anything): the truth – and, since "metaphysics is the truth," metaphysics – unveils the essence of the Seiende, because the very nature of the truth is unveiling, making conscious. It the nature of metaphysics is unveiling the essence of its object, how can Nietzsche's metaphysics "be found in that which he is veiling?"

896 Heidegger, Nietzsche, I, p. 471.

897 Nietzsche, Beyond Good and Evil, p. 97.

898 Nietzsche, Beyond Good and Evil, p. 74. Heidegger, Nietzsche, I, pp. 320, 321. The passage quoted by Heidegger runs as follows: "Whoever, like myself, prompted by

"The God is then only a question? Indeed 'only' a question, that is, the one who is questioned or called. It remains to consider whether the God is more divine if he is questioned or if he is certain and, being certain, may be, if needed, put aside, as it were, in order to be taken back, if needed. [Der Gott ist dann nur eine Frage? Allerdings: 'nur' eine Frage, d. h. der Gefragte, Gerufene. Zu bedenken bleibt, ob der Gott göttlicher ist in der Frage nach ihm oder dann, wenn er gewiss ist und als Gewisser je nach Bedarf gleichsam auf die Seite gestellt werden kann, um nach Bedarf herbei geholt zu werden.]".[899] But

some enigmatic desire, has long endeavored to go to the bottom of the question of pessimism and free from it from the half-Christian, half-German narrowness and stupidity in which it has finally presented itself to this century, namely, in the form of Schopenhauer's philosophy; whoever, with an Asiatic and super-Asiatic eye, has actually looked inside, and into the most world-renouncing of all possible modes of thought – beyond good and evil, and no longer like Buddha and Schopenhauer, under the dominion and delusion of morality, – whoever has done this, has perhaps just thereby, without really desiring it, opened his eyes to behold the opposite ideal: the ideal of the most world-approving, exuberant and vivacious man, who has not only learnt to compromise and arrange with that which was and is, but wishes to have it again *as it was and is*, for all eternity, insatiably calling out *da capo*, not only to himself but to the whole piece and play; and not only to the play, but actually to him who requires the play – and makes it necessary; because he always requires himself anew – and makes himself necessary. – What? And this would not be – *circulus vitiosis deus*?"

899 Heidegger, Nietzsche, I, p. 324. The same typically theological argumentation in Heidegger's Holzwege, pp. 240, 246, where he asserts that "the hardest blow against God is executed not by those who do not believe in God but by the believers and theologians who speak of God as the most *Seiende* without thinking of the *Sein* [being] itself"; "God is dead" in Nietzsche's philosophy. But interpreting this phrase, which Nietzsche in The Joyful Wisdom puts in the mouth of the "madman" (cf. p. 216), Heidegger says in Holzwege, p. 246: This madman "has nothing in common with the way of those who are loafing about in public, 'who do not believe in God.' For they are unbelievers not because God as God has become to them unworthy of belief but because they have themselves abandoned the possibility of belief, in so far as they no longer can seek God ... The madman, however, is ... the one who seeks God crying out for God. [Dieser dergestalt verrückte Mensch hat darum mit der Art jener oeffentlichen Herumsteher, 'welche nicht an Gott glauben,' nichts gemein. Denn diese sind nicht deshalb ungläubig, weil Gott als Gott ihnen unglaubwürdig geworden ist, sondern weil sie selbst die Moeglichkeit des Glaubens aufgegeben haben, insofern sie Gott nicht mehr suchen koennen ... Der tolle Mensch dagegen ist ... derjenige, der Gott sucht, indem er nach Gott schreit.]" The madman, it is true, says: "I seek God!" But the meaning of his speech is that he did not find God, because God does not exist. Those who are loafing about in public saying they do not believe in God, do no longer seek God because they believe that God does not exist. There may be psychologically a difference between men who first believed in God, but later, as a result of a hard struggle, became atheists, and men who never believed in God. But Nietzsche belongs to the latter. He is, according to his own confession in Ecce Homo, an atheist "by instinct" and has been an atheist already "as a child." Cf. Karl Löwith, Heidegger, Denker in dürftiger Zeit (Göttingen, 1960), pp. 89 seqq.

Nietzsche, at many other places, does not – as in the above-quoted statement – only question the existence of God but expressly denies it. If Heidegger could make us believe that the one who questions the existence of God is 'calling' God – and this might even mean that he is invoking God – and that to him God is more divine, is more God, that to the one who firmly believes in his existence, we could accept the view that atheism is belief in God; and if it were admissible to present as the true thought of a philosopher that what he conceals, even if that what he himself expressly and fiercely asserts is just the contrary, then, of course, it is possible to interpret an antimetaphysical philosophy as metaphysics.

In the second volume, chapter on "Nietzsches Metaphysik"[900] Heidegger defines "metaphysics" as "the truth of the *Seiende* as such on the whole [Die Metaphysik ist die Wahrheit des Seienden als eines solchen im Ganzen]." This definition – like the one presented in the first volume, chapter "Die ewige Wiederkehr des Gleichen"[901] – does not contain any reference to the transcendental.

As to Nietzsche's metaphysics he says: "'The will to power,' 'the Nihilism,' 'the eternal recurrence,' the 'superman,' 'the justice' are the five fundamental words of Nietzsche's metaphysics ['Der Wille zur Macht,' 'der Nihilismus,', die 'ewige Wiederkunft des Gleichen,' 'der Übermensch,' 'die Gerechtigkeit' sind die fünf Grundworte der Metaphysik Nietzsches]-".[902] "The hidden unity of the fundamental philosophical doctrines constitutes the essential structure of Nietzsche's metaphysics [Die verborgene Einheit der 'philosophischen Grundlehren' macht das Wesensgefüge der Metaphysik Nietzsches aus]."[903] If metaphysics is the 'truth of the *Seinede*' – and that can only mean true statements about reality – the five doctrines and their unity, whether "hidden" or not hidden, are certainly "metaphysics" in the sense of this insignificant definition. However, later Heidegger says: "Metaphysics begins in the thinking of Plato, who comprehends the *Seiende* as such, that is, the *Sein* of the *Seiende*, as idea. [Platon, mit dessen Denken die Metaphysik beginnt, begreift das Seiende als solches, d. h. das Sein des Seienden, als Idee.]" Hence we are supposed to understand by "metaphysics" a speculation about the transcendental in the sense of Plato's doctrine of ideas in general and of the idea of the absolute Good in particular; and if Nietzsche's philosophy is metaphysics, it is metaphysics in this sense. But Plato's concept of the Good, Heidegger asserts, does not contain the idea of value [Allein Platons Begriff des Guten enthält nicht den Wertgedanken], which is a more than problematical statement. For, if any concept has the character of a value concept it is Plato's idea of the Good. And

900 Heidegger, Nietzsche, II, pp. 257 seqq.
901 Cf. p. 231.
902 Heidegger, Nietzsche, II, pp. 259, 260.
903 Ibid., II, p. 261.

it is not only – as Heideggers asserts – from the point of view of Nietzsche's "metaphysical position" that Platos interpretation of das *Seiende*, the ideas and therefore the transcendental, can be understood as values. ("Indes kann Nieztsche aus *seiner* metaphysischen Grundstellung heraus die platonische Auslegung des Seienden, die Idee und somit das Übersinnliche, als Wert deuten.") "In this interpretation all philosophy since Plato assumes the character of metaphysics. [In dieser Deutung wird alle Philosophie seit Platon zur Metaphysik der Werte.]"[904] But certainly not Nietzsche's philosophy, unless this interpretation means – as Heidegger suggests: "The *Seiende* as such is comprehended as a whole out of the transcendental and the transcendental is recognized as the true *Seiende*; the transcendental may be God as the creator and savior, the God of Christianity, the moral law, the authority of reason, progress or the happiness of the greatest number of men. [Das Seiende als solches wird im Ganzen aus dem Übersinnlichen begriffen und dieses zugleich als das wahrhaft Seiende erkannt; sei dieses Übersinnliche nun Gott als der Schöpfer- und Erlösergott des Christentums, sei das Übersinnliche das Sittengesetz, sei es die Autorität der Vernunft, der Fortschritt, das Glück der Meisten.]"[905] It is evident that Heidegger, in this statement, misuses the term "transcendental [das Übersinnliche]", which means something belonging to the "beyond," to a world other than the empirical world, something like God. A philosophy is metaphysics only if it refers to the transcendental in this sense. The moral law, reason, progress, happiness are or may be conceived of as belonging to this and not to another world, and Nietzsche, who violently rejects the assumption of a transcendental sphere, of another world as a "true" world, in presenting his philosophy, does certainly not use these concepts to designate something transcendental in the only proper sense of this word. But Heidegger continues: "Everywhere the immediately existent reality perceptible by our senses is measured by something desirable, by an ideal ... Every metaphysics is a system of valuations. [Überall wird das unmittelbar vorhandene Sinnliche an einer Wünschbarkeit, an einem Ideal gemessen. Jede Metaphysik ist ein System von Wertschätzungen.]"[906]

But there is a metaphysical and a nonmetaphysical theory of values. According to the one the supreme values are established by the will of God, according to the other by the will of man. Nietzsche's philosophy is or at least contains indeed a theory of values – but an outspokenly nonmetaphysical, even antimetaphysical theory of values. "The desirabilities," says Heidegger, "Nietzsche considers as the 'supreme values.' Every metaphysics is a 'system of valuations,' or, as Nietzsche says, morals, 'understood as doctrine of the relations of supremacy under which the phenomenon 'life' comes into existence'.

904 Ibid., pp. 272–273.
905 Ibid., p. 273.
906 Ibid., p. 274.

[Die Wünschbarkeiten denkt Nietzsche als die 'obersten Werte.' Jede Metaphysik ist ein System von Wertschätzungen' oder wie Nietzsche sagt, Moral 'als Lehre von den Herrschaftsverhältnissen verstanden, unter denen das Phänomen 'Leben' entsteht]".[907] Heidegger refers to *Beyond Good and Evil*, § 19. But in this section, which is dealing with the concept of "will," Nietzsche does not say that all metaphysics is morals but that "willing-as-such" is "included within the sphere of morals." The passage runs as follows: "In all willing it is absolutely a question of commanding and obeying, on the basis, as already said, of a social structure composed of many 'souls' [previously Nietzsche says: "Our body is but a social structure composed of many souls"]; on which account a philosopher should claim the right to include willing-as-such [*Wollen-an-sich*] within the sphere of morals – regarded as the doctrine of the relations of supremacy under which the phenomenon of 'life' manifests itself."[908] In § 2 Nietzsche speaks of metaphysics. He stigmatizes the metaphysicians who consider "the concealed God," the "thing-in-itself" as the "source of the things of the highest value". This mode of reasoning discloses the typical prejudice by which metaphysicians of all times can be recognized; this mode of valuation is at the back of all their logical procedure.[909] The "metaphysics" that is a system of valuations is not Nietzsche's philosophy of values; it is the metaphysics he rejects. It is especially Plato's metaphysics whose theory of values is implied in the doctrine of the transcendental ideas. If morals is, according to Nietzsche, a system of valuations and morals is to be understood as the doctrine of relations of supremacy under which the phenomenon "life" comes into existence, then Nietzsche's theory of values is the contrary of a "metaphysics" of values. For the relations of supremacy and the phenomenon of life, which comes into existence under these relations, take place in this empirical world and not in a transcendental sphere.

Heidegger speaks of a "metaphysics of the will to power [Metaphysik des Willens zur Macht]". He says: "The will to power is the only principle of establishing values [Der Wille zur Macht ist das einzige Prinzip der Wertsetzung]".[910] But the values established by the will to power are definitely not metaphysical but empirical values, established by the will of man. What even the "supreme values" are to Nietzsche shows a statement in *Thus Spake Zarathustra:* "Verily, men have given unto themselves all their good and bad. Verily, they took it not, they found it not, it came not unto them as a voice from heaven. – Values did man only assign to things in order to maintain himself – he created only the significance of things, a human significance! Therefore, called

907 Ibid.

908 Nietzsche, Beyond Good and Evil, p. 28.

909 Ibid., p. 6.

910 Heidegger, Nietzsche, II, p. 274.

he himself 'man,' that is, the valuator,"[911] and the statement in *Beyond Good and Evil*: "Behind all logic and its seeming sovereignty of movement, there are valuations or, to speak more plainly, physiological demands, for the maintenance of a definite mode of life";[912] and finally in *The will to Power*: "The standpoint of 'value' is the same as that of the *conditions* of *preservation* and *enhancement*, in regard to complex creatures of relative stability appearing in the course of evolution ... 'Value' is essentially the standpoint of the increase or decrease of these dominating centers (pluralities in any case; for 'unity' cannot be observed anywhere in the nature of development)."[913] That means that the "values" to which Nietzsche's doctrine refers are immanent in empirical reality because established by the will of man and not by a superhuman, transcendental will. This is the truth about Nietzsche's "metaphysics of the will to power" as "the only principle of establishing values."

Heidegger does not only speak of the "metaphysics of the will to power," but also of a "metaphysical origin of the essence of superman [metaphysischer Ursprung des Wesens des Übermenschen]". He says: "The metaphysical origin of the essence of the superman is unveiled by the rank of reason elevated to an absolute authority as modern metaphysics. [Erst der als neuzeitliche Metaphysik zum Unbedingten entfaltete Rang der Vernunft enthüllt den metaphysischen Ursprung des Wesens des Übermenschen.]".[914] Reason has the ... rank of an absolute authority only if it is considered to be the divine reason in which man participates as created by God. This is the specifically metaphysical concept of reason. But it is not Nietzsche's concept of reason. Heidegger himself refers to the above-quoted statements in *Thus Spake Zarathustra*, where Nietzsche rejects the dualism of body and soul and distinguishes between a big and a little reason, identifying the big reason with the body. It is evident that this reason is not the divine reason in which man as created by God participates. Heidegger correctly says: "The hitherto metaphysical mark of the essence of man, reason, is transferred into animality in the sense of the will to power as bodily function. [Die bisherige metaphysische Wesensauszeichnung des Menschen, die Vernünftigkeit, wird in die Tierheit im Sinne des leibenden Willens zur Macht verlegt.]"[915] Since Nietzsche puts his doctrine of human reason in the mouth of Zarathustra, who "teaches the Superman,"[916] the metaphysical doctrine that reason has the rank of an absolute authority because it is of divine origin cannot "unveil" the metaphysical origin of the essence of the superman. The essence of the superman is not his reason, but his will to power,

911 Nietzsche, Thus Spake Zarathustra, p. 67.
912 Nietzsche, Beyond Good and Evil, p. 8.
913 Nietzsche, The Will to Power, II, p. 182.
914 Heidegger, Nietzsche, II, p. 295.
915 Ibid., pp. 294, 295.
916 Nietzsche, Thus Spake Zarathustra, p. 6.

and his reason is, as Zarathustra emphasizes, his body. In open contradiction to his statement that the essence of the superman is of metaphysical origin Heidegger admits later: "The 'Superman' is not a transcendental ideal. [Der 'Übermensch' ist kein übersinnliches Ideal.]"[917] He quotes *The Will to Power:* "The essential thing is to start out from the body and to use it as the general clue,"[918] and he interprets this statement to mean: "The special sphere of the vital function is conceived of metaphysically as will to power. [Der besondere Bereich des 'Vitalen' ist metaphysisch als Wille zur Macht begriffen.]"[919]

Certainly not "metaphysically" in the sense in which Heidegger uses the word! For Nietzsche says under the heading: "With the body as clue": "In all ages the body, as our actual property, as our most certain being, in short, as our ego, has been more earnestly believed in than the spirit (or the 'soul,' or the subject, as the school jargon now calls it). It has never occurred to anyone to regard his stomach as a strange or a divine stomach; but that there is a tendency and a predilection in man to regard all his thoughts as 'inspired', all his values as 'imparted to him by a God,' all his instincts as dawning activities – this is proved by the evidence of every age in man's history."[920] The concept of a 'divine' reason 'inspired by a God,' is a true metaphysical concept, and it is precisely against this metaphysical concept that Nietzsche opposes his identifications of reason with the body.

It is likewise against the metaphysical concept of man as an image of God that Nietzsche stresses the view that man is an animal. Heidegger says with reference to Nietzsche's statement: "Man is the animal not yet definitively settled. [Der Mensch ist das noch nicht festgestellte Tier.]"[921] "The metaphysical degradation of man to animal means the nihilistic affirmation of the superman. [Die metaphysische Fest-stellung des Menschen zum Tier bedeutet die nihilistische Bejahung des Übermenschen.]"[922] But according to Nietzsche's intention the statement has an outspoken antimetaphysical meaning, and all the more so as it is – according to Heidegger – a "nihilistic" affirmation of the superman. But even Nietzsche's nihilism is interpreted by Heidegger as metaphysics. He refers to a passage in *The Will to Power*, where Nietzsche speaks of an "ecstatic

917 Heidegger, Nietzsche, II, p. 304.

918 Nietzsche, The Will to Power, II, p. 47.

919 Heidegger, Nietzsche, II, p. 300.

920 Nietzsche, The Will to Power, II, p. 133.

921 Nietzsche, Beyond God and Evil, p. 82. Helen Zimmern translates: "The animal not yet properly adapted to his environment."

922 Heidegger, Nietzsche, II, p. 307. Heidegger's phrase: "Feststellung zum Tier" cannot be literally translated. In the usual German language one says: "feststellen etwas," not: "feststellen zu etwas." By saying: "Fest-stellung [putting a hyphen between "fest" and "stellen"] des Menschen zum Tier," Heidegger presumably wants to give to the word "feststellen" the connotation of "herabsetzen [degrade]".

Nihilism."[923] Heidegger asserts that this nihilism has not – as it seems – a purely negative character; for it affirms the "principle of evaluation. ("Dieser [ekstatische Nihilismus] bejaht ... das 'Prinzip der Wertschätzung,' den Willen zur Macht.") Thus "the ecstatic nihilism becomes the 'classical nihilism'. Nietzsche comprehends his metaphysics as 'classical nihilism'. ['Der ekstatische Nihilismus wird zum klassischen Nihilismus. Als solchen begreift Nietzsche seine Metaphysik.']". Heidegger continues: "Where the will to power is the accepted principle of establishing values nihilism becomes the 'Ideal of the highest spiritual power'. [Wo der Wille zur Macht das ergriffene Prinzip der Wertsetzung ist, wird der Nihilismus zum 'Ideal der höchsten Mächtigkeit des Geistes.']"[924] The passage of which Heidegger quotes only the last-mentioned words, runs as follows: "'Nihilism' viewed as the ideal of the highest spiritual power, of the over-rich life, partly destructive, partly ironical."[925] It does not quite confirm Heidegger's view of a nihilism affirming positive values. Then Heidegger says: "In denying every *Seiende* existing in itself and affirming the will to power as the source and measure of the creating force 'nihilism' might be 'a divine way of thinking.' ... The affirmative character of nihilism cannot be expressed in a more definite way. [Indem jedes an sich bestehende Seiende geleugnet und der Wille zur Macht als Ursprung und Maß des Schaffens bejaht wird, könnte 'Nihilismus' 'eine göttliche Denkweise sein.' ... Bejahender lässt sich das bejahende Wesen des Nihilismus überhaupt nicht sagen.]"[926] The words put between quotation marks in Heidegger's sentence are taken from a passage in *The Will to Power*, which runs as follows: "In this respect, nihilism, in that it is the *negation* of a real world and of Being, might be a *divine way of thinking.*"[927] In this statement nihilism has by no means an affirmative, but, on the contrary, a purely negative, destructive character. It is true that Nietzsche calls his doctrine of eternal recurrence "the extremest form of nihilism,"[928] but only as far as the negative aspect is concerned. For he continues: "nothing (purposelessness) eternal! ... We deny final purposes. If existence had a final purpose, it would have reached it."[929] In the above-quoted sentence, Nietzsche does not say that *his* nihilism is a divine way of thinking, nor that nihilism in general *is* such a way of thinking; but that nihilism, as a negation of the real world and of

923 Nietzsche, The Will to Power, II, p. 422.

924 Heidegger, Nietzsche, II, p. 281.

925 Nietzsche, The Will to Power, I, p. 16.

926 Heidegger, Nietzsche, II, pp. 281, 282.

927 Nietzsche, The Will to Power, I, p. 17. Ludovici's translation "a divine view of the world" is not correct. The German text says "eine göttliche Denkweise."

928 Nietzsche, The Will to Power, I, p. 48.

929 In the German text the negative character of this nihilism is more clearly expressed: "Das ist die extremste Form des Nihilismus: das Nichts (das Sinnlose) ewig! ... Wir leugnen Schluss-Ziele: hätte das Dasein eins, so muesste es erreicht sein."

Being, *might* be (*könnte* sein) a divine way of thinking. In the nihilism of Nietzsche's doctrine of eternal recurrence there certainly is no metaphysical element whatsoever.

Even if Nietzsche's nihilism is not only the negation of all moral values, but the affirmation of a new value, established by the will to power, this nihilism has nothing to do with metaphysics as defined by Heidegger. It is expressly directed against this metaphysics: At the beginning of the first book of *The Will to Power*, dealing with the problem of nihilism, we read: "Nihilism, that is, the radical repudiation of value, meaning, desirability... Doubt in morality is the decisive factor. The downfall of the *moral* interpretation of the universe, which loses its *raison d'etre* once it has tried to take flight to a Beyond, meets its end in Nihilism."[930] Radical Nihilism is the conviction that existence is untenable as far as the highest values are concerned which are recognized. It also includes the view that we have not the smallest right to assume a Beyond or things in themselves, which would be either divine or morality incarnate."[931] It is true that the first statement must be understood in the light of the subtitle of *The Will to Power:* "An Attempted Transvaluation All Values," and of the statement made in the preface: "Sooner or later we shall be in need of *new values.*" But there can be no doubt that Nietzsche's nihilism, though not a negation of *all* values, implies the definite rejection of the assumption of a transcendental sphere, that is, of metaphysics in the sense in which Heidegger uses this term.

Among Nietzsche's doctrines which Heidegger interprets as metaphysics he mentions also the doctrine of justice.[932] According to Heidegger, Nietzsche's philosophy closely connects "justice" and "truth": "Because 'justice' is the highest way the will to power works, it is the real foundation of the essence of truth. [Also ist die 'Gerechtigkeit,' weil die höchste Weise des Willens zur Macht, der eigentliche Bestimmungsgrund des Wesens der Wahrheit.]" "In the metaphysics of the absolute and perfect subjectivity of the will to power truth exists as justice. [In der Metaphysik der unbedingten und vollendeten Subjektivität des Willens zur Macht west die Wahrheit als die 'Gerechtigkeit'.]".[933] What Nietzsche says about justice is not very consistent.

Justice is one of the traditional moral values. Because of his radical opposition to them he should reject this value too. However, there is a strong tendency in his philosophy to maintain this value. Most of his statements concerning justice show a great respect for this ideal. For instance: "No one has a higher claim to our reverence than the man with the feeling and the strength for justice. For the highest and rarest virtues unite and are lost in it, as an

930 Nietzsche, The Will to Power, I, pp. 5 seq. Ludovici's translation slightly changed.

931 Nietzsche, The Will to Power, I, p. 8. Ludovici's translation slightly changed.

932 Cf. p. 240

933 Heidegger, Nietzsche, II, p. 325.

unfathomable sea absorbs the streams that flow from every side."[934] Or: "We, who are of a mixed nature, alternately inspired with ardour and chilled through and through by the intellect, want to kneel before justice as the only goddess we acknowledge."[935] Two aphorisms run as follows: "His soul secretly jubilates because in every kind of justice vengeance is still exercised; my soul because ... in all kind of vengeance a spark springs from the anvil of justice." "Who has the passion for justice feels even his most painful affection as a relief."[936] As to the essence of justice Nietzsche's thoughts are not very original. In *Human. All-too-Human* he says: "The character of exchange is the primary character of justice. Each party satisfies the other, as each obtains what he values more than the other. Each one receives that which he desires, as his own henceforth, and whatever is desired is received in return. Justice therefore is retribution [*Vergeltung*] and exchange based on the hypothesis of a fairly equal degree of power, thus, originally, revenge belongs to the province of justice, it is an exchange. Also gratitude."[937]

The same idea is expressed in the following passage: "Equilibrium is, in fact, the basis of justice. When justice in ruder ages says: 'An eye for an eye, a tooth for a tooth,' it presupposes the attainment of this equilibrium and tries to maintain it by means of this compensation ... By means of the *jus talionis* the equilibrium of the disturbed relations of power is restored, for in such primitive times an eye or an arm more means a bit more power, more weight."[938]

Nietzsche accepts the traditional definition of justice as the principles of *suum cuique* and retribution. To coordinate the accepted ideal of justice with his philosophy of power he says in notes published after his death: "Justice, as function of a widely circumspecting power, looking beyond the little perspectives of good and evil, and therefore having a wider horizon of advantage – the intention of preserving something which is more than this or that personality."[939] The chapter "Concerning the History of European Nihilism" in *The Will to Power* contains under the heading "Modern Gloominess" a series of catchwords, among them: "Justice as Will to Power (Rearing)."[940] There is no statement in this work indicating the relationship Nietzsche assumed to exist between justice and the will to power. He certainly did not identify the one with the other. It is very probable that the following statement expresses Nietzsche's thought on this problem: "Right – the will to perpetuate an exist-

934 Friedrich Nietzsche, Thoughts out of Season, Part II, transl. by Adrian Collins, in: Complete Works, V, p. 47.
935 Nietzsche, Human. All-too-Human, Part I, p. 405.
936 Nietzsche, Die Unschuld des Werdens, II, p. 204.
937 Nietzsche, Human. All-too-Human, Part I, p. 90.
938 Ibid., Part II, p. 202.
939 Nietzsche, Die Unschuld des Werdens, II, p. 259.
940 Nietzsche, The Will to Power, I, p. 56.

ing relation of power."[941] This is the well-known principle that "right is might," the obvious consequence of his doctrine of the will to power. Just as this doctrine itself, the idea of justice considered to be involved in it, has nothing to do with metaphysics in the specific sense of this word.

As for the relationship between truth and justice, Nietzsche nowhere says that "justice is the foundation of the essence of truth" or that "truth exists as justice." In *Thoughts out of the Season* Nietzsche says: "The search for truth is often thoughtlessly praised: but it only has anything great in it if the seeker has the sincere unconditional will for justice. Its roots are in justice alone: but a whole crowd of different motives may combine in the search for it, that have nothing to do with truth at all; curiosity for example, or dread of ennui, envy, vanity, or amusement. Thus the world seems to be full of men who 'serve truth': and yet the value of justice is seldom present, more seldom known, and almost always mortally hated."[942] This statement does not refer to the relation between "truth" and "justice," but to a relation between the "search for truth" and the "will for justice," two psychic facts. The value of the search for truth depends on the motive. It is valuable only if its motive is "will for justice." The words: "Its roots are in justice alone" mean that the roots of the value of the search for truth are in the will for justice; the words do not mean that the roots of truth are in justice; nor do they mean that justice is the basis of truth or even that truth exists as justice – an idea which amounts to an identification of the one with the other. Such an identification is hardly compatible with the very different attitude Nietzsche exhibits toward the two ideas. Emotionally in his passionate fight against metaphysics, he rejects the value of truth, but as a logician he must recognize it as a value, although not as an absolute one. Justice, however, he emotionally affirms, but as a relativist, he can maintain it, too, only as a relative value. There is even a statement which may be interpreted as a direct rejection of an identification of truth with justice: "The greatest of all swindles, and self-deceptions: to identify the good, the true, and the beautiful and to *represent* this unity."[943] Since "good" stands for moral value and since justice is – even to Nietzsche – a moral value, by the "good" may well be understood also the "just."

This, however, is probably no argument from the point of view of an interpretation based on the "hidden" thoughts of Nietzsche and applying to his philosophy a concept of metaphysics which is supposed to be "contained and confirmed in his thinking but whose foundation he does not lay and which he nowhere builds up [eines Begriffs der Metaphysik, den Nietzsches Denken zwar erfüllt und bestätigt, aber nicht begründet und nirgends entwirft]."[944]

941 Nietzsche, Die Unschuld des Werdens, II, p. 384.
942 Nietzsche, Thoughts out of Season, II, p. 48.
943 Nietzsche, Die Unschuld des Werdens, I, p. 27.
944 Heidegger, Nietzsche, II, p. 329.

Heidegger is aware of the highly doubtful character of his interpretation. To justify it he proclaims a particular doctrine of interpretation: "Every interpretation, to be sure, must be able to gather the meaning not only from the text, but must be allowed also, without emphasizing it, to add imperceptibly something out of its own. This addition is that which the layman, comparing it with what he considers to be the contents of the text without interpretation, criticizes as imputative and arbitrary interpretation. [Jede Auslegung muss freilich nicht nur dem Text die Sache entnehmen können, sie muss auch, ohne darauf zu pochen, unvermerkt Eigenes aus *ihrer* Sache dazugeben können. Diese Beigabe ist dasjenige, was der Laie, gemessen an dem, was er ohne Auslegung für den Inhalt des Textes halt, notwendig als Hineindeuten und Willkür bemängelt.]"[945]

By discrediting the anticipated criticism of his interpretation of Nietzsche's antimetaphysical philosophy as metaphysics Heidegger cannot obscure the fact that this interpretation based on the presumption to understand Nietzsche better than the philosopher understands himself and wants to be understood, is – just from a professional point of view – a gross misinterpretation.

945 Ibid., II, pp. 262, 263.

Chapter XIII Modern Science

Modern natural science would seem to be the only branch of modern civilization that can escape imputation of theological elements or identification with religion and especially with mystic Gnosticism. For its development is entirely the result of emancipation from theology, religion and mysticism; it constitutes the most radical de-divinization of the world as the object of cognition. With regard to this tendency of modern science, one might be tempted to construct a certain parallelism between the latter and Gnostic speculation, which does not regard the cosmos as a truly divine creation. But since the gnosis supposes that this cosmos is created and governed by an evil demon, the parallelism becomes doubtful. Without ignoring this difference between gnosis and modern science, Jonas remarks that a world de-divinized by the gnosis implies the possibility that future theoretical cognition may conceive of the world as a merely impersonal thing and he adds: "Christianity has permitted to the West only a late realization of this possibility created by the gnosis."[946]

If Gnosticism is misinterpreted as divinization of the world, as in Voegelin's new science of politics, then, of course, even the relation suggested by Jonas between the gnosis and modern science is excluded. However, since Voegelin has made it his task to prove that Gnosticism is the essence of modern civilization, he is forced to pervert its most characteristic element to a "vehicle of Gnostic truth," and that means – according to his concept of Gnosticism – to an instrument of a re-divinization of the world. "With the prodigious advancement of science since the seventeenth century, the new instrument of cognition would become, one is inclined to say inevitably, the symbolic vehicle of Gnostic truth. In the Gnostic speculation of scientism this particular variant reached its extreme when the positivist perfector of science replaced the era of Christ by the era of Comte. Scientism has remained to this day one of the strongest Gnostic movements in Western society; and the immanentist pride in science is so strong that even the special sciences have each left a distinguishable sediment in the variants of salvation through physics, economics, sociology, biology and psychology."[947] The statement that scientism – that is, the apprecia-

946 Jonas, Gnosis und spätantiker Geist, p. 176.
947 Voegelin, The New Science of Politics, p. 127.

tion of science, the readiness to rely on science – is a "Gnostic movement", is utterly different from Jonas's cautious reference to the analogy between a world de-divinized by the gnosis and nature viewed as an impersonal thing by modern science. Gnostic speculation denies the creation of the evil world by the good God, but this does not mean it appreciates science, that is, relies on science. Only by distorting appreciation of science into "immanentist pride" in science, and by distorting reliance on science into a mystic "salvation" through science, is the reinterpretation of modern science as a "symbolic vehicle of Gnostic truth" achieved. What Voegelin calls the "era of Comte" is in truth the era of science, predicted by Comte; but Voegelin objects that this era replaces the era of Christ. Because he deplores this replacement he disqualifies modern science as "Gnostic", meaning heretic.

Brinton's idea of modern science is similar to Voegelin's. He says, of "modern natural science", that it "made possible a whole set of heresies of Christianity."[948] These heresies are "materialism, rationalism, 'humanism', scientism, naturalism, secularism, evolutionism, positivism, ethical culture." In the next sentence he refers to these "heresies" as "great secular religions," associated with the names of Galileo, Newton, Darwin, Locke, Spencer, and Marx. If "scientism" is a heresy, a secular religion, then science itself must have this character. This is indeed what Brinton tries to make the reader believe. He says: "Science and many scientists themselves were not long in coming to the point Laplace at the end of the eighteenth century had arrived at when he could say of God, 'I have no need for that hypothesis.'"[949] This is the answer the French astronomer is said to have given to Napoleon's question about the part God has in his system. The answer means that science is independent of theology and has nothing to do with religion, that is, the belief in God. Brinton comments on this answer: "We need not here consider how legitimate, wise or valuable was this leap from the specific study of scientific problems to a religion, or at least a cosmology, which we commonly call 'materialist' or 'mechanical'. The fact is that men made the leap, and that they were encouraged to make the leap by the extent to which science already had succeeded in accounting for much in nature that had hitherto defied 'rational' accounting". Brinton calls Laplace's advance to a scientific research of the celestial bodies, in spite of its atheistic, antitheological character, the "leap to a religion." By adding: "at least a cosmology," Brinton does not weaken this statement, for he has previously defined religion as what men believe "about the nature of the universe";[950] and if a cosmology is "materialist," it is – according to Brinton's statement about the heresy of "materialism" – a "secular religion." All this means that the more science succeeds in explaining reality without having re-

948 Brinton, A History of Western Morals, p. 275.

949 Ibid., p. 277.

950 Ibid., p. 29; see above p. 28.

course to a transcendent power, the more it assumes the character of a religion. This is not a mere paradox; it is a dangerous attempt to obscure the difference between religion and areligious science.

This attempt manifests itself also in Brinton's presentation of empirical science as revelation. "The most striking of the theological-metaphysical tenets of the new faith [that is, the philosophy of the Enlightenment] is that the *real world* (or just the plain Reality, capitalized) is revealed to the human mind working on data of sense experience, aided by such instruments as microscope, telescope, and the like, in a way best exemplified by what we call 'natural science.' Or, vulgarly, that Science, again with an initial capital, can tell us all we can ever know truthfully about ourselves and the universe." Later he speaks – like Frankel (see above, page 101) – of the "world as conceived by 'the faithful of the Enlightenment' as of the world revealed by human reason working 'scientifically.'"[951] Earlier we pointed out the fundamental antagonism between modern science and revelation, which excludes any similarity between the two. There are, according to a generally accepted view, two essentially different sources of truth about the way we derive our knowledge: either from our own efforts, our sense perceptions and our reason, or from divine revelation recorded in the Bible. "Revelation," in the only proper sense of the word, is the unveiling by an act of God of a reality that by its nature remains hidden without divine intervention. The belief in revelation is a specific element of religion and only possible within religion. In other words: Revelation is the conveyance of a truth to man by a supernatural event, and as such, in direct opposition to the conveyance of truth by science, which is based only on the experience of human senses controlled by human reason and rejecting any kind of superhuman, supernatural source of truth. To call conveyance of truth by science "revelation", to speak of a world or a reality "revealed" to the human mind by science, is the same misuse of terminology as the term "secular religion," and all the other contradictions in terms that are the instruments of the reinterpretation of modern philosophy and science. Brinton speaks not only of a "revelation" through science but also of the "grace" of science. He asserts that in the course of the past two centuries emotional and moral difficulties have been intensified for the enlightened intellectual "by evidence, which is still often unable to face, that the founders of his religion were wrong about human nature, that men are not in fact roughly equal in respect to their capacity to receive the grace of Reason or Science."[952] Just as the belief in God is a "grace," that is, a free gift of God to some men for their regeneration or sanctification, so science is a grace, and hence a free gift of God to some, not to all men. If science is a kind of religion, it may as well be a "grace." To justify this view Brinton refers to the French *Encyclopédie*. He says: "I am not invent-

951 Ibid., p. 447.

952 Ibid., pp. 461–462.

ing this parallel in the famous *Encyclopédie* of Diderot and his colleagues, you will find the following in Volume XII, under the word *philosophe: 'La reason est à l'égard du philosophe, ce que la grace est à l'égard du Chretien. La grace determine le Chretien à agir; la raison determine le philosophe.'*" The article referred to by Brinton does not speak of "science" but of "reason." But even if we accept the identification of science with reason, the passage does not justify Brinton's interpretation of the enlightened science as "grace." For the meaning of the statement is not that reason (or science) *is* grace for the enlightened philosopher, but that he is directed by human reason and not by grace, a divine gift, which directs the Christian. The *Encyclopédie* does not "parallel," as Brinton assumes, reason with divine grace; it opposes the reason of the philosopher to the grace of the Christian, it emphasizes that reason is not grace. Later[953] Brinton says: "Reason does indeed for the Enlightened do the work grace does for the Christian." This is clearly untrue because the work grace does for the Christian is to regenerate or sanctify man, which is certainly not the work of science. "Though Reason is in the determined world view of the Enlightened the free but uncomfortably mysterious gift of Nature, as grace for the Christian is the free and properly mysterious gift of God, so in this moral world of free will the Enlightened individual must *strive* to deserve (attain?) Reason as the Christian strives to deserve grace. We can all get more Reason into this world of human relations if we will only go to work properly, in the missionary spirit, bearing the good news of Reason, Science, Technology." To describe reason as a gift of nature is a figure of speech which, in the philosophy of the Enlightenment, means only that the facts of nature include the fact that man is endowed with reason, and this fact, like all facts of nature, is determined by laws of causality, and therefore not a "free" gift. This fact is no more mysterious than any other fact of nature. There is mystery in nature only to those who imagine something supernatural behind nature. For "mystery" means something that cannot be explained, something beyond human comprehension, because emanating from another, supernatural world and therefore sacred. There are, it is true, and there always will be facts which are not explained by science. But a man of science, though fully aware of this limitation of science, does not assume that behind these facts there are supernatural forces. Consequently, there is no mystery to the enlightened philosopher in his rationalistic approach to nature. Brinton's opinion that the enlightened philosopher feels "uncomfortable" in his rationalistic refusal to see mysteries in nature is an unfounded guess. From his metaphysical point of view Brinton can only say that this refusal should make the enlightened philosopher feel uncomfortable. But even if Brinton's opinion were correct, if the enlightened philosopher really felt uncomfortable, an objective presentation of enlightened philosophy could only ascertain that their representatives, in spite of their al-

953 Ibid., p. 466.

legedly uncomfortable feelings, refused to see a mystery where there is a mystery to a Christian. The grace of God is indeed a mystery; according to Brinton, it must be "deserved," but reason – especially if the term implies "science" – need not be "deserved," a word, which has a strong moral connotation. Only by ignoring all these differences is it possible to speak of "Science" as of the "good news of Reason," that is, of something like a divine message.

If modern science is a religion (even only a "secular" religion), if it is not an objective cognition of reality, free from metaphysical presuppositions, then its conflict with Christianity may well be viewed from Christianity's point of view. Then truth, real truth, the last, the final truth is not on its side but on the other side, and science is disqualified with Brinton as heresy or – what amounts to the same – with Voegelin as Gnosticism. This is perhaps the most disastrous consequence of the attempt to find theological implications in the characteristic manifestations of modern civilization.

Chapter XIV Modern Politics

According to Voegelin's new science of politics, the Reformation with which the modern age begins is to be "understood as the successful invasion of Western institutions by Gnostic movements." Voegelin declares: "The event is so vast in dimensions that no survey even of its general characteristics can be attempted in the present lectures." Consequently, he restricts his task to an analysis of "certain aspects of the Puritan impact on the English public order."[954]

These aspects are the religious ideologies produced in Puritanism's left wing which Voegelin characterizes as a Gnostic revolution. He admits that "Puritanism as a whole cannot be identified with its left wing,"[955] but he justifies his selection of material by the statement that he does not intend "to give a historical account of Puritanism"; that he is concerned only "with the structure of Gnostic experiences and ideas";[956] and that this structure can be found in the material he has chosen. But even if he had demonstrated the Gnostic character of the religious ideology of left-wing Puritanism – which he has not – his interpretation of the Reformation as the revolutionary eruption of Gnostic movements would remain unfounded.[957]

Voegelin's interpretation of Puritanism (which was only one of many components of the Reformation, and not the most decisive one) is not based on an analysis of the movement itself but on its description by Richard Hooker. From this description Voegelin gathers that Puritans, in their criticism of social conditions, insisted on having a "cause"; that the term "cause" was of recent

954 Voegelin, The New Science of Politics, pp. 134–135.

955 Ibid., p. 151.

956 Ibid.

957 Baur, in his work on the Christian Gnosis to which Voegelin refers to justify this use of the term "Gnosticism" (see above, p. 77) sees indeed a Gnostic element in the Reformation. It is "the strict distinction between the law [i. e., the Old Testament] and the Gospels," "the vivid consciousness of the absolute value of the Gospel," "a certain disregard and contempt of the law" (pp. 550–551). This is certainly not a "revolutionary eruption." Baur mentions that Catholic writers tried to interpret the Reformation as "nothing but a renewal of the old Gnosticism." But he considers this view exaggerated (p. 552).

usage; and that probably the Puritans had invented it.[958] To have a "cause" in order to start a movement is interpreted by Voegelin as a "formidable weapon of the Gnostic revolutionaries." How does "having a cause" manifest itself? "In order to advance his 'cause,' the man who has it will, 'in the hearing of the multitude', indulge in severe criticisms of social evils and in particular of the conduct of the upper classes … The next step will be the concentration of popular ill-will on the established government. This task can be psychologically performed by attributing all fault and corruption, as it exists in the world because of human frailty, to the action or inaction of the government… After such preparation, the time will be ripe for recommending a new form of government as the 'sovereign remedy of all evils.'"[959] There is nothing specifically Gnostic in having a "cause" and in advancing it in this way – the way of any political movement, and especially of a revolutionary movement, directed against the established government. It is not specifically Puritan, and not in the least mystic.

Voegelin sees another symptom of the Gnostic character of the Puritan movement in the fact that it "relies on the authority of a literary source," namely, the Scripture, and that "the leaders will then have to fashion 'the very notions and conceits of men's minds in such a sort' that the followers will automatically associate scriptural passages and terms with their doctrine, however ill founded the association may be."[960] This is the attitude of every political movement whose ideology is furnished by Christian theology, and has neither Gnostic nor other mystic implications.

According to Voegelin, the "decisive step in consolidating a Gnostic attitude" is described by Hooker when he accuses the Puritans of "the persuading of men credulous and overcapable of such pleasing errors, that it is the special illumination of the Holy Ghost, whereby they discern those things in the word, which orders reading yet discern them not."[961] Again, there is nothing peculiarly Gnostic in the attempt of a religious leader to make his followers believe that he is illuminated by a transcendent authority. The "special illumination of the Holy Ghost" on which Puritan interpreters of the Scripture tried to base their authority has nothing whatever to do with the mystic experience of a union with God. Only if Voegelin could prove that such mystic experience played an essential role in Puritanism, would his interpretation of this movement as Gnostic (in the sense of mystic) be justifiable. But such a proof is impossible for the simple reason that no social movement can have such a mystic character because mystic experiences are antisocial or at least asocial. A true mystic is far from being even mildly interested in criticism or reform of society,

958 Voegelin, The New Science of Politics, p. 135.
959 Ibid., pp. 135–136.
960 Ibid., p. 136.
961 Ibid.

matters which were the main concerns of Puritanism. A revolutionary mystic is a contradiction in terms.

In order to show that the movement which Voegelin calls the "Puritan Revolution"[962] is a Gnostic revolution, he refers also to "two technical devices ... which to this day have remained the great instruments of Gnostic revolution."[963] The first device is a "Gnostic koran," – and the Gnostic koran of the Puritan movement, as pointed out on page 123, were Calvin's *Institutes*. The Koran is a holy scripture: The Puritans did not regard Calvin's *Institutes* as a holy scripture itself, but as an authentic guide to the right reading of the Holy Scripture. It is, therefore, not appropriate to call Calvin's book a Koran. Nor is there any reason to consider as "Gnostic" an interpretation of the Scripture that claims to be authentic. The fact that Calvin – according to Hooker – claimed to owe his divine knowledge "to non but only to God," is certainly no sufficient basis for such an interpretation. To be the mouthpiece of God was claimed by Moses, Jesus, and Mohammed. If this claim is the criterion of Gnosticism, the three religions founded by these prophets are Gnostic, and then, the term "Gnosticism" means simply religion.

The second device of Gnostic revolution is "putting a taboo on the instruments of critique."[964] This device is used by any religious movement that pretends to possess absolute truth. To hold another than the authentic opinion laid down by the established authority is a punishable crime. The concept of heresy, which plays such a fateful part in the history of the Christian Church, implies this idea. To punish heretics and thus prevent criticism of the authentic doctrine is not practiced solely by "Gnosticism." The example given by Voegelin to illustrate the Puritan taboo on criticism is significant. Hooker was blamed, in the anonymous *Christian* Letter of 1599, a document of Puritan origin, for having used Aristotle against the Scripture.[965] Does Voegelin seriously assert that the Church, the representative of the Christian tradition which he opposes to Gnosticism, does not use this same device – that this Church allowed or allows free criticism of the Scripture? Voegelin cannot deny that the Reformation was directed against the Church, and that the Reformation, at least in its earlier stages, set forth among its aims a free interpretation of the Bible. How, then, can he characterize the whole Reformation as a revolutionary eruption of Gnostic movements if, at the same time, he declares the suppression of this freedom to be a specific Gnostic device?

If the nature of modernity is Gnosticism, and if Gnosticism means the suppression of freedom to criticize, how can the undeniable facts be explained that a characteristic element of modern civilization is the political movement to-

962 Ibid., p. 145.
963 Ibid., pp. 138, 139.
964 Ibid., p. 140.
965 Ibid., p. 141.

ward democracy, which implies the principle of free criticism; and that democratic theories happened to originate with the Puritans of the Left?[966] The new science of politics does not reply to this question, unless the following statement is an answer: "However well the constitutional freedoms of speech and press may be protected, however well theoretical debate may flourish in small circles, and however well it may be carried on in the practically private publications of a handful of scholars, debate in the politically relevant public sphere will be in substance the game with loaded dice which it has become in contemporary progressive societies – to say nothing of the quality of debate in totalitarian empires. Theoretical debate can be protected by constitutional guaranties, but it can be established only by the willingness to use and accept theoretical argument."[967] Does this mean that there is no freedom to criticize in Western democracies? Voegelin cannot claim that the instrument of criticism is tabooed – for how then could Feuerbach's and Marx's critique of religion and other antimetaphysical ideologies have been possible in this civilization? Nor can it be claimed that the democratic creed is based on a Gnostic koran, like Puritanism on Calvin's *Institutes*. Therefore, there is no answer to the question of why in a supposedly Gnostic civilization important societies do not use the specific Gnostic devices. Voegelin considers as a specifically Gnostic element of the Puritan revolution the fact that the Puritan revolutionaries interpreted the society for which they were fighting as the realm to come and as a goal whose attainment required their cooperation by the use of force. On the basis of the disputable statement that "there is no passage in the New Testament from which advice for revolutionary political action could be extracted,"[968] Voegelin assumes that the Puritans falsely justified their revolutionary actions by referring to the Revelation of St. John and arrogated to themselves the function of the angel, who "comes down from heaven and throws Satan into the bottomless pit." To document this view, Voegelin refers to a pamphlet, *A Glimpse of Sion's Glory*, published in 1641, attributed to a Puritan. But the passages quoted by Voegelin[969] contain nothing that can justify the interpretation of the document as a product of Gnosticism. With respect to the relation between the revolutionaries and God – the only relation relevant to the interpretation of the Puritan revolution as Gnostic – the pamphlet, as quoted by Voegelin, says the omnipotent God will come to the aid of the Saints, that is, the Puritan revolutionaries: "[God] shall do these things, by that power, whereby he is able to subdue all things unto himself. Mountains shall be made plain, and he shall come skipping over mountains and over difficulties. Nothing shall hinder him."[970] Voegelin first emphasized as a

966 See A. D. Lindsay, The Modern Democratic State, 5th ed. (New York, 1951), p. 117.
967 Voegelin, The New Science of Politics, pp. 141 seq.
968 Ibid., p. 145.
969 Ibid., p. 145 seqq.
970 Ibid., p. 147.

specific Gnostic element that a Gnostic "will not leave the transfiguration of the world to the grace of God beyond history but will do the work of God himself, right here and now, in history." Voegelin must admit that "the author of the pamphlet knows that not ordinary human powers will establish the realm but that human efforts will be subsidiary to the action of God";[971] whereby he drops this "Gnostic" Element in his picture of the Puritan revolution.

Voegelin is no longer interested in the Gnostic character of the Puritan revolution, but in the fact that the ideology of the English revolution shows similarities with the ideology of the Russian revolution: "In this God who comes skipping over the mountains we recognize the dialectics of history that comes skipping over thesis and antithesis, until it lands its believers in the plain of the Communist synthesis."[972] There are, in fact, similarities between the ideologies of the Puritan and Soviet revolutions; and the results of Voegelin's comparison are indeed interesting. But the ideologies of all revolutions exhibit these similarities. To recognize the God, who comes skipping over the mountains in the Marxian dialectics, is one of the metaphorical exaggerations that play such an unfortunate part in Voegelin's interpretation of social phenomena. Even if Marxian dialectics were identical with the God of the Puritans, and the Russian revolution only a repetition of the English revolution (although the former resulted in a democratic parliamentarism and the latter in a totalitarian dictatorship) there would be no reason to characterize both as Gnostic revolutions and to designate the dictatorship of the proletariat as a concept of "later Gnostics."[973]

How arbitrarily Voegelin uses the term "Gnostic" becomes apparent in his statement on "Gnostic wars." He says: "The revolution of the Gnostics has for its aim the monopoly of existential representation. The Saints can foresee that the universalism of their claim will not be accepted without a struggle by the world of darkness but that it will produce an equally universal alliance of the world against them."[974] It is obvious that this applies only to the Russian, not to the English revolution because only the former has aimed at a world revolution, that is, at the revolutionary establishment of a new social organization of all mankind. The fundamental difference between the two revolutions is obscured by terming them both Gnostic. Voegelin can speak of the split into two worlds as of "the Gnostic mysticism of the two worlds" only on the basis of the unjustified assumption that the Russian revolution is a "Gnostic" revolution, that is to say, on the basis of an unjustified terminology. The split into two worlds is the result of the Russian revolution, but not the result of the "Gnostic" Puritan revolution. Voegelin says: "The two worlds which are sup-

971 Ibid.
972 Ibid.
973 Ibid., p. 149.
974 Ibid., p. 151.

posed to follow each other chronologically will, thus, become in historical reality two universal armed camps engaged in a death struggle against each other."[975] How two worlds that follow each other in time can become two camps existing at the same time, one beside the other, is a mystery; but there is no mystery at all if "two universal armed camps" are engaged in a struggle against each other. Nevertheless, Voegelin continues: "From the Gnostic mysticism of the two worlds emerges the pattern of the universal wars that has come to dominate the twentieth century." But surely not from the "Gnostic" revolution of the seventeenth century! Since both revolutions are Gnostic, Voegelin says (referring to both): "The universalism of the Gnostic revolutionary produces the universal alliance against him," and thus he arrives at the "Gnostic wars" of our time: "The real danger of contemporary wars does not lie in the technologically determined global extent of the theater of war; their true fatality stems from their character as Gnostic wars, that is, of wars between worlds that are bent on mutual destruction."[976] The Gnostic character of these wars consists in the fact that they take place between two worlds "that are bent on mutal destruction." But the two worlds of the Gnostic speculation – the existing and the coming world – are not at all bent on mutual destruction. On the contrary, the one will be replaced by the other, and the other will last eternally.

To speak of Gnostic revolutions and Gnostic wars in the twentieth century is not merely abstruse terminology. There is an important tendency behind it. If the Russian revolution, one of the most significant landmarks of modern times, is regarded as Gnostic, that is, as a heretical religious movement; if one of its most characteristic elements, its antireligious aim, is ignored; if the two World Wars are Gnostic (that is, religious) wars, then, indeed, the Middle Ages have not yet come to an end.

The last chapter of Voegelin's work on the new science of politics is entitled "The End of Modernity."[977] Since he says that the nature of modernity is Gnosticism, we can expect to learn how Gnosticism, and therefore modern civilization, will come to an end, and perhaps also what kind of civilization will come in the future. Indeed, Voegelin identifies the end of modernity with "the end of the Gnostic dream" which, as he says, "is perhaps closer at hand than one ordinarily would assume."[978] What does he mean by "Gnostic dream"? The idea of an everlasting state of perfection. Gnosticism, he says, destroys the oldest wisdom – that "what comes into being will have an end," and that "the mystery of this stream of being is impenetrable." Although he said before: "The revolution of the Gnostics has for its aim the monopoly of *existential* re-

975 Ibid.
976 Ibid.
977 Ibid., pp. 162 seqq.
978 Ibid., p. 173.

presentation," he now says that Gnosticism is a "*counterexistential* dream world."[979] As a consequence of "its disregard for the structure of reality," Gnostic politics "is self-defeating" because this disregard "leads to continuous warfare."[980] This is a doubtful statement because continuous warfare may have many different causes and is a phenomenon by no means restricted to "Gnostic" modernity. But this statement is not the most questionable point in Voegelin's theory of the end of modernity. Even more questionable than this "self-defeating" factor are other dangers of Gnosticism, such as "the destruction of the truth of the soul" and the "search for civil theology" (p. 166). We have already pointed out that Gnosticism cannot be accused of destroying the truth of the soul because, according to Voegelin's own characterization of this religious movement, it aims at opening the soul to God (see above, p. 73); and we have shown that nothing could be more alien to the historic gnosis than a search for "civil theology," that is, the principle of making religion the instrument of government. When Voegelin is speaking of Gnosticism as a civil theology, he has in mind the policy of the Bolshevik and Nazi governments which, indeed, are characterized by that element of civil theology which Voegelin formulates as putting a taboo on the instrument of criticism. He says: "As far as our experience with totalitarian empires goes, their characteristic feature is the elimination of debate concerning the Gnostic truth which they themselves profess to represent. The National Socialists suppressed debate on the race question, once they had come to power; the Soviet government prohibits debate and development of Marxism. The Hobbesian principle that the validity of Scripture derives from governmental sanction and that its public teaching should be supervised by the sovereign is carried out by the Soviet government in the reduction of communism to the 'party line.'"[981] Speaking of the end of modernity, Voegelin says: "The totalitarianism of our time must be understood as journey's end of the Gnostic search for a civil theology."[982] By the totalitarianism of our time he can only mean nazism and bolshevism. These political systems are "journey's end of the Gnostic search for a civil theology" or – as he formulates later – "Gnosticism as a civil theology."[983] The Gnostic character of the two totalitarian regimes is also apparent from the statements that Gnostic movements, in their origin and development from Joachim to the Puritans closely connected with Christianity, "tended to abolish Christianity";[984] that the destruction of the truth of the soul "is the cause of the bleak atrocity of totalitarian governments in their dealings with

979 Ibid., pp. 151, 167.
980 Ibid., p. 173.
981 Ibid., p. 187.
982 Ibid., p. 163.
983 Ibid., p. 166.
984 Ibid., p. 163.

individual human beings";[985] and that it is difficult to foresee "the probable reaction of a living Christian tradition against Gnosticism in the Soviet empire."[986] Since the National Socialist empire has already disappeared, the end of the Gnostic dream and, thereby, the end of modernity, seem to coincide in the main with the end of the Soviet empire.

It would be a mistake to interpret the "Gnostic dream" of totalitarianism as referring only to the political ideology of National Socialist Germany and the Soviet state. It refers also to political reality. Voegelin speaks of a "Gnostic dream world." He admits, it is true, that "the nonrecognition of reality [which in Gnosticism] is a matter of principle," does not prevent the Gnostic politicians from remaining aware "of the hazard of existence in spite of the fact that it is not admitted as a problem in the Gnostic dream world; nor does the dream impair civic responsibility or the readiness to fight valiantly in the event of an emergency. The attitude toward reality remains energetic and active, but neither reality nor action in reality can be brought into focus; the vision is blurred by the Gnostic dream. The result is a very complex pneumopathological state of mind."[987] This statement may be true to some extent with respect to the Nazi regime, but there is insufficient basis for the opinion that the Soviet government's vision of reality is "blurred by the Gnostic dream," that is to say, by its political ideology. The leaders of this "Gnostic empire" are not dreamers, and their state of mind is not at all "pneumopathological," if this word has anything to do with the penuma of Gnostic speculation. But later we read: "[Whereas in] the sixteenth century the dream world and the real world were still held apart terminologically through the Christian symbolism of the two worlds," later, "with radical immanentization the dream world has blended into the real world terminologically."[988] This "identification of dream and reality as a matter of principle has practical results which may appear strange but can hardly be considered surprising." But, surprising, indeed, they are! "The critical exploration of cause and effect in history is prohibited; and consequently the rational co-ordination of means and ends in politics is impossible. Gnostic societies and their leaders will recognize dangers to their existence when they develop, but such dangers will not be met by appropriate actions in the world of reality. They will rather be met by magic operations in the dream world; such as disapproval, moral condemnation, declarations of intentions, resolutions, appeals to the opinion of mankind, branding of enemies as aggressors, outlawing of war, propaganda for world peace and world government, etc. The intellectual and moral corruption which expresses itself in the aggregate of such magic operations may pervade a society with the weird, ghostly at-

985 Ibid., p. 164.
986 Ibid., p. 165.
987 Ibid., pp. 168–169.
988 Ibid., p. 169.

mosphere of a lunatic asylum, as we experience it in our time in the Western crisis."[989] It is hardly possible that Voegelin considers the imperialistic policies of the Nazi and Soviet governments as magic operations in a dream world, characterized by moral condemnations, declarations of intention, outlawing of war, propaganda for world government. It is now evident that the Gnostic dream world to which the quoted statements refer is not the world of the totalitarian states whose political ideology is the civil theology of an everlasting realm of perfection; instead, it is the politics of the Western powers directed against the totalitarian states that he castigates as "the manifestations of Gnostic insanity in the practice of contemporary politics."[990] Here, again, it is not now totalitarianism that is accused by Voegelin of identifying dream and reality, of prohibiting critical exploration of cause and effect in history, of establishing its political ideologies as civil theology by putting a taboo on the instrument of criticism. He does not now criticize Gnosticism as a civil theology of the *Soviet* society but wants to expose "the dangers of Gnosticism as a civil theology of Western society."[991] Now not only the totalitarian autocracies of nazism and Communism, but also the liberal democracies of the West are condemned as "Gnostic." Is it really possible to maintain that the political system of the Western democracies contains anything that is comparable to the system that he calls "the civil theology of the totalitarian states"? If radical contrasts, such as those between the liberal-democratic regimes of the United States, Great Britain, France, and the totalitarian-autocratic regimes of the Nazi and Soviet states, are comprised in the concept of Gnosticism, this word can only mean the expression of political disapproval. Voegelin says that the "nonrecognition of reality" in the Gnostic dream world has as a consequence "types of action which in the real world would be considered as morally insane because of the real effects which they have will be considered moral in the dream world because they intended an entirely different effect. The gap between intended and real effect will be imputed not to the Gnostic immorality of ignoring the structure of reality but to the immorality of some other person or society that does not behave as it should behave according to the dream conception of cause and effect. The interpretation of moral insanity as morality, and of the virtues of *sophia* and *prudentia* as immorality, is a confusion difficult to unravel. And the task is not facilitated by the readiness of the dreamers to stigmatize the attempt at critical clarification as an immoral enterprise."[992] The reader might think that these statements refer to the Gnostic dream world of the totalitarian states. But the following passages show that Voegelin is speaking of the "liberals" of Western civilization: "As a matter of fact, practically every great political thinker who recognized the

989 Ibid., p. 170.
990 Ibid., pp. 170–171.
991 Ibid., p. 173.
992 Ibid., pp. 169 seq.

structure of reality, from Machiavelli to the present, has been branded as an immoralist by Gnostic intellectuals – to say nothing of the parlor game, so much beloved among liberals, of panning Plato and Aristotle as Fascists."[993] It is not the Nazi Gnostics who stigmatized Plato as a fascist and branded Machiavelli as an immoralist – Machiavelli, whose *Principe* is the Gnostic symbol of the leader, according to Voegelin;[994] and it is not the Nazi and Soviet theorists whom Voegelin accuses of establishing a "continuous Gnostic barrage of vituperation against political science in the critical sense."[995] Does he seriously maintain that outside the totalitarian states a barrier exists against any kind of criticism in political science, and does his statement imply that in the Western democracies a "political science in the critical sense" – which he evidently identifies with an antipositivistic and antirelativistic school of thought – is not permitted to develop freely? Can he seriously deny that this science, of which his new science of politics is a significant product, is now even more *en vogue* in Western society than its opponents; and is it not vituperative to stigmatize these opponents as "destructive"? By publishing his anti-"Gnostic" book in a "Gnostic" society of the West he makes ample use of the essential difference between his society and the "Gnostic" society of the East, which difference he tries to eclipse by calling both "Gnostic." As a "manifestation of Gnostic insanity in the practice of contemporary politics [of] Western society," Voegelin points to the attitude toward the National Socialist movement as to "the Gnostic chorus wailing its moral indignation at such barbarian and reactionary doings in a progressive world – without, however, raising a finger to repress the rising force by a minor political effort in proper time."[996] Has he forgotten that the "Gnostic insanity" of the Western societies destroyed the Nazi movement after a very short existence? "Gnostic politicians," he says with indignation, "have put the Soviet army on the Elbe, surrendered China to the Communists, at the same time demilitarized Germany and Japan and in addition demobilized our own army."[997] This means that the new science of politics disapproves of the policies of liberal administrations of the Franklin D. Roosevelt type and thus shows that it is a "political" science, not a science of politics.

Voegelin considers the "evolution of mankind toward peace and world order" "mysterious" and does not believe in "the possibility of establishing an international order in the abstract without relation to the structure of the field of existential forces."[998] Gnostic immanentization "with increasing theoretical illiteracy ... may assume the form of various social idealisms, such as the aboli-

993 Ibid., p. 170.
994 Ibid., p. 112.
995 Ibid., p. 170.
996 Ibid., pp. 171 seq.
997 Ibid., p. 172.
998 Ibid.

tion of war, of unequal distribution of property, of fear and want."[999] Who but the late President Roosevelt can be meant by the reference to these ideals, stigmatized as a result of "increasing theoretical illiteracy"? Professor Voegelin is against disarmament, which, he says, is based on the erroneous view that armies are "the cause of war and not the forces and constellations which build them and set them into motion."[1000] It would be easy to show that the democratic politicians and liberal intellectuals he tries to ridicule as Gnostic dreamers do not believe in a predestined evolution of mankind; that they try, instead, to bring about peace and world order, without having illusions about the difficulties inherent in such policy because they are fully aware of the forces operating against it; that they suggest disarmament or reduction of armament not because they are so stupid as to assume that armies are "the" cause of war, but because they know that the existence of an army makes war possible and that the militaristic mentality that is inevitably connected with the maintenance of armies is an additional motive for a policy that uses war as its instrument. Voegelin cannot hide the fact that he distorts the ideas of his political opponents by referring to them as "Gnostics." The meaning which this word assumes in the new science of politics becomes evident when Voegelin deals with the thesis "that Western society is ripe to fall for communism."[1001]

Voegelin should know that this pessimistic opinion has been expressed by a great economist, Joseph Schumpeter, whose anti-Communist attitude is beyond doubt.[1002] Without referring to this author, Voegelin says of this opinion that it "is an impertinent piece of Gnostic propaganda,"[1003] that is, Communist propaganda. Now we understand what Voegelin really means when he, on the basis of his new science of politics, calls the Roosevelt politics and the movement for peace, world order, and disarmament, "Gnostic." It is the same tactic as smearing as Communists those who do not conform with one's own opinion.

One of the main concerns of Voegelin's theory of identifying modernity as Gnosticism is to accuse not only the Soviet state, but also the allegedly civil theology of Western societies, of having destroyed "the truth of the soul," and to condemn the policy of these democracies as "Gnostic insanity."[1004] Among the Western societies "the American and English democracies" represent, according to his own testimony, "the oldest, most firmly consolidated stratum

999 Ibid., p. 121.
1000 Ibid., p. 172.
1001 Ibid., p. 176.
1002 See Joseph A. Schumpeter, Capitalism, Socialism and Democracy (New York and London, 1942); and the same author's paper: "The March into Socialism," American Economic Review, XL, 2 (1950), pp. 446 seqq.
1003 Voegelin, The New Science of Politics, p. 176.
1004 Ibid., p. 170 seq.

of civilized tradition."[1005] England and the United States are certainly the most prominent, and the most representative among the Western societies; and if the Western societies are guilty of Gnosticism, this accusation must be directed in the first place at these two democracies. As a matter of fact, Voegelin has directed it, expressly at least, against the United States in the period of the Roosevelt administration. But, finally, Voegelin admits: "Of the major European political societies, however, England has proved herself most resistant against Gnostic totalitarianism; and the same must be said for the America that was founded by the very Puritans who aroused the fear of the Hobbes."[1006] In the catastrophic situation into which Gnosticism, with its destruction of the truth of the soul, has driven modern civilization, he sees, at the end of his book, "a glimmer of hope, for the American and English democracies which most solidly in their institutions represent the truth of the soul are, at the same time, existentially the strongest powers."[1007] This is the – wholly contradictory – truth of Gnosticism as the nature of modernity. It is the end of Voegelin's Gnostic dream. How entirely arbitrary this theological interpretation of modern politics is, is apparent in the fact that although Voegelin disqualifies democratism as "Gnosticism" as a false, heretical religion Brinton characterizes it as the right, the "orthodox" religion, in relation to which Marxian communism is to be considered "heresy." Brinton speaks of democracy and communism as of "our great conflicting secular faiths";[1008] but he tries to show that "democratic nationalism" is "the first, or early orthodox *church*, form of the religion of Enlightenment."[1009] The "church," called democracy, is Rome. But: "The socialists and the other radicals are the protestants of the new faith in the principles of 1776 and 1789, principles tarnished, compromised in the eyes of the protestants by the new Rome of nationalist popular government or semidemocracies."[1010]

Why is democracy a religion? Democracy is a specific form of government by men exercised over men on this earth. It is characterized by the fact that the government is determined, directly or indirectly, by those who are to be governed. As such it has nothing to do with religion, neither as liberal nor as totalitarian democracy. Atheists, as well as men who believe in God, can be and are in favor of democracy. If there is any relation at all between the religion of men and their political attitude, it can be seen in the fact that men, who believe in a God who rules the world without its consent, as an absolute autocrat, are more

1005 Ibid., p. 189.
1006 Ibid., p. 187.
1007 Ibid., p. 189.
1008 Brinton, A History of Western Morals, p. 339.
1009 Ibid., p. 322.
1010 Ibid., p. 366. On Brinton's comparison of Marxist socialism with Protestantism, see above p. 165.

inclined to accept as well an autocratic government by other men than atheists or religiously indifferent people. There can be little doubt that in modern times democratism goes hand in hand with emancipation from religion.[1011] The same is true of nationalism which is difficult to reconcile with the belief in a God who loves all men without regard to their nationality, – a God before whom all men are equal. The statement that to some nationalists their nation is their God is a figure of speech, which expresses the idea that the sentiments which unite men to their conationals and hence to their community are as intense as those that unite men to the god in whom they believe! To identify – for this reason – nationalism with religion is the logical fallacy that is the foundation of the theological interpretation of modern philosophy, science, and politics.

By this fallacy Brinton justifies calling democratic nationalism a religion. He says: "It is surely impossible even for those who find terms like 'religion of nationalism' misleading, inexact, or simply offensive, to deny that the individual does have this emotional relation to the common thing, that much of the hymns, symbols, and public ceremonies of the nation-state at least suggest religious ritual, and that there are national holy writings, declarations, bills of rights, consecrated orations by a Webster, a Danton, a Farewell Address, other pronunciamentos, that are comparable to canonical writings in recognized religions."[1012] The only reason why Brinton calls the hymns, symbols, and public ceremonies of the nation-state "religious ritual," the declarations, bills of rights "holy writings," and the orations by Webster and Danton "consecrated", is the fact that individuals have certain "emotional relations" to the common thing, called nation or nation-state. But Brinton seems not to be certain that this reason is sufficient, for he says that the ceremonies of the nation-state only "suggest" religious ritual, that its pronunciamentos are only "comparable" to canonical writings. In the next sentence, however, he again resumes his usual identification of nationalism with religion. "There are clearly national saints – Washington, Lincoln, Lenin – and those near-saints, the cultural heroes – Shakespeare, Dante, Goethe." He uses the words: "there *are* national saints and near-saints," not "there are personalities who are as highly appreciated, as saints of a religion are worshiped by its believers." In the following sentence he again uses only an "analogy" between nationalism and religion: "But, those who reject the analogy with recognized religions ask, where is your armature of theology, eschatology, ethics, all essential to a true religion? The answer is partly, of course, that nationalism is clearly not a theistic religion, and if you so define religion as to make a *theos* and a supernatural view of the cosmos the essential mark of a religion, you must abandon the analogy between religion and nationalism. You will, however, have thereby abandoned a useful tool for understanding human conduct." However, it is not a mere

1011 See my Foundations of Democracy, pp. 40 seqq.

1012 Brinton, A History of Western Morals, pp. 331 seqq.

analogy, but an identity that, as Brinton asserts, exists between the Enlightenment and its offspring Marxian communism and democratic nationalism on the one hand and religion on the other. He again and again asserts that the Enlightenment and its offspring *are* religions. Abandoning this "analogy," raised to an identification, does not mean abandoning a useful tool for understanding human conduct, but, on the contrary, abandoning a highly dangerous misinterpretation of the essential elements of modern civilization.

Conclusion

This book might meet with the objection that it overestimates the importance of the interpretation against which its polemic is directed. To see theological implications in certain philosophies of history and sociologies of our time and to discover religion in modern science and politics might be considered to be merely a more or less exaggerated presentation of certain similarities, a *façon de parler* chosen because of its effect on the reader, a quasi poetical license, without serious consequences.

However, this is a dangerous error in the author's opinion. The purpose – and if not the purpose, the inevitable effect – of the interpretation stigmatized in this book is to undermine the powerful dam which has been erected to protect science and politics from being flooded by metaphysico-theological speculation. This speculation is not the product of man's rational cognition, but of his imagination rooted in his wishes and fears. The interpretation against which the author is fighting is part of an intellectual movement within Western civilization which can be understood only by recognition of its social function. Provoked by the social instability following the two World Wars, the Russian revolution, and the establishment of communism in great parts of the world, this movement is aiming at returning religion to politics, and theology to science. For it is assumed that only by this return, and that means by the belief that the capitalistic-democratic social order maintained in the Western Hemisphere corresponds to the will of a transcendent and hence absolute authority, can this social order be absolutely justified in its conflict with communism.

Whether such a justification is possible, however, is no concern of science, scientific philosophy, or political theory. For science is not, as the Marxists pretend, a mere intellectual superstructure over political reality – a view which the anti-Marxists, without being aware of it, confirm by attributing to science the function of justifying a definite political system. Science can only describe and explain; it cannot justify reality. It has the immanent tendency to be independent of politics and, as a rational and objective cognition of reality, cannot presuppose in the description and explanation of its object the existence of a transcendent authority beyond any possible human experience.

Bibliography

Aeschylos. *Prometheus* Chained in: *The Tragedies of Aeschylos*. Transl. by Theodore Alvis Buckly, London: 1863.

D'Alembert, Jean le Rond. *"Discours préliminaire de l'Encyclopédie"*, in: D'Alembert, Jean le Rond: *Œuvres Philosophiques, Historiques et Littèraires*. Vol I. Paris: 1805.

Arnim, Hans von. *Die europäische Philosophie des Altertums*, Part 1: *Kultur der Gegenwart*, Berlin and Leipzig: 1909.

Aron, Raymond. "L'Avenir des religions seculières", *La France Libre*, Vol. VIII, London: 1944. No. 45, pp. 210–217; No. 46, pp. 269–277.

Augustine. *The City of God*. Transl. by John Healey, with an introduction by Ernest Baker. London: Everyman's Library, 1947.

– *The City of God*. Transl. by Marcus Dodd. New York: The Modern Library, 1950.

– De *Trinitate*.

– *Enchiridion*.

Balthasar, Hans Urs von. *Prometheus*. Heidelberg: 1947.

Barth, Hans. *Wahrheit und Ideologie*. Zürich: Manesse-Verlag, 1945.

Baur, Ferdinand Christian. *Die christliche Gnosis; oder die christliche Religionsphilosophie in ihrer geschichtlichen Entwicklung*. Tübingen: 1835.

Becker, Carl L. *The Heavenly City of the Eighteenth-Century Philosophers*. New Haven: Yale University Press, 1932.

Benz, Ernst. *Ecclesia Spiritualis*. Stuttgart: 1934.

Bett, Henry. *Joachim of Flora*, London: Methuen, 1931.

Bible. The Holy Bible, Revised Standard Version. London: Thomas Nelson, 1952.

Bindschwedler, Maria. "Meister Eckharts Lehre von der Gerechtigkeit", *Studia Philosophica*. Vol. XIII. Basel: 1953.

Bloch, Ernst. *Naturrecht und Menschenwürde,* in: Bloch, Ernst: *Gesamtausgabe*. Vol. VI. Frankfurt a. M.: 1961.

Bodin, Jean. *Les Six Livres de la Republique*. N. p. [Geneva?]: Gabriel Cartier, 1599.

Bosanquet, Bernard. Article "Religion, Philosophy of," in Baldwin's *Dictionary of Philosophy and Psychology*. New York and London: 1911.

Bousset, Wilhelm. *Hauptprobleme der Gnosis*. Göttingen: 1907.

Brinton, Crane. *A History of Western Morals*. New York: Harcourt, Brace, 1959.

Buber, Martin. *Paths in Utopia*. Transl. by R. F. C. Hull, London: 1949.

Büdinger, Max. *Die Universalhistorie im Alterthume*. Wien: 1895.

Bultman, Rudolf. *History and Eschatology*. Edinburgh: 1957.

Burnet, John. *Early Greek Philosophy*. 4th ed. London: A. and C. Black, 1930.

Bury, J. B. *The Idea of Progress*. New York: Macmillan, 1932.

Calvin, John. *Commentaries on the Epistles of Paul to the Galatians and Ephesians.* Transl. by Rev. William Pringle. Grand Rapids, 1948.

Cassirer, Ernst. *Die Philosophie der Aufklärung*. Tübingen: 1932. English Translation: *The Philosophy of the Enlightenment*, transl. by Fritz C. A. Koelln and James P. Pettegrove, 1955.

Chambers, Clark A. "The Belief in Progress in Twentieth-Century America", *Journal of the History of Ideas*. Vol. XIX. April 1958.

Chastellux, Marquis de. *De la Félicité Publique ou Considérations sur le Sort des Hommes dans les Différentés Époches de l'Histoire*. Nouvelle édition. Paris: 1822.

Collingwood, R. G. *The Idea of History.* Oxford: Clarendon Press, 1951.

Comte, Auguste. *The Catechism of Positive Religion*. Transl. by Richard Congreve. London: J. Chapman, 1858.

– *Système de Politique Positive*, Paris: 1851–1854.

– *Cours de Philosophie Positive* [1830–1842]. 4th ed., Paris: 1877. English Translation: *The Positive Philosophy of August Comte*, transl. by Harriet Martineau. New York: 1858.

Condorcet, A. N. *Esquisse d'un tableau historique des progrès de l'ésprit humain* [1793]. Paris: Bibliothéque de Philosophie, 1933.

– *Sketch for a Historical Picture of the Progress of the Human Mind.* Transl. by June Barraelough with an introduction by Stuart Hampshire, London: Weidenfeld and Nicolson, 1955.

Crusius, Chr. A. *Entwurf der notwendigen Vernunft-Wahrheiten,* 2nd ed. Leipzig: 1753.

Daniélou, Jean. "The Conception of History in the Christian Tradition", *The Journal of Religion*, 1950.

D'Arcy, M. C., S. J. *The Sense of History: Secular and Sacred.* London: Faber and Faber, 1959.

Dempf, Alois. *Sacrum Imperium*. München and Berlin: 1929.

Der Grosse Herder. 5th ed. Vol. IV. Freiburg: 1954.

Diderot, Denis. *Pensées Philosophiques,* in: Diderot, Denis: *Œuvres Complètes*, Vol. I. Paris: 1821.

Diodorus of Sicily. Books I and II, 1–34, with an English translation by C. H. Oldfather. London and New York: The Loeb Classical Library, 1933.

Draper, John W. *History of the Conflict Between Science and Religion*, 3rd ed. New York: 1875.

Ducasse, C. J. A *Philosophical Scrutiny of Religion*. New York: Ronald Press, 1953.

Eibl, Hans. *Metaphysik und Geschichte*. Leipzig and Wien: 1913.

Eisler, Rudolf. *Nietzsches Erkenntnistheorie und Metaphysik*. Leipzig: 1902.

– *Wörterbuch der philosophischen Begriffe,* 4th ed. Berlin: 1927.

Engels, Friedrich. "Die Lage Englands", in Karl *Marx*-Friedrich Engels: Historisch-Kritische Gesamtausgabe. Vol. I-II. Berlin: 1930.

– *The Development of Socialism from Utopia to Science*, in: *Socialism, Utopian and Scientific.* Transl. by E. Aveling. New York: 1901.

– "On the History of Early Christianity", *Die Neue Zeit.* Vol. XIII. 1894–1895, pp. 4–13, 36–43.

Evans, David Owen. *Social Romanticism in France*. Oxford: Clarendon Press, 1951.

Festugière, A. M. J. *La Revelation d'Hermès Trismégist*. Vol. IV. *Le Dieu inconnu et la Gnose*. Paris: 1954.

Feuer, Lewis. "What is Alienation?", *New Politics*, Vol I. 1962.

– Ed. *Marx and Engels: Basic Writings on Politics and Philosophy.* Garden City, N. Y.: Another Books, Doubleday, 1959.
Fitthogen, Gottfried. "Der Streit um Lessings Erziehung des Menschengeschlechts", *Preussische Jahrbücher.* Vol. CLIV. 1913.
Frankel, Charles. *The Faith of Reason: The Idea of Progress in the French Enlightenment.* New York: King's Crown Press, Columbia University, 1948.
– *The case for Modern Man.* New York: Harpers, 1956.
Fulton, W. Article "Trinity", in: *Encyclopedia of Religion and Ethics*, Vol. XII.
Gans, Eduard. *Rückblick auf Personen und Zustände.* Berlin: 1836.
Gerlich, Fritz. *Der Kommunismus als Lehre vom tausendjährigen Reich.* München: 1920.
Gilson, Etienne. *Les Metamorphoses de la Cité de Dieu.* Louvain and Paris: 1952.
Grundmann, Herbert. *Studien über Joachim von Floris.* Leipzig: 1927.
Guthrie, W. K. C. *In the Beginning.* London: Methuen, 1957.
Haller, Karl Ludwig von. *Restauration der Staatswissenschaft.* Winterthur: 1816–1834.
Harnack, Adolf von. *Marcion: Das Evangelium vom fremden Gott.* Leipzig: 1921.
Hayek, F. A. *The Counter-Revolution of Science.* Glencoe, Illinois: Free Press, 1952.
Heidegger, Martin. *Was ist Metaphysik?* Bonn: 1930.
– *Holzwege.* Frankfurt am Main: Klostermann, 1951.
– *An Introduction to Metaphysics.* Transl. by Ralph Manheim. New Haven: Yale University Press, 1959.
– *Nietzsche.* 2 Vols. Pfullingen: Neske, 1961.
Helvetius, C. A. *Œuvres completes.* Vols. II and IV. Paris: 1795.
Hobbes, Thomas. *Leviathan.* Edited with an introduction by Michael Oakshott. Oxford: Blackwell, 1960.
Holbach, P. H. T. *Système de la Nature ou Des lois du monde physique et du monde moral.* London: 1771.
– *Systéme Social; ou Principes Naturels de la Morale et de la Politique.* Paris: 1822.
– *The System of Nature; or Laws of the Moral and Physical World.* Transl. by H. D. Robinson. Boston: 1868.
Huck, Johannes Chrysostomus. *Joachim von Floris und die joachitische Literatur.* Freiburg im Breisgau: 1938.
Hume, David. *An Enquiry concerning Human Understanding.* La Salle, Illinois: Open Court Publication Co., 1949.
– *Dialogues concerning Natural Religion.* Reprinted with an introduction by Bruce M'Ewen. Edinburgh and London: 1907.
– *A Treatise of Human Nature.* With an introduction by A. J. Lindsay. London and New York: Everyman's Library. n. d.
Huxley, Julian. *Religion without Revelation.* New York: The New American Library, 1957.
Huxley, Thomas. "Scientific Aspects of Positivism", in: Huxley, Thomas: *Lay Sermons, Addresses and Reviews,* 5th ed. London: Macmillan, 1894.
Irenaeus. *Five Books against Heresies.* Transl. by John Keble. Oxford: 1872.
Jaspers, Karl. *Nietzsche* und das Christentum. Hameln: n. d.
– *Der philosophische Glaube.* München and Zürich: 1948.
– *The Perennial Scope of Philosophy.* Transl. by Ralph Manheim. New York: Philosophical Library, 1949.
– *Nietzsche.* Berlin: 1950
Jonas, Hans. *Gnosis und spätantiker Geist.* Vol. I: *Die mythologische Gnosis.* Göttingen: 1934.
– "Gnoticism and Modern Nihilism", *Social Research*, Vol. XIX. 1952.
– *The Gnostic Religion.* Boston: 1958.

Kamlah, Wilhelm. *Christentum und Geschichtlichkeit*. Stuttgart: 1951.
Kant, Immanuel. *Prolegomena zu einer jeden künftigen Metaphysik, die als Wissenschaft wird auftreten können*, in *Kants Gesammelte Schriften*, published by Königliche Preussische Akademie der Wissenschaften. Vol. IV. Berlin: 1903.
– *Critique of Pure Reason*. London and New York: Everyman's Library, 1934.
Kaufmann, Walter. *Critique of Religion and Philosophy*. New York: Harper, 1958.
– *Nietzsche, Philosopher, Psychologist, Antichrist*. New York: Meridian Books, 1959.
Kelsen, Hans. *Der soziologische und der juristische Staatsbegriff*. Tübingen: 1922.
– "Platonic Justice", *Ethics*. Vol. XLVIII. 1937–1938.
– "Foundations of Democracy", *Ethics*. Vol. LXVI. 1955.
– *The Communist Theory of Law*. New York: Praeger, 1955.
Kierkegaard, Soren. *The Point of View*. Transl. by Walter Lowrie. London and New York: 1939.
– *Works of Love*. Transl. by David F. Swenson and Lillian Marvin Swenson. New Jersey: Princeton University Press, 1946.
Knoll, August M. *Katholische Kirche und scholastisches Naturrecht*. Wien: 1962.
Köhler-Zürich, Walther. *Die Gnosis*, Tübingen: 1911.
Kraft, Julius. "Die Selbstentfremdung des Menschen", in: *Geist und Tat*. Vol. XL. March 1956.
Lange, F. A. *Geschichte des Materialismus*, 7th ed. Leipzig: 1902.
Leisegang, Hans. Article. "Gnosis" in: *Die Religion in Geschichte und Gegenwart*. Vol. II. Tübingen: 1927.
– Die *Gnosis*. Leipzig: 1924.
– *Denkformen*, 2nd ed. Berlin: Walter de Gruyter, 1951.
Lessing, Gotthold Ephraim. *The Education of the Human Race*. Transl. by the late Rev. Fred W. Robertson, M.A., 4th ed. London: 1883.
Lessing, Theodor. *Geschichte als Sinngebung des Sinnlosen*, 2nd ed. München: 1921.
Leuba, James H. A. *Psychological Study of Religion*. New York: 1912.
Lindsay, A. D. *The Modern Democratic State*, 5th ed. New York: Oxford University Press, 1951.
Lipsius, R. A. *Der Gnosticismus, sein Wesen, Ursprung und Entwicklungsgang*. Leipzig: 1860.
Löwith, Karl. *Meaning in History: The Theological Implications of the Philosophy of History*. Chicago: The University Press, 1949.
– *Heidegger, Denker in dürftiger Zeit*. Göttingen: 1960.
Lubac, Henri de, S. J. *Proudhon et le Christianisme*. Paris: 1945.
– *The Un-Marxian Socialist: A Study of Proudhon*. Transl. by T. E. Scantlebury. New York: Sheed & Ward, 1948.
– *The Drama of Atheist Humanism*. Transl. by Edith M. Riley. London: Sheed & Ward, 1949.
MacKinnon, D. M., ed. *Christian Faith and Communist Faith. A Series of Studies of Members of the Anglican Communion*. London: 1953.
Maritain, Jacques. *On the Philosophy of History*. Ed. by Joseph W. Evans. New York: Scribner, 1957.
Marsilius of Padua. *The Defensor Pacis*. Transl. with an introduction by Alan Gewirth. New York: Columbia University Press, 1956.
Martineau, James. *A Study of Religion*. New York: 1888.
Marx, Karl. *A Contribution to the Critique of Political Economy*. Transl. by N. J. Stone. Chicago: 1904.

– "Manifest der Kommunistischen Partei", in: Marx, Karl: *Die Frühschriften*. Ed. by Siegfried Landshut. Stuttgart: 1953.
– "Nationaloekonomie und Philosophie", in: Marx, Karl: *Die Frühschriften*. Ed. by Siegfried Landshut. Stuttgart: 1953.
– "Zur Kritik der Hegelschen Rechtsphilosophie", in: *Die Frühschriften*. Ed. by Siegfried Landshut. Stuttgart: 1953.

Marx, Karl and Engels, Friedrich. *The German Ideology*. Part I and III. Ed. with an introduction by R. Pascal. New York: International Publishers, 1939.

Matter, Jacques. *Histoire critique du gnosticisme et son influence sur les sects religieuses et philosophiques des six premières siècles de l'ère chrétienne*. 2 vols. Paris: 1828.

Mauthner, Fritz. *Der Atheismus und seine Geschichte im Abendland*. Stuttgart and Berlin: 1920–1923.

Meister Eckhart. *A Modern Translation* by Raymond Bernard Blackney, New York: Harper Tochbooks, 1957.

Meister Eckhart. *Selected Treatises and Sermons*. Transl. from Latin and German with an introduction and notes by James M. Clark and John V. Skinner. London: 1958.

Metzger, Wilhelm. *Gesellschaft, Recht und Staat in der Ethik des deutschen Idealismus*. Heidelberg: 1917.

Moeller van den Bruck, Arthur. *Das Dritte Reich*, 3rd ed. Hamburg: 1931.

Mommsen, Th. E. "St. Augustin and the Christian Idea of Progress", *Journal of the History of Ideas*, Vol. XII. 1951.

Monnerot, Jules. *Sociologie du Comminism*. Paris: Gallimard, 1942. Engl. Translation: *Sociology and Psychology of Communism*. Transl. by Jane Degras and Richard Rees. Boston: The Beacon Press, 1953.

Mosheim, Johann Lorenz von. *Versuch einer impartheiischen und gründlichen Ketzergeschichte*, 2rd ed. Helmstaedt: 1748.

Mühl, Max. *Die antike Menschheitsidee in ihrer geschichtlichen Entwicklung*. Leipzig: 1928.

Müller, Adam. *Von der Notwendigkeit einer theologischen Grundlage der gesamten Staatswissenschaft* [1820], in: Müller, Adam: *Schriften zur Staatsphilosophie*. Ed. by Rudolf Kohler with an introduction by P. Erich Przywara, S. J. München: Theatiner Verlag, n. d.

Neander, August. *Genetische Entwicklungen der vornehmsten gnostischen Systeme*. Berlin: 1818.

Niebuhr, Reinhold. *Faith and History: A Comparison of Christian and Modern Views of History*. New York: 1949.

Nietzsche, Friedrich. *Beyond Good and Evil*. Transl. by Helen Zimmern, in: Friedrich Nietzsche, *Complete Works*. Vol. XII. London and Edingburgh: 1911.
– *Human. All-too-Human*. Transl. by Helen Zimmern, in: Nietzsche, Friedrich: *Complete Works*. Vol. VI. London and Edingburgh: 1900–1911.
– *The Dawn of the Day*. Transl. by J. M. Kennedy, in: Nietzsche, Friedrich: *Complete Works*. Vol. IX. London and Edingburgh: 1911.
– *Ecce Homo*. Transl. by A. M. Ludovici, in: Nietzsche, Friedrich: *Complete Works*. Vol. XVII. London and Edingburgh: 1911.
– *Philosophy during the Tragic Age of the Greeks*. Transl. by A. Mügge, in: Nietzsche, Friedrich: *Complete Works*. Vol. II. London and Edingburgh:1911.
– *The Antichrist*. Transl. by Anthony M. Ludovici, in: Nietzsche, Friedrich: *Complete Works* Vol. XVI. London and Edinburgh: 1911.
– *The Genealogy of Morals*. Transl. by Horace B. Samuel, in: Nietzsche, Friedrich: *Complete Works*. Vol. XIII. London and Edingburgh: 1910.

- *The Joyful Wisdom.* Transl. by Thomas Common, in: Nietzsche, Friedrich: *Complete Works.* Vol. X. London and Edingburgh: 1910.
- *Thus Spake Zarathustra.* Transl. by Thomos Common, in: Nietzsche, Friedrich: *Complete Works.* Vol. XI. London and Edingburgh: 1909.
- *The Twilight of the Idols.* Transl. by A. M. Ludovici, in: Nietzsche, Friedrich: *Complete Works.* Vol. XVI. London and Edingburgh:1915.
- *Thoughts out of Season.* Transl. by Adrian Collins., in: Nietzsche, Friedrich: *Complete Works.* Vol. V. London and Edingburgh: 1909.
- *The Will to Power.* Transl. by Anthony M. Ludovici, in: Nietzsche, Friedrich: *Complete Works.* Vols. XIV and XV. London and Edingburgh: 1909–1910.
- *The Unschuld des Werdens,* in: *Der Nachlass.* Ed. by A. Baeumler. Stuttgart: 1956.
- *Gesammelte Werke.* Vols. VI, XI, XIV, XV. München: Musarion Verlag, 1920–1929.
- *Nietzsches Werke.* Vols. VI, XII, XIII, XIV. Leipzig: C. G. Naumann, 1901–1913.

Noyes, Alfred. *Voltaire,* 3rd ed. London: 1939.

Otto, Rudolf. *Das Heilige: Über das Irrationale in der Idee des Göttlichen und sein Verhältnis zum Rationalen,* 14th ed. Gotha: 1926. English Translation: The Idea of the Holy, transl. by John W. Harvey. London: Oxford University Press, 1925.
- *Reich Gottes und Menschensohn.* München: 1934.

Piesch, Herma. *Meister Eckharts Ethik.* Luzern: 1935.
- "Meister Eckharts Lehre vom 'Gerechten'", in *Festschrift der Nationalbibliothek in Wien.* Vienna: 1926.

Plato. *Protagoras.*
- *Republic.*
- *Seventh Letter.*
- *Laws.*

Popitz, Heinrich. *Der entfremdete Mensch,* in: *Philosophische Forschungen.* Neue Folge, ed. by Karl Jaspers. Vol. II. Basel: 1953.

Proudhon, P.-J. *Systeme des Contradictions Économiques ou Philosophie de la Misère,* in: Proudhon, P.-J.: Œuvres completes. Vol. IV. Paris: 1867. English Translation: *System of Economic Contradictions or the Philosophy of Misery,* transl. by Benj. R. Tucker in: *The Works of P. J. Proudhon.* Vol. IV. Boston: 1888.

Reichenbach, Hans. *The Rise of Scientific Philosophy.* Berkeley and Los Angeles: University of California Press, 1951.

Reisner, Erwin. *Die christliche Botschaft im Wandel der Epochen.* München: 1935.

Robertson, J. M. A *History of Free Thought in the Nineteenth Century,* 4th ed. London: Watts, 1936.

Rocholl, R. *Rupert von Deutz.* Gütersloh: 1886.

Rockwood, Raymond O., ed. *Carl Beckers Heavenly City Revisited.* Ithaca, N. Y.: Cornell University Press, 1958.

Rosenstock, Eugen. *Die europäischen Revolutionen.* Jena: 1931.

Rosenstock-Huessy, Eugen. *The Christian Future; or The Modern Mind Outrun.* London: Student Christian Movement Press, 1947.

Rousseau, Jean Jacques. *Du Contrat Social.* With an introduction by Maurice Halbwachs. Aubier: Editions Montaigne, n. d.

Russel, Bertrand. *A History of Western Philosophy.* New York, 1945.
- *Religion and Science.* London, New York, Toronto: The Home University Library of Modern Knowledge, 1956.

Ryazanoff, D., ed., *Karl Marx, Man, Thinker and Revolutionist.* A Symposium. New York 1927. German Translation: Karl *Marx* als Denker, Mensch und Revolutionär. Berlin: 1928.
Saint-Simon, Claude Henri, Comte de. *Introduction aux Travaux Scientifiques du Dix-neuvième Siècle,* in *Œuvres Choisies.* Brussels: 1859.
– *Selected Writings.* Ed. by F. M. H. Markham. Oxford: Basil Blackwell, 1952.
Saint-Simon and D'Enfantin. *Œuvres de Saint-Simon et D'Enfantin.* Vol. XIX. Paris: 1869.
Schmidt, Erich. *Lessing,* 3rd ed. Berlin: 1909.
Schmitt, Carl. *Politische Theologie: Vier Kapitel zur Lehre von der Souveränität.* München und Leipzig: 1922.
Scholz, Heinrich. *Glaube und Unglaube in der Weltgeschichte.* Leipzig: 1911.
Schott, E. "Die Gedanken des Abtes Joachim von Floris", *Zeitschrift für Kirchengeschichte.* Vol. XXIII. 1902 pp. 157–186.
Schumpeter, Joseph A. *Capitalism, Socialism and Democracy.* New York and London: Harper, 1942.
– "The March into Socialism", *American Economic Review.* Vol. XL. 1950
Sertillanges, Antoine-Gilbert E. O. P. *Le Christianisme et les Philosophies.* Vol. I: *Le Ferment Évangelique: L'Élaboration Séculaire: La Synthése Thomiste.* 2nd ed. Paris: n. d.; Vol. II: Les Temps Mo-dernes, Paris: 1941.
Sophocles. *Antigone.*
Spengler, Oswald. *The Decline of the West.* Transl. by Charles Frances Atkinson. New York: Knof, 1932.
Steffes, J. P. *Das Wesen des Gnostizismus und sein Verhältnis zum katholischen Dogma.* Forschungen zur christlichen Literatur- und Dogmengeschichte. Vol. XIV. Paderborn: 1922.
Talmon, J. L. *The Rise of Totalitarian Democracy.* Boston: Beacon Press, 1952.
Taubes, Jakob. *Abendländische Eschatologie.* Bern: A. Francke, 1947.
Thyssen, Johannes. *Geschichte der Geschichtsphilosophie.* Berlin: Junker und Dünnhaupt, 1936.
Tindal, Mathew. *Christianity as old as Creation or the Gospel a Republication of the Religion of Nature,* 2nd ed. London: 1731.
Tocqueville, Alexis de. *L'Ancien Régime et la Révolution.* Paris: 1866.
Toynbee, Arnold J. *A Study of History.* London, New York, Toronto: Oxford University Press, 1954.
Troeltsch, Ernst. *Der Historismus und seine Probleme,* in: Troeltsch, Ernst: *Gesammelte Schriften.* Tübingen: 1922.
Tucker, Robert C. *Philosophy and Myth in Karl Marx.* Cambridge: The University Press, 1961.
Vaihinger, Hans. *Die Philosophie des Als Ob,* 7th and 8th ed. Leipzig, 1922.
Vellay, Charles. *Discours et Rapports de Robespierre.* Paris: 1908.
Voegelin, Erich. *The New Science of Politics: An Introduction.* Chicago: University of Chicago Press, 1952.
– *Wissenschaft, Politik und Gnosis.* München: Kösel Verlag, 1959.
Voltaire, F. M. A. "Remarks on M. Pascal's Thought", *The Works of Voltaire.* Vol. XXI. Paris, London, New York, Chicago: Edition de la Pacification, 1901.
– *Œuvres Complètes.* Vol. XXII. Paris: Gamier Frères, 1877–1885.
Waller, Martha. *Lessings Erziehung des Menschengeschlechtes,* in: *Germanische Studien,* 160. Berlin: 1935.
Weldon, T. D. *The Vocabulary of Politics.* Penguin Books, 1955.

White, Andrew Dickson. *A History of the Warfare of Science with Theology in Christendom.* New York: 1896. Reprinted New York: 1960.
White, William Allen. *A Theory of Spiritual Progress.* Emporia, Kansas: 1910.
Willy, R. *Friedrich Nietzsche.* Eine Gesamtdarstellung. Zürich: 1904.
Wilson, R. McL. *The Gnostic Problem.* London: Mowbray, 1958.
Windelband, Wilhelm. *An Introduction to Philosophy.* Transl. by Joseph McCabe. London: 1921.
Woodcock, George. *Pierre-Joseph Proudhon.* New York: 1956.

Index of Subjects

G

H

I

J

K

O

P

R

S

T

U

V

W

Index of Names

W

X

Z